# Budapest

THE BRADT CITY GUIDE

**Adrian Phillips**
**Jo Scotchmer**

Bradt Travel Guides Ltd, UK
The Globe Pequot Press Inc, USA

**First published October 2004**

Bradt Travel Guides Ltd
19 High Street, Chalfont St Peter, Bucks SL9 9QE, England; www.bradtguides.com
Published in the USA by The Globe Pequot Press Inc, 246 Goose Lane, PO Box 480,
Guilford, Connecticut 06437-0480



A catalogue record for this book is available from the British Library

ISBN-10: 1 84162 110 2   ISBN-13: 978 184162 110 4

*Cover* The Fishermen's Bastion (William Courage)
*Text photographs* Luis Castaneda/Tips Images (LC), Angelo Cavalli/Tips Images (AC), Guido Alberto Rossi/ Tips Images (GAR)
*Maps* Steve Munns   *Illustrations* Carole Vincer

Typeset from the author's disc by Wakewing
Printed and bound in Italy by Legoprint SpA, Trento

# Authors

**Adrian Phillips** and **Jo Scotchmer** spent six months travelling around Hungary, pestering museum curators and losing themselves (literally!) among its highways and byways. Adrian is senior editor at Bradt – which he joined in 2001 after completing a PhD in English literature – and co-author of *Singapore: The Bradt Travel Guide.* Jo is a public-relations manager whose portfolio includes travel resorts; she also dabbles in freelance journalism, and has written articles for magazines including *Cosmopolitan* and *Time Out*. Budapest is a pleasure they indulge at every opportunity, dragging friends and family in tow. Their guide to Hungary is published in 2005.

## CONTRIBUTORS

We are grateful to the following for their invaluable assistance: **Lucy Mallows** (various), **Marti Andrews** (spas, food), **Stuart Candy** (music) and **Jo Kidd** (festivals, facts).

# Contents

# Acknowledgements

Never has so much been owed by so few to so many – we salute you all. Thank you to Tsvia Vorley, Ildikó Balogh and Melinda Stein for smoothing the initial path; to Sally Brock, Steve Munns, Selena Dickson and all at Bradt for making sense of endless scribbles; to Carole Vincer for her lovely sketches; to Annalisa Rellie and Tim Burford for brochures and notes scrawled on airline sick bags; to all on the July tour party for earnest research into the city's bars; to our families and friends for their support, and especially Janet, Tony and Duncan for some welcome distraction; and to Tricia Hayne and Hilary Bradt for the faith to entrust us with the project. Above all, thank you to Erzsébet and William Courage, and Péter and Zsanett Koltai, who were selfless in their help and guidance, and proved that friendships can grow in spite of endless impositions.

***LIST OF MAPS***

# How to Use this Book

**Symbols** are used where appropriate to indicate transport routes:

B bus
M1/M2/M3 metro (number indicates line)
T tram
TB trolleybus

**Map references** (eg: [2 CI]) relate to the colour maps at the end of this guide.

**Hotels** are divided initially by price, and then subdivided between Buda and Pest.

**Restaurants** are divided between Buda and Pest, and then further subdivided between districts or convenient areas. All prices were verified within a period of four months, so use them as a comparative guide.

**Opening hours** are included for restaurants, bars, museums and sights.

**Chapters 10** and **11** guide you to the sights as you walk the streets of Buda and Pest. They include cross-references to **Chapter 12**, containing full entries for museums, galleries and major sights. **Chapter 13** is dedicated to Budapest's nature.

**Time** is given using the 24-hour clock in the usual way. (Hungarians refer to the full hour to come rather than that passed. Thus 6.30 is expressed as 'half to seven' (*fél hét óra*); in shorthand/24-hour forms, it may therefore appear as 'f7', 'f19', '½7' or '½19'. The same applies to ¼- and ¾-hour intervals.)

# Introduction

Our first view of Budapest was through shaking fingers, slumped greenly in the back of an airport taxi driven by a man resolute in his commitment to overtaking on blind corners. The southern approach to the city was unpretty, characterised by blurred advertising boards and blared car horns; residential blocks were grey, stolid and utilitarian. We stumbled out of the car and into a restaurant, playing diners' roulette with a Hungarian-language menu, and settling our stomachs with glasses of Bull's Blood and plates of what we later learned were cockerels' testicles. Almost inevitably, the tatty hotel's cheerless manager had no record of our booking, and indicated as much by shrugging his shoulders and picking his ear.

But romantics know that love can blossom from unpromising first meetings. As we trudged off to find a bed for the night, a yellow tram rumbled and screeched beside us. We passed a faded 19th-century mansion, and peeked through its broad archway to a wooden-cobbled passage and a pretty garden courtyard. We turned a corner and crossed a woman taking her Hungarian puli for its evening walk, a dreadlocked dog that looked more mat than mutt. And then we reached the river, with the palace lording it on the opposite bank and illuminated bridges casting white lights upon the surface. It has been said that Hungary 'grows on you and seems to squirt a divine soda water into your blood'. In that moment by the Danube, our hearts were caught, and the city only tightened its grip as the days passed.

We read about its tragic past, placed our hands in walls pocked with the bullet scars of '45 or '56, and strolled castle walls that had borne the brunt of 30 sieges.

We struggled hard to hear history's echoed screams among such beauty and elegance, and wondered at the resolve of a people prepared time and again to put the pieces back together. We drank strong coffee and stronger fruit brandy, browsed market halls for salamis and lace, rode the clattering cogwheel railway into the hills and wallowed warmly in thermal baths. The city had entered our blood. It wasn't that our first impressions had been wholly inaccurate; Hungarians *do* drive with suicidal impatience, and service *can* be tardy in an industry still recovering from 40 years of communist rule. Once such raw spirit is tempered with the city's soda, however, it creates a colourful blend of grace and charm and underlying attitude. It's an intoxicating thing; we know we shall never agree to a final visit.

***FEEDBACK REQUEST***

We've strived to tramp and nag and eat our way to accuracy. However, cities are living and breathing things in perpetual states of change. Would you lend us your ears and eyes to ensure that subsequent editions keep pace? What was new or different during your visit? What did you like or dislike about the book? Please drop us a line at hungarytravelguide@yahoo.co.uk, or write to us c/o Bradt Travel Guides, 19 High St, Chalfont St Peter, Bucks SL9 9QE. We'd love to hear from you, and will be sure to reply personally.

Best, Adrian and Jo

# Contexts

1

## INTRODUCTION TO THE CITY

Great cities are forged from moments of tragedy as well as triumph, but Budapest has seen more than its fair share of blood and bullets. For much of its modern history, when Hungary dropped the toast it landed buttered-side down. The Turks strutted here in the 16th and 17th centuries, Austria ruled during the 18th and 19th, and the 20th century saw the country lurch from one terror regime to another. The citizens did not subject meekly; the capital has witnessed several revolts and some ding-dong street battles, and the nation's revered heroes are those who've fought for freedom.

As we write, however, Hungarians are in charge, and the only gangs of foreigners are coach parties. It's immediately evident that tourism is thriving in the capital; entry to the EU and the sudden interest from low-cost airlines suggests the boom will get boomier still. Budapest is big enough to take it. Areas like Váci utca and the Castle District already cater for tourists, and can look after themselves. Elsewhere, one of the city's strengths is the elbowroom around its sights. While there are quaint narrow streets on Castle Hill, Budapest is characterised more typically by the broad and the bold. These are features of nature, such as Buda's craggy hills and caves, and the sweeping river; they are also features of architecture, such as Pest's historicist and art-nouveau mansions and Parisian boulevards, which replaced the medieval and baroque during 19th-century expansion. Another strength is the diversity of attractions. The city is significant both for its museums and its nightclubs, for its opera house and its contemporary music festivals; it suits both the flâneur and the hill walker. For all the exoticism of its Turkish baths and the impact of its communist past, this is a cosmopolitan capital that has always looked longingly westward. However, with the odd smoking Trabant, rumbling tram, and flower-selling *néni* comes destinational bite, and a flavour quite unique.

## HISTORY

### The early years

Peering through history's early mists, excavations suggest that the site of the capital was inhabited as long ago as the **fourth millennium BC**. There were communities here during the Bronze and Iron ages, including Celts who arrived in the 4th century BC and constructed a citadel on Gellért Hill. In around 35BC the area's strategic advantages were properly exploited for the first time when the **Romans** extended their imperial boundary eastward to the Danube, occupying the Celtic settlement of Ak-Ink (adopting the Latinised form of Aquincum). A legionary camp was established in today's Óbuda and a civilian town to its north; the river formed a natural barrier to attacks from Asiatic tribes, and a couple of advanced fortified positions were constructed on the other bank – including Contra-Aquincum, remains of which still stand in Március 15 tér. Aquincum flourished and became the capital of Pannonia Inferior, one half of the Roman province of Pannonia; as provincial governor, Hadrian built himself a palace on Shipyard Island.

During the 4th century the empire declined, and the Romans finally abandoned Buda at the beginning of the 5th century. This triggered the **second age of**

**migrations** as peoples from the east moved into the Carpathian Basin. Initially the Huns filled the vacuum under the notorious Attila, followed by other tribes including the Avars and the Slavs. Seven tribes of **Magyars** – ancestors of the contemporary population – arrived in 896AD, probably from lands between the River Volga and the Urals; these skilled horsemen fanned out across the region, the chieftain Árpád settling in Hungary. It was under the **Árpád dynasty** and King István (crowned in 1000) that the country became a Christian state, the king ruthlessly dispatching of pagan claimants to the throne and recognising the unifying potential of the church. His right hand is a holy relic on display in Szt István Basilica. Budapest actually lacked real clout at this point for the religious centre was in Esztergom and the royal palace in Székesfehérvár.

István's only son Imre was killed in a hunting accident, and so the king's death in 1038 sparked a lengthy period of instability between a succession of feeble kings and the nobility; it was in the immediate aftermath that pagans stuffed Bishop Gellért, Imre's spiritual tutor, into a spiked barrel and tossed him from the hill that now bears his name. In 1222 the '**Golden Bull**' was signed, a sort of Magna Carta that acknowledged Hungary as a nation, decreed a yearly meeting (Diet) of nobles in Pest and curtailed the powers of the king. Trade began to thrive on both sides of the river (at the time separate towns), but the good times were swiftly curtailed by the **Mongol invasion** of 1241–42, when the country was razed and vast swathes of the population massacred. King **Béla IV** (1235–70) returned from exile determined to protect Hungary from future hostility. He fortified Castle Hill, moved the populations of Buda and Pest behind the safety of its walls, and in doing so was lauded as the second state founder. Castle Hill was subsequently ranked a city and named Buda (the area to its north relegated to Óbuda – 'Old Buda'), while Pest developed as a commercial centre and attracted immigrant craftsmen from other corners of Europe.

## The Golden Age

At the beginning of the 14th century, the Árpád line petered out with the death of the heirless András III. The ensuing power struggle was won by **Károly Robert** (1308–42), a French Angevin king with the backing of the pope. It was under the Angevin kings that the royal court was moved from Visegrád to Buda. Subsequent monarchs enlarged upon the regal residence, in particular **Zsigmond of Luxembourg** (1387–1437) who constructed the beautiful Gothic Friss Palace. Zsigmond's reign coincided with Turkish expansionist ambitions in Europe; the Ottoman advance was halted at the Battle of Nándorfehérvár (now Belgrade) in 1456, when Hungary's greatest general, the Transylvanian Prince János Hunyadi, achieved a famous victory. Pope Callixtus III declared that the noon Angelus should be prayed, and church bells rung across Catholic Europe in grateful remembrance. Hunyadi succumbed to the plague shortly afterwards, but in 1458 his teenage son **Mátyás** (1458–90) took the throne. His reign proved something of a historical purple patch. The economy prospered, and Mátyás and his Italian wife Beatrice made Buda one of the centres of Renaissance art and learning. For men of letters, he put together a stunning library in one wing of the palace; for men of action, he set up the Black Army, one of Europe's first professional units. Hungary's political and cultural influence never again blossomed so fulsomely.

There was the familiar feudal infighting following Mátyás's demise, climaxing in the **Peasant Revolt** of 1514. The revolt united the ruling classes, who savagely crushed the peasants – the leader György Dózsa was burnt to death on a metal throne – and enforced a Tripartitum law that reduced the peasants to the status of serfs. Such turbulence, though, was as nothing compared with that to come.

## First Turks, then Habsburgs

For Hungarians, August 29 1526 is the most tragic date in a past littered with them. On that day the Turks obliterated the Magyar army at Mohács in southern Hungary. Fifteen years later the **Ottomans** had conquered Buda, Óbuda and Pest, and settled in for the long haul. During their 150-year stay they built little of lasting value beyond thermal baths, some of which remain today, and Buda stagnated under the pashas. There were several attempts to re-take Buda before a **European army** united under the command of Archduke Charles of Austria and Prince-Elector Maximilian of Bavaria eventually vanquished the Turks in 1686, after a siege that lasted months. Buda was reduced to rubble by the fighting, and Pest was by now a virtual ghost town. The combined population of the three towns was just 1,000. There was a massive process of rebuilding and re-population ahead (the latter with German, Slovak and Serbian settlers, as well as Hungarians from other parts of the country). However, Hungary still hadn't secured freedom – it had merely swapped one master for another.

The Catholic **Habsburgs** placed Hungary under military rule, rigorously persecuting Protestants and determinedly undermining the privileges of the native nobility. At the start of the 18th century, during the War of the Spanish Succession, the country embarked on an eight-year rebellion led by Prince **Ferenc Rákóczi**. The struggle eventually failed, but Rákóczi had been the first to draw together all Hungarians in opposition to Habsburg rule.

After the wars, the Habsburgs invested heavily in developing the towns, and the enlightened absolutism of rulers like Empress **Maria Theresa** (1740–80) led to a period of sustained growth. Pest became an important trading centre and a wealthy town, attracting fresh groups of immigrants including Serbs and Jews. The first decades of the 19th century also witnessed the so-called **Age of Reform**, in large part spurred by Count **István Széchenyi** – 'the greatest Hungarian'. His broad, progressive bourgeois vision was influenced by visits to England, and he inspired the construction of the Chain Bridge, the founding of the Hungarian Academy of Sciences and the laying of the first railway line. It was also during this period that Pest took on its current face. The Great Flood of 1838 had an effect as dramatic as London's fire of 1666, flattening the neoclassical and baroque dwellings and making way for the broad Parisian boulevards that replaced them. Some surviving churches bear markers recording the height reached by the waters.

This all coincided with turbulence in Europe and a revival of nationalist feeling in Hungary. On March 15 1848 **revolution** broke out on Pest's streets, its spokesmen the poet Sándor Petőfi and his fellow radicals. A National Assembly convened in Pest, led by Kossuth Lajos – the 'Moses of the Hungarians' – who spearheaded the **War of Independence**. The Habsburgs prevailed in 1849 after Emperor **Ferenc József** (1848–1916) enlisted the help of a Russian force. Petőfi had died in battle and Kossuth went into exile. Lajos Batthyány, the first independent prime minister, was executed. The Habsburgs built a citadel looking down from the Buda bank, and the Hungarians were rudely awoken from their dreams of freedom.

However, renewed hope came more swiftly than expected. The Austrians suffered several defeats to Italian, French and Prussian armies, and – anxious to shore up the Habsburg empire – acceded to an agreement drawn up by the liberal politician Ferenc Deák. The **Compromise** (*Ausgleich*) of 1867 established a dual monarchy, whereby Hungary had its own government, parliament and even small army, but operated jointly with Austria in matters of foreign policy and defence. In 1873 Buda, Óbuda and Pest were **unified** to form Budapest, a union that had been inevitable since the erection of the Chain Bridge linking both banks. The city developed a capitalist infrastructure, the population grew rapidly, Pest became a place of great municipal construction and the hub of the empire's rail system, and cultural output rivalled that of Vienna. This spirit of energy and independence was evident during the **millennial celebrations** of 1896 commemorating the Magyar conquest. An exhibition featured 220 halls showcasing Hungarian achievements, while lasting monuments like City Park, Heroes' Square, the first underground railway line, Mátyás Church and the Museum of Applied Arts were also born of this staggeringly ambitious and productive moment.

## The World Wars

The Austro-Hungarian empire was decisively defeated in **World War I**, and the Habsburg monarchy collapsed. In the aftermath, a short-lived communist regime known as the **Republic of Councils** was established for 133 days under Béla Kun – using 'Red Terror' to impose nationalisation of land. On June 4 1920 Hungary was forced by the victorious powers to sign the uncompromising **Treaty of Trianon**, which handed two-thirds of its territory to neighbouring countries that even included Austria. Three million Magyars found themselves sudden exiles in foreign states. This division of countryman from countryman had a lasting impact on Hungarian culture and sense of self, and the memory of 'Greater Hungary' – and the current treatment of ethnic Hungarians in Romania and elsewhere – remains a hot topic to this day.

In November 1919, Admiral **Miklós Horthy** rode into Budapest at the head of a counter-revolutionary army. Kun fled abroad, ultimately to be executed by Stalin, and on March 1 1920 Horthy was elected Regent (as the self-declared representative of exiled Habsburg Emperor Karl IV). Horthy led a right-wing dictatorship whose policies were conservative, anti-Semitic and nationalistic. Its primary aim was to retrieve the lands stripped from Hungary at Trianon, an ambition supported universally by Hungarians. This and the government's right-wing bent inevitably pushed it towards alliance with fascist Germany.

In 1941 – against the advice of Prime Minister Teleki, who subsequently committed suicide – Horthy supported Germany in the unprovoked attack upon Yugoslavia. Hungary was rewarded with the return of some lost lands, but it was now inextricably and actively involved in the conflict, and its army suffered very heavily on the eastern front. When Horthy secretly entered into negotiation with the Allies, the Germans learned of the betrayal and **occupied** the country in March

1944. They installed the leader of the Hungarian Nazis (the **Arrow-Cross Party**) at the head of the government, ushering in the horrors of the Holocaust. A ghetto was established in the area around the Great Synagogue and troopers executed Jews on the Danube banks. Twenty percent of the capital's inhabitants were Jews, and only the intervention of Horthy and the actions of Raoul Wallenberg (the Swedish diplomat), Carl Lutz (the Swiss consul) and the Catholic Church saved them from the wholesale deportation that occurred in the rest of the country. Allied aerial bombardment took a serious toll on the city, and this was worsened when the Germans made a desperate last stand against the advancing Russians, destroying all the bridges and holing up on Castle Hill. Budapest was surrounded on December 24 1944, and Hitler ordered the 22,000 mainly SS troops to defend it to the last soldier; on February 12 1945, down to just 1,800, they finally succumbed. Three-quarters of Budapest's buildings bore the scars of battle, over a third were destroyed and 25,000 civilians had been killed.

## The communist years

The daunting process of reconstruction began; historic buildings were restored, and drab, utilitarian residential blocks raised on the outer city limits. The communists came to power in 1947 on the back of a campaign of intimidation and a rigged election. Mátyás Rákosi imposed a **Stalinist dictatorship** between 1947 and 1953, emulating his mentor in the brutal use of spies, torture and murder. Memorials to communist and worker heroes appeared on boulevards whose names were changed in honour of the 'liberators'; the symbols of ideology were inescapable. Rákosi's position was undermined by Stalin's death in 1953, and **Imre Nagy** – a reformist in the Communist Party – took over as prime minister. He was expelled for introducing mild reforms, but the spectre of a kindly, humane communism had been raised.

On October 23 1956 a student demonstration demanded Nagy be reinstated; some of the demonstrators were fired upon by members of the secret police (ÁVO) and peaceful protest flared into **revolution**. The statue of Stalin that stood to the south of City Park was broken to pieces. Nagy set up an administration, declared the country's withdrawal from the Warsaw Pact, and looked hopefully to the West for recognition and assistance. However, Western powers were focused upon the Suez crisis, and – after bloody street fighting – Soviet tanks brutally suppressed the revolution. **János Kádár** was placed in charge; 20,000 people were arrested, 2,000 executed, and many more shipped off to labour camps. Nagy was exterminated two years later.

Initially repressive in consolidating his position, and hated for being the Soviets' man, Kádár went on to institute a raft of liberal policies that were nicknamed '**Goulash Communism**'. In 1989 the Communist Party, recognising the shape of things to come, announced that there would be **free elections**. In 1990, with a quiet simplicity wholly alien to significant events in Hungary's history, the communists were voted out. The People's Republic of Hungary became the Republic of Hungary, and the contemporary era of parliamentary democracy had begun. Budapest has enjoyed heavy investment from the West ever since, and on May 1 2004 Hungary became a member of the **European Union**. (For fuller details of the political and economic landscape from 1956 to the present day, see *Politics* and *Economy* below.)

# POLITICS

## The fall of communism

The sign that the worm had turned irrevocably in the modern history of Hungarian politics came during the **reburial of Imre Nagy** in 1989. Nagy was a reformist, the face of a kinder, more flexible communism. Installed as leader in 1953, when Stalin's death brought about a crisis in Hungary, he had been ousted in 1955, reinstated at the start of the uprising in 1956, and then imprisoned and quietly executed by the Soviets after the revolution was crushed. His body, along with many others, was lain in a distant corner of the Újköztemető (New Public Cemetery), in overgrown 'Plot 301'.

In the aftermath of 1956, Moscow's man took power. **János Kádár** managed a delicate balancing act, both appeasing Soviets and proving popular with Hungarians. He instituted a platform of national reconciliation, and from 1968 implemented a programme of radical economic reforms. This 'market socialism' was nicknamed 'Goulash Communism' abroad, and led to strengthened relations with the West. It also relieved domestic tensions and gradually improved living standards; Hungary was known as the 'happiest barracks in the Bloc'. Kádár died in 1989, and the country began to move positively towards **democracy proper**. The MSZMP (Hungarian Socialist Workers' Party) permitted a series of 'round table' discussions with 'non-official' new 'opposition' parties. In a reconciliatory act in November,

Nagy (and other victims of the revolution) were reburied in a spruced-up Plot 301. During the ceremony a young hippie of a student, Viktor Orbán, gave voice to what many were thinking in demanding that Soviet troops leave his country. The last soldier did so on June 19 1991, a day celebrated each year (see page 35).

As the Iron Curtain began to draw back, Hungary played a significant role in pulling the cord. Gyula Horn (the foreign minister) allowed East Germans to climb into their Trabants and sputter through the country to reach the West. A picnic was held on the border with Austria, after which East Germans crossed a field where the dividing barbed wire had been symbolically cut. In 1989, the reform communists declared the advent of **party-political democracy**; the first free elections in March 1990 resulted in a coalition led by the Hungarian Democratic Forum (Magyar Demokrata Forum – MDF), who campaigned on a blend of conservative and nationalist policies. The first president of the new democracy was the enduringly popular Árpád Göncz, a Free Democrat (SZDSZ) translator and author who had been imprisoned by the Soviets.

## Democratic Hungary

In the 14 years since the ***rendszerváltás*** (change of political system), Hungarian politics has been consistent only in its swinging backwards and forwards between left and right (or, more accurately, centre-left and centre-right). In 1994, the **Socialist Party** (Magyar Socialista Párt – MSZP) returned to power on the back of a feeling of nostalgia for past stability and dissatisfaction at rising unemployment, rising inflation and rising crime. The MSZP and its liberal Free Democrat (Szabad

Demokrata Szövetség – SZDSZ) coalition partner were led by Gyula Horn, the man who had waved through the soap dishes on their journey to the West five years earlier. The government introduced an 'austerity package' to set the country back on course towards EU membership.

A policy with 'austerity' as its mantra – however well meant – is rarely a vote winner, and in 1998 (when the four-year tenure came to an end) the country inevitably looked rightwards once more in electing a third party, **Fidesz** (Fiatal Demokraták Szövetsége). This Alliance of Young Democrats was originally formed in the late 1980s by Viktor Orbán – who had spoken with such passion and charisma at Nagy's funeral – from a group of law students. In the early days the party was characterised by youthful liberalism, but it became increasingly conservative in the ensuing decade. Orbán began to promote staunchly conservative, Christian family values – 'God, Homeland, Family' ('*Isten, Haza, Család*'). In a move rich with political, religious and social meaning, Orbán shifted the iconic symbol of Hungary – the crown of Szt István – from the National Museum to the Parliament building.

During the four years that Fidesz ruled, the relationship between the government and the capital scraped rock bottom. Gábor Demszky, who is now in his fourth term as SZDSZ mayor of Budapest (he was first elected in 1990), is a former dissident who had to drive a taxi when forced from a succession of jobs under communism in the late '70s. Demszky and Fidesz fought a series of bitter battles over the cost of large projects in the city, including the construction of the fourth metro line and the site of the National Theatre – or the 'National Pit' (see page 176), as the empty hole

## A CAR FOR THE PEOPLE

**Q** *'How do you double the value of a Trabant?'* **A** *'Fill it with petrol.'*

The Berlin Wall fell in 1989, but the blue-smoke-belching Trabant – symbol of the old communist era – is still a visible presence. City governments have tried to run it off the road, but people love their 'soap dishes'. Owners were offered a BKV transport pass worth 30,000Ft in 1995 as an incentive to trade in their Trabis; of 300,000 on the road, just 200 were handed in. The city government recently increased the reward to 200,000Ft.

During the 1960s and '70s, the waiting list for a Trabi was 15 years long. It cost a year's wages for an average Hungarian worker, and came in beige, light blue or olive green. On delivery, new owners were advised to tighten visible screws and grease all working parts. In actual fact it was never meant to be a car, but a rainproof motorcycle with a boot, and thus cheap transport for all the family. It was an innovation in the 1950s, the engine so light it could be lifted out by one man – rally-racing Trabants often carried a spare in the boot. In a 'reindeer test' – which simulates the ability of a car to avoid an obstacle (such as an animal) at speed – the Trabant apparently bettered a Mercedes. It was handmade of

became known. At the heart of this were contrasting views of the very capital itself, which Demszky promotes as a 'world city' and Fidesz sees as the embodiment of dangerous, non-Magyar forces of cosmopolitanism and liberalism.

Duroplast – a mixture of compressed resin and polyester – and is light, rust-proof and cheap. However, it is also totally non-recyclable, has the acceleration of an overweight slug and gets reduced to smithereens in a collision.

In the last days of the Berlin Wall, rickety East German Trabants escaping to the West through Hungarian territory became symbols of freedom. Consumerism, however, and the competing claims of shiny Audis and Fiats, meant it quickly reverted to a sad symbol of socialism: inefficient and dull. There were even small ads in local papers offering to swap cars for packets of cigarettes. The Trabi gained cult status in the West, though; in the early 1990s, U2 took a fleet of them on tour as part of their *Achtung Baby* set.

The last Trabant was made in 1992, but Zwickau in the former East Germany (where it was manufactured) remains a place of pilgrimage for the annual rally, attended by enthusiasts from all over Europe. The proudly ugly Trabi has outlived the demise of the system and the factory, and remains the most communist car of all – a true car for the people.

As for international ties, Hungary joined **NATO** in 1999, and for many years there was a US military base at Taszár. Opened in 1995, it attracted its share of controversy. Although built to provide backup for peacekeepers serving in Bosnia, in 1999 it was used as a launch pad for NATO air strikes against Serbia during the Kosovo crisis. The action was unpopular in Hungary, where there was much sympathy both for Serbs and for the Hungarian minority living in the Vojvodina region. The US air force withdrew in June 2004.

In 2002, the country elected the socialist **MSZP** once more (again with coalition partners SZDSZ). The elections were savage and the socialists' victory tiny (178 seats, of which SZDSZ won 20), with a majority of just ten. So narrow was the margin that Fidesz refused to accept the result, and established local action groups, Civic Circles (Polgári Kör), to drum up support in the countryside (where conservative values still predominate). However, while the majority of the centre-left coalition – similar in many respects to a Western European social-democratic government – is slender, it is nevertheless stable.

The present prime minister, Péter Medgyessy, is a banker and former finance minister who is not a member of any political party (ministers need not be MPs, simply requiring the backing of the governing party). Medgyessy steered Hungary into the **EU** on May 1 2004 (see page 19) and has announced Hungary's intention to adopt the euro as currency in 2010. In August 2000, Parliament elected Ferenc Mádl – a law professor and minister in the conservative MDF government of 1990–94 – to be its president. The president has relatively little executive power under the constitution, but does provide a check on the constitutionality of government legislation. His official residence is now in the Sándor Palace in the Castle District (see page 239).

While smooth and unbloody, the transition from the rule of state to democratic government was nevertheless a significant social, ideological and political change that took place just 15 years ago. The swing-ball nature of the country's elections is an understandable feature of a system still bedding in. Parliament is a more exciting place, and a centre of lively argument; it is also a place where debate is often confrontational, and focused upon political points-scoring rather than genuine policy differences. Where consensus comes in the parliamentary chamber is over Euro-Atlantic integration and the development of a free-market economy. And always hovering in the background is the cultural issue of the Treaty of Trianon, the territory Hungary lost after World War I and the millions of ethnic Hungarians living beyond the re-defined borders.

The main political parties are the Hungarian Socialist Party (MSzP), Alliance of Free Democrats (SzDSz), Hungarian Civic Alliance (Fidesz-MPP), Hungarian Democratic Forum (MDF), Hungarian Workers' Party (MMP), Hungarian Justice and Life Party (MIEP), Christian Democratic People's Party (KDNP), and Hungarian Democratic People's Party (MDNP).

## Budapest politics

Budapest has a complicated **dual self-government** system. In addition to the Budapest Municipality (the local government of Budapest, with its chief mayor of the city), the 23 districts have their own governments, each with an elected mayor and a body of representatives. Neither the municipal nor the district governments has primacy, and in essence their roles have come about through division of labour. Local-government tasks are generally implemented by the district governments, while tasks stemming from national policies, those relating to multiple districts of the city or to the city as a whole are undertaken by the Budapest Municipality. Fights between the two governmental representatives are common, and usually centre on issues of funding. Budapest is usually independent of national politics, but investments in large city projects have to be jointly agreed by the Parliament and the City Hall, and this has caused significant squabbles in the past (see page 13). In addition, Budapest tends to lean to the left of the political divide – and faces increased difficulties when a right-wing government is in power.

## ECONOMY

Hungary has made the transition from a centrally planned to a **market economy**, and continues to demonstrate strong growth. It has brought under control the high inflation that characterised the early years after its change of political system – from 14% as late as 1998 to under 5% in 2003 – and its reward has been admittance to the EU. The **private sector** accounts for over 80% of GDP, and foreign investment in (and ownership of) Hungarian firms has been a primary force in this economic success. Since 1989, direct foreign investment has amounted to around US$25 billion, attracted by relatively low working costs and wages, and an educated workforce. The national unemployment rate is just 6%, although there are wide regional variations. Germany is Hungary's most significant economic partner.

Standing at its crossroads, **Budapest** has emerged as the financial and commercial hub of central Europe. It is inevitably at the forefront of Hungary's economy, and consequently of its economic growth. It is here that the country's important transport arteries are gathered and it is here that 60% of foreign capital investment is funnelled. The unemployment rate is just 2.4%, the GDP per capita is a staggering 90% higher than the average, and the capital generates 35% of the national income.

## EU Membership

On May 1 2004, ten acceding eastern European and Mediterranean countries joined the European Union. Hungary was among them, and the economic effect of this membership is likely to be profound. On accession, Hungary's 10.1 million population had a per capita GDP of £6,975/US$12,515. Average earnings were €5,870. And of all the joining countries, Hungary's Northern Great Plain enjoys (or doesn't!) the lowest per capita GDP at only 34% of the existing EU states' average. Compared with the £16,192/US$29,052 per capita GDP of the existing 15 member states at date of entry, Hungary clearly has some catching up to do. Her prospects are encouraging. As the EU expands eastwards, it is likely that inward investment will see the establishment of increased manufacturing to take advantage of the freedom of movement of goods inherent in the principle of single-market free trade, combined with the benefits of a cheaper and energetic young workforce.

Having said that, the transition may be a tough one. Hungary's lingering Soviet-era state bureaucracy may find itself unprepared to enforce the EU's legally binding regulations and directives. EU rules on food, water control and pollution may challenge Hungary's current political administration and business culture – and these apply from day one, while the advantages of Common Agricultural Policy food subsidies and generous state benefits will not equal that of the existing states for ten years. It is to be hoped that the dynamism of Hungary's educated youth will rapidly overcome the current gap in living standards, as happened when Spain and Portugal joined the EU in the mid-1980s.

## PEOPLE

> When a Hungarian enjoys himself, he will cast himself on to a bench, lean his arms on the table amidst the bottles and glasses, put his head down on them and sob audibly… But this is only when he is having a good time and thoroughly enjoying himself.
>
> H Ellen Browning, *A Girl's Wandering in Hungary* (1897)

Pick up a guidebook – any guide to any destination – and you'll invariably read of a country whose people are unrivalled in toothy bonhomie. Well, the Hungarians don't fit this global community of Cheshire cats. They are a rare and intriguing breed that looks on the gloomier side of life, who notice the cloud from afar but develop myopia when it comes to its lining. They acknowledge this trait, although typically describing it as 'realism'. They are more Eeyore than Tigger, and hooray for that.

We can look to history to make sense of this tendency towards pessimism. Foreign nations (Ottomans, Habsburgs, Germans and Soviets) and nature herself (devastating 19th-century flood) have conspired to subject the people and destroy their precious monuments. The Treaty of Trianon stripped the country of two-thirds of its territory. Borders have buckled through the ages, and five million ethnic Hungarians are now 'exiles', dividing families and isolating pockets of the populace. The upshot is a social psyche that expects to be dealt the rough cards in any hand. On an individual level, this melancholy can manifest itself in tragic ways. It is estimated that alcoholism is a problem for ten percent, and Hungary used to top the 'suicide league table'.

It is therefore surprising that Hungarians are neither lethargic nor submissive; on the contrary, they are fiercely patriotic and take deep pride in their past heroic struggles against oppression. The Castle District is standing proof of a willingness to rebuild – repeatedly – from conflict's rubble. They have been resourceful, energetic and inventive, claiming a clutch of Nobel prizes and making a bigger splash in the spheres of science, music and medicine than their population size entitles them. As the proverb states, 'only a Hungarian can enter a revolving door behind you and come out in front'. Such nationhood and high achievement stem from a desperate urge to resist forces that might snuff them out.

The issue of where the country stands in relation to its past divides Hungarians. Some – more usually city folk – are westward-facing Europeans. Others are fervent nationalists who believe in a Greater Hungary. They stress the importance of ancient tradition, of their Asiatic roots, and are frequently suspicious of the liberal cosmopolitanism (by which they usually mean 'Jewish-ness') of Budapest. Some right-wing politicians have played upon geographical insecurities, positioning Hungary as an island in a sea of Slav, surrounded by neighbours they cannot trust. This fear of anything that isn't 'pure Magyar' can seem strange when common surnames like

### *THE NAME GAME*

What's in a name? Nothing, it seems, as long as it's not that of Belgian movie star Jean-Claude van Damme or former communist leader János Kádár. These were among those submitted to – and rejected by – the Interior Ministry last year. Hungarians are obliged to choose names from an official list, a practice introduced under the communists; while Rózsa would no doubt smell as sweet by any other name, that other name had better be in the approved 'Ládó' book.

Those wishing to deviate from the list must apply for permission, and unusual or foreign-sounding names are often turned down. There are exceptions; 'Jennifer', for instance – very possibly popularised by singer Jennifer Lopez – has made it into the 1,900 permitted first names as 'Dzsenifer'. Historical names are also protected, and applicants would usually have to

Németh (meaning 'German'), Tóth ('Slovak), Horváth (Croatian) and 'Orosz' (Russian) are indicative of a more mixed heritage. Nevertheless, such isolationist views make prejudice common; while there is growing public discussion about the shame of the Hungarian Holocaust, anti-Semitism is not unusual and dislike of the Roma minority is often openly expressed. Hungary also lags behind some Western countries in its ready acceptance of feminist views and alternative lifestyles (such as homosexuality).

If it seems paradoxical (even oxymoronic) to talk of people as proud prove a familial link. Typical requests for name changes come from married women starting in business who want to free themselves of '*né*' (see below), or from Roma looking to disguise their roots after marrying non-Roma.

Registered forenames are assigned a calendar 'name day' (*névnap*), which is celebrated with cards and gifts. (The name-day calendar can be found at www.behindthename.com/namedays/hungarian.) A married woman may either retain her maiden name or adopt her husband's with the appendage '*né*' ('belonging to'). As such, if Szabó Anna married Kovács János, she could call herself one of four versions: Kovács Jánosné, Kovácsné Szabó Anna, Kovács Jánosné Szabó Anna or just Szabó Anna. Confused? Well you'll be dismayed to hear that, in addition to all this, in Hungary surnames appear in front of forenames...

pessimists or suicidal self-improvers, there are other ways in which the coin of the Hungarian national character has two apposite sides. As we've said, Hungarians – even urbanists and the young – are inherently conservative and home loving, preferring the Magyar way of life. Yet they can also be wholly lacking in prudery. The pornography business is strong in Budapest, and porn stars like Michelle Wild and Monique Covet household names who appear regularly on breakfast television. And while the people are reserved, their social codes based on formality and politeness, you may find this difficult to credit in some restaurants, where it is quickly clear that the service industry has yet to recover fully from 40 years of communism.

The Hungarian character evades simple stereotypes. This is a race of people made tough by repeated slaps from history's hand; it is also one with stamina, with resourceful answers to difficult questions, and with a little less of the commercial superficiality so familiar in the West. Tourists will find that the Budapest boulevard is a purposeful place where people hurry about their business. There are few exchanged smiles on the metro. However, there is never any sense in which this is intimidating or uncomfortable, and it masks a genuine and earnest helpfulness that lurks close beneath the surface. A terse face can be transformed by '*köszönöm*' from a foreign tongue, and more sustained interaction reveals an openness, an engaging and sophisticated humour, and a commitment to friendship that is all the more valuable because not casually offered.

The **ethnic make up** of Hungary is 89.9% Hungarian, 4% Roma, 2.6% German, 2% Serb, 0.8% Slovak, 0.7% Romanian.

## CULTURAL DOS AND DON'TS

**Tipping** It is customary to give a tip (*borravaló*, meaning 'something to buy wine with'...!) to waiters, hotel porters, bath attendants, bar staff, taxi drivers, hairdressers and tour guides. As in most countries, the amount to tip is something of a grey area. Ten to 15% is generally acceptable, although with bar and café bills and taxi fares it is common simply to round up to the nearest 'convenient' amount.

Give porters 300–500Ft, masseurs 200Ft and locker attendants 50Ft. When paying the bill in a restaurant, do not leave your tip on the table. Instead tell the waiter precisely how much you would like to pay (including the tip); if you say 'thank you' as you pass over payment, the waiter will assume that you don't want any change. Check whether service is included before paying – the staff are unlikely to point out your error if you tip twice – and shelve any embarrassment about refusing to tip if the service is poor. Service in Hungary is variable to say the least, and will not change while disinterested staff know they'll get paid regardless.

**'Cheers!'** The convivial toast when drinking is '*egészségedre*' – a twister for the foreign tongue thickened with wine. However, the clinking of beer glasses is something of a social *nem-nem*. Why? After crushing the rebellion against Habsburg rule in 1849, the Austrian military leader Haynau – known as the 'Hyena of Brescia' – toasted the execution of 13 Hungarian generals by clinking his beer glass. Angry Hungarians swore that for the next 150 years they would refrain from clinking their own glasses out of disgust for what they had seen. The period has passed but the custom continues.

**Bars** Most bars in Budapest offer table service. Open a tab and settle the bill with the waiter or waitress before you leave.

**Smoking** Smoking is popular in Hungary, and you'll see many a Budapester drawing on a thin, white-tipped cigarette and lingering over a coffee. A law was passed in 1999 stipulating that restaurants must provide a non-smoking section;

hunt out the sign reading '*tilos a dohányzás*' (no smoking) – it usually marks the tiny area shoved away at the back.

**Thanks Doc** Hungarian doctors were paid meagre salaries by the state during the communist period, and it became customary for grateful patients to offer physicians a tip (*hálapénz*, or 'gratitude money'), given discreetly in a plain envelope, for their help and advice. Doctors are much better off today, but many Hungarians still adhere to this tradition – a friend recently gave 50,000Ft, for example, after a small operation.

**What's the point?** As a rule of thumb, Hungarians consider it rude to point at other people with the index finger – it is OK, however, to point at an object. When counting on their hands, Hungarians start with the thumb. As such, if a shop assistant wants to check that you really only want one banana, she will give what looks like a thumbs-up sign. Two bananas would be thumb and index finger, and so on.

**Train escalators** Unlike escalator etiquette in the UK, Hungarians do not stand to the right to allow others to pass on the left. If you're in a hurry and fear dawdlers ahead, you'll have to grin and stair it.

**House visits** If invited to a Hungarian's home for a meal, take a bottle of good Hungarian wine with you – a fine Tokaji is always well received – and perhaps some flowers or chocolates. You may be expected to remove your shoes before entering. Few topics of conversation are off limits, but remember that the average Hungarian salary is considerably lower than those of many other Europeans, so be sensitive that discussions of your earnings might cause discomfort. Budapesters are also fiercely – and rightly – proud of their capital; adverse comments should be served with a healthy dollop of tact.

**Shopping** When entering a chemist or food shop, you must pick up a basket – even if you plan to buy just one item or simply to browse. Large electrical stores often ask customers to leave their bags in secure lockers before they shop to make theft more difficult.

## GIVING SOMETHING BACK/LOCAL CHARITIES

**Education for Blind Children** (*Vakok Szolgáltató Központja*) XIV, Ajtósi sor 39; tel: 1 363 3343; email: latasserultek@vakisk.hu; www.vakisk.hu. From nursery through to specialised secondary school.

**Foundation for the Women of Hungary** (*Magyarországi Női Alapítvány*) 1537Bp, PO Box 453/277; tel: 1 350 1311; email: mona.fwh@matavnet.hu; www.mona-hungary.org

**Károlyi István Children's Centre** (*Gyermekközpont*) Web (in English): www.gyermekkozpont.hu.

**Foundation for School Meals** (*Gyermekétkeztetési Alapítvány*) XX, Mária utca 3; tel: 1 283 2510; www.gyea.hu. Foundation providing school meals for needy (mostly Roma) children.

**White Cross** Tel (in English): 06 20958 2545; www.feherkeresztliga.hu. Does excellent work rounding up the absurdly high number (two million) of cats and dogs that go astray annually in Hungary.

## BUSINESS

Budapest's location makes it a popular place for international business conferences, and there are plenty of hotels that cater for these. Many four- and five-star hotels have business centres and even individual internet access in their rooms. The financial district is in Pest.

Business etiquette is similar to that in western Europe and the US. The suit is the standard uniform, the handshake is used for greeting (it is customary to wait until the woman offers her hand), business cards (*névjegy*) are exchanged (although Hungarian cards will list the holder's surname before his/her forename), and it is common to give a token gift. The principal language of business is English, although on occasion a translator may be required; it is prudent to ask about this beforehand, and the British embassy can advise on interpretation services. While the usual hours of business are 08.00–16.30 during the week, companies (and especially government offices) often close early in the afternoon on Friday, and spring and autumn are the main business seasons.

### Useful contacts

**American Chamber of Commerce** V, Deák Ferenc utca 10; tel: 1 266 9880; email: info@amcham.hu; www.amcham.hu

**British Chamber of Commerce** V, Bank utca 6; tel: 1 302 5200; email: bcch@bcch.com; www.bcch.com

**Hungarian Chamber of Commerce and Industry** V, Kossuth tér 6–8; tel: 1 474 5100; email: mkik@mail.mkik.hu; www.mkik.hu

**ITD Hungary** VI, Andrássy út 12; tel: 1 472 8100; email: info@itd.hu; www.business2hungary.com. The headquarters of the Hungarian government's investment and trade-development agency, which offers consulting, business match-making services, trade directories, conference facilities and a business library. *Open Mon–Fri 09.00–16.30.*

## RELIGION

Churchgoers are a minority in Hungary, particularly in Budapest and other cities. **Roman Catholicism** (*Katolikus*) is the main religious denomination (67.5% of Hungarians). István, Hungary's first king, introduced Christianity as the religion of state over a thousand years ago, and it survived in spite of sustained Turkish occupation (when many Hungarians converted temporarily to Islam) and the secularity of communist rule. The largest **Protestant** denomination is the Calvinist or Reformed Church (*Református*; 20% of the population), followed by the Lutherans/Evangelicals (*Evangélikus*; 5%).

Seven percent are listed as affiliated to other religious orders that include **Serb** and **Greek Orthodox** (*Szerb/Görög ortodox*) and **Judaism** (*zsidó vallás*). Before World War II, Budapest had one of the most significant Jewish communities in the world, estimated at 200,000. However, over half perished during the Holocaust, and after the war only 90,000 Jews remained in the city. Numbers dwindled further under communist rule, particularly following the 1956 revolution. The demise of communism saw a revival of sorts, and today 80,000 Jews live in the city (the biggest community in central Europe), a number that continues to grow. In addition, as in most post-communist countries, Hungary is seen as fertile ground for the '**new**'

**religions**; Mormons, Hari Krishna, Faith Congregation and Scientologists are all commonly found on the streets and subways.

## CULTURE

Hungary has a proud cultural history, but much of its output remains closed to a world that can't speak the tongue. Some of the finest **literature** is set in regions now beyond the country's borders, and represents the constant prick of loss. An early narrative of roaming Magyars fleeing hostile foes in their own land has a strong hold, while there's a tradition of rebellion, isolation and despair among the popular songbooks. The most renowned writers hark from the Romantic age, kings among them being the young revolutionary poet Sándor Petőfi (see page 278) and his friend János Arany. Others you'll come across – often through the names of streets or squares – are the Romanticists Ferenc Kölcsey (author of the national anthem) and Mihály Vörösmarty, the late-19th-century realists József Eötvös and Mór Jókai, the anguished Endre Ady and the expressionistic, avant-garde Attila József. In October 2002, Imre Kertész – author of *Sorstalanság* (*Fateless*), a shocking Holocaust novel – won the Nobel Prize for Literature. Head for the Hungarian National Gallery (see page 306) for a survey of the nation's **artistic** contribution.

As for classical **music**, Ferenc Liszt, Béla Bartók and Zoltán Kodály are established names in the canon of European composers. These days, the minimalist textures of modern composer György Ligeti are helping to carry on the Hungarian claim to musical preeminence – his compositions featured in *2001 A Space Odyssey*, and his was the eerie piano music in Stanley Kubrick's *Eyes Wide Shut* and Márta Sebestyén's haunting vocals at the beginning of *The English Patient*. However, fewer will have encountered contemporary Hungarian music, although this scene is one of the most intriguing faces of cultural change underway in the country.

In the second half of last century, while rock and roll boomed in the West, Hungarians only had access to it via Radio Luxembourg and Radio Free Europe (which were illegal). Communism prohibited commercial radio, and the musical diet was officially limited. During this era underground radio played a crucial counter-establishment role, both cultural and political (indeed, some people partly attribute the bloody 1956 Hungarian uprising to its subversive influence).

As a consequence, Hungarians are even now 'catching up' with some of the music that passed them by. And it hardly needs stating that Hungarian classic rock is unknown in the West. Although local rock bands required a permit to play for live audiences, there were some very successful home-grown artists in the 1960s and '70s (such as Bikini, LGT, Illés, Metró and Omega).

Popular music underwent a rapid change in the late 1980s. The cultural influx that came with the political shift has continued unabated since. Young Hungarians are generally fashion conscious and up to date. Nevertheless, seismic cultural change has inevitably resulted in generational differences. Those in their 30s and 40s tend to go out less frequently as family and work commitments take precedence; older Hungarians arguably hold a limited definition of 'culture', partly due to the entrenched Soviet practice of 'cultural houses', which served for the staging of everything from poetry readings to chess games. The established view in Hungary is that pop is a subculture belonging to the commercial – not the cultural – domain, and full acceptance will take time.

To try to isolate and define Hungarian music would be to overlook the fact that its *diversity* is intrinsic to understanding this corner of the world. The musical landscape in central Europe reflects a tangled web of historical relationships and influences. The mutual borrowing from musical traditions in this region – Slavonic, Romany, Jewish and more – may seem bewildering at first.

**Folk music** – stifled under communism because nationalistic songs were out of keeping with the professed internationalist ethic – now thrives again. Try listening to Kaláka, or Muzsikás with Márta Sebestyén. In some restaurants, musicians play traditional tunes on string instruments, including the Hungarian *cimbalom*. To hear the instrument's capabilities explored in full, try Balogh Kálmán and the Gipsy Cimbalom Band. Other notable groups exemplifying distinctive regional music styles include the renowned ambassadors of *klezmer* (a Jewish folk tradition originating in central and eastern Europe) the Budapest Klezmer Band; purveyors of Croatian dance Vujicsics; and Parno Graszt, Romano Drom, Kalyi Jág and Ternipe, bands that exemplify the Romany (gypsy) strand of Hungarian musical tradition. Or the Hungarian strand of the Romany tradition, depending on your point of view.

**Jazz** fans might try the Dresch Mihály Quartet or the Balázs Elemér Group, while the upcoming group The Next Generation is made up of highly talented young musicians in their teens and 20s. Admirers of instrumental virtuosity should make a note of pianist Béla Szakcsi Lakatos and his son Robi, the latter a rising star in his own right. Dynamic young violinist Lajkó Félix – imagine a kind of Balkan Nigel

Kennedy – from northern Serbia now lives and regularly performs in Budapest.

Among well-regarded **DJs** active in Budapest, and at the cutting edge of Hungarian sounds, are turntable veteran Palotai and the talented young Yonderboi. Electronic and dance artists you can pursue in record shops (or perhaps catch live) include Anima Sound System, Korai Öröm, Zagar, Másfél and Yonderboi (again). These acts are notable for fusing global and local elements in a way that is original and eclectic, but avoids seeming contrived. The fusion of new and old is emblematic of the meeting of world and local cultures occurring in this part of Europe. Contemporary Hungarian music is especially interesting for the way many of the artists disregard, and so transcend, boundaries between musical genres and traditions.

## HOLIDAYS, FESTIVALS AND EVENTS

### National holidays

Businesses and shops close for national holidays.

| | |
|---|---|
| **January 1** | New Year's Day |
| **March 15** | Independence Day |
| **March/April** | Easter Monday |
| **May 1** | Labour Day |
| **May/June** | Whit Monday |
| **August 20** | St Stephen's Day (founding of the state) |
| **October 23** | Republic Day (anniversary of the 1956 revolution and the 1989 proclamation of the republic) |

| | |
|---|---|
| **November 1** | All Saints' Day |
| **December 25–26** | Christmas (*Karácsony*) (usually December 24 too) |

## Festivals and events

Budapest celebrates a range of festivals devoted to sport and the arts. The country's two biggest cultural events are the Spring (Tavaszi) and Autumn (Őszi) festivals. Tickets are available from the Budapest Spring-Autumn Festival Office (V, Egyetem tér 5; tel: 1 486 3300; email: info@festivalvaros.hu; www.festivalcity.hu). Tourinforms and listings magazines will offer precise details of the attractions on offer and their venues.

**New Year's Day Concert (Jan 1)** The Dohnányi Orchestra Budafok and the Danube Folk Ensemble perform classical pieces during an extravaganza of music and dance at the State Opera House. See www.hungariakoncert.hu.

**Independence Day (Mar 15)** Commemorates the anniversary of the 1848 revolution, when Hungarians revolted – ultimately unsuccessfully – against Habsburg rule. The poet Sándor Pétőfi famously recited his 'Nemzeti Dal' ('National Song') from the steps of the National Museum. The date is often marked by political gatherings and soap-box rants by the far-right around Heroes' Square.

**Budapest Spring Festival (around Mar 19–Apr 4)** A 17-day national arts festival. The capital hosts 200 events, including orchestral recitals, and opera, ballet and folk-dancing performances. See www.festivalcity.hu.

**National Dance House Gathering and Crafts Fair (around Mar 27–28)** A celebration of traditional dancing and art, with performances from folk artists, musicians and dancers, plus an arts-and-crafts sale. In 2004 it was held at the Körcsarnok, one of the stadia near Puskás Ferenc Stadion. See www.tanchaz.hu.

**Labour Day (May 1)** During the communist era, Labour Day was commemorated with great street parades; today there are parties in City Park and on Margaret Island. The country joined the EU on May 1 2004, so celebrations now have added significance.

**Danube Carnival International Cultural Festival (around Jun 11–20)** The capital jigs to a ten-day festival of music and dance, held at various locations. See www.dunaart.hu/carnival.

**Ferencváros Festival (around Jun 18–Jul 12)** Lively summer music and arts, with various concerts and a grand opera première. Held at Bakáts tér open-air stage, at the southern end of Ráday utca, or in Bakáts tér church. See www.szinhaz.hu/fesztival.

**Budapest Equestrian Summer Festival (Jun 26–27)**
Thousands of spectators flock to Shipyard Island for thrilling displays of equestrian martial arts, show-jumping, dressage, stunt shows and carriage driving. See www.karneval.hu.

**Budapest Farewell (Búcsú) (last weekend of Jun)** A series of outdoor concerts that commemorate the day the last Soviet troops left Hungarian soil in 1991.

**Chain Bridge Festival (end of Jun)** A recent addition to the events calendar, this two-day festival involves the closure to traffic of Budapest's most famous bridge. It enrages motorists. However, it's short in duration and small in scale, with stalls selling food and items of folk art, and performances of traditional music and dance.

**Sziget Festival (end July/start August)** Budapest's very own Glastonbury is held on Shipyard Island. There's a broad spectrum of music from some of Europe's best bands –

## *EASTER*

The week leading up to Easter is a busy one for the women of Hungarian households, who perform a thorough spring clean and go into baking overdrive. In addition, they paint hard-boiled eggs with folksy motifs and patterns, and present them to visitors as Easter gifts. The celebrations themselves begin on Good Friday, with mass services held at 15.00 in churches all over the city. On Easter Sunday, following morning services, children are treated with chocolate eggs and small presents from the Easter Bunny. The real fun, though, comes on Easter Monday, when the traditional 'sprinkling' (*locsolkodás*) takes place. Men customarily 'sprinkle' their female relatives and friends with cheap perfume, in return for which they receive a reward – a painted egg, some chocolate coins or a shot of *pálinka* (potent fruit brandy). The latter reward means that by mid-afternoon there can be some rather giddy sprinklers! Originally this ritual was a fertility rite, when men visited the single women of the village and sprinkled their friends and relatives along the way. Even today it is used as a form of courtship. It is less sodden than it was in the past, however – when buckets of water were used in the villages rather than cologne.

dance, trance, pop, hard rock, jazz and blues – and those who fancy it can camp. In addition, there are extreme sports, a fun fair, theatre, discussion groups, dance, film, pubs, bars, restaurants, World Music, African Village, Hari Krishnas – in short, everything and everyone! See www.sziget.hu.

**St Stephen's Day (Aug 20)** A public holiday in honour of Hungary's patron saint and first king, Szent István (1000–1038). His mummified right hand is paraded through the streets, and church services are held across the capital, along with plays, shows, dances and a craft fair in the Castle District (see www.nesz.hu). The day climaxes with a spectacular river procession and fireworks on Gellért Hill.

**Budapest Parade (around Aug 28)** A thumping carnival and street party modelled on Berlin's Love Parade, with colourful floats and parades, and a massive disco afterwards in the Stadionok complex. See www.sziget.hu/budapestparade and www.sziget.hu/afterparty.

**Jewish Summer Festival (around Aug 29–Sep 5)** A celebration of Jewish culture, music, dance, cuisine and film. A good opportunity to watch a concert inside the breathtaking Great Synagogue. See www.jewishfestival.hu.

**Budapest International Wine Festival (around Sep 5–15)** A merry festival concentrated on the Castle District (with smaller events in Budafok and Szentendre), and featuring a wine auction, a harvest procession and, of course, plenty of sniffing, gargling and tasting! Stalls offer nibbles to complement the tipples. See www.winefestival.hu.

**Autumn Festival (around Oct 15–31)** Contemporary arts festival that has been running for 20 years.

**Republic Day (Oct 23)** A national holiday marking the anniversary of the outbreak of the 1956 uprising. It also commemorates the 1989 proclamation of the Hungarian republic.

**Budapest Antiques Fair (last weekend of Nov)** Held in the Palace of Arts (Műcsarnok) on Heroes' Square. See www.antik-enterior.hu for details on Antik Enteriőr.
**New Year's Eve Gala Ball (Dec 31)** The capital's glitterati dig out their penguin suits and ball gowns, and step out to the State Opera House for a wonderful gala concert performed by some of the country's leading musicians and dancers. In addition, they gorge on a banquet prepared by the Gundel chefs, and risk indigestion by tripping the light fantastic until dawn. Not surprisingly, tickets are sought after and very expensive. See www.viparts.hu.

## GEOGRAPHY

The Republic of Hungary lies in the Carpathian Basin in central eastern Europe. It occupies 93,030km$^2$, is landlocked and bordered by seven others: Austria, Slovakia, Romania, Serbia and Montenegro, Croatia, Slovenia and Ukraine. Budapest is the country's capital and largest city, occupying a central-northern position and taking up 525km$^2$. The Danube runs through the country for 417km, slicing Budapest into two halves; on its western bank is the green and hilly Buda, while on the eastern is the flat and built-up Pest.

## CLIMATE

Hungary enjoys a temperate continental climate, although seasonal variations are significant. Winter (December–February) is icy cold, with temperatures often dropping below freezing and some snowfall possible. Spring arrives and the temperatures begin to perk up properly in April, although showers are also common. You should expect ten hours of sunshine during the summer months (June–August), which are at least warm and can be very hot – the August average is 22°C, but temperatures often break the 30°C barrier. It is also noticeable that temperatures do not peak at midday, but appear to continue rising well into the afternoon, and humidity can be high. March and November are the wettest months, and are neither warm nor bitingly cold.

For detailed **weather reports**, log on to the Hungarian Meteorological Service website at www.met.hu (which has information in English).

BUDAPEST
N
Bradt
III
II
XIII
XIV
Margaret Island
Újlipótváros
0 2km
0 1ml
Nyugati Railway Station
City Park
Király Baths
Városmajor Station (Cogwheel Railway)
Parliament
VI
Puskás Ferenc Stadium (Népstadion)
Lipótváros
Terézváros
Víziváros
St Stephen's Basilica
VII
I
Erzsébetváros
XII
Széchenyi Lánchíd
V
Déli Railway Station
Kerepesi Cemetery
Buda Castle Palace
Belváros
Józsefváros
Tabán
Hungarian National Museum
VIII
Keleti Railway Station
Szabadság híd
Citadella
Big Market Hall
Wolf's Meadow Cemetery
Sas Hill
XI
IX
Ferencváros
© Bradt Travel Guides Ltd
Népliget bus station

# Planning

2

## THE CITY: A PRACTICAL OVERVIEW

The first thing to ask yourself is 'On which side of the river am I?' The 525km² city is divided in two by the blue Danube, which runs through here for 28km and is spanned by seven road and two rail bridges. If you're among narrow streets or leafy hills to the west, you are in Buda, which makes up a third of the city; if you're in the more built-up area to the east, with shops, businesses, broad boulevards and squares, you're in Pest. If you're wet and treading water, you've fallen between the two.

Administratively, Budapest is carved into 23 districts (I–III, XI–XII and XXII in Buda, IV–X, XIII–XXI and XXIII in Pest; see map opposite). The tourist is most likely to spend time in districts V (the downtown), I (where you'll find the Castle District), VI (Terézváros, which holds Andrássy út), XIV (home of City Park), VII and VIII (Erzsébetváros and Józsefváros respectively), III (where the Roman ruins of Aquincum lie) and II and XII (the Buda hills). Districts or areas within them often also bear historic names (such as Erzsébetváros – or Elizabeth Town).

The city's street plan is well laid out. In essence, the centre of Pest is defined by two ring roads – the Kiskörút (the Small Boulevard), a semicircular thoroughfare that links the Chain and Liberty bridges and hems in the Belváros (city centre), and the Nagykörút (Great Boulevard), which runs outside it between Petőfi and Margaret bridges. Radiating outward from the Kiskörút are several broad avenues that cut through the Nagykörút and beyond. The result is

## HIGHLIGHTS/SUGGESTED ITINERARIES

### *If you're staying a weekend*

- Make an early-morning trip to the bustling Big Market Hall, with its salamis and lace and glass and caviar.
- Ride the funicular railway up Castle Hill, trawl a leisurely course around the Castle District, and scoff a cake at the Ruszwurm.
- Pick a museum and gallery or two – choose from extensive holdings at the Museum of Fine Arts, the Hungarian National Museum and the Hungarian National Gallery, or more specialised exhibitions like the polished Varga Imre Collection or the sombre, compelling and stylised House of Terror.
- Soak away your aches in a thermal spa – and admire the proud art-nouveau architecture and wide-girthed men of the Gellért or Széchenyi baths.
- Wrap yourself around a pastry in a *fin-de-siècle* coffee house.
- Take in the sights and shops of the city centre, including the Szt István Basilica and the Parliament building.



an easily navigable spider web of tarmac. Buda is characterised more by its features than its roads, with Castle and Gellért hills dominating the immediate riverscape. On a map, Margit körút makes a teasing play of continuing the natural

- Join the metro to Heroes' Square and City Park, with its ducks, zoo and eclectic castle.
- Eat *gulyás* soup, Hortobágy pancakes, and paprika chicken with dumplings.
- Try a shot of fruit brandy, and a glass or three of sweet Tokaji Aszú.
- Watch the day draw to a close in a café-bar on Liszt Ferenc tér.

### *And longer…*

- Hire a bike and pedal around Margaret Island.
- Take the cogwheel and children's railways into the Buda hills, and return by chairlift from János hegy.
- Visit the Cave Church dug into the side of Gellért hegy, and then push on up to the Freedom Monument and Citadella on top.
- Take in a performance at the stunning State Opera House, or an outdoor concert in front of the Szt István Basilica.
- Book an evening river trip.
- Travel to Statue Park, the dumping ground for communist statues.
- Eke out the Roman amphitheatres and mosaics of Óbuda.

line of the ringroad, before leading off towards Lake Balaton. Attila út, Hegyalja út, Bartók Béla út and Fő utca are Buda's main roads – the first three busy and noisy – while Moszkva tér and Móricz Zsigmond körtér are the transport hubs. In addition to all this, there are three metro lines (all serving Pest, one of which crosses the river to the north of Castle Hill), suburban railways, and three main railway stations (Déli in Buda, and Keleti and Nyugati in Pest) that run trains to national and international destinations.

### Addresses

Hungarian addresses are written with the postcode first, followed by the street and building number. In the case of Budapest, the two central numbers in the four-digit postcode indicate the building's district (*kerület*); thus 'H-1014 Budapest, Fő utca 4' falls in district I (in the Castle Hill area of Buda). Clearly this filling in the postcode sandwich provides a useful indicator as to the location of an address. Floors of buildings (*emelet*) are numbered from the level above ground upwards (as in Britain), written as III *emelet* (third floor), IV *emelet* (fourth floor), etc.

## WHEN TO VISIT

There's no bad time to visit Budapest, although March and November – wet months and neither hot nor cold – are at the bottom of the pile. Traditionally locals ship out of the capital in the sticky months of July and August, when temperatures can hit 32°C. As cities go, though, Budapest caters well for lovers of summer sunshine. There are several outdoor spas and swimming pools in which to cool down, and most hotels have air conditioning. If you want to avoid the risk of traipsing around in the wake of beetroot-red gaggles of tourists, come in spring or autumn, when you can also enjoy the music, dance, theatre and art on offer during one of the capital's two major cultural festivals (see pages 34–8). Hotel rates are lower outside the summer season. Autumn provides the light to watch nature by, and the hills form a pleasing backdrop to walks among falling leaves. The weather generally remains warm enough for strolling, although it can be drizzly from April through to mid-May. The cold settles in from the end of October until the middle of March, and bites in December and January, with the sun setting at 15.45 and temperatures plummeting below freezing. But it's a cold heart that turns from the romance of Budapest in winter, with snow under foot and Christmas markets selling hot wine. Just bring your scarf and gloves.

## TOUR OPERATORS (WORLDWIDE)

Package holidays, city breaks, tailor-made tours and flights are readily available through UK- and US-based tour operators specialising in eastern Europe. In addition to those below, see also *Local tours* and *Local travel agents* (page 83), some of which can arrange accommodation etc.

### In the UK

**CME Travel** 39 Spencer Rd, Rendlesham, Woodbridge IP12 2TJ; tel: 0870 128 0636; email: mike.silford@cmefortravel.co.uk; www.cmefortravel.co.uk. City breaks to Budapest and excursions to the Hungarian countryside.

**Cycle Riders** Victoria Works, Lambridge Mews, Bath BA1 6QE; tel: 01225 428452; www.biketours.co.uk. Group tours to Budapest (and beyond) on two wheels.

**Fregata Travel** 83 Whitechapel High St, London E1 7QX; tel: 020 7375 3187; email:

fregata@commodore.co.uk; www.fregatatravel.co.uk. Concise tour of Budapest includes all the city's main attractions.

**Great Rail Journeys** Saviour House, 9 St Saviourgate, York YO1 8NL; tel: 01904 521900; email: grj@greatrail.com; www.greatrail.com. Runs several rail tours departing from Waterloo to European cities including Budapest.

**Jules Verne Tours** 21 Dorset Sq, London NW1 6QG; tel: 020 7616 1000; email: sales@vjv.co.uk; www.vjv.com. Tours include a four-night programme taking in all the main city sights, as well as longer tours that feature Budapest, Vienna and Prague.

**Interchange (The Spirit of Travel)** Interchange House, 27 Stafford Rd, Croydon, Surrey CR0 4NG; tel: 020 8681 3612; email: interchange.uk.com; www.interchange.uk.com. Can arrange flights, transfer, car hire, accommodation and excursions. Spa, golf and horse-riding programmes are available, as is a six-day steam-engine-driving course in Budapest!

**Kirker Holidays** 4 Waterloo Court, Theed St, London SE1 8ST; tel: 0870 112333. Specialises in short/city breaks.

**Martin Randall Travel** Voysey House, Barley Mow Passage, London W4 4GF; tel: 020 8742 3355; email: info@martinrandall.co.uk; www.martinrandall.com. Culture vultures can join a musical or historical tour of Budapest.

**Operas Abroad** The Tower, Mill Lane, Rainhill, Prescot, Merseyside L35 6NE; tel/fax: 0151 493 0382; email: info@operasabroad.com; www.operasabroad.com. Specialist packages featuring three opera performances.

**Regent Holidays** 15 John St, Bristol BS1 2HR; tel: 0117 921 1711; email: regent@regent-holidays.co.uk; www.regent-holidays.co.uk. Respected independent operator specialising in eastern European destinations.

**Trailfinders** 194 Kensington High St, London W8; tel: 020 7937 1234; www.trailfinders.com. A one-stop shop for advice, flights and tailor-made packages to Budapest.

## *Nature*

**Earthwatch Institute** 267 Banbury Rd, Oxford OX2 7HT; tel: 01865 318838 *(general enquiries)*, 01865 318831 *(project enquiries)*; email: projects@earthwatch.org.uk; www.earthwatch.org/europe. A non-profit-making organisation assisting with research into the decline of songbirds migrating from Europe to sub-Saharan Africa. At the research centre in the Ócsa wetland (30km southeast of Budapest; see page 371) volunteers learn to set up and patrol mist nets, assess birds' health, and conduct vegetation surveys. Be aware that while such projects are rewarding they are aimed at proper research, and are not guided tours.

**Ecotours** See page 84.

## In the USA

**Abercrombie & Kent** 1520 Kensington Rd, Suite 212 Oak Brook, Illinois 60523-2156; tel: +1 630 954 2944; www.abercrombiekent.com. High-end tailor-made private tours for individuals and small groups.

**Earthwatch Institute** 3 Clocktower Place, Suite 100, PO Box 75, Maynard, MA 01754; tel: +1 (978) 461 0081 or +1 (800) 776 0188; email: info@earthwatch.org. For description, see above.

**Forum Travel International** 91 Gregory Lane, Suite 21, Pleasant Hill, Calfornia 94523; tel: +1 (800) 252 4475; email: fti@foruminternational.com; www.foruminternational.com. Offers a biking tour from Vienna to Budapest, tracing the course of the Danube.

### In Australia

**Earthwatch Institute** 126 Bank Street, South Melbourne, VIC 3205; tel: +61 (0) 3 9682 6828; email: earth@earthwatch.org. For description see page 47.

## RED TAPE

### Entry requirements

European Union (EU) nationals, including those from Britain, may visit Hungary as indefinite tourists providing they have valid passports; visitors from France, Germany, Italy and Spain require only an identification card. Tourists from all other European countries (excluding Albania, Turkey, Macedonia and Bosnia-Herzegovina), the USA, Canada, Australia and New Zealand can visit without a visa for up to 90 days.

Travellers wishing to exceed a 90-day stay should apply for a visa from their country's consulate and allow at least four weeks for it to be processed. Visas can also be issued at Hungarian border crossings (not rail crossings) and at Budapest Ferihegy Airport. In order to apply for a visa you'll need your passport (valid for at least six months from the time of exit from Hungary) and two recent passport-sized photos. A single-entry visa currently costs US$40, double-entry US$75 and multiple-entry US$180. Transit visas are valid for up to 48 hours and are compulsory for visa-requiring travellers who pass through Hungarian borders. A single-entry transit visa costs US$38, double-entry US$65 and multiple-entry US$150. For additional visa information, log on to Hungary's foreign ministry website at www.mfa.gov.hu.

### Customs regulations

Visitors aged 16 or over may take 250 cigarettes, 50 cigars or 250g of tobacco, two litres of wine, one litre of spirits and five litres of beer, 250ml of cologne and 100ml of perfume out of the country. Export of museum pieces or antiques requires an export permit, registered in your name; such permits can usually be obtained from the shop of purchase (see www.muemlekvedelem.hu for more details). If you buy an antique at auction, the organisers will give you an invoice and, for a charge of 2–4% of its selling price, a relevant museum issues the *kiviteli engedély* (export permit). Specialist companies can arrange all this paperwork for you, if you're willing to pay; try Jeff Taylor of First European Shipping (tel: 06 20 958 2545; www.firsteuropeanshipping.com), who speaks English. The special *bírálati csoport* (appraisal team) evaluates the art work if you do not have an invoice. Importation of any currency worth more than one million forints must be declared, and raw meat or milk products and potted or rooted plants cannot be brought in or out of Hungary. Unsurprisingly, it is prohibited to import pornography, drugs and unlicensed weapons. Now that Hungary has joined the EU, you can only claim back VAT (ÁFA) on goods over a certain value if you are a non-EU citizen. Hand the refund form (available from shops) to customs on leaving the country.

## HUNGARIAN EMBASSIES AND CONSULATES ABROAD

**Australia** 17 Beale Crescent, Deakin, ACT 2600; tel: +61 (2) 628 22 555; email: hungcbr@ozemail.com.au; www.matra.com.au/~hungemb

**Canada** 299 Waverley St, Ottawa, Ontario, K2P 0V9; tel: +1 (613) 230 2717; www.docuweb.ca/hungary

**Germany** Unter den Linden 76, 10117 Berlin; tel: +49 (30) 203 100; email: info@ungarische-botschaft.de; www.ungarische-botschaft.de

**Ireland** 2 Fitzwilliam Place, Dublin 2; tel: +353 (1) 661 2902; email: hungarian.embassy@eircom.net; www.kum.hu/dublin

**Italy** Via dei Villini 12–16, 00161 Roma; tel: +39 064 423 0598; email: titkarsag2@huembrom.it; www.huembit.it

**UK** 35 Eaton Place, London SW1X 8BY; tel +44 (20) 7235 5218; email: office@huemblon.org.uk; www.huemblon.org.uk/index.htm

**USA** 3910 Shoemakers St NW, Washington DC 20008; tel: +1 (202) 362 6730; email: office@huembwas.org; www.hungaryemb.org

## GETTING THERE AND AWAY

There are 56 road crossings, and 26 rail, five water and 17 air entry points into Hungary. Ensure all your documentation is at hand when crossing borders as guards have the right otherwise to refuse entry.

### By air

As with air travel to most European destinations, ticket prices to Budapest are at their highest during the summer period (June–August), and at Christmas and New Year. Costs may also rise during city festivals, and especially during the Hungarian Grand Prix (see page 225). The cheapest season is winter, between the months of November and March. Shop around for cut-price flights and last-minute bargains on the internet.

Websites like www.expedia.com, www.travelocity.co.uk, www.lastminute.co.uk and www.cheapflights.co.uk can offer good savings.

### *From the UK*

The no-frills airline revolution has made deep in-roads into eastern Europe. Before Hungary's admission to the EU, only British Airways and the Hungarian carrier Malév offered direct flights to Budapest from London; now a host of budget airlines are getting in on the act, including easyJet, Sky Europe and Wizz Air. Incredibly, there are now (in 2004) three times more seats available between London and Hungary than there were in 2003, and prices are increasingly competitive.

There are plans by easyJet to open routes between Budapest and Newcastle and Bristol on November 1 2004. At the moment of going to press, however, direct flights from the UK are available only from London airports (taking around 2½ hours). Those who live away from the capital can choose to make a connection to Budapest from another European city. For example, indirect flights operate from Manchester with a stop over in Amsterdam and take approximately six hours. KLM (tel: 0870 507 4074; www.klm.com) schedules direct flights from Amsterdam, Air France (tel: 0845 359 1000; www.airfrance.com) from Paris, and Lufthansa (tel: 0870 837 7747; www.lufthansa.com) flies via Frankfurt. However, while this was a well-worn route in the past, there's no doubt that the more cost-effective way now to fly to Budapest from another airport in the UK is by booking a connecting flight to London on one of the budget airlines from around £40 (standard return) upwards, or by speaking to British Airways about 'add-on' fares, which usually start at £70. It may be cheaper still to catch the train to London and make your way to one of the London airports from there. Be aware, though, that this could add hours to your journey time.

**Air Berlin** Tel: 0870 738 8880; www.airberlin.com. Germany's second-largest air carrier operates a daily direct connection between London Stansted and Budapest, costing from £64 return.

**British Airways** Tel: 0870 850 9850; www.ba.com. Operates two flights a day from London's Heathrow to Budapest (Terminal 2B) for around £100–250 return. You can get a discount on your flight if you book online and use BA's excellent 'e-ticketing' system, which also allows a speedier check in.

**easyJet** Tel: 0870 600 0000; www.easyjet.com. The popular low-cost airline celebrated Hungary's accession to the EU by opening a daily service between London Luton and Budapest, with return tickets from £41. A second service from Gatwick costs about the same. From November 1 2004, the airline will run daily services from Newcastle and Bristol, and fly twice-daily from Luton.

**Malév Airlines** Tel: 0870 909 0577 *(customer reservations)*; www.flymalev.co.uk. Fly twice-daily direct from London Stansted and London Heathrow to Budapest (Terminal 2A). The airline also runs two indirect flights a day from Manchester. You can expect to pay around £79 for a return ticket from Stansted. A return from Heathrow costs £100–250, and a standard return from Manchester is from £250.

**Sky Europe** Tel: 020 7365 0365; www.skyeurope.com. The Slovakian carrier runs a once-a-day service between London Stansted and Budapest, with return flights costing from as little as £51. Flights land at Ferihegy Terminal 1.

**Wizz Air** Tel: 0048 22 500 9499; www.wizzair.com. New budget European airline with flights between London Luton and Budapest (Terminal 2B). A return flight costs from £60, but there is currently only one evening flight per day. Wizz Air doesn't distribute paper tickets; you'll be issued with a registration number provided at the time of booking, which must be presented at check-in along with your passport.

## *From the US*

Only Malév runs direct flights between New York's JFK Airport and Budapest. There are seven flights a week, taking just over nine hours, and you can expect to pay roughly US$725 return. KLM operate non-direct flights from the US via Amsterdam.

## *From the rest of the world*

There are no direct flights from **Australia**; the cheapest way to reach Budapest is to fly to London from Sydney or Melbourne and transfer to a budget airline from there. Qantas offers daily flights direct to London for around US$2,500.

Malév operates five direct flights a week between **Canada** (Toronto) and Budapest costing around US$750 standard return. You could also try Air Canada and Lufthansa for indirect flights from Vancouver and Montreal. In **Ireland**, Malév flies direct from Dublin at least once daily, and twice daily on Mondays, Wednesdays and Saturdays. Costs start from around £200 return. No direct flights are available from **New Zealand**; you'll need to take a flight to London or Paris (with Air New Zealand), and get a connection from there.

In addition to the above, you can catch direct Malév flights to Budapest from

**Lyons** (seven flights a week), **Ljubljana** (12 a week), **Vienna** (twice daily) and **Dubrovnik** (three a week). Other international airlines that operate in and out of Ferihegy include Turkish Airlines, Alitalia, Finnair, Czech Airlines and Aeroflot.

## Airline/airport contact numbers

**Aeroflot** +36 1 318 5955
**Air France** +36 1 318 0411
**British Airways** +36 1 411 5555
**Central airport info** +36 1 296 9696
**Finnair** +36 1 317 4296
**Flight information** +36 1 296 7000
**KLM** +36 1 373 7737
**Lost luggage Terminal 2A** +36 1 296 8108
**Lost luggage Terminal 2B** +36 1 296 7948
**Lufthansa** +36 1 266 4511
**Malév** +36 1 235 3222/3888

## Airport transfer

Ferihegy International is Hungary's only commercial airport, located 25km southeast of Budapest. There are two adjacent terminals: Terminal 2A services Malév flights, while Terminal 2B looks after most other airlines. The airport is compact and clean, and contains a handful of souvenir and duty-free shops, a bar, coffee shop and restaurant, and currency exchange bureaux (that in Terminal A charges no commission, whereas that in Terminal B charges around 250Ft). The old Terminal 1 (tel: +36 1 296 0427/8/9 or +36 1 296 0424/5), located on the same road as Ferihegy 2 but closer to town, is used primarily by private aircraft and budget airlines (eg: Sky Europe). On landing, passengers have the following options for travelling to the city centre:

**Airport Minibus Service** Tel: 1 296 8555. For those travelling in ones or twos, the minibus shuttle is hassle-free and affordable. The counter is open daily (05.00–01.00) and the bus will drop you off at any address in Budapest. Book your seat at the minibus desk (there is one in the arrivals hall of each terminal). A one-way ticket costs 2,100Ft, and a return 3,600Ft. For your return journey, call the office 24 hours in advance, and quote your flight number and hotel location. (Note that while we have never encountered difficulties, we recently spoke to tourists stranded at their hotel when the return minibus failed to turn up. As well as booking 24 hours ahead, you are advised to telephone on the day to check your booking has been logged.)

**Airport bus** The public bus is the cheapest transfer (145Ft, or 180Ft if you pay the driver). It leaves every 10–15 minutes (between 05.00–23.00 daily) from the stop marked 'BKV Plusz Reptér busz' outside Terminal 2. Disembark at the very last stop, Kőbánya Kispest metro, and from there take the underground blue metro line 3 into the heart of Pest (Deák Ferenc tér station) and beyond. Buses back from Kőbánya Kispest run between 04.30 and 23.45, and the trip takes around 20 minutes. Bus 94 leaves for Kőbánya Kispest every half-hour from Terminal 1.

**Taxi** For three passengers or more, a taxi should work out a cheaper option per person than the Airport Minibus. Be wary, though, of hailing a cab outside the airport – there is a real danger of being stung. Either telephone a taxi firm from the airport, or agree a price before getting into the vehicle (see page 94). A realistic fare for a journey into the centre of the city is around 4,000–5,000Ft. Many taxi companies offer a flat-rate airport fare if you order by telephone.

## By train

Travelling from the UK to Budapest by train is only worth the time and effort if you're planning a round-Europe trip, would like to stop off along the way, or are afraid of flying. With the rise of the low-cost airline, flights are now considerably cheaper than return rail tickets; for example, a 2nd-class return ticket from London Waterloo (via the Eurostar) to Budapest Keleti costs approximately £300. The journey from London takes 22 hours (including the three-hour journey on the Eurostar), and you can travel via Cologne and Munich, Frankfurt and Nürenberg or Paris and Vienna. Tickets are usually valid for around three months, allowing you to get off to explore along the way (although you can't depart from your booked route). For information on crossing the Channel from London, contact Eurostar (tel: 08705 186186; email: info@eurostar.com; www.eurostar.com). Rail tickets to Budapest can be booked through the Rail Europe Travel Centre (178 Piccadilly, London W1; tel: 0870 830 2000; email: reservations@raileurope.co.uk; www.raileurope.co.uk), who can also help to plan your trip.

There are three main train stations in Budapest that serve both domestic and international destinations. The **Eastern Railway Station** (*Keleti pályaudvar*; VIII, Baross tér) is the point of arrival and departure for most international trains, the **Western Railway Station** (*Nyugati pályaudvar*; VI, Nyugati tér) was the city's first main station, built in 1877 by Eiffel, and there's also the **Southern Railway**

**Station** (*Déli pályaudvar*; I, Krisztina körút). Each has a connection to the underground system.

Trains operated by the Hungarian state railway company MÁV (Magyar Államvasutak) certainly can't be described as modern, but – like a favourite pair of slippers (or Jimmy Choo-choos?!) – they are plain, roomy and comfortable. See www.mav.hu or www.elvira.hu for details of international rail timetables and ticket costs, or call 1 322 9035.

Rail tickets can be purchased from the above stations or from the **MÁV Ticket Office** (VI, Andrássy út 35; tel: 1 461 5400; email: informacio@mav.hu; open Mon–Fri 09.00–17.00). Unfortunately the staff may speak little English; if you want to take the hassle out of booking, deal instead with a travel agent like Vista (see page 88).

## *Rail passes*

The **InterRail pass** (see www.interrail.com) divides Europe into eight zones (see www.raileurope.co.uk/inter-rail for details); Hungary resides in zone D. Passes vary according to the number of zones you wish to cover (adults from £223 to £415), and can be bought from Rail Europe (see opposite), international rail stations and STA Travel Centres.

A classic **Eurail Pass** (see www.eurailnet.com; email: info@eurailnet.com) allows limitless travel across 17 European countries, including Hungary. Prices range from £323 to £900. If you're under 26 then you are eligible for a Eurail Youthpass, which dramatically cuts the cost. Holders of both the above passes are entitled to discounts on Eurostar travel.

## By coach

Travel to Budapest by coach is an exhausting proposition. It used to be the cheapest option, but is now under severe pressure from the budget airlines. **Eurolines** (tel: 0870 5143219; www.eurolines.co.uk or www.nationalexpress.co.uk) operates in over 30 other countries, and under the National Express banner in the UK and Volánbusz in Hungary. In England, direct and indirect coaches depart from London Victoria Coach Station and Dover Eastern Docks to Budapest Népliget – the capital's main coach station. The journey takes a mind-numbing 28½ hours. Coaches depart daily from both coach stations in peak season (June 26–September 11), and every day except Wednesday and Saturday the rest of the year. Standard fares are single £82 (£78 for under 26s) and return £113 (£102).

If you are planning a European tour, it could be worth investing in a **Euroline Pass**, which gives holders unlimited deluxe coach travel for between 30 and 60 days to 18 major European cities (including Budapest). Passes range from £129 to £259. For more information, visit the Euroline website, the Euroline ticket office at Népliget, the Volánbusz Travel Office (V, Erzsébet tér 1; tel: 1 318 2122 or the central office at Népliget Bus Station) or any National Express agent in the UK.

The three primary **bus stations** for national and international services are all found on the Pest side of the city. Each station has its own connecting metro station.

**Népliget Bus Station** (*autóbuszállomás*) IX, Üllői út 131; tel: 1 219 8080
**Stadion Bus Station** XIV, Népstadion; tel: 1 252 2995 *(domestic)*, 1 252 1896 *(international)*
**Árpád híd Bus Station** XIII, Forgách utca; tel: 1 329 1450

## By car

The overland drive from the UK to Budapest would certainly make an epic of a road movie – all 1,684km (1,047 miles) of it – but there's a certain romanticism and some wonderful scenery. Once on mainland Europe the easiest route to Budapest is via Ostend, Belgium, Cologne, Frankfurt and Vienna. On a good day the journey should take around 17 hours but, obviously, this doesn't take into account food (and ablution) stops, sleep breaks, traffic problems, border queues, etc. See www.michelin.com for a detailed route planner. It's important to keep to hand your driving licence, vehicle insurance and registration documents (as well as your passport), and to display your country-identification letter on your vehicle. Third-party insurance is compulsory in Hungary, but cars with licence plates and national-identification letter for A, B, CH, D, DK, E, F, FL, GB, HR, I, IRL, IS, L, NL, P, S, SK, SLO countries will already be covered. If your country is not listed above then you'll have to produce a Green Card and may be asked to buy the insurance at the border if you don't already have it.

It is vital to take out adequate breakdown cover in case the unthinkable happens. The AA (tel: 0800 085 2840/ 0870 600 0371; www.theaa.com) operates a European Breakdown Cover policy that will protect you on your trip. Finally, be aware that tolls and high fuel prices in mainland Europe can considerably inflate your anticipated expenses.

There's little joy for the driver in the centre of Budapest, with the congestion and maze of one-way streets that you expect from major capitals. The system of public transport is by far the better option. However, a car can be useful for trips into the hills or to towns and villages beyond the capital.

### By hydrofoil

**Mahart Passnave** V, Belgrád rakpart; tel: 1 484 4013/4010; email: hydrofoil@mahartpassnave.hu; www.mahartpassnave.com
Mahart operates a daily hydrofoil service between Budapest and destinations on the Danube Bend, leaving from Vigadó tér landing stage every Saturday, Sunday and bank holiday from June 5 to August 29. It also runs a service linking Budapest to Vienna via Bratislava between April and November.

## HEALTH

### *with Dr Felicity Nicholson*

Generally the standard of public health in Hungary is good, the tap water is safe to drink and no vaccinations are legally required. However, it is wise to be up to date with routine vaccinations such as diphtheria, tetanus and polio. Hepatitis A should also be considered.

If you are planning to visit deep-forested areas outside the capital, consult your doctor about getting immunisation against encephalitis, which is carried by forest ticks (*kullancs*). Take precautions by using tick repellents, wearing long-sleeved clothing and a hat, and tucking trousers into boots. After a day in the forest it is important to check yourself for ticks, or get someone else to do it for you. For those travelling with children, concentrate particularly on checking their hair. The other primary irritant is the mosquito, which whines around the riverside on summer evenings, and is particularly tiresome when you're trying to enjoy a nice piece of fish at the Római part. Cover exposed skin with a DEET-based insect repellent (*rovarirtó*) and they'll feast on some other suckee.

For those who are going to be working in hospitals or are to be in close contact with children, hepatitis B vaccination is recommended. Pre-exposure rabies vaccine (ideally three doses given over a minimum of 21 days) should also be considered for anyone who is specifically going to be working with animals.

For emergency telephone numbers, see page 78.

## Travel clinics and health information

A full list of current travel clinic websites worldwide is available on www.istm.org. For other journey preparation information, consult www.tripprep.com. Information about various medications may be found on www.emedicine.com/wild/topiclist.htm.

## In Hungary

Free emergency health care is available to foreigners, but any required medication or follow-up treatment will have to be paid for. It is therefore important to ensure that your travel insurance covers medical costs. Take a copy of your policy certificate with you and keep the policy number to hand in case you are obliged to quote it. In an emergency, contact **Főnix SOS Ambulance** (II, Kapy utca 49; tel: 1 200 0100), which provides round-the-clock health care and has its own ambulance service. The private **Rózsakert Medical Center** (II, Second Floor, Gábor Áron utca 74–78; tel: 1 391 5905) is housed in the shopping mall of the same name and has helpful, American-trained doctors in residence; it is closed at weekends.

Hungarians swear by the curative properties of thermal baths (*gyógyfürdő*), and doctors will frequently prescribe dips for conditions ranging from skin problems to arthritic pains.

## Pharmacies

For those minor ailments, you'll find Budapest has a rash of pharmacies (*gyógyszertár* or *patika*). It is nevertheless worth bearing in mind that some medicines available over the counter in the UK and US – like antihistamine – require a prescription in Hungary. If you suffer from allergies, take such medication with you. Most pharmacies close between 18.00 and 20.00, but at least one in every district is open 24 hours a day. If it's very late you may have to ring the bell for admittance (and you may also be charged a small fee). Some pharmacies running non-stop services can be found at the following addresses:

VIII, Rákóczi út 39; tel: 1 314 3695/3694
VI, Teréz körút 41; tel: 1 311 4439
XII, Alkotás utca 1B; tel: 1 355 4691/4727
II, Frankel Leó út 22; tel: 1 212 4406/4311
IX, Üllői út 121; tel: 1 215 8947/3900

## Dentists

Hungary has a first-rate and highly affordable dental service, of which many Austrians make use during trips here. The *Budapest Sun* and *Budapest Times* often contain advertisements for private dental practices. If you're in need of urgent dental care, contact **SOS Dental Service** (VI, Király utca 14; tel: 1 267 9602), which operates 24 hours a day.

## SAFETY

Happily Budapest is a safe city with a low rate of violent crime, particularly by Western standards. However, like many other European capital cities, pick-pocketing, mugging, car theft and overcharging with threats are sadly on the increase. The bulging tourist wallet is inevitably at greatest risk, so it is wise to stay vigilant when travelling on public transport, strolling in busy and built-up areas, shopping in markets and malls, and relaxing in restaurants and bars. As a general rule, don't let your belongings out of your sight, try not to flash around valuable items and make use of your hotel safe. Never walk the streets with large sums of cash, or – as we learnt to our cost – leave your cellphone in an unzipped shoulder bag as you peer at the bus timetable.

It is not unknown for criminals to go to more extreme lengths to extort money from tourists. There have, for example, been instances of conmen posing as policemen and demanding cash. If in any doubt, ask for the 'officer's' credentials and insist on being taken to a police station with access to a translator. Theft of cars and the possessions inside them is not uncommon, so don't tempt opportunists by leaving things of value on the seats. Drivers should be cautious about stopping to help apparent breakdowns.

Gentlemen, if an attractive young woman approaches and asks you to join her for a drink, consider the possibility that she is drawn by more than your irresistible masculine charms. Unwary, strutting men have lost both their swagger and their swag when, after tripping over their tongues into a seedy joint with a 'consume girl', they have been forced by burly bouncers to pay an extortionate price for the drinks.

On a more mundane level, check your bills in restaurants and bars carefully for 'mistakes' in the maths. Never order from a menu that does not display prices alongside its fare. Always use a recognised taxi firm, and agree a price or check the meter is cleared before climbing in (see page 94). And resist dealing with unlicensed moneychangers in the street.

We must stress again that by Western standards Budapest is extremely safe, and you are unlikely to feel threatened. Please don't have nightmares, do sleep tight. For up-to-date security information, check the Foreign and Commonwealth Office website at www.fco.gov.uk.

## Women travellers

There is a typical central European machismo to Hungarian men, and they can hold attitudes that many in the West would consider sexist. Such thinking tends to manifest itself in high-blown compliments rather than anything more sinister. Women will find men unafraid to 'check them out' as they pass in the street and perhaps less inhibited in approaching them in bars than in more reserved cultures such as Britain; however, provided women take sensible precautions they should encounter no harassment.

## Terrorism

The threat of terrorist activity is a current danger in Hungary as elsewhere in the world. Obvious targets such as the British and American embassies are presently protected with concrete barriers and armed guards. Tourists are advised to behave as they would at home and be alert to any suspect behaviour, especially in busy public places. The FCO website (see opposite) offers up-to-the-minute advice.

## The law

It is now legal for prostitutes to stand in a 'tolerant zone' (*türelmi zóna*), wait for customers to stop their cars, and then 'conduct their business' in the cars or nearby bushes. You may see scantily clad women beside some of the main roads leading out from the city. Other more solid trappings of the trade – pimps and madams, brothels etc – remain illegal (although some strip joints are rather feeble covers for prostitution rackets). Recreational drug use is prohibited. Tourists are most likely to brush with the law as a result of motoring offences. Random road blocks are extremely common – during a four-month period we were pulled over on seven occasions in a Hungarian car. You will be asked to show your passport, driving licence and car registration papers. Minor offences can be punished with on-the-spot fines, while fines for speeding (usually 10,000Ft) must be settled at a post office. It is illegal to drink any alcohol at all prior to driving.

## The police

While the police force (*rendőrség*) has enjoyed a better reputation than counterparts in other eastern European nations, it has nevertheless been regarded with suspicion by Hungarians. Accusations of corruption have plagued the constabulary for years. In 2003 the director of police in Budapest went so far as to

offer his officers cash rewards in return for their blowing the whistle on instances of bribery in an attempted clean up. On the whole, though, the situation is improving and tourists are unlikely to encounter any problems in their dealings with officers, which will primarily come in being stopped at road blocks (see page 65) or very occasionally during passport inspections. There is a good police presence on the streets of Budapest during high season, when patrols aim at deterring thieves. Officers usually speak little or no English, but in July, August and September such patrols are often accompanied by translators.

Lost **passports** should be reported immediately to the Office for Immigration and Citizenship (XI, Budafoki út 60; tel: 1 463 9165), which is open 24 hours a day. If your passport has been stolen you'll need to report it to the police either by calling one of the emergency numbers or via the tourist police office (in the Tourinform at V, Sütő utca 2; 24-hour tel: 1 438 8080).

For **emergency telephone numbers**, see page 78.

## WHAT TO TAKE

There is little that isn't readily available in Budapest. Pack your swimsuit for a spa visit, your driving licence if you are looking to hire a car, and a jacket and tie if you're a gentleman who wants to dine at the Gundel (see page 153). It can be very cold in winter and very hot in summer, so choose your clothes accordingly; there are winds and occasional storms in summer, and a jumper is worthwhile for those cave or cellar visits. Take out comprehensive travel insurance before your trip to cover lost baggage, theft and medical emergencies, and bring copies of the documentation with you. Beyond that, bring some comfortable shoes, a patient frame of mind and a packet of indigestion tablets.

## ELECTRICITY

Hungary's electrical current is 220 Volts/50Hz, accessible via the European two-pin plug. Plug adaptors for use with three-pronged plugs are generally available from large supermarkets and chemists in the city.

## MONEY AND BUDGETING

### Money

The **forint** (Ft or HUF) is Hungary's official unit of currency and is issued in banknote denominations of 200, 500, 1,000, 2,000, 5,000, 10,000 and 20,000 and coins of 1, 2, 5, 10, 20, 50 and 100. Small shops, cafés or taxis may have difficulty with notes worth more than 5,000Ft, and you'll be treated with incredulity in most places if you present a 20,000Ft note. With this in mind, request notes of no higher value than 10,000Ft when changing money, and ask your hotel to break down larger denominations before going out for the day.

While Hungary joined the EU on May 1 2004, the country will not be embracing the euro in the immediate future. However, some businesses have been accepting the euro for some time, and hotels at the upper end of the price range will often list their prices in euros because of the changing value of the forint.

The current **exchange rate** (September 2004) is £1 = 370Ft, US$1 = 206Ft, €1 = 248Ft.

## BUDGETING

Budapest is no longer a total bargain-bucket destination, and is more expensive than the rest of Hungary. Prices vary by area, and a beer in a prime tourist location will cost over double that of a beer elsewhere. In general, though, you'll get far more for your money in shops, restaurants, hotels and on public transport than you will in the West. The following rough guide lists daily budgets per person; the calculation is based on two people sharing accommodation (and therefore paying half each of the room cost) – a single traveller may find the accommodation cost slightly higher:

**Strapped** Church mice can scrape by on around 5,500Ft (£15.00/US$28) per day by staying in a hostel dorm, eating in a basic *büfé* and getting around on foot. There might even be change for a decilitre of wine in a backstreet *borozó*.

**Modest** If you can't splash out but can afford a minor ripple, you'll get along comfortably with 13,000Ft (£35/US$64) a day by seeking out a cheap *panzió* (10,000Ft for a double). This will allow you to have a light snack for lunch, visit



For information on banks, exchanging currency, ATMs and travellers' cheques, see pages 71–2. For information on tipping, see page 24.

Any goods purchased in Hungary require the payment of a value-added tax levy known as AFA (between 11 and 25%). Most quoted prices in shops include this tax the odd museum and gallery, travel around by public transport, and eat a two-course meal with wine at an inexpensive restaurant.

**Comfortable** A daily allowance of 30,000Ft (£80.00/US$148) will permit a stay in a four-star hotel, ample sightseeing, cake stops, a meal in a decent restaurant, some late-night drinks in a bar, and a taxi back to your room.

**Indulgent** For 50,000Ft (£133/US$246) you can kick off your shoes and live the city high life. Stay in a luxury hotel, drink cocktails, eat well and make merry, travel where you want to go and see most of what you want to see. You'll rarely need to check the restaurant prices before taking a table, and you should still have a bit of loose change at the end of the day.

**Hey, big spender** If money is no object, book a plush room at the Four Seasons, dine at the Gundel, drink top Tokaji Aszú until it's coming out of your ears, take in a performance at the State Opera House, bet bravely at the Várkert Casino and set about the shops of Váci utca. If you want to spend a fortune in Budapest it is quite possible to do so – it will simply take a little longer than in London or Paris.

but it's worth checking in case. Non EU country members can claim this tax back if purchasing goods worth over 50,000Ft within six months of purchase. See page 100 for hotel tax rates.

# Practicalities

3

## BANKS

The greatest concentration of banks is in downtown Pest. Banks are generally open 08.00–16.00/17.30 on weekdays and 08.00–12.00 on Saturdays (although some are closed altogether at weekends); all are shut on Sundays. Banks to look out for are Budapest Bank, OTP, K&H and Postabank. Twenty-four-hour automated teller machines (ATMs) are fairly commonplace – if in doubt, head to the busy shopping areas of Váci utca or the Great Boulevard. Most ATMs accept American Express, Visa and Mastercard, as well as debit cards from Cirrus and Maestro. Check with your bank before you travel whether you'll be charged a commission fee.

## EXCHANGING CURRENCY

Numerous bureaux de change booths can be found on Váci utca and the Great Boulevard, as well as in hotels, railway stations and shopping centres. However, they may charge commission and their rates of exchange vary considerably – be sure to shop around. The Interchange counters offer poor rates, and should be avoided. Always ask how much it will cost to change £1 or US$1 – some booths mislead customers by quoting a rate that only applies if you change over a certain amount of money. The safest place to exchange cash is at a bank, where you should get an acceptable rate. There are also foreign-currency exchange machines at several points around the city (including at II, Margit körút 43–45, V, Károly körút 20, and

VI, Andrássy út 49). Dealing with black-market money-changers is illegal, and you run a high risk of being ripped off.

## Travellers' cheques

The profusion of ATMs means that travellers' cheques are increasingly rare things, and many bureaux de change do not deal with them. You should, in any case, avoid such booths as the rates on offer are likely to be very low. Banks will exchange travellers' cheques at decent rates without fuss; travel agencies like Ibusz may be able to exchange them, though usually for a commission. You can also try the post office. Remember to take your passport as a means of identification.

**American Express Exchange** V, Deák Ferenc utca 10; tel: 1 235 4330. Exchanges AmEx travellers' cheques commission-free and also dispenses cash to its cardholders. A smaller branch in the Castle District at the Sisi Restaurant has a currency exchange that operates daily from March to mid-January. *Open Mon–Fri 07.00–17.30, Sat 09.00–14.00.*

## Visa TravelMoney

A safe and convenient alternative to carrying cash or travellers' cheques is the Visa TravelMoney scheme (offered through Travelex; tel: 020 7837 9580; email: customerservices@travelex.com). The system is based on a pre-paid travel card that allows holders 24-hour access to their money in any local currency. You simply load the card up with funds before your trip and draw the cash out as you go along from ATM machines. Once you've exhausted your funds you throw the card away.

## CREDIT CARDS

Although locals tend to pay for goods and services in cash, major credit cards are accepted in Budapest, particularly in tourist-heavy shops, hotels and restaurants. However, smaller outlets – including some supermarkets, museums and transport ticket offices – may not take them. If your card is lost or stolen, notify your credit-card company immediately to prevent the possibility of fraud.

**American Express** Tel: 1 235 4330
**Visa** Tel: 0800 963833 (UK 24-hour hotline)
**Mastercard (Hungary)** VI, Westend City Center, Tower C, Floor 6, Vaci út 1–3; tel: 1 238 75 00; fax: 1 238 7930

## MEDIA

### Print

The Hungarian press is independent (foreign and locally owned), but journalism is not very daring, critical or investigative. Budapest is – relatively speaking – a small town, and tends to be nepotistic and incestuous. Everyone knows everyone and there is a reluctance to give (as well as receive) criticism, however constructive. Items such as restaurant reviews tend to be bought off in advance and lack objectivity. Of the Hungarian-language press, ***Pesti Est*** is probably the only publication of any practical use to the foreign tourist. This is the weekly pocket-sized listings guide to the best bars, clubs and events in town, and can sometimes help with addresses and opening hours; it's also a good prop for affecting an air of

Magyar cool in bars. There are some English translations on the website (www.est.hu). Among the mainstream nationals, ***Blikk*** is now the most widely read daily – full of gossip, naked women, film stars, and no obvious news. It has supplanted the perennial favourite ***Népszabadság*** (*People's Freedom*), the serious broadsheet and former organ of the one-party ruling MSZP.

## English-language press

There are a number of English-language publications, several of which are available free of charge from hotels, tourist offices and coffee houses. Major international newspapers and lifestyle magazines can be picked up from larger newsagents and bookshops, although you should expect to pay considerably above the cover price and foreign newspapers are usually at least a day out of date. For details of shops that sell dailies on their date of publication, see page 207.

***Budapest Business Journal*** The weekly *BBJ* concentrates on business with some news and lifestyle features. Founded in 1992 by an American-owned company. The online edition can be found at www.bbj.hu.

***Budapest Sun*** A weekly, running since 1993; traditionally popular with ex-pats, many feel it has lost its way in the last few years, and it has come under pressure from the *Budapest Times*. It contains local news – at times a little late – as well as restaurant reviews, arts and entertainment listings, business and sport. Associated Newspapers owned. There is also an online edition (www.budapestsun.com). The cover price is 359Ft, but complimentary copies are available in most hotels of three stars or more.

***Budapest Times*** A newish weekly (since September 2003) with good news and business and a growing culture section. Formed independently as a sister paper to the *Budapester Zeitung*. Retails at 360Ft.

***Where Budapest*** A glossy monthly distributed free through hotels, tourist offices, embassies and restaurants. Information on shopping, dining, entertainment, nightlife and cultural events, together with regularly updated listings and a sprinkling of well-informed features.

## Television

On the whole, the fare on the Hungarian goggle box makes for pretty depressing viewing. The state owns two television channels: **MTV1** (Magyar Televizio 1 – not to be confused with the American music channel!) and **MTV2** (Magyar Televizio 2). During the communist period, these were used as tools for political propaganda, and even today parliament has a strong influence over their content. They air very conservative programmes that have changed little since the '80s, often featuring serious-looking men with droopy moustaches who pontificate on political or literary topics. Occasionally, the schedule is jazzed up with a variety show, invariably wheeling out the same old performers.

The state-run stations come off very badly in competition with two newer and fresher commercial stations. **Duna TV** is run by a foundation (very conservative in nature) that places emphasis on the 'larger Hungary' of times pre-Trianon Treaty (see page 8). The channel concentrates on more artistic programmes, and has reasonable European art films (but only shown after 23.00). **RTL Klub** is run by

RTL in Germany and shows the same low-brow chat shows, reality shows, shock shows, daytime drivel and Hollywood action movies. A third commercial station is **TV2** (the country's first national commercial channel), which has similar programming. When TV2 ran a Hungarian Big Brother, RTL Klub hit back with its own version – 'Való Világ' ('Real World') – with slightly different rules. It proved considerably more popular, and is now in its third season.

There are many more local independent stations: **Bp TV** (run by local celebrity Anettka, who often appears naked during live phone-ins), **Hír TV** (a right-wing news channel), **Film Múzeum** (showing old Hungarian films) and **Spektrum TV** (a kind of 'National Geographic' channel). Almost everyone in Budapest has either cable or satellite, offering dozens of foreign channels (usually German) and dubbed channels such as National Geographic, Hallmark, Club TV, and the Discovery Channel. At 23.00, the Travel Channel suddenly changes to hardcore porn with local 'stars' performing in tourist spots such as the Gellért Hotel or Fishermen's Bastion – a novel way of showcasing the city's sights…

## Radio

Since the fall of communism, the airwaves have been flooded with commercial stations. **Rádió 1** (103.9fm), **Danubius** (103.3fm), **Est FM** (98.6fm) and **Juventus** (89.5fm) offer a mix of local and international popular music. **Bridge FM** (102.1fm) plays rock. **Tilos Rádió** (90.3fm) started off as a pirate radio station (*tilos* means 'forbidden') and is liberal in style. It was once taken off the air for several weeks after a drunken radio-show host said something derogatory about Christianity during a Christmas broadcast. **Rádió C** (88.8fm) is a new station for the Roma minority, and popular with younger listeners seeking an alternative to the tired old rotation lists of Juventus and Danubius. There are three state radio channels: **Kossuth Rádió** (107.8fm) broadcasts mainly news and politics, **Petőfi Rádió** (94.8fm) is more mixed, with culture, entertainment and news, and **Bartók Rádió** (105.3fm) is devoted to classical music. **Info Rádió** (95.8fm) is a news channel, seemingly conservative in influence (and Fidesz-biased).

You can listen to BBC World Service at certain times on **BBC-RFI Budapest** (92.1fm), a non-profit-making station launched in 2003 in collaboration with Radio France Internationale. For programme schedules, log on to www.bbc.co.uk/worldservice.

## COMMUNICATIONS

### Telephone and fax

Most public telephones in Hungary are operated by **phone cards** (*telefonkártya*), which can be purchased from newsagents, hotels, tourist offices and post offices (800Ft/50 units and 1,800Ft/120). The fewer coin-operated public phones take 20Ft, 50Ft and 100Ft pieces. Main post offices (see page 80) offer a **fax** service, as do hotels with business centres and some internet cafés (see page 80).

Local areas in Hungary each have a two-digit prefix code – except Budapest, whose **area code** is '1'. Budapest telephone numbers are seven digits long (excluding the area prefix), those of other areas six. Local calls can be made by directly dialling the required telephone number. For those beyond Budapest, dial '06' (the inter-area code), wait for a slightly different-sounding dialling tone, and then enter the specific area code and telephone number. (For cellphones, see below.) For calls out of the country, dial the international access code '00', listen for the second tone, and proceed with the relevant country code and number. Some country codes are listed below:

| | | | | | |
|---|---|---|---|---|---|
| **Australia** | 61 | **Hungary** | 36 | **UK** | 44 |
| **France** | 33 | **Ireland** | 353 | **USA/Canada** | 1 |
| **Germany** | 49 | | | | |

### *Useful/emergency telephone numbers*

**Ambulance** 104
**Domestic operator and directory inquiries** 198
**Fire brigade** 105
**General emergency** (for English, German and French speakers) 112
**International operator and international directory inquiries** (English spoken) 199
**Police** 107
**Tourinform 24-hour hotline** (info and reporting crimes; English speakers) 1 438 8080

### *Cellphones/mobiles*

The three cellphone providers are Westel, Pannon and Vodaphone. To call a cellphone from a landline, you must prefix both the standard intercity code (06) and the provider's regional code – 30 or 60 (Westel), 20 (Pannon) or 70

(Vodaphone). Calls between same-network cellphones do not require either of these codes, while a call to a mobile on a different network only requires the regional prefix.

## Post office

Post offices (*posta*) are usually open Monday–Friday 08.00–18.00, Saturday 08.00–12.00. You can post letters and parcels, buy stamps (*bélyeg*) – although you'll save queue time by getting these at newsagents – pay parking and speeding fines, send faxes (main branches only), and exchange Eurocheques, American Express travellers' cheques and postal orders. If you're **sending a letter**, head for the desk marked with an envelope symbol. Letters or postcards to other European destinations will take around five or six days, while those to the US take eight to ten. Letters/postcards within Hungary cost 33/30Ft, to Europe 170/120Ft, to the US 180/130Ft. Be aware that it's far from unusual for 'interesting-looking' packages to go walkabout in the Magyar postal system – a postman somewhere, for instance, is doing his rounds in a fetching pair of pastel M&S knickers. Always send anything of value to or from Hungary by registered post. To do this in Hungary, ask for an *ajánlott levél* form; its instructions are in Hungarian, but it's fairly straightforward to fill out (name, address, weight, value, etc) – the clerk can usually help, especially in larger post offices. You keep the form, which is stamped and numbered, while the letter or parcel is marked with an identification number.

A few main branches keep later hours:

**Posta** V, Petőfi Sandor utca 19. *Open Mon–Fri 08.00–20.00, Sat 08.00–14.00.*
**Posta** V, Városház utca 18. *Open Mon–Fri 08.00–20.00, Sat 08.00–14.00.*
**Keleti Pályaudvar Posta** VIII, Baross tér 11/c. *Open Mon–Sat 07.00–21.00.*
**Nyugati Pályaudvar Posta** VI, Teréz körút 61. *Open Mon–Sat 07.00–21.00, Sun 08.00–20.00.*

## Internet

Most hotels offer internet access, but there are plenty of cheaper internet cafés all over Budapest. For useful website resources, see *Further Reading*, page 386.

**City Press Café** V, Petőfi Sándor utca 17–19. Newsagent and café with internet access. You are issued with a card that is charged up with credit and can be used during subsequent visits. *Open daily 07.00–22.00.*

**Hotel Charles** (see page 114) has a small internet café, with three terminals. Very reasonably priced for a hotel. *Open 24 hours, daily.*

**Internet Café** VI, Andrássy út 46; tel/fax: 1 331 9102. Functional, 17-terminal café. You can also copy CDs, send faxes, and print and photocopy documents here. *Open 24 hours daily.*

**Kiber@Buda** XI, Budafoki út 22; tel: 1 209 9257. A dingy little student place with eight stations. *Open 24 hours daily.*

**Szakkönyváruház** VI, Nagymező utca 43; tel/fax: 1 373 0500. Large Hungarian bookshop with 12 stations. Other internet shops forming part of this chain can be found at VIII, József korut 52; VII, Rákoczi utca 14 (in the Fokusz bookstore); and VI, Liszt Ferenc tér 9. *Open Mon–Sat 10.00–18.00, Sun 09.00–13.00.*

**VideoMania & Internet Kávézó** VI, Andrássy út 29. Small eight-terminal office above a video store. *Open Mon–Thu 10.00–22.00, Fri–Sat 10.00–24.00, closed Sun.*

**Vista kávéház** VI, Paulay Ede utca 7; tel: 1 429 9999. A pleasant café with internet access. *Open Mon–Fri 09.00–18.30, Sat 09.00–16.30, closed Sun.*

**Yellow Zebra** V, Sütő utca 2; tel: 1 266 8777. This friendly English-speaking tour company (see page 86) has five terminals, due to double in number in 2005. *Office open daily 09.00–20.00 (high season), 10.00–19.30 (other times)*

## EMBASSIES (LOCAL)

**Australia** XII, Királyhágó tér 8–9; tel: 1 457 9777; www.ausembbp.hu. *Open Mon–Fri 09.00–12.00.*

**Canada** XII, Budakeszi út 32; tel: 1 392 3360; www.kanada.hu. *Open Mon–Thu 08.30–10.30, 14.00–15.30.*

**France** VI, Lendvay utca 27; tel: 1 374 1100. *Open Mon–Fri 09.00–12.00.*

**Germany** I, Úri utca 64; tel: 1 488 3500. *Open Mon–Fri 09.00–12.00.*

**Ireland** V, Szabadság tér 7; tel: 1 302 9600. *Open Mon–Fri 09.30–12.30, 14.30–16.00.*

**UK** V, Harmincad utca 6; tel: 1 266 2888. *Open Mon–Fri 09.30–12.30, 14.30–16.30, closed weekends and British and Hungarian bank holidays; telephone enquiries Mon–Fri 09.00–12.00, 14.00–17.00.*

**USA** V, Szabadság tér 12; tel: 1 475 4400; www.usis.hu. *Open Mon–Fri 08.15–17.00; emergencies out of hours, call 1 475 4703.*

## TOURIST INFORMATION

The easiest way to obtain useful and up-to-date tourist information *(turista információ)* is by visiting a Hungarian tourist office, or **Tourinform**. There are around 140 of these in the country, manned by (usually) multilingual staff who can offer advice and help on accommodation, restaurants, transport, events and attractions. They also distribute free brochures, leaflets and listings magazines (be sure to pick up the English-language publications *Where Budapest* and the pocket-sized *Budapest Guide* if you can), as well as selling tourist discount cards, local transport tickets, phone cards and so on. For further details, tel: 1 438 8080 (24-hour hotline) or 00800 36 000 000 (from abroad); email: hungary@tourinform.hu; www.tourinform.hu or www.hungarytourism.hu.

Tourinform offices in Budapest can be found at:

I, Szentháromság tér; tel: 1 488 0475; email: var@budapestinfo.hu. Known as 'Várinfó (castle information), this office stands adjacent to the Mátyás Church (see page 342). *Open daily 09.00–21.00 (Jun–Sep), 09.00–19.00 (Oct–May).*
V, Sütő utca 2 (just off Deák tér); tel (24-hour): 1 438 8080; tel: 1 317 1248. *Open daily 24 hours.*
VI, Liszt Ferenc tér 11; tel: 1 322 4098. *Open daily 09.00–19.00 (Apr–Oct), 10.00–18.00 (Nov–Mar).*
VI, Nyugati pályaudvar (Western Railway Station); tel: 1 302 8580. *Open daily 09.00–19.00 (Mar–Oct), 09.00–18.00 (Nov–Feb).*

Computerised **information touch points** are found at Blaha Lujza tér, the upper terminus of the funicular railway, Déli Railway Station, both terminals of Ferihegy Airport, the Big Market Hall, Tourinform (Sütő utca 2), Moszkva tér and Keleti Railway Station.

# LOCAL TOURS

There's no shortage of organised tours of the city and beyond, both for those who pre-book and for impulsive types. As well as the buses, boats and balloons, there are cycling, nature, walking and horse-riding tours.

**Absolute Walking Tours** V, Sütő utca 2; tel: 1 266 8777; www.absolutetours.com. A variety of alternative tours (costing 3,500–5,000Ft) depart from outside the Lutheran church on Deák Ferenc tér, including a whizz around some communist sites (Mon, Wed, Fri–Sat 10.30; Jan–Feb Sat only) and a stagger around Budapest's bars (Mon, Wed, Fri–Sat 20.00; Jan–Feb Sat only). Conventional sightseeing walks leave daily from outside the Exhibition Hall on Hősök tere, as well as from the Lutheran church. No need to book. *Office open daily 09.00–20.00 (high season), 10.00–19.30 (other times).*

**Budapest Eye** VI, West End Shopping Centre Roof Garden, Váci út 1–3; tel: 1 238 7623; email: budapestballon@muber.hu; www.budapestkilato.hu. A tethered hot-air balloon that takes passengers 150m above the city. You'll pay extra for permission to take a camera with you, which will be strapped to your wrist; we learnt it's best if the nominated cameraman is not the trembling one with his eyes tight shut. Adult 3,300Ft, child 1,000Ft, concessions 2,000Ft, discount with Budapest Card. Call 06 20 589 7907 or 06 20 589 7915 for more information. Flights subject to weather. *Open daily 10.00–20.00 (Nov–Apr), 10.00–24.00 (May–Oct).*

**Budatours** VI, Andrássy út 2; tel: 1 374 7070; email: btours@budatours.hu; www.budatours.hu. Standard sightseeing buses (open-topped or covered) with recorded commentaries in various languages (including English). Depart from outside Andrássy út 3 (daily 10.30, 11.30, 13.30, 14.30 and 15.30; adult 4,800Ft, child 2,400Ft).

**Cityrama Sightseeing Tours** V, Báthori utca 22; tel: 1 331 0043; email: cityrama@cityrama.hu. Sightseeing by bus or boat. The ten-hour Danube Tour visits the Danube Bend, and includes a three-course lunch and guided walk (adult 16,000Ft, child 8,000Ft). Private tours by minibus are also available for small groups. *Open Mon–Fri 08.00–18.00, Sat–Sun 09.00–15.00.*

**Ecotours Hungary** XII, Varosmajor utca 10; tel: 1 214 2376; www.ecotours.hu. UK contact: Shena Maskell; tel: 01903 200584; email: ecotours@tiscali.co.uk. Specialist operator offering pre-arranged and bespoke eco tours.

**EUrama Sightseeing Tours** V, Apáczai Csere János utca 12–14; tel: 1 327 6690; www.eurama.hu. Half- and full-day tours by bus and on foot. The kids' tour (8,000Ft/person) visits the Tropicarium (see page 323) and the summer bobsleigh run (see page 230). Also folklore events, horse shows and Jewish-theme tours.

**Hubertus** II, Ady Endre utca 1; tel: 1 316 0469; email: andrea@hubertus.com; www.hubertus.com. Specialist tour company that organises equestrian, hunting and angling tours.

**Koltour Bt** XI, Rákó utca 3; mobile: +36 20 935 9511; email: koltour@axelero.hu; www.koltour.hu. Péter was our tour guide on an early visit to Budapest. He is knowledgeable, helpful and abundantly energetic. He and his family offer English- and German-language sightseeing trips, and can arrange restaurants, hotels, airport transfers and personalised tours ranging from city walks and boat rides to searches for the graves of relatives.

**Legenda Travel Agency** V, Vigadó tér, Pier No 7; tel: 1 266 4190; www.legenda.hu. Two hour-long boat trips along the Danube with recorded commentaries. The daytime tour on the *Duna Bella* costs 3,600Ft, while the evening excursion on the *Duna Legenda* costs

4,200Ft (and includes a couple of glasses of wine).

**Mahart Passnave** V, Belgrád rakpart; tel: 1 484 4000; email: passnave@mahartpassnave.hu; www.mahartpassnave.hu. Local programmes include a two-hour sightseeing folklore evening (May 1–Sep 29, every Wed and Sat at 20.00) at a pricey 9,500Ft/person, and a one-hour city cruise (ten per day in summer) for a more affordable 2,400Ft/person (discounts for children). *Ticket and information office open Mon–Fri 08.00–16.00, closed weekends.*

**MÁV Nosztalgia** V, Belgrád rakpart 26; 1 302 3580; email: nostalgia_trains@mail.matav.hu; www.mavnosztalgia.hu. Nostalgic railway excursions (to destinations in Hungary and beyond) on 50 restored vintage trains. Trains to the Danube Bend leave from Nyugati station at 09.40 (May 6–Sep 30) and arrive at the final destination of Szob at 11.48.

**Paul Street Tours** Tel: 06 20 958 2545; email: faurestk@mail.datanet.hu. American Kristin Faurest runs personally tailored neighbourhood tours of Budapest, focusing upon the architecture and culture, as well as taking tourists on antiques-shopping trips. For a specialised tour, call a few days in advance.

**Program Centrum City Tours** Le Meridien Hotel, Erzsébet tér 9–10; tel: 1 327 0055; email: agency.programcentrum@axelero.hu; www.cityrama.at. Sightseeing, wine-tasting, Parliament and folklore tours, as well as excursions beyond the capital. Three-hour city tour costs 6,000Ft/person (half price with Budapest Card). *Open Mon–Fri 09.00–14.00; also open Sat 09.00–15.00 (Apr–Oct).*

**TGV Tours** VI, Hajós utca 23; tel: 1 354 0755; email: info@tgvtours.hu; www.tgvtours.hu

**To-Ma Tour** V, Budapest, Október 6 utca 22; tel: 1 353 0819; email: tomatour@axelero.hu;

www.tomatour.hu. Friendly company specialising in tailor-made and group tours of the city, as well as offering a range of private apartments (see page 123).

**Yellow Zebra** V, Sütő utca 2; tel: 1 266 8777; email: yellowzebrabikes@yahoo.com. Night

## *THE GREAT AND THE GOOD*

Think you haven't been touched by the brilliance of the Hungarian mind? Consider some of the following contributors to the worlds of science, culture, art and entertainment. And think again.

**Ede Teller** (1908–2003) Born in Budapest, Teller was a physicist who co-developed the atomic bomb and invented the hydrogen bomb.

**Albert Szent-Györgyi** (1893–1986) Awarded a Nobel Prize in 1937 for discovering vitamin C.

**Oszkár Asbóth** (1891–1960) A flight-obsessed engineer who invented the propellor helicopter.

**Ernő Rubik** (1944–) Mathematician and creator of the irritating '80s cubic puzzle the Rubik Cube, which baffled and frustrated millions around the world.

**László József Bíró** (1899–1985) Not content with inventing the ball-point pen (or *Biro*), he also fashioned the automatic gearbox.

**Imre Kertész** (1929–) Acclaimed Jewish writer, deported from Budapest during World War II (aged 11). His novel *Sorstalanság* (*Fateless*) documented his and day, rain or shine, the Yellow Zebra 4-hour bike tours cover the city's main sights. Adult 4,000Ft, student 3,500Ft; bike hire from 3,000Ft (excluding deposit). *Office open daily 09.00–20.00 (high season), 10.00–19.30 (other times)*

experiences in Nazi concentration camps, and won him the Nobel Prize for Literature in 2002.

**Harry Houdini** (1874–1926) Real name Ehrich Weisz. Perhaps the most-accomplished escapologist the world has known.

**Ferenc Liszt** (1811–86) Renowned 19th-century composer and pianist who founded his own music academy in Pest.

**Béla Bartók** (1881–1945) Discovered by Liszt, Bartók was one of Hungary's greatest composers of classical and folk music.

**Zoltán Kodály** (1882–1967) A popular composer and teacher who, with Bartók, collected Hungarian folk music. Kodály also devised his own method of music study to encourage the less talented to learn and play.

Hungarians were also responsible for inventing colour television, the hologram, the phosphorus match and the horse-drawn coach. Actors Tony Curtis, Drew Barrymore, Freddie Prinze Junior and Zsa Zsa Gabor have Hungarian ancestry, as do fashion designer Calvin Klein, singer Paul Simon and comedian Jerry Seinfield.

## LOCAL TRAVEL AGENTS

Travel agents can offer assistance with accommodation, programmes and excursions, car rental, and with tickets for shows and international and domestic travel; they can also often provide information, brochures and tourist maps, while some offices exchange travellers' cheques.

**Express** V, Semmelweis utca 4; tel: 1 266 3277; email: expresstravel@mailbox.hu; www.expresstravel.hu. *Open Mon–Fri 08.00–18.00, Sat 09.00–13.00, closed Sun.*

**Ibusz** *Main office:* V, Ferenciek tere 10; tel: 1 485 2700; www.ibusz.hu; *other offices:* VII, Dob utca 1 and V, Vörösmarty tér 6. The largest travel-bureau network in Hungary. *Open Mon–Fri 08.30–16.30, closed weekends.*

**Kata Tourist** V, Régi Posta utca 12; tel: 1 486 0147. Small but helpful office that's great for those on a budget. *Open daily 10.00–20.00.*

**Koltour Bt** See page 84

**Vista Travel Club** VI, Paulay Ede utca 2; tel: 1 429 9766. Bilingual staff assist with outbound travel. There is also internet access, and travel bits and bobs for sale. At the junction with Andrássy út. *Open Mon–Fri 09.00–18.30, Sat 09.00–14.30.*

**Vista Visitor Centre** VI, Paulay Ede utca 7; tel: 1 429 9950; email: incoming@vista.hu; www.vista.hu. Located in a modern coffee house, the second Vista centre (on the same road) handles incoming travel and is the place to head for excellent travel help and advice about Hungary. *Open Mon–Fri 09.00–23.00, Sat 10.00–23.00, Sun 11.00–20.00.*

## DISCOUNT CARD

If you're exploring the city to the full, the **Budapest Card** is a wise investment. It offers free admission to over 60 museums and sights, half-price sightseeing tours, discounts in some restaurants, shops and thermal baths, plus free and unlimited use of public transport. Cards are valid for 48 hours (4,350Ft) or 72 hours (5,450Ft), cover one adult and one child (up to the age of 14), and can be purchased from tourist offices, the airport, travel agencies, hotels and main metro ticket offices. Sign the card and fill in the date from the moment you want to start using it (you can choose when the period begins). A brochure listing the places where the card is accepted can be picked up from Tourinform offices. See www.budapestinfo.hu/card for more information.

## PUBLIC TOILETS

There is a distinct shortage of places to spend a penny in Budapest. When you do find somewhere, you're likely to have to spend more precisely 20–100Ft, as there is usually a charge – indeed, in summer even some restaurants (like McDonalds) request a fee. Doors are marked with *nők* or *női* (women) and *férfiak* or *férfi* (men).

# Local Transport

Here are the statistics: 180 buses (*autóbusz*), 14 trolleybuses (*trolibusz*), 29 trams (*villamos*), three underground metro lines, and a suburban railway (HÉV) – in addition to the Hungarian State Railway (MÁV), which takes passengers to national and international destinations beyond the city. Oh, and there are taxis, and funicular, children's and cogwheel railways. Of course, 89% of statistics mean absolutely nothing, but Budapest is genuinely blessed with an efficient and punctual public transport network, both easy to navigate and cheap to travel on. Getting around is a doddle.

If you wish to **report an incident** that occurs on the transport system, contact the Traffic Security Department of Budapest Transport Limited (VIII, Baross utca 132; tel: 1 461 6500). If an **item goes astray**, contact the Budapest Public Transport Company's (BKV) lost-and-found office (VII, Akácfa utca 18; tel: 1 267 5299; *open Mon–Thu 07.00–15.00, Fri 07.00–14.00*). Up-to-date **public transport information** is available in English from the BKV website at www.bkv.hu/angol.

## PUBLIC TRANSPORT

### Tickets

Public transport in Budapest is primarily based on good faith. Passengers purchase their tickets (*jegy*) before boarding the metro, bus, tram or trolleybus – tickets are not available on the vehicles – and are trusted to validate them by inserting them into 'punching' machines. On the underground, these machines are automated and are usually found at the top of the escalators, while buses and trams have them on board (where you have to pull down on the slot to operate the puncher). Inspectors (with red armbands) sometimes patrol to check tickets, and may also wait at the metro station exits; they will issue fines for fare dodgers (2,000Ft if paid on the spot, 5,500Ft if paid within 30 days). A few of the newer transport vehicles have ticket-issuing machines on board, but these are far between.

Tickets are available individually or in books, and can be purchased from hotels, newsagents and train stations. The same type of ticket can be used on the underground, trams, buses and trolleybuses; one ticket allows one journey on one transport system (without changing). If you're travelling on the underground and intend to change lines then you'll require a transfer ticket that needs to be validated. A Budapest Card allows free use of public transport. The standard single ticket is valid on the HÉV up to the city limits, but you'll need to buy a separate ticket for travel onward. Ferry tickets can be purchased from ticket machines at the docking points.

## *Ticket prices*

**Single** 145Ft
**Book of 10/20** 1,250/2,450Ft
**One-day ticket** 1,150Ft
**Tourist ticket** (for three days) 2,300Ft
**Metro section ticket** (valid for up to three stops only) 105Ft
**Metro section transfer ticket** (up to five stops with one line change) 160Ft
**Metro transfer ticket** (as many stops as you like with one line change) 240Ft

## By metro

Budapest's metro was the first underground transport network in continental Europe – the second in the world after London's – and consists of three lines: yellow (M1), red (M2) and blue (M3). The yellow line, which travels the entire length of Andrássy út to City Park and beyond, is the oldest and was built to celebrate the country's millennium in 1896. It is affectionately known as the '*kisföldalatti*' (or 'little underground'), and its stations are decorated with patterned tiles. All three lines are reliable and safe, and the trains arrive at frequent intervals of a few minutes. The metro runs from 04.30 until around 23.00 every day. The three lines intersect at Deák Ferenc tér station in the heart of Pest. Plans are afoot to add a fourth metro line that will run between Kelenföld and Keleti railway stations (and possibly as far east as Bosnyák tér). You can visit a small museum dedicated to the metro (see page 326).

## By bus, tram and trolleybus

The blue single-decker **bus** service is frequent and dependable. Busier bus routes have express services – indicated by a red (rather than black) number – that only stop at major bus stops, while those with an 'E' suffix run direct from terminal to terminal. Day buses operate between 05.00 and 23.00, and can get very crowded during the rush hour. They are particularly useful for getting into the Buda hills; Buda's main terminals are at Moszkva tér and Móricz Zsigmond körtér. **Night buses** (*éjszakai járatok*) run between 23.30 and 04.30, following the routes of the red and blue underground lines and the main tram paths. Night buses bear the accented letter 'É' after the bus number (eg: 52É). Budapest has three bus stations for national and international services (see page 58).

There's something slightly special about riding a **tram**; Budapest's enjoy some of the city's choice cuts, running over four of the bridges, along both riverbanks and around the Great Boulevard. It's a great, unsung, yellow rumble of a way to see the city's various aspects.

The transport brainchild of the '40s, the **trolleybus** is still surging onward along its overhead cables. It was introduced to commemorate Stalin's 70th birthday in 1949, which is why the first working bus was numbered '70'; each succeeding route was numbered upwards.

Trams, buses and trolleybuses run from around 05.00 to 23.00 daily (excluding night buses). Most stops have a printed **timetable** (*menetrend*).

## By HÉV

The suburban railway, known as the HÉV, consists of four lines that run to the outer reaches of the capital and nearby towns of Szentendre, Gödöllő, Csepel and Ráckeve. The green trains are used predominantly by commuters, although the 45-minute journey between Batthyány tér and the picturesque town of Szentendre is very popular with day trippers, and also passes through Óbuda and Aquincum on the way. In daylight hours trains for Szentendre leave every 20–30 minutes.

## OTHER TRANSPORT

### By taxi

Taxis are everywhere in Budapest, but tourists are vulnerable to unscrupulous drivers who charge significantly over the odds. The best way to avoid this is to order a taxi by telephone from a reputable firm. If you call from a public telephone, you can usually quote the number in the booth and the taxi will know precisely where to collect you. If you must hail a cab in the street, always ensure it is a marked car (with a company name on the side), ask for an approximate cost from the driver, and ensure the meter is visible and re-set. Remember that the driver is unlikely to be able to change large currency bills, and that you should give a tip (either 10% or round the fare up to the nearest convenient amount). Legally, taxis are allowed to charge up to the following rates: (06.00–22.00) 200Ft basic fee, 200Ft/km, 50Ft/minute for waiting; (22.00–06.00) 280Ft basic fee, 280Ft/km, 70Ft/minute for waiting. Firms will usually have a standard charge for the journey to the airport from Pest or Buda.

**Reputable taxi firms** include **Fő** (tel: 1 222 2222), **Buda** (tel: 1 233 3333), **City** (tel: 1 211 1111), **Rádió** (tel: 1 377 7777), **6x6** (tel: 1 266 6666), **Tele5** (tel: 1 355 5555) and **Taxi 2000** (tel: 1 200 0000).

## By ferry

A pleasant way to enjoy the riverbank sights is to board a ferry. These operate between Boráros tér on the Pest side to the Római part in Buda via Batthyány tér; don't expect to get there in a hurry – the full journey takes an hour. Ferries depart from Boráros tér May 1–September 3 Thursday–Sunday at 09.00, 11.40, 12.40, 15.20 and 16.20 (the last of these only as far as Batthyány tér). The final boat from the Római part leaves at 17.20, and goes to Jászai Mari tér (by Margit híd) via Hajógyári-sziget (Shipyard Island) and Margit-sziget (Margaret Island).

## By car

Most areas of this compact city are easily reached by public transport or on foot. Furthermore, driving is not for the fainthearted. Traffic can be very heavy, particularly in rush hour, one-way streets make navigation infuriating, and other road users are unforgiving of the hesitant (and unafraid to show their displeasure). However, a car can be useful in the Buda hills or for visiting towns on the Danube Bend.

In Hungary you must drive on the right and wear a seatbelt (even if seated in the back). In addition, vehicles are required to have their dipped headlights on, even during the day, although this is generally ignored in cities (including Budapest). Ensure that you have at least third-party insurance if you are bringing your own car – check with your insurance company that you are covered in Hungary. The speed limit is 50km/h in towns, villages and built-up areas, 90km/h outside built-up areas, 110km/h on dual carriageways and 130km/h on motorways. Police regularly stop motorists to check their documentation, so have your passport, driving licence and vehicle registration papers to hand. It is illegal to use a cellphone while driving or to have any alcohol at all in the bloodstream. Pedestrians should note that cars almost always fail to stop at zebra crossings.

Finding somewhere to **park** can seem a Herculean task, particularly in Pest. You pay for a space at coin-operated meters or through pay-and-display machines. Time restrictions on parking in the downtown area are enforced by wheel clampers. Multi-storey car parks can be found at V, Szervita tér 8; V, Aranykéz utca 4; VIII, Futó utca 52; and VII, Osvát utca 5.

To **rent a car** in Hungary you need to be 21 years old or over, and in possession of a driving licence (valid for at least a year) and a passport. You will need to leave a deposit – usually a temporary debit from your credit card. Some companies will deliver the car to your hotel (and pick it up again); the car will have a full petrol tank on delivery, and you must ensure it is full when returned.

The following companies have good reputations:

**Avis** V, Szervita tér 8; tel: 1 318 4240; www.avis.com. Reliable company whose office is located in the underground car park of Szervita tér. Fiat Seichentos are available from €26/day, and Opel Corsas from €33/day.

**Fox Autorent** XI, Vegyész utca 17–25; tel: 1 382 9000; email: wbartesch@fox-autorent.com; www.fox-autorent.com. Full range of cars, most with A/C. There's airport service or home/hotel delivery, and 24-hour road assistance. Cars from €35/day.

**Worldwide Rent A Car** V, Sas utca 10–12; tel: 1 302 0431. Situated in front of the

Basilica, on the corner of Sas Utca and Zrínyi utca. This is the place to try if you want to pay very little and don't mind an older, unflashy car with a high mileage.

## By bicycle

While cycling is fraught with danger in the city centre, and bikes are prohibited on most major roads, there are cycle lanes along the Buda bank running to Szentendre and beside Andrássy út up to City Park. Furthermore, cycling is a good way to explore the greener areas of Buda. You can carry bicycles on the HÉV and the Cogwheel Railway (you will have to pay extra), but not on buses, trolleybuses, trams or the metro. For further information and details of bike hire, see page 229.

# 5 Accommodation

During excavations of Aquincum, several cubicles were unearthed just outside what was then the south gate. Together they represented the city's earliest known 'hotel', a resting place for weary travellers who arrived too late to pass through the walls and had to hunker down until sunrise. Thankfully, in later years guests got more for their money. The boom in elegant hotels came towards the end of the 19th century, a time of economic prosperity and the millenary celebrations, when the country was keen to make a showcase of its capital. The ravages of 20th-century war put paid to many – although several historic hotels remain, most notably the Gellért (though with a slightly different façade) – and for two decades following World War II not a single new one was constructed. It was in the 1980s that the second wave proper rolled in; the state monopoly was undone, and high-class and mid-range hotels sprouted. The wave has yet to break.

At the turn of the 20th century, the pension (*panzió*) also took off, bed-and-breakfast-style accommodation for holiday visitors or workers seeking jobs in the capital. Nationalisation and post-war housing policy saw the larger of these places carved into low-grade apartments. Between the 1950s and 1980s, manual workers stayed at grim, socialist hostels (*munkás szállók*). Pensions bounced back though, and today flourish in the hills; unfortunately there are fewer in the city centre, and those there are tend to be considerably more expensive than their counterparts beyond the capital. Indeed, there's certainly no surplus of truly cheap accommodation for budget travellers anymore. The best bet is to head for one of the few hostels, stay in an empty college dorm, arrange a private room or bring a tent (see pages 122–4).

## HOTELS, PENSIONS AND HOSTELS

So, where do you lay your hat? If it's velvet-lined with a feather on top, you'll have no trouble putting it down in a top-end hotel targeting the business and affluent-tourist dollar. The desirable locations are along the river, in the Castle District, in or around the Belváros and near City Park. These hotels are based on Western models, and are often priced as such. Be aware, however, that the hotel star-rating system in Hungary is a less reliable guide to facilities; you may find, for instance, that a four-star establishment has a swimming pool where a five-star does not. Nor can a star rating account for character, and some of the historic hotels fall outside the top bands. Because Budapest sits on hot spring water, several hotels offer thermal treatments. While these in part cater to guests with specific medical complaints, there has been a big push towards 'wellness' tourism in Hungary, and provision for those who want to be cleansed, pummelled or pampered. There are also a good number of mid-range hotels. If you come across a *panzió* in Pest, it is likely to be a hotel of this ilk in all but name; the more personal, family-run guesthouses are to be found in the Buda hills. At the lower end of the budget range are hostels and basic hotels or pensions, usually located either in shabbier neighbourhoods or in suburbs beyond the tourist centre.

Because of the vagaries of the star system, and the blurred division in Budapest between pensions and hotels, we've sorted our listings by price (with sub-categories of Buda and Pest). These are walk-in rates for a double room during high season – generally May/June–September/October (although some hotels exclude parts of July and August, when the heat means visitor numbers drop) and the period over New Year. Low-season rates fall by around 30%. In addition, advance reservations, group bookings, and stays of more than one night will bring room charges down, and most of the better hotels offer discounted deals on weekend breaks. (Keep an eye on websites like www.lastminute.com and www.expedia.com.) The flipside of the coin is that during days around the Formula 1 Hungarian Grand Prix (in August) rates climb extravagantly, often to two or three times the high-season rate. VAT (12%) and City/Tourist Tax (3%) are payable on tourist rooms; these are included in our accommodation prices unless we state otherwise. Accommodation fills up in high season, so book ahead where possible. Demand is also fierce during festival periods.

The facilities you can expect in each category are laid out below. Breakfast is a buffet spread; a peculiar (irritating!) quirk is that while it is generally included in the price of budget and mid-range accommodation, you may be charged extra in the higher-cost places. Many hotels can arrange bike hire, theatre trips and excursions.

## Luxury (£125/US$224 and upwards)

You can assume that luxury hotels will have en-suite rooms with a bath and/or shower, television with satellite channels and pay-per-view movies (some in English), telephone, mini bar, room safe, air conditioning, internet-access point or business centre, restaurant and bar, fitness facilities and sauna; they may also have a swimming pool, solarium, shops and café.

## *Buda*

**Art'otel** I, Bem rakpart 16–19; tel: 1 487 9487; email: budapest@artotel.hu; www.artotel.hu [1 C3]

When a hotel gets someone in to add a lick of paint, you don't usually expect a contemporary American artist to turn up. The walls of the Art'otel display 600 works by Donald Sultan, creating a modern, sophisticated and clean-lined interior. The rooms are jazzy and spacious; request one with a river view. The Chelsea Restaurant is well worth a look (see page 138). 164 rooms. Superior €198, executive €218, suite €298 (incl breakfast).

**Corinthia Aquincum Hotel** III, Árpád fejedelem útja 94; tel: 1 436 4100; email: info@aqu.hu; www.corinthiahotels.com

B 86; HEV *Árpád híd*

It's not as plush as its sister hotel in Pest (see page 103) and views over the grounded boats of Shipyard Island are less enticing than its riverside location might suggest. The Corinthia Aquincum's trump card, however, is its spa. The thermal pools are filled with water pumped from Margaret Island, and are free for guests to use (although wellness treatments are extra). Non-guests may access the spa for 3,500Ft. 310 rooms. Swimming pool. Single €210, double €228, executive rooms €248, apartment €380 (excl City Tax, but incl breakfast). Stands at the foot of Árpád Bridge.

**Hilton Budapest** I, Budapest, Hess András tér 1–3; tel: 1 889 6600; email: sales_budapest@hilton.com; www.budapest.hilton.com [1 C4]

Location, location, location; the Hilton is the property gurus' mantra made flesh. Nestled next to the Mátyás Church, with eastern-facing rooms offering unrivalled views over the Danube, it is the envy of every other hotel in the city. As for the structure itself, the modern meets the historic in one of the most ambitious and provocative architectural projects you'll find in a hotel. Its design incorporates rows of metallic-tinted windows with the baroque façade of a 17th-century Jesuits' college, and the ruins of a 13th-century Dominican monastery. (For further history, see pages 245–6.)

While it lacks the haughty grandeur of some 5-star establishments, and the sensitive position doesn't allow for a swimming pool, it remains one of Budapest's best-known hotels. Robert Redford has laid tousled locks on the pillow of the presidential suite. In summer, the centrepiece Dominican courtyard hosts exhibitions, concerts and plays, while the fabulous Dominican Restaurant offers the very cream of views to go with its goose-liver specialities. Guests can park in the Castle District for no charge – ensure you have your ticket stamped at reception before exiting. The rooms are not enormous, but are elegant and suitably well equipped. 322 rooms. Deluxe €220–250, executive €270–300, suites €450–2,000 (all excl VAT and City Tax). Excellent buffet breakfast €20.

## Pest

**Andrássy Hotel** VI, Andrássy út 111; tel: 1 462 2100; email: welcome@andrassyhotel.com [2 G2]

M1 *Bajza utca*; B *4*

Once a state-owned hotel putting up foreign communist delegates (including Gorbachev), the Bauhaus building was designed by architect Alfréd Hajós, who was also an Olympic swimmer. It's now a charming sophisticate, with a limousine service and tinkling fountains in the lobby. There's a cheerful, Mediterranean-café feel about the place, and it's well situated for City Park and the State Opera House. The new Zebrano restaurant is also very good, serving a kind of international fusion. 70 rooms. Ask for one with a balcony. Single 38,000Ft, double 51,250Ft, deluxe 65,000Ft, suites 79,000–105,000Ft. Breakfast 3,700Ft/person.

**Corinthia Grand Hotel Royal** VII, Erzsébet körút 43–49; tel: 1 479 4000; email: royal@corinthia.hu; www.corinthiahotels.com [2 G4]
T 4, 6
The building is over a century old, and once contained the Café Royal – a beacon for Bohemians and the literati. After grey days as an office block it emerged in 2003 as the brightest of butterflies. There's yesteryear dignity about the marble lobby, sweeping staircase and heritage-protected ballroom, but any stuffiness is tempered by an airy modern layout that pits rooms around atrium courtyards. While the main restaurant has sturdy leather chairs and continental and Hungarian cuisine (including reasonably priced set lunches), there's also a luxurious oriental restaurant and sushi bar. There are plans to add thermal baths – wrangles with the heritage committee are ongoing – but for the moment guests are transferred to the spa of the sister Hotel Aquincum (see page 101). 414 rooms. Rooms are comfortably sized and smartly furnished, the executives offering marble surfaces, access to the executive lounge, and views over the inner atrium or boulevard rather than the rear of the hotel. All have bath and separate shower. Single €240, double €280, executive single €300–340, suites €400–3,000 (all excl 12% VAT). Breakfast €20.

**Four Seasons Hotel** V, Roosevelt tér 5–6; tel: 1 268 6000; www.fourseasons.com/budapest [1 D4]
Utterly stunning; this hotel will smack the gobs of the most difficult to please. The Gresham Palace started life as a temple to capitalism, created in 1907 for the London Gresham Life Assurance Society. Fashioned during Hungary's Golden Age, this was one of the finest examples of art-nouveau architecture in the world, housing company offices and luxury apartments. During the winter of 1944–45 Soviet soldiers occupied the palace, burning furniture to keep warm while the residents huddled in the cellar. It declined desperately after 1948 and nationalisation by the Hungarian communist government. Half a century later – after painstaking restoration and an outlay of US$110 million – the country's most luxurious hotel was opened in 2004. It is five-star-plus, with rooms furnished in Secessionist style (many with balconies and vaulted ceilings), and a spa with swimming pool. The Páva (Peacock) Restaurant serves Mediterranean and contemporary Hungarian cuisine. 179 rooms. Singles from €270, doubles €290–340, suites €950–3,700 (excl taxes).

**Hotel Helia** XIII, Kárpát utca 62–64; tel: 1 889 5800; email: helia@danubiusgroup.com; www.danubiusgroup.com/helia
B *133*; TB *76*; M3 *Dózsa György út*
This conference, wellness and thermal hotel is located slightly to the north of the centre, on the riverbank overlooking Margit-sziget . Rooms lack trappings of luxury but your money gives access to some serious liquid therapy. It is popular with older guests and those recovering from injuries; however, with a swimming-pool complex, a brace of thermal baths, a sauna and steam baths, a two-level fitness centre, and treatments that include a Cleopatra

bath of milk and honey, there's certainly room here for the tourist in search of a little pampering. 262 rooms. Some rooms have balconies (pay an €11 supplement for a river view), and a couple of the suites have their own private saunas (a legacy of former Finnish owners). Single €149–159, double €168–178, suite €258–367 (incl breakfast).

**Intercontinental Budapest** V, Apáczai Csere János utca 12–14; tel: 1 327 6333; email: budapest@interconti.com; www.interconti.com [1 D4]
When voted the best view of Budapest, the judges were clearly inside looking out. In fairness, it's less of an eyesore than the Budapest Marriott next door (V, Apáczai Csere János utca 4; www.marriotthotels.com/budhu), but nor does it do the Pesti riverscape near the Chain Bridge any favours. Both hotels target business travellers, and neither have the gravitas of luxury. Nevertheless they are superbly equipped and located precisely where you want to be. The Marriott also has an all-you-can-eat cake buffet in its lobby lounge (which raises it considerably in our estimations). 398 rooms. Swimming pool. Double €270–310, deluxe €350, business room €300–380, suites €570–600 (excl VAT and City Tax). Breakfast €20.

**Kempinski Hotel Corvinus** V, Erzsébet tér 7–8; tel: 1 429 3777; email: hotel.corvinus@kempinski.com; www.kempinski-budapest.com [1 E4]
Madonna hid here when filming *Evita* and Michael Jackson fans camped outside during his stay. Perhaps the pretty-headed A-listers come for the breakfast, which includes over 150 items on a sumptuous buffet menu; perhaps they drink the night away in the brick Bavarian beerhouse or enjoy a meal in the Bistro Jardin (see page 146). The hotel itself emerged in 2003 from a thorough spruce up, its rooms taken in hand by a designer who introduced tasteful furnishings

of beige, aqua, gold and black. Each suite is unique in style, and has a music system. Overall the hotel is immaculate, and has a five-star-plus rating. 365 rooms. Swimming pool. Wellness centre opening 2005. A gallery in the corridors of the first floor showcases contemporary Hungarian artists. Single €250–400, double €290–440, suites €420–2,600 (excl VAT and City Tax). Breakfast (Mon–Fri 06.00–10.30, Sat–Sun 06.00–11.00) €26; you don't have to be a guest to join the gorging fest.

**Le Méridien Budapest** V, Erzsébet tér 9–10; tel: 1 429 5500; email: reservations@lemeridien.hu; www.lemeridien-budapest.com [1 E4]
Opened in 2000 – and housed in the protected Adria Palace – this is a classically furnished hotel with genuine star quality. There are chandeliers in the lobby, brown marble in the rooms, and an art-deco glass-domed glory of a Parisian brasserie-restaurant. 218 rooms, decorated to a high standard with walnut and woven damasks. Small pool with a glass roof. Singles €235–385, doubles €275–425, suites €360–1,600 (excl VAT and City Tax). Breakfast €19.

## *Margaret Island*

**Grand Hotel Margitsziget** XIII, Margit-sziget; tel: 1 889 4700; email: grandmargitsziget.reservation@danubiusgroup.com; www.danubiusgroup.com/grand
*B 26 runs between the hotel and Nyugati station every 15 minutes. Ferry operates between the island and downtown in summer. Car access via Árpád Bridge.*
The stocky, mansion-like Grand was designed by Miklós Ybl in 1873, attracting literary greats like János Arany (for six years) and Sándor Bródy, and gatherings of early-20th-

century socialites. Guests may use the spa and medical facilities of the adjacent hotel (see below), which is linked to the Grand via an underground corridor. (Rooms in the Grand are smaller, but also 10% cheaper.) Each room has period features and a pleasing view of the island's greenery or the river running around it, while some of those on the second and third floors have terraces. 164 rooms. Single €149–164, double €168–184, suite €194–244 (incl breakfast).

**Thermal Hotel Margitsziget** XIII, Margit-sziget; tel: 1 889 4700; email: resind@margitsziget.danubiusgroup.com; www.danubiusgroup.com/thermalhotel
The Thermal Hotel is less noble of aspect than its neighbour – in fact, prior to 1979 it functioned as a hospital – but it is here that guests get down to the serious business of health, fitness and beauty. The spa complex makes use of three hot springs that feed the island, and there are indoor and outdoor swimming pools. You can choose from a truly bewildering list of treatments. If you want to know just how much of you is fat, they'll tell you the percentage with no holds barred; if you dream of a healthier spine, this is the place to come; the 'drinking cure' is warmer, eggier and altogether less alcoholic than you might have hoped. 267 rooms. Single €164–174, double €184–194, studio €184–204, suite €244 (incl breakfast). Bike hire 500Ft/day. Non-residents may use the spa for 4,500–5,500Ft/day.

## Expensive (£75–124/US$135–222)

You can assume that expensive hotels will have en-suite rooms with a bath or shower, television with satellite channels, telephone, mini bar, restaurant and bar, fitness facilities and sauna; they may also have pay-per-view channels, room safe, air conditioning, internet-access point or business centre, a swimming pool, solarium and café.

## Buda

**Congress Park Hotel Flamenco** XI, Tas vezér utca 7; tel: 1 889 5600; email: flamenco.reservation@danubiusgroup.com; www.danubiusgroup.com/flamenco [3 C7]
*T 61 from Moszkva tér, T 49 from Deák Ferenc tér or T 19 from Batthyány tér to Kosztolányi Dezső tér; B 7, 7A, 27, 12, 86*
The Hotel Sport was built on the western side of Feneketlen-tó (Bottomless Lake) (see page 259) in the 1960s, one of the first hotels to emerge for 20 years and characterised by the ungainly functionalism typical in buildings of the period. It's now the Flamenco and has conferences in mind, allowing guests to take a stroll around the reedy (and somewhat whiffy) lake in between seminar dozes. The facilities are excellent, including a swimming pool and access to nearby tennis courts. 358 compact rooms with A/C. Single/double €120–140, suite €220 (incl breakfast). Bike hire €5/2 hours.

**Hotel Gellért** I, Gellért tér 1; tel: 1 889 5500; email: gellert.reservation@danubiusgroup.com; www.danubiusgroup.com/gellert [3 E7]
If a turn-of-the-20th-century dandy were to meet Medusa's eye, the Hotel Gellért might be the result. This is an old-money aristocrat in stone. Ironically it was completed in 1918, and its first guests were political officials of the Hungarian Republic of Soviets. However, it recovered to become a favourite of the inter-war party set, offering food prepared by the great János Gundel and air-boat flights to Lake Balaton from the embankment outside.

Among more recent luminaries attracted by its high-blown art-nouveau style have been Andrew LLoyd Webber, Richard Nixon and Pele. With a grand history comes a disdain for homogeneity; this is a hotel for lovers of faded noble charm rather than wall-to-wall comforts. Rooms (divided into three categories) vary considerably in size and shape. Those facing the river offer wonderful views – although light sleepers should note that trams rumble along the road below – while others overlook an inner courtyard. A long-term programme of renovation means that some rooms await their overhaul. The hotel's café and terrace serves great cakes and snacks, and the recently renovated Gellért sörózö operates as a beer garden and sun trap. 234 rooms. Most without A/C. Single €75–190, double €170–210, suite €250–270 (incl breakfast and use of the adjacent Gellért Baths; see page 220). Bike hire 1,000/5,000Ft (hour/day).

**Hotel Gold Buda** I, Hegyalja út 14; tel: 1 209 4775; email: goldbuda@goldhotel.hu; www.goldhotel.hu [3 C6]
B *8, 112 stop outside*
With its distinctive conical turret, this is an appealingly quirky and asymmetrical little hotel. It's fairly well located near Erzsébet Bridge, at the western foot of Gellért Hill, although a busy road runs past the doorstep. 24 rooms. Single €84–141, double €94–141, tower room €100–147 (incl breakfast, excl City Tax).

**Hotel Lido** III, Nánási út 67; tel: 1 436 0980; email: lidohotel@elender.hu; www.bestwestern-ce.com/lido.
B *106 from Árpád Bridge;* HEV *Rómaifürdő*

This is one for sporty types, with squash and tennis courts, a swimming pool, fitness centre and bowling alley. Stands near the river, just behind the Római part. 54 rooms. Single €96, double €126, apartment €225 (incl breakfast).

## *Pest*

**Astoria** V, Kossuth Lajos utca 19–21; tel: 1 889 6000; email: astoria.reservation@danubiusgroup.com; www.danubiusgroup.com/astoria [4 F5]
The Astoria retains much of its *fin-de-siècle* elegance, boasting chandeliers and a marbled lobby in green and gold – indeed, it is often used by film-makers producing period pieces. It was cutting edge when it first opened, with lifts and even a central vacuum-cleaning system (whatever that may have been). Its walls could tell a tale or two; in 1944 the basement was used as a detention centre for prisoners of the Gestapo, and ironically it formed the Soviet HQ during the 1956 revolution. In addition, it was here that the first democratic Hungarian government declared independence from Austria in October 1918. Today the rooms vary in size, but are comfortable and classically furnished. 131 rooms. Single €100–110, double €110–120, suite €170. Breakfast €13.

**Grand Hotel Hungaria** VII, Rákóczi út 90; tel: 1 889 4400; email: grandhungaria.reservation@danubiusgroup.com; www.danubiusgroup.com/grandhotel-hungaria [2 H4]
M2 *Keleti;* B *7 and 78 (stop outside)*
This Goliath of a hotel – the country's biggest – stands a 5-minute walk from Keleti station, and it's a good bet for larger tourist parties. It occupies the site of two early-20th-century

hotels; the gypsy musician Rácz Laci would play at the Centrál, reportedly taking two cabs home afterwards (one for himself and one for his fiddle). The ongoing renovation programme is something of a labour of Hercules, but refurbished rooms are neutral and understated; those at the front of the building have terraces. Solarium, A/C, underground parking (€15/day). 499 rooms. Single €110, double €130, apartment (for 2) €200, suites €130–150 (incl breakfast).

**Hotel Erzsébet** V, Károlyi Mihály utca 11–15; tel: 1 889 3710; email: erzsebet.reservation@danubiusgroup.com; www.danubiusgroup.com/erzsebet [4 F5]
This fabulously central hotel was originally built in 1872, and was named after the queen of the time. The cellars were transformed into a beer hall in 1927, the walls decorated with murals illustrating an epic poem – 'János Vitéz' ('John the Valiant') by revolutionary poet Petőfi Sándor. The hall features live gypsy music from 19.00. 123 rooms. Rooms basic but comfortable. A/C. Single €110, double €120 (incl breakfast).

**NH Budapest** XIII, Vígszínház utca 3; tel: 1 814 0000; email: nhbudapest@nh-hotels.com; www.nh-hotels.com [1 E2]
T *4, 6;* B *26, 91, 191*
The Budapest arm of this Spanish-owned hotel chain keeps the downtown within easy grasp, and is newly out of its wrapper – it only opened at the end of 2003. The furnishings have not had time to get tatty, and remain sharp, clean and contemporary. Solarium, A/C, underground parking. 160 rooms. The smart rooms look either outwards or over an inner courtyard atrium; some have balconies. Located directly behind the Vígszínház (Comedy Theatre) on the Great Boulevard. Rooms €88–135. Breakfast €16.

**Radisson SAS Béke Hotel Budapest** VI, Teréz körút 43; tel: 1 889 3900; email: sales.budapest@radissonsas.com; www.radissonsas.com [2 F3]
*T 4 and 6 stop almost outside*
The novelist Ferenc Móra considered the Britannia – the Radisson in its previous incarnation – his second home. During the mid-1900s, the fashionable flocked to the hotel's vaunted nightclub for live jazz and dancing. The façade remains, and the Zsolnay Café is turn-of-the-century elegant, but otherwise this is a modern hotel with swimming pool, sauna, solarium and massage treatments. You're right in the thick of the city here, on the busy Nagy körút, and well placed for both the Belváros and City Park. 247 rooms. Rooms comfortable, without knocking any socks off. A/C. Single/double €180, suite €340 (excl all taxes). Breakfast €17. Parking €21/day.

## Mid-range (£35–74/US$63–133)

Hotels and pensions in the middle range will generally have en-suite rooms with a bath and/or shower, television and telephone; they may have mini bar, air conditioning, restaurant, bar and sauna.

### *Buda*

**Ábel Panzió** XII, Ábel Jenő utca 9; tel/fax: 1 381 0553/372 0289 [3 C7]
*T 61 (from Moszkva tér or Móricz Zsigmond körtér) stops near top of Ábel Jenő utca*
A pretty villa with creeper-covered walls, shuttered windows and a veranda overlooking a well-kept garden. It's a very high-class guesthouse whose interior radiates old-fashioned elegance, and is ideal for those after some last-century peace and relaxation. On a quiet

backstreet off Villányi út. 10 rooms. No TV, but radio. Single €65, double €70 (incl breakfast).

**Burg Hotel** I, Szentháromság tér 7–8; tel: 1 212 0269; email: hotel.burg@mail.datanet.hu; www.burghotelbudapest.com [1 C4]
Lacking the river views of its illustrious neighbour the Budapest Hilton (see page 101), this hotel nevertheless has its own piece of courtyard history – a segment of castle wall dating back 300 years – and is very reasonably priced considering the desirability of its location. Most of its rooms overlook the square, are decorated with lightwood furnishings, and are as you would expect from a 3-star establishment – functional and lacking in trimmings. 26 rooms. A/C. Single €99, double €109, suite (for 2) €129 (incl breakfast).

**Hotel Budapest** II, Szilágyi Erzsébet fasor 47; tel: 1 889 4200; email: budapest.reservation@danubiusgroup.com; www.danubiusgroup.com/budapest [1 A2]
*T 18 and 56 (from Moszkva tér); B 5 (from Erzsébet Bridge)*
This satisfying cylinder of a hotel was innovative in the 1960s, and remains a striking landmark at the point where grey meets green in Buda. Opposite is the lower terminus of the Cogwheel Railway (see page 356), sending its clacking carriages away into the hills. There are no inconvenient pillars or square corners to get in the way of panoramic views, and on a clear day those near the top of the 15 storeys will set your heart doing the quickstep. There is no extra cost for rooms on upper levels – so make sure you aim high when booking. Sauna. 289 rooms. A/C. Single/double €95, suite €120 (incl breakfast).

### *COMMIE LOVE*

Durex, the condom manufacturer, conducted a survey in 2003 to find the nation that most enjoyed sex. The French? The Italians? Oh, *nem nem*. Hungarians topped the poll as the Buda-best lovers, followed by citizens from Serbia and Montenegro, Croatia, Bulgaria and the Czech Republic. Perhaps a communist past is the Viagra of central Europe…

**Hotel Charles** I, Hegyalja út 23; tel: 1 212 9169; email: reservation@charleshotel.hu; www.charleshotel.hu [3 C6]

*B 112 and 8 stop outside*

The Charles was originally built to cater for visiting businessmen who wanted to burn their own dinner after a hard day at the office. Each of the sizeable studio rooms and apartments has a little kitchen with a hob, fridge, sink and cutlery. The location isn't the prettiest, but it's fairly convenient for the main tourist areas, the staff are courteous and helpful, and the value is excellent. Bike hire (see page 229). 70 rooms. Single €49, double €66, triple €90, apartment (for 1–4 people) €72–114 (incl breakfast).

**Hotel Normafa** XII, Eötvös út 52–54; tel: 1 395 6505; email: registration@normafahotel.com; www.normafahotel.com

*B 21 (from Moszkva tér) stops outside*

Just a few metres from the southern entrance to the wooded Normafa lejtő (see page 357)

on Sváb hegy, and 2km from János hegy with its biking and walking routes, this handsome alpine-style hotel is a great base for families exploring the Buda hills. Fitness centre, sauna, outdoor swimming pool (with a children's pool and play area). Bike hire 1,000Ft/hour or 2,000Ft/day (20,000Ft deposit). The adjacent Normafa Café and Grill (tel/fax: 1 395 1771) serves international cuisine of good repute. 61 rooms. Single €85, double €95, suite €115 (incl breakfast).

**Kulturinnov Hotel** I, Szentháromság tér 6; tel: 1 355 0122/375 1651; email: mka3hotel@dbassoc.hu [1 C4]

The interior of this neo-Gothic palace (see page 243) on the northern side of the square has a faded splendour, but don't expect royal luxury from the small hotel in its wings. This aristocrat has had to tighten his belt. Owned by the Hungarian Culture Foundation, the hotel's rooms are very basic. Nevertheless, as for the Burg Hotel (page 113), one can't help but feel fortunate to find relatively affordable rooms within fly-casting distance of the Fishermen's Bastion. Parking 2,500Ft/day (accessed via the barrier at the northern end of Dísz tér or via Bécsi kapu). 16 rooms. Most look inward over the building's central courtyard; no TV. Single 13,000Ft, double 20,000Ft, triple 22,000Ft (incl breakfast).

**Vadvirág Panzió** II, Nagybányai út 18; tel/fax: 1 275 0200/394 4292; email: vadvirag.panzio@axelero.hu

*B 5 (from Március 15 tér) to Pasaréti tér, then 8-minute walk in direction of Bartók memorial house (see page 321)*

Much care has gone into this super *panzió*, divided between two buildings and tucked into

Buda's green belt. All rooms have period elegance, with rich reds and drape curtains, and some have balconies offering hill views. The beautifully tended garden is a pleasure in summer months, and there's also a terrace for sunbathing and a sauna. It's a touch pricier than some pensions, but it's plusher too. 18 rooms. Single/double €49–70, apartments €70–80 (incl breakfast).

## *Pest*

**Hotel Fiesta** VI, Király utca 20; tel: 1 328 3000; www.ahotelfiesta.com [2 F4]
M1, M2, M3 *Deák Ferenc tér;* T *47, 49*
Daylight floods the lobby atrium, with its transparent roof and suspended stained-glass panels, and signals a stylish, modern hotel. Spacious rooms are unfussy, colourful and clean. 112 rooms, the superior larger than the standard. A/C. Located 400m from Deák Ferenc tér. Single €90, double €100, suite €120.

**Hotel Gold Panzió** XIV, Pándorfalu utca 15 (near Ungvár utca); tel: 1 252 0470; email: panzio@goldhotel.hu; www.goldhotel.hu
TB *74 stops a few minutes' walk away;* M1 *Mexikói út; near M3 motorway.*
On a quiet suburban backstreet 1km northeast of City Park, this *panzió* is friendly, cosy and competitively priced. 22 tasteful and roomy rooms, with small balconies. Single €49–90, double €57–90 (incl breakfast, excl 3% Tourist Tax).

**Hotel Liget** VI, Dózsa György út 106; tel: 1 269 5300; email: hotel@liget.hu; www.liget.hu [2 G1]
TB *75, 79 or* B *20, 30 stop close by*

Well positioned for City Park and Heroes' Square, less so for the downtown. The rooms are muted and uninspiring, but large and comfortable enough. Sauna, solarium, bike rental. 139 rooms. Single €96, double €112 (incl breakfast).

**Hotel Queen Mary** VII, Kertész utca 34; tel: 1 413 3510; email: info@hotelqueenmary.hu; www.hotelqueenmary.hu [2 G4]
*TB 70, 78 to top of Kertész utca; M1 Oktogon, M2 Blaha Lujza tér, then T 4, 6 a short way to junction with Király utca, and walk*
Opened in 2003, the Queen Mary remains as eager as a puppy. There are few decorous frills, but all is fresh, unsullied and as yet un-dog-eared. Just off the Nagy körút, it's a short elope to the café-bars of Liszt Ferenc tér. 26 rooms. A/C. Single €50, double €55, triple €70 (incl breakfast).

**Hotel Stadion** XIV, Ifjúság útja 1–3; tel: 1 889 5200; email: stadion.reservation@danubiusgroup.com; www.danubiusgroup.com/stadion [2 K4]
*M2 Népstadion*
In the heart of the sport district, near the Puskás Stadium on the outskirts of town, the Stadion inevitably receives its fair share of athletes, spectators and school touring teams. High-tech fitness room, swimming pool, sauna, solarium. Rooms are a good size, newly refurbished, many with balconies. 379 rooms. Single/double €110 (incl breakfast).

**Leó Panzió** V, Kossuth Lajos utca 2/A; tel: 1 266 9041; email: panzioleo@mail.datanet.hu [4 F5]
With Váci utca a mere 30m away and the Franciscan church at Ferenciek tere opposite, she can go shopping while he prays the credit card can take it. You couldn't ask for a more central

location; it's on the second floor of a shabby-looking building with a cage lift, but the rooms are spacious and well furnished. A/C. 14 rooms. Single €66, double €82 (incl breakfast).

## Budget (£34/US$61 and under)

Hotels, hostels and pensions in the budget category will generally have en-suite rooms with a bath and/or shower and telephone (except in hostel dorms); in addition, they may have television, air conditioning, internet access and sauna. Youth hostels (*ifjúsági szálló*) may be open during the summer only, although this is unusual in Budapest. (The Hungarian Youth Hostels Association can provide further information, and make reservations; VII, Almássy tér 6; tel: 1 413 2065 or 1 343 5167; www.youthhostels.hu). A final bargain-basement option is to stay in college accommodation during the summer recess (July and August). The Tourinform should be able to provide a list of these, although local tourist agencies (see under *Private rooms*, page 122) can also make bookings for you.

### *Buda*

**Back Pack Guesthouse** XI, Takács Menyhért utca 33; tel: 1 209 8406; email: backpackguest@hotmail.com; www.backpackbudapest.hu [3 B8]
B *7, 7A;* T *19, 49. Alight at Tétényi út and then short walk.*
Jungle murals, rainbow colours, a decked 'chillout' garden and a room called the 'love shack'. This is a fun-time commune of a guesthouse, where you're likely to join a social soup of English speakers on the move – from committed hippies to students doing the GAP-Year tour. Some backpacking places leave you feeling in need of a good shower, but here the

rooms are clean, comfortable and cheerful. Doubles have TV, basin. Shared toilets, showers, kitchen, laundry facilities. 15 minutes by bus from the centre. 8 rooms. Double 6,600Ft, dorms 2,200–2,800Ft/person.

**Büro Panzió** II, Dékán utca 3; tel: 1 212 2929; email: buro-panzio@axelero.hu [1 B3]
M2 *Moszkva tér;* T *4, 6*
Fairly basic and a touch bleak, the Büro is just off Moszkva tér, convenient for public transport and less than 10 minutes on foot to the Castle District. Considering this, it's cheap as chips, but don't expect modern furnishings. 10 rooms, some with TV. Single 5,000Ft, double 10,000Ft, triple 15,000Ft (incl breakfast).

**Hotel Citadella** I, Citadella sétány; tel: 1 466 5794; email: citadella@citadella.hu; www.citadella.hu [3 D6]
B *27 as far as Búsuló Juhász Étterem and then 300m walk.*
Those who fancy doing a bit of holiday porridge should head for the chunky ramparts of the former Habsburg fortress (see page 342). There are few home comforts here – it's more hostel than hotel – but can prison have been all that bad with views like these from the walls? Most rooms sleep 2–4, and there is a dorm for 14. 12 rooms. Shower and basin, but shared toilets. No TV. Rooms €46–51, dorm €10/person.

**Hotel Korona** XII, Sasadi út 123; tel: 1 319 1255; email: korona.pension@axelero.hu; www.koronapension.hu [3 A7]
B *53 (from Karinthy Frigyes út) stops outside;* T *59 (from Moszkva tér) runs to Farkasréti tér, at northern end of Sasadi út*

A well-equipped villa-style hotel on the cusp of the Buda hills, with beautifully maintained gardens and modern, clean rooms. Excellent value. Sauna. 24 rooms, some with balconies, some with A/C. Single 10,200Ft, double 12,750Ft, triple 15,300Ft, apartment 22,950Ft (incl breakfast).

**Hotel Papillon** II, Rózsahegy utca 3/B; tel: 1 212 7450; email: rozsahegy@axelero.hu; www.hotelpapillon.hu [1 B2]
B *11 from Batthyány tér*
More family guesthouse than hotel, with homely, modern rooms and a welcoming owner. There's room to dip little more than a toe in the tiny swimming pool at the back, but the garden allows you to relax after the sapping climb up Rose Hill. 20 rooms. Single €36, double €46, triple €56 (incl breakfast, excl Tourist Tax).

## Pest

**Best Hostel** VII, Podmaniczky utca 27; tel: 1 332 4934; email: bestyh@mail.datanet.hu; www.besthostel.hu [2 F3]
T *4, 6 (from Moszkva tér);* B *72;* TB *73;* M3 *Nyugati tér*
A calm and comfortable hostel near Nyugati station. Ring doorbell 33 for access to the inner courtyard of the block, and the hostel is on the first level. Communal kitchen, common room (with TV), internet access, shared showers and toilets. Dorms (for 6, 8 and 9) 2,800Ft/person, twin/quad 4,000Ft/person, triple 3,400Ft/person (incl breakfast).

**Marco Polo Hostel** VII, Nyár utca 6; tel: 1 413 2555; email: info@marcopolohostel.com; www.marcopolohostel.com [2 F4]
TB *74 stops close by;* M2 *Blaha Lujza tér (3 streets away)*

Upper-end hostel in the business district, with cheerful rooms, a washer and dryer, and a disco bar open into the wee hours. Rooms (not dorms) are en-suite and have TV and telephone. Free minibus from Keleti station. Single 12,000Ft/person, double 8,000Ft/person, triple 6,000Ft/person, quad 5,000Ft/person, dorms (for 12) 4,200Ft/person. 10% discount with student or IYHF cards.

**Medosz Hotel** VI, Jókai Mór tér 9; tel: 1 374 3000 [2 F3]
B *4 along Andrássy út;* T *4, 6;* M1 *Oktogon*
As drab and utilitarian as they come, the Medosz is nevertheless an affordable option right on top of the bars and restaurants of Liszt and Jókai squares. Rooms are spartan but well enough equipped, and there's a decent breakfast. Credit cards are not accepted. 70 rooms. Single 10,000Ft, double 13,000Ft, triple 15,500Ft, suite 20,000Ft (incl breakfast).

**Red Bus Hostel** V, Semmelweis utca 14; tel: 1 266 0136; www.redbusbudapest.hu [4 F5]
M2 *Astoria,* M3 *Ferenciek tere, then few minutes' walk*
No nonsense here – basic hostel accommodation owned by a friendly South London geezer and his Hungarian wife. It's on the first floor of a residential block; climb the stairs around the inner courtyard after you've passed through the main entrance. Standard dormitories, as well as single, double and triple rooms, communal kitchen and laundry facilities, internet access, and shared toilets and showers. Dorms (for 4, 6 and 8) 2,800Ft/person, twin 7,500Ft/room (incl breakfast). Centrally located just inside Károly körút, on the corner of Gerlóczy utca and Semmelweis utca. The owners run a second hostel in summer (VII, Szövetség utca 35; tel: 1 321 7100), offering dorm beds only.

## PRIVATE ROOMS

Bagging a bed in someone else's house is usually a far cheaper alternative to hotel or *panzió* accommodation, and also allows you a peek behind domestic curtains. Rooms are available in most districts, although beyond the downtown or surroundings of the Castle District there's the risk of a run-down neighbourhood or a high-rise block. Double-check with the agency concerned – you're very much in their hands. Your hostess is likely to be a retired lady with but a smattering of English, so don't bank on any meaningful chitchat. Rooms usually have TV, bedding and towels. Expect to pay 4,000–6,000Ft for a single room and 5,000–9,000Ft for a double. Rates should include heating and electricity (but not food), and are dependent upon the season and duration (there may be a minimum length of stay to qualify for the quoted rate). The following places can organise a private room on your behalf:

**Ibusz** V, Ferenciek tere 10; tel: 1 485 2767; email: accommodation@ibusz.hu; www.ibusz.hu. Rooms 4,000–6,500Ft/person/night. *Office open Mon–Fri 09.00–17.00, closed weekends.*

**Kata Tourist** V, Régi Posta utca 12; tel: 1 486 0147. Helpful tourist office that can organise cheap accommodation in hostels and dorm rooms in universities. *Open 10.00–20.00 daily.*

**To-Ma Tour** V, Október 6 utca 22; tel: 1 353 0819; email: tomatour@axelero.hu; www.tomatour.hu. Singles 4,500–6,000Ft, doubles 5,500–8,000Ft. *Open Mon–Fri 09.00–12.00, 13.00–20.00, Sat–Sun 09.00–17.00.*

**Tribus Hotel Service** V, Apáczai Csere János utca 1; tel: 1 944 2455; email: tribus.hotel.service@mail.datanet.hu. Rooms 5,000–9,000Ft/night. *Office open 24 hours daily.*

## PRIVATE APARTMENTS

Self-contained apartments are an alternative for families and small groups. Most come with a fully equipped kitchen, bed linen and towels, television and radio. Rates include all utility costs. Try one of these companies for bookings:

**Boulevard City Apartments** XII, Virányos utca 10/A; tel: 1 214 6262; www.aktivtours.hu. Superior 2- and 3-room accommodation in a modern apartment building just beyond the Nagy körút. Apartments €66–88/night depending upon size and length of stay (min 2 nights). Tourist tax of €1.5/person/night.

**To-Ma Tour** See page 85. Although the 1-, 2- and 3-bedroom apartments are not luxurious, they are centrally located, clean and well equipped. There's wiggle room over prices, but expect to pay from €45/60/85 for 1/2/3 rooms.

**Tribus Hotel Service** See opposite. Pleasant apartments for 1–6 people, mainly in downtown Pest. 10,000–20,000Ft/apartment/night.

**www.budapestrooms.com** Tel: 30 454 3017; email: info@budapestrooms.com. Website contains apartment details; complete the online registration form to secure your booking. €40–70/night (1–2 people), €50–80/night (3–4), €80–100/night (5–6).

## CAMPING

The best places to pitch up are on the Buda side of the river. Sites are well equipped without giving Eurocamp undue cause for worry, and can be crowded in high season.

**Csillebérci Camping** XII, Konkoly Thege Miklós út 21; tel: 1 275 4033
B *21 (from Moszkva tér) or Children's Railway to Csillebérc terminus*

Not the most modern campsite, but it has excellent sports facilities (outdoor pool, tennis courts etc), and is beautifully situated on Széchenyi hegy. Tent and caravan camping, bungalows and youth hostel; showers, cooking appliances, on-site café and restaurant. Daily fee €4/person; tent €5/night, caravan €11/night. Bungalows (bathroom, fridge, radio) €38/48 (for 2/3). Youth hostel rooms (shared bathrooms) double €16–20, triple €21–27; apartment (for 4, kitchen, bathroom) €36–45. *Camping open May 1–Sep 30; bungalow/youth hostel open all year.*

**Római Camping** III, Szentendrei út 189; tel: 1 368 6260; www.hotels.hu/romai_camping
HEV *Rómaifürdő station*
Large campsite with all-dancing facilities – swimming pool, decent showers, a restaurant and shop – and open all year. Opposite the Római Strand, on the road running northwards to Szentendre. A 15-minute train journey to the centre of Buda and 30 minutes into Pest. Daily fee 990Ft/person; tent 1,950Ft/night, caravan 2,970Ft/night, bungalows 1,690–15,000Ft/night (class I–III). *Reception open Mon–Fri 08.00–15.00 (call at site restaurant 15.00–22.00).*

**Zugligeti 'Niche' Camping** XII, Zugligeti út 101; tel: 1 200 8346; www.campingniche.hu
B *158 (from Moszkva tér) stops by entrance*
The campers' favourite, and understandably so. Small but inviting, well kept, and attractively located. Very good restaurant. 9km from the city centre. *Open Mar–Nov.*

# 6 Eating and Drinking

*I am not a glutton – I am an explorer of food.*

Erma Bombeck (1927–1996)

You can't properly enjoy rooting around a city without the anticipation of good food and drink to come. Budapest doesn't disappoint. Coffee and cake is the cement between sights in a day spent wandering, and you'll reflect fondly on that evening passed people-watching on a terrace with a glass of beer and a bowl of bean soup. Hungarian food fuelled shepherds, hunters and fishermen, and it more than fills the legs of today's tourists; it is characteristically hearty, oily and rich, heavy with protein and carbohydrate. Prepare to loosen the belt and lose a few buttons.

## FOOD

**Hungarian cuisine** (*Magyar konyha*) has been influenced by the kitchens of Serbia, France and Turkey; the Renaissance court of King Mátyás introduced Italian ingredients like garlic, onion and dried pasta; the Germans and Austrians muscled in during the Austro-Hungarian period with their cream-filled desserts, sauerkraut and dumplings. All these tastes add nuances to a no-nonsense, homely tradition of peasant cookery.

Pork became a staple of the Hungarian diet after the Turkish invasion, when the Muslim occupiers left pigs wholly to the natives. 'Be not afraid of scooping in the piquant sour cream' one of the Gundels once cried, and his advice was not ignored;

it is handsomely applied to soups and sauces, as well as dishes of meat, cabbage and sweet pasta. Vegetable accompaniments are pickled or from the freezer, and salads plate-edge afterthoughts. The vegetarian diner may feel put upon in traditional restaurants, where the choice is often restricted to fruit soups and cheese or mushrooms in breadcrumbs. The Hungarian phrase for 'add spices' (*trágyázd meg*) literally translates as 'fertilise with manure'; cumin, caraway, black pepper and marjoram are frequent fertilisers, but when you think Hungary it's red (*piros*) paprika that sets the tastebuds tingling. Probably introduced from Spain in the 16th century (although not widely used until the 19th), it imparts vivid culinary colour, and ranges in taste from sweet and fruity (*édes*) to fiery (*erős*), the latter proffering a kick like a hussar's horse. And woe betide he who gets between a Magyar and a piece of fresh bread (*kenyér*); it is regarded as the greatest of feasts.

While many busy Hungarians may just grab a roll on the run, if they greet the day properly then it is early and with a **breakfast** (*reggeli*) of open sandwiches. Salami (*szalámi*) or dried, chorizo-like sausage (*száraz*), ham, cheese, yellow pepper and tomato are eaten with white bread. The weekend may see omelettes on the table, while at Easter there is gammon-like ham with boiled eggs and horseradish. The reviving morning brew is hot (often black) coffee or tea with lemon (not milk).

**Lunch** is the main event, and comprises two courses. The first is likely to be soup (*leves*). Freshwater lakes like Balaton provide the specimens for fish soup (*halászlé*) – a customary dish on Christmas Eve. Chicken soup (*tyúk húsleves*) is packed with vegetables and light pasta (similar to Italian *vermicelli*), while fruit soup (*hideg gyümölcsleves*) is a refreshing summer slurp, flavoured with cherry or strawberry, topped with cream and served cold. The meaty Hortobágy pancake (*Hortobágyi húsos palacsinta*) is a speciality of the Great Plain; seasoned minced pork or poultry is folded into thin pancakes and baked in a sauce of paprika and sour cream. Please don't miss this one – it shades the number-one spot on our Hungarian-dish wish list.

The second course is invariably a meat-based rib sticker. The international superstar is, of course, goulash (actually *gulyás*, and pronounced 'gooyash'), strictly a soup rather than a stew, and containing beef or pork, pinched dumplings, vegetables and the ubiquitous paprika. Cooked in a cauldron (*bogrács*), its roots can be traced to the country's nomadic ancestors. While today's Hungarians at home tend to treat it as a main course, in restaurants you'll find it among the starting line up. The same applies to the smoky, meaty and gorgeous kidney-bean soup (*jókai bableves*). Each of the above should be mopped up with a hunk of dunking bread, but other specialities are served with weighty side dishes including egg dumplings (*galuska* or *nokedli*), couscous-type pasta (*tarhonya*), potato croquettes (*krokett*) and rice. A traditional stew (*pörkölt*) might be concocted from any of the main meats, but our vote goes to that with chicken (*csirkepaprikás*) – creamy, golden as toffee, and occasionally with the coxcomb thrown in! Other popular choices are stuffed cabbage (*töltött káposzta*) or pepper (*töltött paprika*) filled with minced meat, a piece of the earthy-tasting pike perch (*fogas*), and a plate-sized slab of Wiener schnitzel (*bécsi szelet*). The latter is often eaten for Sunday lunch.

**Pudding** (*édességek* or *desszertek*) requires a healthy appetite and a sweet tooth. Any room for a cake, an ice-cream, a strudel or a crêpe? At times savoury becomes sweet; *túróscsusza* is a hot pastry with ricotta, sour cream and – believe it or not – pork crackling. Pastas, too, are familiar dessert dishes. *Rétes* is an Austrian strudel filled with either fruit, walnut, peppery cabbage or poppy seeds and ricotta, while walnut cream and chocolate sauce is the heavenly mix in a Gundel pancake (*Gundel palacsinta*). For other sweet options, see box, page 158.

## DRINK

Thirsty? Big-name fizzy **soft drinks** are available everywhere, as are bottled mineral waters (*ásványvíz*) and fruit juices. Hungarians satisfy regular coffee cravings (see page 156); although they are less enamoured with tea, which is sipped straight or with lemon, teahouses are popping up with growing frequency. For something stronger, fruit **brandy** (*pálinka*) is a popular tipple – even at breakfast time for rural diehards. It's distilled from apricots (*barack*), plums (*szilva*), pears (*körte*), cherries (*cseresznye*) or peaches (*őszibarack*), although if you try a home brew – a common hobby of the older generation – you'll get some fire with your fruit. Another apéritif is the herbal and distinctive Unicum, said to have been invented by the court physician to József II, and distilled by the Zwack family for 200 years. Many claims have been made for this bitter liquid – that it is an aid to digestion, a restorative and even an aphrodisiac; the only undeniable truth is that it is an acquired taste. Drink it straight, with cola or even as a hot toddy. And give it as many second chances as you feel able. (There is a small museum at the Budapest Zwack plant at Soroksári út 26. Contact them on 1 476 2308 to arrange a visit.)

Much **beer** (*sör*) is imported from the Czech Republic or brewed under the licence of foreign companies like Tuborg and HB, but Hungarian beers are deserving of attention. They might be bottled or on tap, and fall into two types – lager (*világos*) and brown (*barna*), the latter similar in colour to English bitter but with a sweet flavour. The leading breweries are Dreher and Borsodi, the first marginally our preferred choice, while other regional brands can be found in the supermarkets. The word for 'cheers!' – *egészségedre* – is a mouthful at the best of times, but becomes a particular trial after a drink or two. Remember not to clink together those beer glasses (see page 25).

It is said that Hungarians can be divided into the few who produce **wine** and the many who would dearly love to. For much of the 20th century, you'd be forgiven for thinking the amateurish majority had been let loose on the vineyards. There was a massive decline in quality behind the Iron Curtain; vineyards were neglected, fine sites abandoned, and state co-operatives devoted themselves to mass production. During the 1980s, Hungary's main export, Bull's Blood, became a byword for vinegar; the Soviets were the sole bulk buyers. However, change has been rapid since the advent of privatisation. Joint ventures with foreign vintners and investment in technology have resulted in some fine wineries, many of them family-owned.

Some facts. There are 22 wine regions and around 20 Hungarian grape varieties. Seventy-five percent of wines are white (*fehér bor*), although recently it is the reds (*vörös bor*) that have attracted attention. In very rough terms – there are exceptions – white is produced in the north and red in the south. Grapes include Hungarian

***WINNING WINES***

What should you plump for with dinner? Aged in networks of mould-clad cellars, **Tokaji Aszú** is long-lived and nectar sweet, with a volcanic mineral edge. It was favoured by Europe's royal houses, and Louis XIV declared it 'the king of wines, the wine of kings' – which must have had the marketing people gleefully rubbing their hands. It suffered under the state economy, but is heralded as back to its freshest and fruitiest. Aszú is created from grapes affected by noble rot, and the number of hods (*puttonyos*) of such grapes added to a dry base wine determines the wine's sweetness. Most is produced at levels of between three and six *puttonyos*, with Aszú Esszencia sweeter still. Top recent vintages were 1996 and 2000, while those of 1993 and 1999 are judged to be classics. Dry Tokaji wines are also available – look out for those of 2000 and 2002 – but more readily acclaimed are the light and young-drinking whites from **Lake Balaton** (especially the Olaszrizling of Badacsony). If you fancy something bubbly, the country's main sparkling wine (*pezsgő*) is the relatively inexpensive **Törley** champagne. It's produced by Hungary's largest wine

and imported varieties. Good-to-fine white wines are made from Furmint (the base wine of Tokaji Aszú), Királyleányka, Hárslevelű, Irsai Olivér and Olaszrizling, along with Sauvignon, Chardonnay and Tramini. Quality home-grown reds include Kékfrankos (the most widely planted) and Kadarka, while Cabernet, Merlot and company, Hungarovin, and compares favourably with versions from New World countries.

**Bull's Blood** (Bikavér) derives its name from the period of Turkish occupation; the sober Ottomans thought that their opponents were made brave by consuming flagons of animal blood, when the Hungarians were actually more sensibly seeking Dutch courage in flagons of red wine. Moves are underway to protect Bull's Blood, which became synonymous with a Hungarian product ruined by commercialism, but its definition remains loose – simply encompassing 'quality' blended red wine from Szekszárd or Eger. One problem is that large companies continue to cling to its potential as a brand, looking enviously at the success of Australian Rosemount or Jacob's Creek. A leading firm even attempted to spark success by replacing its bull's head logo with a rather Spanish-looking matador. Stick to bottles from small producers who take time over the product rather than the branding and you'll find some excellent wines. Alternatively, reds from **Villány** are expressive, full-bodied and rightly rated.

Pinot Noir have all been produced at very respectable levels. Reds are characteristically light because of the country's cold winters, and they are often served at a lower temperature than you might usually expect. There is a Hungarian equivalent of the French *appellation controlée*, so before buying check for *minőségi* (quality) or *különleges minőségi* (special quality) on the bottle. During the day and in bars, wine is sometimes mixed with soda or sparkling water to make a spritzer (*fröccs*).

## WHERE TO EAT

There is no shortage of places to fill your face. Restaurants, cafés and pâtisseries are dealt with below (see pages 133–63). Light bites of pickles, cold meats and sandwiches are available to take away from delicatessens, while those who want to take the weight off for a short while seek out a *bisztró*, *snackbár* or *büfé*, which offer small selections of hot food alongside filled rolls. Burger and sandwich (*szendvics*) stands are burgeoning, together with global fast-food giants that vie with cheaper kebab shops and Chinese buffets. Otherwise seek out a place selling *főzelék*, puréed dishes of vegetables (not unlike baby food) that are cooked in the home but generally overlooked by restaurants. They can be made from whatever vegetables are in season and make great bar food. The pumpkin version is very tasty, if you like gloop. One popular snack on the move is a *perec*, a large and salty piece of pretzel-shaped bread (try to avoid stands where they are uncovered and therefore likely to be stale), and another a *lángos*, something of a bulky hybrid of the Yorkshire pudding and the doughnut. A *lángos* is often topped with ladlefuls of runny garlic sauce, sour cream and cheese, and is enough to give your heart an attack just looking at it. Fresh produce is available in supermarkets, but head instead for outdoor markets or market halls, which have an excellent array of meat, fish, vegetables and fruit (see pages 199).

# RESTAURANTS

Greek, Italian, French, Chinese, Japanese, Indian, Mexican, Russian – the whole gamut of global fare is represented in Budapest. You'll even find Hungarian. Such culinary internationalism is relatively recent and, as such, the range and sophistication of some menus are slightly limited. Prices at the bottom and top ends are higher than elsewhere in the country, considerably so where *haute cuisine* is concerned, and eateries in Váci utca and the Castle District will charge what they know they can get. Nevertheless, the average cost of a meal in any of the brackets remains significantly lower than in Western capitals. Eat-all-you-like brunches and fixed two- or three-course tourist menus offer added value.

There are several words for different types of restaurant, although in reality some are used interchangeably. *Étterem* or *vendéglő* indicate a restaurant, the latter supposedly a cheaper establishment than the former (although this is by no means always true), while you can usually expect traditional Hungarian specialities in a *csárda* ('inn'). Lunch is customarily the main meal of the day, but restaurants in the capital cater equally for the evening crowd; despite this, you risk bed without supper if you arrive much later than 22.00. What, then, can you expect from the dining experience? How long's a piece of string? There are courtyard gardens and river terraces, brick cellar restaurants and dining rooms, modern lounges and rustic spaces strung with dried paprika. Traditional restaurants range from classy and intimate to cavernous coach-party traps. You might be treated to the lively strains of a gypsy violinist, or suffer the tinny torture of a cheap synthesiser. These days Hungarians are less likely to double-take on passing a vegetarian restaurant, but the choice is usually stark in those places specialising in native cuisine; even the obligatory fried vegetables are sometimes cooked in animal fat. Beyond the top restaurants, the biggest unknown is likely to be the quality of service. While many owners are waking up to tourist expectations, it remains far from unusual for a waiter to don the proverbial blinkers. If this is the case, don't tip.

What else to bear in mind? You shouldn't have difficulty securing a table in the majority of restaurants, although it is worth booking at the best. Dress codes are generally relaxed; Gundel (see pages 153–4) is the exception rather than the rule in requiring diners to wear jacket and tie. Don't order if food or drink menus are missing prices, and always check your bill carefully. Despite the brilliance of the Hungarian mind, errors of calculation are common and curiously tend to fall above the line rather than below it. Ask whether a service charge is included – it usually isn't – and tip ten–15 percent if you're satisfied. (For tipping etiquette, see page 24.) Major credit cards are usually accepted, but always ask in advance if you haven't got cash in reserve.

We've chosen to divide restaurants by area; entries include the average cost of a main course, together with the upper and lower limits.

## Buda

### *Castle District*

**Arany Kaviár** I, Ostrom utca 19; tel: 1 201 6737/225 7370; www.aranykaviar.hu [1 B3]
Renovated in 2003, this intimate restaurant specialises in Russian, Armenian, Ukrainian and

Georgian cuisine; its rich decoration emulates the dining-rooms of the 19th-century Russian bourgeoisie. Have your tastebuds tickled by fine caviar and your head befuddled with frozen glasses of syrupy vodka, thick enough to spread on toast. By comparison with the West, caviar remains relatively inexpensive here. It is worth bearing in mind that the sturgeon is endangered; if you want to do your bit to ensure its survival, choose red caviar, which is from the salmon. Just outside Bécsi kapu. Caviar specialities 4,500–8,990Ft, other mains 2,250–4,500Ft (avg 3,200Ft). *Open 12.00–24.00 daily.*

**Articsóka Vár** I, Szentharomság tér 6; tel: 1 488 7416; www.articsoka.hu [1 C4]
Baby sister of its popular namesake over the river (see page 149). The décor is tasteful, with displays of contemporary art from the adjoining gallery, while the Mediterranean food is good without quite living up to the promise of the sharp surroundings. Lunchy snacks settle alongside a monthly selection of more substantial meals like grilled lamb with Tuscan tomato sauce and steak with truffle sauce. There are wines from France and Italy, and a cigar club for committed puffers that runs every second Thursday. Pastas 1,090–1,490Ft, salads 1,190Ft. Mains 1,990–3,790Ft (avg 2,500Ft). *Open 10.00–24.00 daily.*

**Budavári Fortuna** I, Hess András tér 4; tel: 1 375 6857; www.miwo.hu/fortunarest [1 C3]
A 14th-century building and a choice of three sumptuous main dining-rooms, each with its own regal castle 'theme'. Before wolfing down some traditional Hungarian food – goose liver, goulash, Hungarian fish – you can turn vintner and bottle your own sparkling wine. The process takes just a few minutes, costs 8,000Ft, and has encouraged some rather glamorous

figures to stain their manicured fingers with the grape. ABBA, Otto Habsburg, Antonio Banderas, Melanie Griffith, Roger Moore and Gloria Gaynor all have autographed bottles in the cellar waiting to accompany their next meals. Mains 1,800–4,500Ft (avg 3,200Ft). *Open 12.00–16.00 and 19.00–24.00 daily.*

**Rivalda** I, Színház utca 5–9; tel: 1 489 0236; www.rivalda.net [1 C4]
The Rivalda is highly rated by luvvies and foodies alike. A colourful interior pays homage to those who have trodden the boards, and there is also a very pretty dining area in the Carmelite courtyard. Outdoor theatrical productions are held here in August, and for an additional charge you can eat while enjoying a performance. Contemporary Mediterranean and international cuisine, and a distinguished wine list. Prices lean towards the expensive, but the food is good. Just off Dísz tér, next to the National Dance Theatre (see page 187). Mains 1,600–3,800Ft (avg 2,800Ft). *Open daily 11.30–23.30.*

## *Gellért Hill, the Tabán and surrounds*

**Aranyszarvas** I, Szarvas tér 1; tel: 1 375 6451 [3 D5]
We'd read good things about the 'Golden Stag', but it put up a patchy performance during our visit. A venison goulash starter promised much and sturdy puddings filled empty drums, but the main game courses didn't fire, and the service felt perfunctory rather than efficient. Perhaps – like the duck – we're being a little tough, but we found our thoughts drifting to the Villa Doria (see opposite) a few short steps away. Mains 1,800–2,900Ft (avg 2,300Ft). *Open 12.00–23.00 daily.*

**Hemingway** XI, Kosztolányi Dezső tér 2, Feneketlen-tó; tel: 1 381 0522; www.miwo.hu/hemingway [3 DB]
B̄ 12; T̄ 19, 49
The owner's a Hemingway nut; Latin, Mediterranean and African motifs evoke the writer's world, and photos and furniture his epoch. This large and popular open restaurant has a decked terrace overlooking the reedy 'Bottomless Lake'. Its international menu specialises in grilled dishes, and fishy dishies in particular. There are good selections of teas, coffees and cigars too. Mains 1,350–3,200Ft (avg 2,400Ft). *Open daily 12.00–24.00.*

**Tabáni Terasz** I, Apród utca 10; tel: 1 201 1086; www.tabaniterasz.hu [3 D5]
There's a Parisian-style restaurant and café, a decked terrace at the front, a quieter courtyard garden complete with walnut tree, and a wine cellar for tastings. It's popular both with the coffee crowd and the pre-dinner cocktailers, while a diverse international spread makes room for cajun steaks, venison, paella, lasagne and shrimps. Outside is a memorial statue to Benedek Virág (see below). Mains 1,200–3,800Ft (avg 2,000Ft). *Open 12.00–24.00 daily.*

**Villa Doria** I, Döbrentei utca 9; tel: 1 225 3233; www.villadoria.hu [3 D5]
Few 18th-century buildings remain in the Tabán; this neoclassical house of 1700 is where the Pauline poet Benedek Virág (1754–1830) – who is buried in the Cave Church (see page 340) – spent the last years of his life. It is now home to the Villa Doria, with its high-ceilinged dining rooms, polished floors you could skate on, and cobbled courtyard bar. The Italian chef prepares a large selection of excellent dishes from his native land. Mains 1,100–4,500Ft (avg

2,300Ft). Some more expensive choices are planned – including langoustine for two at a wallet-weeping 29,000Ft. Set buffet lunch available at weekends (12.00–17.00; 3,000Ft). Also accessible from Apród utca (through Tabáni Terasz). *Open 12.00–23.00 daily.*

## *Víziváros*

**À la Carte étterem** I, Iskola utca 29; tel: 1 202 0580 [1 C3]
During the fairer months, pavement seating is in high demand and the staff enjoy little time for quiet contemplation. The Hungarian selection is enormous, and the food a real bargain. It's also cheering to see that the waiters can trade a smile while being rushed off their feet. Tucked behind Batthyány tér. Mains 490–2,050Ft (avg 1,000Ft). *Open 12.00–23.00 daily.*

**Chelsea Restaurant** I, Bem rakpart 16–19; tel: 1 487 9487; www.artotel.de [1 C4]
Clean, chic, fashionably understated, the Chelsea has something of a gallery feel to it – unsurprising since it is part of the Art'otel (page 101), itself a paean to American painter Donald Sultan. The menu is refreshingly brief, featuring delicate international dishes that bend towards Mediterranean and Asian flavours and won't sit heavy on the stomach. Entrance on Fő utca or through the hotel lobby. Mains 1,600–3,350Ft (avg 2,200Ft). A weekly menu offers discount dishes. *Open daily 12.00–15.00 and 18.00–23.00.*

**Kacsa Vendéglő** II, Fő utca 75; tel: 1 201 9992; www.kacsavendeglo.hu [1 C2]
B *11;* T *4, 6*
Well, pluck a duck! Move over Disney, with your Daffy and your Donald, for there are higher artists at work in the kitchen of 'Duck Restaurant'. The chef has over 60 duck dishes

in his portfolio; on request, he'll put together a plate featuring a 'taste' of several. The menu is interspersed with other international choices, and the goose-liver starter melted on the tongue. The waiters are attentive, respectful and knowledgeable. Let them guide you. This is exclusive, expensive dining, and very much all it's quacked up to be. Opposite the Király Baths. Mains 2,700–5,900Ft (avg 3,500Ft). *Open Mon–Fri 12.00–15.00 and daily 18.00–01.00.*

**Le Jardin de Paris** I, Fő utca 20; tel: 1 201 0047 [1 C4]
You look for a top eatery and two come along at once. After leaving the Kacsa (see previous entry), Le Jardin de Paris is just a few hundred metres away, near the French Institute; if you lack the stomach to be a two-dinner diner you'll have to save it for another time. Make it an evening meal, for the garden is at its most atmospheric after dark. There are fairy lights in the trees, oil lamps on the tables, an al-fresco kitchen and an open-fronted cellar bar. Among the French offerings are snails, calamari, sweet breads, truffles and lobster. The goose breast is a favourite. Mains 1,650–3,500Ft (avg 2,700Ft). *Open daily 12.00–24.00.*

**Margitkert** II, Margit utca 15; tel: 1 326 0860; www.margitkert.com [1 C2]
T *4, 6*
The Margitkert tempts diners with a big cheese. The bald-headed Lajos Boross is the 'Gypsy King' – the chief violin soloist (*primás*) – of the Budapest Gypsy Symphony Orchestra (www.100violins.com). The orchestra is the largest of its type in the world, and was born at the funeral of the legendary *primás* Sándor Járóka in 1985, when leading gypsy musicians struck up a spontaneous tune as a mark of respect. The restaurant's food is traditional, wholesome and well priced, the speciality of the rather kitsch house a wooden platter of

grilled meats (for two or more). Make some room for all this by walking to the restaurant, which is up a steep hill opposite Margaret Bridge. Mains 840–2,680Ft (avg 1,600–1,800Ft). Gypsy music daily from 18.00 (Boross usually from 19.30). *Open 12.00–24.00 daily.*

**Seoul House Korean Restaurant** I, Fő utca 8; tel: 1 201 7452 [1 C4]
OK, Budapest isn't overflowing with Korean restaurants, but this is where smartly dressed Asian diners come for their *kimchi*. It's upmarket and a touch pricey, selling top traditional Korean food and Hungarian wines. At the corner with Apor Péter utca. Mains 2,000–4,500Ft (avg 2,200Ft). *Open Mon–Sat 12.00–15.00/18.00–23.00, closed Sun.*

## Moszkva tér

**Marxim** II, Kis Rókus utca 23; tel: 1 316 0231; www.extra.hu/marxim [1 B2]
M2 *Moszkva tér;* T *4, 6*
This communist-themed pizzeria near Moszkva tér throws up the usual paradoxes, revelling in a certain nostalgia for iconography and agitprop murals while dividing booths with barbed wire. There's a mixed bag of clientele too: young-buck students after cheap beer, bearded 'thinkers' smoking roll-ups, and middle-class 40-somethings gorging on pieces of Gorbi Gorbi or Pizza à la Kremlin. Loud and lively, it's the only restaurant you'll visit that requests diners not to scrawl on the walls. Pittas and pastas alongside good-value pizzas. Mains 540–1,190Ft. *Open Mon–Thu 12.00–01.00, Fri–Sat 12.00–02.00, Sun 18.00–01.00.*

**Szt Jupát** II, Dékán utca 3; tel: 1 225 0339; www.stjupat.hu [1 B3]
M2 *Moszkva tér;* T *4, 6*

In the morning's early hours, when the sensible of Budapest are long abed, the Szt Jupát is a beacon for those more committed to an active nightlife. They've danced, they've revelled, they've imbibed with suitable relish; duvets await, but first some steps towards dulling hangovers to come. Take a polished booth, cast a bleary eye over the never-ending story that is the menu, and prepare to line the stomach with daunting wooden platters of Hungarian specials. Quantity lords it very slightly over quality here, and our starters had barely started before the main courses crashed the party, but it's busy, buzzy and the prices please the tightest of wallets. A litre of beer costs just 740Ft. Mains 890–3,800Ft (avg 1,300Ft). Just behind Moszkva tér. *Open 12.00–06.00 daily.*

## Óbuda

**Új Sipos Halászkert** III, Fő tér 6; tel: 1 388 8745
HEV *Árpád híd;* B *18, 37, 42*
Slap in the middle of the peaceful Fő tér, this grand fish restaurant serves Hungarian and international dishes. Be tempted by grilled prawns in honey and cognac or trout fillets with red wine and prunes. Mains 1,450–2,950Ft (avg 2,300Ft). *Open daily 12.00–24.00.*

## The Buda hills

**Náncsi Néni** II, Ördögárok út 80; tel: 1 398 7127; www.nancsineni.hu
T *56 or* B *56 from Moszkva tér to Hűvösvölgyi terminus, then* B *157, which stops outside*
A sailor tired of the sea and determined to establish a restaurant. He'd strive to make guests feel 'they were in their grandmother's kitchen'. The result screams old-fashioned comfort in any language, from its frilly curtains to its check tablecloths. The owner asks

that if you enjoy the food you recommend it to your friends, and if not that you recommend it to your mother-in-law. Friends, it's worth the trip. The dishes are Hungarian and international (including seafood), and the extensive menu is not for the indecisive. It's good to see *főzelék* included (only on Mon, Wed and Fri). Mains 1,250–6,666Ft (avg 2,600Ft). Booking advised. *Open Mon–Fri 12.00–23.00, Sat–Sun 09.00–23.00.*

**Remíz** II, Budakeszi út 5; tel: 1 275 1396; www.remiz.hu
B *22;* T *56 from Moszkva tér*
You'll want to lick your plate clean. You'll yearn to hug the chef tightly to your breast, and listen to whispered secrets of aubergine mousse, of crispy catfish and truffles, of venison and blueberries. The Remíz (Tram Depot) blends past and present; tram paraphernalia and tinkling ivories evoke an era of silent movies and full moustaches, while traditional dishes are infused with modern international influences on the monthly menu. It's low-lit and graceful without a hint of stuffiness. One of the city's best; if only it were more central. Mains 1,620–3,280Ft (avg 2,500Ft). *Open 09.00–24.00 daily.*

**Serpenyős Vendéglő** II, Szépvőlgyi út 62; tel: 1 335 5361; www.reziserpenyos.hu
B *65 stops almost outside*
Take along a hearty hunger and an elasticated waistband and you'll be well satisfied with the portions. If your appetite is daintier, the restaurant offers its dishes in smaller sizes too. Among the homely Hungarian choices during our visit was a plate of crispy goose leg, roasted goose liver, mashed potato and onion. Smack those lips. Mains 900–2,480Ft (avg 1,700Ft). *Open 12.00–24.00 daily.*

# Pest

## *Downtown and beyond*

**Bangkok House** V, Só utca 3; tel: 1 266 0584 [4 F6]
We feel a little guilty faulting a restaurant for an excess of enthusiasm, but any self-respecting Bangkok homeowner would start and run screaming from the clichéd Asiana. If you can lever yourself into a seat among the intense clutter of rattan work and Buddhist statuettes, you'll find some decent enough Thai food on a heaving menu. Mains 1,350–4,550Ft (avg 1,750Ft). *Open 12.00–23.00 daily.*

**Baraka Restaurant** V, Magyar utca 12–14; tel: 1 483 1355 [4 F5]
The Baraka is tucked away on a back street, but it's worth hunting out. Dark-wood furnishings and soft cone lighting make the setting polished but cosy. Excellent food, influenced by French and Asian flavours, is brought to you by attentive staff. Large selection of plonk. Mains 1,900–4,000Ft (avg 3,000Ft). *Open Mon–Sat 18.00–23.00, closed Sun.*

**Biarritz Restaurant and Café** V, Balassi Bálint utca 2; tel: 1 311 4413 [1 D2]
The interior is rustic and uncomplicated, the modern European cuisine first class, and the service correct. It's not cheap, however; you'd think mashed potato was a delicacy at 1,500Ft for three dollops. Near the Parliament building. Mains 1,250–3,150Ft. *Open 09.00–24.00 daily.*

**Fakanál Étterem** V, Vámház körút 1–3; tel: 1 217 7860 [4 F5]
Take a break from browsing at the Big Market Hall, and fill up on typical Hungarian food at

very cheap prices. Long wooden tables overlook the bustling shoppers below. Located on the first-floor gallery. *Open Mon–Fri 10.00–17.00, Sat 10.00–14.00, closed Sun.*

**Fatál** V, Váci utca 67; tel: 1 266 2607/2608 [4 F6]
There have been discontented rumbles of late at the 'Wooden Plate'. Not from stomachs, you understand – food mountains on wooden boards and brim-filled bubbling pans leave no room for those. Instead it is said that the cellar restaurant has become a production line. There's some truth in the complaint; the service is rushed and impersonal, and this certainly isn't the place for lovers' whispers or business deals. It's a cacophonous brick cauldron of chatter and whirring fans, where you'll fight for elbowroom on wooden benches and suffer waiters who ignore and lean across you by turns. The silence rings when you exit. Cheap, super-sized dishes ooze Hungarian rusticity and manliness, the fare of tough-skinned farmers with big hands: liver sausage, black pudding, beef bouillon, dumplings, deep-fried brains, red cabbage. You'll love every minute. Mains 900–1,500Ft. Entrance on Pintér utca. *Open 11.30–02.00 daily.*

**Firkász** XIII, Tátra utca 18; tel: 1 450 1118 [1 E2]
T̲ *4, 6*
The Firkász (Scribbler) is something of a modern variation on the literary theme of early 20th-century coffee houses, paying tribute to the age of wireless and inky fingers. There's even the odd jobbing journo. Filling Hungarian specialities at a fair price, and twice-monthly wine tastings. Just north of the downtown. Mains 1,500–2,800Ft (avg 2,000Ft). *Open 12.00–24.00 daily.*

**Focaccia** Pest V, Apáczai Csere János utca 19; tel: 1 266 1234 [1 D4]
We'll spare blushes by naming no names, but the restaurant of the Sofitel Atrium was a whispered recommendation from the manager of a rival hotel. Thank heaven for treacherous staff; Focaccia brings the Mediterranean sun and *joie de vivre* to the banks of the Danube, with a piazza-like fountain, an authentic wood-fired oven, and fresh sea fish, vegetables and olive oil. Near the Chain Bridge. *Open Mon–Sat 12.00–23.30, Sun 18.00–23.30.*

**Govinda Vegetarian Restaurant and Salad Bar** V, Vigyázó Ferenc utca 4; tel: 1 473 1309 [1 D4]
Hare Krishna Indian restaurant serving a large selection of vegetarian and vegan options. Dishes for around 400Ft, a big plate selection for 1,500Ft. Just off Roosevelt tér. *Open 12.00–21.00 Mon–Sat, closed Sun.*

**Kárpátia** V, Ferenciek tere 7–8; tel: 1 317 3596; www.karpatia.hu [3 E5]
A Pest institution. With hand-painted vaulted ceilings and a smattering of stained glass, this is the closest you'll get to dining in the Mátyás Church. You can eat more cheaply in the booths of the brasserie at the front, but that is to dip a toe instead of diving in; choose rather the main dining room or the marquee terrace in the courtyard of the former monastery. The gypsy musicians thoroughly enjoy themselves, while smart waiters serve with a flourish. For all its rich formality, there's no snootiness here. The only regret is that the décor far outshines the food. Mains 2,800–6,900Ft (avg 3,000–4,000Ft). A two-course meal for two (with wine) in the brasserie is around 8,500Ft. *Open 11.00–23.00 daily.*

**Kempinski Restaurants** V, Erzsébet tér 7–8; tel: 1 429 3777 [1 E4]
The Kempinski's glass conservatory becomes something of a goldfish bowl in the evening; wave a cheery fin at the ogling masses on Deák Ferenc utca and get your gills around some delectable food. There are two restaurants (Ristorante Giardino and Bistro Jardin), offering Italian or international and Hungarian. You're unlikely to go wrong whatever your choice, but, just for the record, the lamb fillet baked in herb bread was aromatic, pink and juicy. Quite delicious, if expensively so. There's an outdoor summer terrace. Booking essential. Mains 3,200–5,600Ft (avg 4,000–4,500Ft). *Open 06.30–23.00 daily.*

**Lou Lou** V, Vigyázó Ferenc utca 4; tel: 1 312 4505; www.lou-lou.hu [1 E4]
Pest's answer to Buda's Le Jardin de Paris (see page 139), Lou Lou attracts the city crowd with its refined bistro styling. There are French, Italian and Spanish wines alongside the Hungarian bottles. Excellent pan-fried foie gras. Mains 1,950–4,500Ft (avg 3,500Ft). Next to the Govinda (see previous page). *Open Mon–Fri 12.00–15.00, 19.00–23.00, Sat 19.00–23.00, closed Sun.*

**Mokka Café and Restaurant** V, Sas utca 4; tel: 1 328 0081 [1 E4]
Hookahs and woven throws convey Moroccan funkiness, but the menu is international with a Mediterranean flavour. Alongside the marinated duck slices and lamb ribs are a few meatless options, including a veggie lasagne. A set lunch for around 1,000Ft gives added value on weekdays. Mains 1,450–4,950Ft (avg 2,600Ft). *Open daily 12.00–24.00.*

**Óceán bár & grill** V, Petőfi tér 3; tel: 1 266 1826; www.oceanbargrill.com [3 E5]
Mussel chowder, tiger prawns, monkfish? New England cod and chips? Opened in 2003, the

capital's only dedicated seafood restaurant is still a pup, but the earnest commitment of its Norwegian owner deserves reward. He was still in the honeymoon period during our visit, all flushed cheeks and excited talk of monthly themed specials and Sunday-brunch buffets served in a lifeboat full of ice. While the interior mimics the deck of a ship, and there must have been mutiny in the air when staff were introduced to their sailor suits, it avoids being overly camp. The seafood is imported from all over the world, but the focus is Scandinavian – Nordic delicacies are sold in the adjacent delicatessen. A gem – and one of the few places you can turn up at 23.00 and not raise waiterly eyebrows. Mains 1,690–7,490ft (avg 2,700Ft). *Restaurant open 12.00–24.00 daily; deli open Mon–Sat 10.00–21.00.*

**Okay Italia** XIII, Szent István körút; tel: 1 349 2991 [1 E2]
*T 4, 6*
A popular spot among young Hungarians and ex-pats, who chow down on decent pizza and pasta at reasonable prices. On the Great Boulevard. Mains 1,200–2,730Ft (avg 1,300Ft). *Open Mon–Fri 11.00–24.00, Sat–Sun 12.00–24.00.*

**Shakespeare Theatre Pub** V, Sas utca 4; tel: 1 266 8758; www.shakespeare.hu [1 E4]
'To eat or not to eat, this is not a question!' Thus does the restaurant open its tribute to the bard by murdering him. Suppress the urge to brain the owner with his lady's fan, and make your choice from a playbill menu offering good-quality and imaginative international vittles. The 'all the world's a stage' theme is played out with gusto and attention to detail. Let good digestion wait on a spicy goulash starter and duck pepper steak in rosemary sauce. Mains 1,200–2,600Ft (avg 1,700Ft). *Open 11.30–24.00 daily.*

**Spoon Café and Lounge – The Boat** V, by the Chain Bridge, in front of the InterContinental Hotel; tel: 1 411 0933; www.spooncafe.hu [1 D4]
Very much a new kid on the dock, the gleaming Spoon is moored next to the Columbus (see page 169). In contrast to its neighbour, this is sophisticated dining for captain rather than crew, with candlelight and international choices like garlic octopus and goose liver. Mains 1,690–4,950Ft (avg 3,500Ft). *Open daily 12.00–02.00.*

**Taverna Dionysos** V, Belgrád rakpart 16; tel: 1 318 1222 [3 E6]
We last visited this faux taverna in winter and it was bursting at its whitewashed seams – testimony to its enduring local popularity. All the Grecian specialities are represented here but, like many such outposts in Hungary, there are misses to balance the hits. Beware Greeks bearing dayglo wallpaper paste masquerading as taramasalata. By contrast, moussaka and dolmades with tzatziki were delicious, the staff spirited and the music cheerful. Mains 1,250–2,740Ft (avg 1,700Ft). *Open 12.00–24.00 daily.*

**Trattoria Toscana** V, Belgrád rakpart 15; tel: 1 327 0045; www.toscana.hu [3 E6]
Tuscan cooking by an Italian chef in a cosy villa facing the Danube. The food wasn't piping hot when we sat down here for lunch, but the restaurant's reputation is strong and so we'll assume an off-day in the open kitchen. Wild boar, pizza, pasta and fish. Mains 1,190–3,900Ft (avg 1,800–2,000Ft); pizzas 1,290–1,950Ft. Between Erzsébet and Szabadság bridges. The adjacent wine shop (L'Enoteca) serves Tuscan-speciality food and wine. *Restaurant open 12.00–24.00 daily; wineshop open Mon–Sat 12.00–21.00.*

## Terézváros

**Articsóka** VI, Zichy Jenő utca 17; tel: 1 302 7757; www.articsoka.hu [2 F3]
M3 Arany János utca; TB 70, 78

Green fingers went to town in Articsóka. With its creepers, potted palms and skylight, you'll be forgiven for thinking you've intruded upon a biosphere project. Fortunately we don't suffer from hayfever, and love the foliage and airy feel. The cuisine is primarily – though not exclusively – Mediterranean, with emphasis on fish, and is inventive, good looking and fine tasting. Mains 1,390–3,990Ft (avg 2,700Ft). *Open 12.00–24.00 daily.*

**Belcanto** VI, Dalszínház utca 8; tel: 1 269 2786; www.belcanto.hu [2 F4]
M1 *Opera*

It's fortunate that music is the food of love, for the food itself at Belcanto is not. Even though the cuisine is nothing to sing about, the waiters do their level best, assembling around the piano at times to distract you from your plate. This used to be a private club for opera performers, and the restaurant makes much of the connection. It is this that attracts a mainly foreign crowd, and justifies the cost of what is otherwise an over-priced international and Hungarian menu. Buffet lunch 1,900Ft; mains 3,500–4,500Ft (avg 4,000Ft). Music from 20.00 onwards. *Open daily 12.00–15.00, 18.00–02.00.*

**Bombay Palace** VI, Andrássy út 44; tel: 1 332 8363 [2 F3]
M1 *Oktogon;* B *4*

Indian eateries are few and far between in Hungary; this one is part of an international chain, and serves Budapest's Bombay best. Mains 800–4,500Ft, lunch/supper set menus 2,000/3,000Ft. On corner of Jókai Mór tér. *Open 12.00–14.45, 18.00–23.00 daily.*

**Chez Daniel** VI, Szív utca 32; tel: 1 302 4039 [2 F2]
M1 *Kodály Köröndt;* TB 72

Pay no heed to the tatty homes around it; Daniel's house is very much in order. The staple of the French food is fresh produce from local markets, and there's a sunny courtyard with open-fronted bar. In addition to exclusive à-la-carte options – like smoked salmon with caviar sauce – there are exclusive set menus for 2,900–8,400Ft (the latter six courses). If you feel inspired, the restaurant has a bookstore devoted to the gastronomical arts. *Restaurant open daily 12.00–15.00, 19.00–23.00.*

**Dzsungel Étterem** VI, Jókai utca 30; tel: 1 302 4003; www.dzsungelcafe.hu [2 F3]
T *4, 6*

Unique, riotously over the top, this one's for the child or the chest-beating Tarzan in your party. Swing into a jungle of vines, plastic animals and pools, of taped squawks and chirrups and a real-life parrot. The adjoining bar and café is deforested, and positively peaceful by comparison. Mains 1,190–2,590Ft (avg 2,000Ft). *Open 12.00–01.00 daily.*

**Két Szerecsen** VI, Nagymező utca 14; tel: 1 343 1984; www.ketszerecsen.com [2 F4]
TB *70, 78*

The 'Two Saracens' was a coffee shop in the 18th century. Today it blushes terracotta from head to toe, and provides a popular glass-fronted spot for theatregoers. Tapas, black spaghetti with cockles and other Mediterranean selections are very reasonably priced. Try to snag a window table in the raised section. Mains 1,270–2,470Ft (avg 1,400–1,500Ft). *Open Mon–Fri 08.00–01.00, Sat–Sun 09.00–01.00.*

**Mare Croaticum** VI, Nagymező utca 49; tel: 1 311 7345 [2 F3]
TB 70, 78
Tiled basement restaurant offering specialities from Croatia. Gorge on the 'all-you-can-eat' menu, which includes drinks, or go more à-la-carte easy. Fixed menu 2,000Ft (Mon–Fri 12.00–17.00) or 3,000Ft (Mon–Fri 18.00–24.00, Sat–Sun throughout); à-la-carte mains 950–5,890Ft (avg 2,200Ft). Entrance on Weiner Leó utca. *Open 12.00–24.00 daily.*

**Marquis de Salade** VI, Hajós utca 43; tel: 1 302 4086 [2 F3]
TB *70, 78*
This cellar restaurant – arching and intimate, with woven wall hangings – serves an extensive range of well-prepared and sizeable specialities from Azerbaijan, Russia and Hungary. Alongside the lamb and fish is a fair vegetarian selection, and above the restaurant is a bar and coffee house. Mains 1,100–2,800Ft (avg 1,800Ft). *Open 11.00–01.00 daily.*

**Művészinas** VI, Bajcsy-Zsilinsky út 9; tel: 1 268 1439; www.directinfo.hu/muveszinas [1 E4]
M1, M2, M3 *Deák Ferenc tér*
If you're a city slicker with a high-maintenance lady to impress, Művészinas is high on your list. It radiates turn-of-the-20th-century romance, while among the international dishes are uppercrust classics like Russian caviar, goose liver and chateaubriand. This is blue-blooded chic, and perfect for candlelit supping and wooing. Mains 1,800–6,900Ft (avg 3,200Ft). *Open 12.00–24.00 daily.*

**Premier Étterem és Terasz** VI, Andrássy út 101; tel: 1 342 1768; www.premier-restaurant.hu [2 G2]
M1 *Bajza utca*
Premier's art-nouveau mansion is also home to the Association of Hungarian Journalists, so expect to find the odd hack lurking among the velvet curtains. There is piano music in the theatre-inspired dining room during winter months, while the terrace is the popular spot once spring has sprung. Stop here for a coffee, or order something more substantial from a menu featuring international food – including a weekly changing seafood selection – and Hungarian specialities. Mains 1,900–3,500Ft (avg 2,800Ft). *Restaurant open 12.00–23.00 daily; coffee house open 08.00–23.00 daily.*

**Sir Lancelot** VI, Podmaniczky utca 14; tel: 1 302 4456; www.sirlancelot.hu [2 F3]
TB *72, 70, 78*
There are no forks here, so ditch your inhibitions, grab a bib and prepare to get greasy, medieval style. Busty wenches flit between the benches of this feasting hall, bearing wooden platters of meat and goblets of wine, while in the evening there are displays by jousting knights. Sophisticated? Erm…no. There's a sister restaurant on the Buda side – King Arthur's (III, Bécsi út 38–44; tel: 1 437 8243). *Open daily 12.00–01.00.*

**Vörös és Fehér** VI, Andrássy út 41; tel: 1 413 1545; www.vorosesfeher.com [2 F3]
M1 *Oktogon;* B *4*
We couldn't decide between the *vörös* or the *fehér*, so we raised several glasses of each to the chef and a dish of meaty butterfish. The portions tend towards the moderate in size,

but the quality is unquestionable. Bustling atmosphere; we recommend it highly. Some tapas choices on an international menu. Mains 1,780–5,140Ft (avg 2,300Ft; tapas average 1,200Ft). *Open 12.00–24.00 daily.*

**Yu Yuan Kínai Étterem** VI, Andrássy út 28; tel: 1 269 2057 [2 F4]
B *4*
One of the city's numerous cheap Chinese joints, offering a buffet downstairs and à-la-carte dining on the first floor. Mains 150–2,300Ft, set menu 3,100Ft/person. Near the opera house. *Open 10.00–23.30 daily.*

## *Heroes' Square and City Park*

**Bagolyvár** XIV, Állatkérti út 2; tel: 1 468 3110; www.bagolyvar.com [2 H1]
M1 *Hősök tere;* TB *75, 79*
'Owl's Castle' was established by Hungarian-American restaurateur George Lang, who also revived Gundel after communism. While the baroque and Biedermeier furnishings radiate 19th- rather than 21st-century charm, Bagolyvár is consciously less formal in atmosphere than its neighbour, as well as less imposing on the pocket. The canopied terrace is a joy in summer months, and the all-female staff are at the heart of the restaurant's lightness of touch. Mild, but traditional, Hungarian flavours dominate; the strudel desserts are a particular pleasure. Mains 1,170–4,000Ft (avg 2,500Ft). *Open 12.00–23.00 daily.*

**Gundel** XIV, Állatkerti út 2; tel: 1 321 3550; www.gundel.hu [2 H1]
M1 *Hősök tere;* TB *75, 79*
It's fashionable to decry Gundel. 'You'll get more for your money at the sister restaurant

next door,' they drawl. For all the merits of Bagolyvár – and there are many (see previous entry) – it's like comparing a strawberry gateau with a chocolate sponge. Eating at Gundel is an event, it's something worth mentioning, it's the city's culinary rite of passage, it's the cream on top. Queen Elizabeth II and Pope John Paul II have loaded their forks here. In 1939, while run by the great Károly Gundel, the *New York Times* wrote that the restaurant was 'the most convincing advertisement of all for Budapest'. Ask Budapesters to name three restaurants and Gundel will be one of them. Guaranteed.

The main dining room evokes high *fin-de-siècle* grace, with rosewood pillars, polished furnishings and oil paintings, and there's also a beautiful garden. The menu offers refined creations based upon Hungarian classics, as well as dishes from France and elsewhere. The gypsy musical ensemble is as accomplished as any you will find. What about the cost? Well, all this comes at a very high price by Hungarian standards, but it remains low when compared with fine dining in western Europe. Enjoy a five-course set menu with wine for 15,500Ft, six courses for 18,900Ft or a Sunday brunch buffet (11.30–15.00) for around 5,000Ft. Mains 2,980–8,890Ft (avg 5,000Ft). Gents require a jacket. *Open 12.00–16.00, 18.30–24.00 daily.*

**Robinson** XIV, Városligeti tó; tel: 1 422 0222 [2 H1]
M1 *Hősök tere;* TB *75, 79*
On a sun-drenched day, life seems tickety-boo from under a pagoda on Robinson's decked jetty. The lake and its water life are all about, while in front is an expensive menu that makes a good stab at being truly international – Hungarian broth, Thai prawn soup, French onion soup, New Zealand beef. In fact, it's an appealing place during winter too, toasty warm next to the fire in the pavilion's hearth. Mains 2,000–5,800Ft (avg 3,600Ft). The Caffé Vergnano

above the restaurant offers a lofty view of the park while you lick your ice-cream. *Restaurant open 12.00–16.00, 18.00–24.00 daily; café open 12.00–24.00 daily.*

## *Erzsébetváros*

**Fausto's** VII, Dohány utca 5; tel: 1 269 6806 [2 G4]
T *47, 49;* TB *74*
Established by an ex-pat restaurateur, Fausto's is the city's Italian stallion. The décor is immaculate, the chef concocts delicate regional dishes, and the bill is on the steep side. Mains 3,000–6,000Ft (avg 4,000Ft). *Open Mon–Sat 12.00–15.00, 19.00–23.00, closed Sun.*

**Fészek Klub** VII, Kertész utca 36; tel: 1 322 6043 [2 G4]
TB *70, 78*
With a courtyard to grace a Shakespearean romance, it's the Fészek Klub we dream of on those balmy summer nights. The exterior offers few clues to the restaurant within; the building is owned by an artists' guild, and the gallery a popular haunt for rehearsing actors and musicians. The food is very cheap, but not special, and the service makes the tortoise seem positively sprightly, but the courtyard… Mains 550–2,200Ft. *Open 11.00–24.00 daily.*

**Green's Söröző és Főzelékbár** VII, Dob utca 3; tel: 1 352 8515 [2 G4]
T *47, 49*
There's something refreshingly uncomplicated about *főzelék*, food that's pulped into submission (see page 132). This cellar bar, with its back-to-back booths, also includes some

cheap international choices and several Bavarian meals. Mains 699–1,999Ft (avg 1,300Ft); *főzelék* 300–400Ft. *Open 10.00–24.00 daily.*

**M** VII, Kertész utca 48; tel: 1 342 8991 [2 G4]
TB *70, 78*
The owner was economical with the alphabet when naming this place, and he saved a few forints when decorating it too. The walls are covered with brown parcel wrap, and the furnishings ink sketches on top. It's like joining your picnic in its paper bag. Unfortunately, during our visit there was also some economising in the kitchen. A limited selection of international and Transylvanian-influenced dishes changes regularly on the menu. It's quirky and cucumber cool, but don't go there hungry. Mains 1,100–1,700Ft (avg 1,200Ft). *Open 18.00–24.00 daily.*

## COFFEE AND CAKE

### Pâtisseries and coffee houses

Hungarians love sugar and caffeine in equal measure. By rights, they should spend their days bouncing off the walls and their nights in wide-eyed insomnia. **Pâtisseries** (*cukrászda*) display a tempting selection of cakes, pastries and ice-creams. Some are shops selling sticky things to take away, while others allow you to have your cake and eat it amid chandeliers and marble, and with a coffee at your elbow. You'll find cakes in **coffee houses** (*kávéház*), too. At the turn of the 20th century, there were nearly 1,000 coffee houses in the Hungarian capital, with a staggering 64 places along the Nagy körút alone to drink the 'black soup' (*fekete leves*). As in many continental countries, these places were traditionally kaleidoscopes of social colour where newspapers were read, politics discussed, poems composed and rebellions plotted. The young revolutionaries of 1848 are said to have penned their demands for reform in the Pilvax kávéház, while two decades later Ferenc Deák negotiated the terms of the 1867 Compromise in the coffee house of the Queen of England hotel. Some establishments even had their own notepaper for artists to use; where they didn't, an impoverished poet would scrawl a sonnet on a napkin in lieu of payment for his drink. The importance of the coffee house as a forum for social discussion and expression diminished in the 1940s, and the more staunchly working-class and socialist coffee bar took hold (see page 163), but many of the classics of the era remain. Furthermore, a hundred years on there's been a Renaissance, with a crop of new venues. Some – like the Centrál, which re-opened in 2000 – fall within the grand Pesti tradition, while others are modern, trendy interpretations that are more properly café-bars (see pages 163–6). Coffee still very much matters. The standard cup is a small and strong espresso (*eszpresszó* or *kávé*). You can order it with milk (*tejeskávé*), but beyond that the standard varies. A cappuccino may be little more than a filter coffee with whipped cream, and isn't worth a scribbled couplet.

## *Buda*

**Angelika kávéház** I, Batthyány tér 7; tel: 1 212 3784 [1 C3]

Housed in the former crypt of the adjacent Szt Anna Church, the Angelika is bathed with a

## *SWEET STUFF*

You'll have no problem sating that craving for sweetness. Hungary's restaurants, cafés and (especially) pâtisseries promise things naughty but nice. If you can forget the scales, the doctor's orders and your conscience's wagging finger, below are some of the treats that await you.

### Cake

*Dobos torta* (cake) Dobos József, a master chef, prepared his cake for the Hungarian National Exhibition of 1885, and it worked gourmets and confectioners into a drooling frenzy. Competitors were desperate to learn the recipe, and orders flooded in from home and abroad. It became Hungary's most famous cake. Five layers of white sponge filled with chocolate cream and glazed caramel on top.

*Sacher torta* Rich chocolate cake with jam running through the middle. Originated in Vienna.

*Gyümölcs torta* Sponge cake with fruits and whipped cream.

*Rigó Jancsi* A two-inch-square sponge cake with chocolate cream and chocolate glaze atop.

stained-glass orange wash, while the sprawling terrace outside combines cobbles and elevated platforms. At night, the candlelit tables are particularly inviting. *Open 8.00–21.00 daily.*

*Somlói galuska* Layers of sponge cake, rich chocolate sauce, walnuts, raisins and a whirl of whipped cream served in a bowl.

## Pancakes, pastries and strudels

*Palacsinták* Crêpes with a choice of fillings, such as sweet cottage cheese, nuts, fruit, chocolate cream or jam. The classic dish of this family is the *Gundel palacsinta*, a folded pancake containing walnut and rum filling and drenched in chocolate sauce and more rum. It may be served flaming. Flaming good.

*Krémesek* Square flaky pastries with French pâtisserie and whipped creams.

*Rétesek* Strudels are available with a range of fillings, including cherry *(meggyes)*, sweet cottage cheese *(túrós)*, and poppy seeds *(mákos)*.

## Ice-creams

*Fagylaltok* There can be no nation more committed in its devotion to ice-cream. Roadside vendors, pâtisseries and ice-cream parlours (*fagylaltozó* or *fagyizó*) really are hubs of the community in summer, and they'll do a very respectable trade in winter too. *Fagyi* (the slang term) is served in cones and you pay by the scoop (*gombóc*). The range of flavours can be daunting – anything from vanilla to poppy seed.

**Auguszt cukrászda** II, Fény utca 8; tel: 1 316 3817; XI, Farkasréti tér, XI Sasadi utca; tel: 1 249 0134; www.augusztcukraszda.hu [1 B3]

The name Auguszt is synonymous with fine pastry in Budapest. Since 1870, five generations have strived to maintain the family reputation. The dynasty operates from three locations (see also opposite), each managed by a family member and each selling fine sweets, ice-creams and pastries made on the premises. (To get to the Farkasréti tér outlet, take tram 59 from Moszkva tér.) *Open Tue–Sat 10.00–18.00, closed Sun–Mon.*

**Coffee-Inn** I, Apor Péter utca 2; tel: 1 201 2935 [1 C4]
Just a couple of years old, this coffee house and bar is a peaceful little find, where people enjoy relaxing over a game of backgammon or cards. *Open 11.00–23.00 daily.*

**Daubner cukrászda** II, Szépvölgyi út 50
It ain't much to look at, but this is the city's sugar daddy. Devotees queue down the road to have flasks filled with creamy ices, and perch on steps to wrap themselves around buttery pastries. Recollections of banoffee-pie ice-cream make us dribble. *Open daily 09.00–19.00.*

**Nagyi palacsintázója** I, Batthyányi tér 5; tel: 1 212 4866 [1 C3]
Delicious savoury or sweet pancakes at any time of day or night. *Open around the clock.*

**Ruszwurm cukrászda** I, Szentharomság utca 7; tel: 1 375 5284; www.ruszwurm.hu [1 C4]
Ruszwurm is the oldest café in Budapest, operating since 1827, and the simple elegance of its interior presents a fine example of the Biedermeier style popular during the period. The cakes are traditional and homemade, and in the past graced the tables of palatines and duchesses; Sisi (Empress Erzsébet) came here for hot chocolate. Look out for the lion with

a bridle in its paw on the arch of the building's gate; a former trader here boasted that the leather belts he made were strong enough to hold a lion. It is not recorded how he met his end… *Open 10.00–19.00 daily.*

## Pest

**Auguszt cukrászda** V, Kossuth Lajos utca 14–16; tel: 1 337 6379; www.auguszztcukraszda.hu [4 F5]
Pesti branch of the family chain (see previous page). *Open Tue–Sat 10.00–18.00, closed Sun–Mon.*

**Café intenzo és étterem** IX, Kálvin tér 9; tel: 1 219 5243; www.cafeintenzo.hu [4 F6]
This building housed the Two Lions Inn until 1881, but it is now a popular pavement café next to the lean Calvin statue. Avoid the noise of traffic by sitting in the garden courtyard.

**Centrál kávéház** V, Károlyi Mihály utca 9; tel: 1 266 4572 [4 F5]
In 2000, the Centrál reopened after half a century. In its pomp during the late 1800s and early 1900s, this was a hub of intellectual – and particularly literary – life. Men of letters were seated on a special gallery (now part of the no-smoking section) so that ordinary mortals could watch them as they worked, like so many specimens in a cerebral zoo. The artist József Rippl-Rónai scrawled 'I drew this in the Centrál Coffee House' on one of his paintings. Today you'll find high ceilings, polite service and snacks for the modest purse (*zóna ételek*, at the 700Ft mark) alongside more expensive Hungarian and international dishes. Located on the corner of Ferenciek tere. *Open 08.00–24.00 daily.*

**Cukrászda kávézó** VI, Andrássy út 14; tel: 1 332 4559 [2 F4]
An Italian parlour serving whacking portions of ice-cream, including a spaghetti ice dressed up to look like a dish of bolognese. *Open 09.00–24.00 daily.*

**Európa kávéház** V, Szent István körút; tel: 1 312 2362 [1 D2]
Upmarket, Austrian-style café with a takeaway bakery and ice-cream shop next door. *Café open 09.00–23.00 daily; shop open Mon–Fri 07.00–20.00, Sat 09.00–20.00, Sun 10.00–20.00.*

**Gerbeaud** V, Vörösmarty tér 7–8; tel: 1 429 9000 [3 E5]
Hungary's most famous café, Gerbeaud is a refined behemoth in marble, walnut and wicker, a favoured rendezvous spot, an exquisite must in the tourist top ten, and always – always – busy. Emile Gerbeaud – the Swiss pâtissier who managed the place from 1884 – brought the Parisian taste to Budapest. He gave birth to the cognac cherry (*konyákos meggy*), and was the first to use chocolate boxes for bonbon treats to take away. Foreign princes were drawn by his artistry. As the trains of the Kisföldalatti ('little underground') rumble below, get around a Gerbeaud layered cake. In the café's cellar, accessed via Dorottya utca, is a beer hall serving home-brewed drinks. *Café open 09.00–21.00 daily; Gerbeaud Sörház open Sun, Tue–Thu 11.00–24.00, Fri-Sat 11.00–02.00, closed Mon.*

**Lukács cukrászda** VI, Andrássy út 70; tel: 1 302 8747
It's changed much since being refurbished during the 1990s, but this used to be where secret policemen ate pastries in between interrogations at their headquarters (Andrássy út 60; see page 305). *Open Mon–Fri 9.00–20.00, Sat–Sun 10.00–20.00.*

**Művész** VI, Andrássy út 29; tel: 1 352 1337 [2 F4]
'The Artist' was a favourite of the upper middle classes during the communist era. It exudes old-world grandeur, and the terrace on a warm evening is great for a pastry before watching the fat lady sing at the State Opera House opposite. *Open 09.00–23.45 daily.*

**New York kávéház** VII, Erzsébet körút 9–11 [2 G4]
Designed by Alajos Hauszmann in 1894, the New York Palace was an Italian Renaissance showcase for the New York Insurance Company. The New York kávéház occupied the ground floor, and could justly claim to be at the birth of modern Hungarian literature. Ferenc Molnár is said to have tossed the café's key into the Danube in protest at its closing at night; he went on to write his great work *Liliom* here. Regulars were provided with paper and unlimited coffee, while impoverished authors lingered over the 'writers' dish' – a bargain plate of bread, cheese and salami. The café declined after World War I and was ignominiously rammed by a Russian tank in 1956. It is now being restored to its turn-of-the-century best, and will re-open in 2005 as a luxury hotel and coffee house. Near Blaha Lujza tér.

**Palacsinta Porta** VI, Liszt Ferenc tér 3; tel: 1 343 1263 [2 F3]
The place to go if you're dying for a crêpe. Have a savoury main with mushroom and corn, and then a sweet one with cinnamon and plum. *Open Mon–Fri 12.00–22.00.*

## Coffee bars

The *presszó* or *eszpresszó* is less traditionally highbrow than the *cukrászda* or *kávéház*. The author Sándor Márai complained in 1940 that in *eszpresszó* bars 'one can only chat – one cannot write a great work as there is no space on the table.' It is instead a communal place for the local working class, where groups of ladies enjoy cakes and gangs of workmen play dominoes and eat *somlói galuska* with their beer. Its floor is stone or covered with beige linoleum, and there are net curtains, tiled walls and little gnome stools. Surly waitresses wear long, lace-up boots that give support during endless hours of standing. A proper old-style *presszó* has a neon sign proclaiming a socialist name such as 'Terv' (Five-Year Plan), 'Béke' (Peace), 'Haladás' (Progress) or even 'Májas' (Liver Sausage). But the *eszpresszó* is an endangered species. One by one, they have closed as rent soars and the fast-food chains and banks move in.

Budapest was once the city of *eszpresszó* bars, where elderly couples would drink brandy and have sing-songs on Friday nights, where old *bácsis* danced with little girls and *nénis* danced together, where workers spent their wages on beer, and the air was thick with the fog of Munkás (Worker) cigarettes. In 1937, the Quick in Vigadó utca was the first coffee bar to open (it is an office now), and was followed by many more. After 1956, social-realist architecture began to wane. Shops destroyed during the uprising were rebuilt in the modern style. There was a craze for neon, and for radical slogans like 'Prosperity' and 'Spartacus'. While some of the 1950s *eszpresszós* still exist, the original style is harder to find. The neon lights are fading, the Traubi (grape) and Márka (cherry) soft drinks are hard to find, the Bambi pop has disappeared, the wheels of progress grind on. However, the following are hanging on in there:

**Bambi** II, Frankel Leó út 2/4.
One of the few untouched interiors dating back to the 1960s. Red leatherette seats and old men playing dominoes on a Sunday afternoon.

**Ibolya** V, Ferenciek tere 5 [4 F5]
Very popular with students, enjoying a quick *eszpresszó* before heading into the main library opposite. Smoky.

**Mester** IX, Mester utca 45 [4 G7]
A real *eszpresszó* announced by wonderful tableau signs and a massive ceramic stove. Waitresses take no nonsense from behind the '60s counter. On a street of craftsmen (see box, pages 204–5).

**Terv** V, Nádor utca 19 [1 D4]
Smartened up, but *cukrászda* pretensions are undermined by working men drinking beer and spirits in the morning.

**Tik-Tak** XII, Böszörményi út 17/C [3 G1]
Neon cuckoo clock above the doorway. Refined, silver-haired gentlefolk of the vicinity used to drop in for coffee and cognac.

**Tulipán** V, Nádor utca 32 [1 D4]
Belongs to the group of *presszós* in District V bearing the names of flowers – the Ibolya

(Violet) and the Muskátli (Geranium) tourist trap on Váci utca. Back room of high stools, mushroom tables and walls turned beige by cigarette smoke.

## WHERE TO DRINK

You'll have no trouble finding a place for a proper drink in Budapest, but the various categories of watering hole might confuse the raw Western recruit. Far from upmarket, a wine bar (*borozó*) often equates to a den of men drinking rough vintages ladled from metal drums for 30Ft a decilitre. You might find spit and sawdust in a beer hall (*söröző*), too, but you are just as likely to find a well-turned-out pub. The word *pince* indicates a cellar, be that a brick beer tavern with wooden benches or a place for tasting wine (*borospince*) from regional vineyards. Some wineshops (*italbolt*) also offer tastings. Modern bars often bear the name 'café', and are contemporary reinterpretations of an earlier coffee-house culture that declined in the mid-20th century; they may serve food and coffee, and have music and dancing, but they are more bar than traditional café or club (both of which are dealt with elsewhere; see pages 156–63 and 187–91). The primary clusters are on the Pest side of the river, and on Liszt Ferenc tér and Ráday utca in particular. During summer, such areas make a very Parisian use of public space as tables spill on to pavements, squares and courtyards. All of the above are generally open daily from 11.00 or 12.00 until 24.00, although closing times often extend into the early hours on Fridays and Saturdays. When wetting your whistle, you can order draught beer by the half-litre (*korsó*) or smaller (*pohár*) glass, while wine is served by the bottle (*üveg*), by the glass (*pohár*) or – usually in wine bars – by the decilitre.

# BARS AND PUBS

## Buda

**Café Miró** I, Úri utca 30; tel: 1 375 5458 [1 C4]

A self-consciously contemporary wine-bar-cum-café. Inspired by the work of Catalan artist Joan Miró, its bold splashes of colour and wiry metal furnishings draw the fashionable and young like moths to its flame. The waitresses appear to feel that cheerful and attentive service is very last season, however, and could do with a slap from the smile fairy. Good view of Mátyás Church – and of old 'golden balls' (see pages 243–4). *Open 09.00–24.00 daily.*

**Club Casanova Bar** I, Batthyány tér 4; tel; 1 212 9717 [1 C3]

Academics may debate the authenticity of the disco mirror ball, but there's historical justification for the sequinned masks. In the 18th century, this hostelry was the venue for grand masque balls attended – it is said – by Casanova himself. Happy 'hour' between 12.00 and 21.00 offers 50% off a range of drinks. Just below street level at the western side of Batthyány tér. *Open Mon–Sat 12.00–06.00, closed Sunday – even the great Lothario needs a rest.*

**Dokk Café** II, Mammut II, 2nd Floor, Lövőház utca 2–6; tel: 1 345 8531; www.dokkcafe.com [1 B2]

The main event is later at the Dokk Club (page 189), but this is the swanky starting point for the élite and beautiful of Budapest. If you want to avoid the judgemental eye of the self-appointed fashion police, steer well clear. Sells the inevitable cocktails, together with international snacks. *Open Sun–Thu 11.00–01.00, Fri–Sat 11.00–02.00.*

**Oscar Bar** I, Ostrom utca 14; tel: 1 212 8017 [1 B3]
Dingy, below-street (but air-conditioned) drinking-hole devoted to the world of American film. A favoured haunt of ex-pats. Just below the Castle District and a short walk from Moszkva tér. *Open Sun–Thu 17.00–02.00, Fri and Sat 17.00–04.00.*

## Pest

**Becketts** V, Bajcsy-Zsilinsky út 72; tel: 1 311 1033; www.becketts.hu [1 E3]
It's named after Samuel Beckett, there is passable Guinness in the taps and a *Commitments* poster on the wall, which all adds up to about as authentic an Irish pub as Hungary has to offer. Ex-pats love the place, drawn by the siren sound of pool balls clinking, the promise of 14 draught beers, and live music and half-price whiskies from 20.00 on Thursdays. The pub grub is also excellent. *Open Sun–Thu 12.00–01.00, Fri–Sat 12.00–03.00.*

**Box utca** VI, Bajcsy Zsilinsky út 21: tel: 1 354 1444; www.box-utca.hu [1 E4]
You may or may not have heard of him, but the Hungarian boxer István 'Ko-Ko' Kovács was an Olympic gold-medal winner in 1996 and a world champ in 2001, and he's since made a pretty good fist of this upmarket sports bar and restaurant. This is a place of plasma screens and soft lighting, of sports jackets rather than string vests; chunky chips make way for breaded chicken roulade. During his visit, David Coulthard carelessly left behind his racing car in the restaurant. Very child-friendly. Opposite the Arany János metro. *Open Mon–Fri 08.00–24.00, Sat–Sun 10.00–24.00.*

**Champs Sports Pub** VII, Dohány utca 20; tel: 1 413 1655; www.champs.hu [4 F5]
A massive cellar bar swathed in sporting paraphernalia and with raised television screens for sporting nuts. Decent portions of grub at reasonable prices. *Open 12.00–02.00 daily.*

**Columbus Pub** V, Vigadó tér 4; tel: 1 266 7514 [3 D5]
We're not sure what Columbus would have made of the neon drinks adverts, nor what the Celts make of its claim to Irishness. By contrast, we are very sure what the staff make of their sailors' neckerchiefs, which must shiver their timbers. Beyond that, however, this moored theme pub scrubs up well as the deck of a 15th-century galleon, and makes a surprisingly relaxed place for a yo-ho-ho and a bottle of rum. There's also international pub fare. *Open 12.00–late daily.*

**Darshan Café** VIII, Krúdy Gyula utca 8; tel: 1 266 7797 [4 G6]
A young and hippyish crowd sprawl among the stone-chip mosaics of this small café. The exotic Darshan Udvar, a colourful, Asian-inspired bar, club and concert venue, is set back in the parade opposite. Just off Lőrinc pap tér. *Café open Mon–Sat 07.00–24.00, Sun 16.00–24.00; bar open Mon–Wed 10.00–01.00, Thu–Fri 10.30–02.00, Sat 18.00–02.00, Sun 18.00–24.00.*

**Etno Coffe & Lounge** V, Fehérhajó utca 5; tel: 1 411 0643; www.etno.hu [3 E5]
Don a pair of shades and a cool expression, and relax in the knowledge that you're among the trendy set. Sip cocktails, coffees, milkshakes or flavoured teas. Statuettes of Hindu elephant gods look on as you tuck into food with an Asian bent. Fits the bill for an afternoon break, an informal meal or an evening drink. *Open 11.00–23.00 daily.*

**Irish Cat** V, Múzeum körút 41; tel: 1 266 4085 [4 F6]
One of the city's good-time meat markets. There's flat Guinness and thumping chart music, but also a surprisingly diverse crowd and an unthreatening atmosphere. Opposite the National Museum. *Open Mon–Thu 11.00–02.00, Fri–Sat 11.00–04.00, Sun 17.00–02.00.*

**Janis's Pub** V, Királyi Pál utca 8; tel: 1 266 2619 [4 F6]
A blessed refuge from the teeny-boppers, Janis's (Joplin, obviously) emanates creaky-kneed maturity. Perfect for an inoffensive sup of Kilkenny or a 15-year-old malt. *Open Mon–Thu 16.00–02.00, Fri–Sat 16.00–03.00, Sun 18.00–24.00.*

**John Bull Pub** V, Podmaniczky tér 4; tel: 1 269 3116 [1 E4]
With gold-patterned wallpaper and cream drapes, English visitors may find this rather smarter than the typical boozer back home. It's also quieter and less smoky. Unfortunately, the inflated prices are depressingly familiar. *Open 12.00–24.00 daily.*

**Leroy Café** VI, Westend City Center, 1st Floor, Váci út 1–3; VI, Sas utca 11; tel: 1 266 5248 [2 F2]
Two in a chain of bar-restaurants popular with 20- and 30-somethings; that on Sas utca is a very recent link, and is well located overlooking Szent István tér. Sushi is supplied by the posher parent establishment, the Tom-George Restaurant (V, Október 6 utca 8; tel: 1 266 3525; www.tomgeorge.hu). *Open 12.00–24.00 daily.*

**Longford Irish Pub** V, Fehér Hajó utca 5; tel: 1 267 2766 [3 E5]
Longford is one of several bars and cafés that have sprung up around Szomory Dezső tér,

offering a diluted version of Liszt Ferenc tér for those who can't face the trip out of the centre. To call it 'Irish' is a load of blarney, but it's modern, smart and a favourite for those who enjoy people watching . *Open 11.00–02.00 daily.*

## *Liszt Ferenc tér and Jókai Mór tér*

Liszt tér is the established scratching post for the city's young and trendy. It is here that they gather in real concentrations around the café-bars that line either side of the square, perched at the tables and chairs that litter it in summer months. (For further history etc, see page 287.)

**Buena Vista** VI, Liszt Ferenc tér 4–5; tel: 1 344 6303; www.buena-vista.hu [2 F3]
This is an elegant club sandwich of a place, with a tavern at the bottom, a café in the middle and a restaurant (serving Hungarian, French and Italian) in the gallery atop. Wine lovers can choose from an extensive selection that runs from 1,800Ft to 35,000Ft a bottle; those with simpler tastes slouch at wooden tables in the cellar and draw their own pints of beer from individual taps. *Open 10.00–01.00 daily.*

**Cactus Juice** VI, Jókai Mór tér 5; tel: 1 302 2116 [2 F3]
A western-themed bar that is, as you'd expect, lively, loud and popular with stag parties. *Open Mon–Thu 12.00–02.00, Fri–Sat 12.00–04.00, Sun 16.00–02.00.*

**Café Vian** VI, Liszt Ferenc tér 9; tel: 1 268 1154 [2 F3]
Café Vian hogs the sun's first rays. Head here early for a hearty breakfast, with English,

American, Hungarian and continental on the menu. The place is named after the 20th-century French author and poet, Boris Vian, and has a small stage for regular art exhibitions and theatrical evenings. *Open 09.00–24.00 daily.*

**Karma Café** VI, Liszt Ferenc tér 11; tel: 1 413 6764 [2 F3]
If karma is the result of the actions of a life, you'll need to sacrifice a few merit points in jostling for a seat at the square's most popular café-bar. Show no mercy, for pavement tables are rare things of an evening. The Buddhist-inspired interior is calm and intimate. If you're peckish, plump for some Asian and Mediterranean cuisine. Live music at weekends. There's a sister bar in the Westend City Centre (see page 209). *Open 11.00–02.00 daily.*

**Pesti Est Café** VI, Liszt Ferenc tér 5; tel: 1 344 4381 [2 F3]
There's a downstairs nightclub where parties are hosted every few weeks (check *Pesti Est* magazine for forthcoming events). Otherwise the café-bar serves a range of cocktails and snacks. *Open 11.00–02.00 daily.*

**Winston's Bar** VI, Jókai Mór tér 3; tel: 1 331 1955; www.winstons.hu [2 F3]
Comfortable English-pub atmosphere, with dark wooden tables, groaning bookshelves and shepherd's pie. *Open 12.00–24.00 daily.*

## *Ráday utca*

Linking Kálvin tér and the lower reaches of the Nagykörút, the regenerated Ráday utca is the upstart challenger to the hegemony of Liszt Ferenc tér, sustained by the custom of students from the three universities near by. Look elsewhere for picture-postcard prettiness – there's a gritty edge about the place, and an absence of pavement posing – but the number of restaurants and bars has doubled in the last few years and the road is consolidating its new status as a leading nightspot. We've plucked a couple of bars from the group, but there are many more.

**Soul Café** IX, Ráday utca 11–13; tel: 1 217 6986; www.miwo.hu/soulcafe [4 F6]
One of the leading lights on the busy strip, Soul has an open fireplace and a terrace, which makes it popular in winter and summer alike. Media types enjoy weekend lunches of fresh fish and chocolate cake from the international menu. *Open 12.00–01.00 daily.*

**Time Café and Lounge** IX, Ráday utca 23; tel: 1 476 0433; www.timecafe.hu [4 F6]
Despite arriving 30 minutes late, our colleagues insisted they were 'on time' as they stood on the clock face sunk into the floor of the café-bar. How they chuckled! We found it less amusing, but were quickly calmed by Mediterranean colours, soothing jazz and cool beers.

# 7 Entertainment and Nightlife

There's no excuse for calling it a day when the sun sets over Budapest. No city wears night's cloak with more elegance. The castle turns on its illuminations, bridges follow suit, lights ride the river's ripples and romance's stage is set. Choose a bar for that post-dinner digestif, and decide upon where next. Since the 19th century, culture has been an important touchstone of Hungarian self-identity – initially as a means of tacit resistance to occupation – and there are plenty of places to let dinner settle over performances of folk music, opera or dance. Alternatively, you can listen to Hungarian takes on jazz, blues and rock, or let good digestion wait on some energetic clubbing. There are few people whose darkness hours Budapest can't find a way to fill.

There are several publications listing what's on, available (often free) from Tourinforms, hotels, pubs and bars. *Pesti Est* (page 73) and *Pesti Műsor* give information on arts and entertainment, but are mainly in Hungarian. Grab a free copy of *Súgó* for theatre listings that are translated into English in July and August. In general, the best bet for English speakers are titles like *Where Budapest* (page 75), the *Budapest Sun* (page 74), or the *Budapest Times* (with its 11-day calendar detailing upcoming events at bars, cultural houses etc; page 75).

## TICKET OFFICES

Most venues have their own box offices, but the following agencies (*jegyiroda*) sell tickets to sporting events, opera and ballet, concerts (including pop, jazz, classical), theatre performances, and folklore programmes.

**Jegyiroda** VI, Nagymező utca 19; tel: 1 302 3841; www.ticket.matavnet.hu
**Mérleg Jegyiroda** V, Mérleg utca 10; tel: 1 485 0473. *Open Mon–Wed 10.00–18.00, Thu 10.00–14.00, Fri 10.00–18.00*
**Music Mix 33** V, Váci utca 33; tel: 1 266 1651. *Open Mon–Fri 10.00–18.00, Sat 10.00–13.00*
**Ticket Centrum** V, Vigadó utca 6; tel: 1 318 3862. *Open Mon–Fri 10.00–16.00*
**Ticket Express** VI, Andrássy út 18; tel: 1 312 0000; www.tex.hu. Also a branch in the Ibusz office at Ferenciek tere 10 (tel: 06 3030 30999; open Mon–Fri 09.00–17.00). *Open Mon–Fri 09.30–18.30*
**Vigadó Jegyiroda** V, Vigadó tér 5; tel: 318 9903. Specialises in concerts at the nearby Vigadó theatre. *Open Mon–Fri 10.00–18.00*
**www.online.jegymester.hu/index_eng.html** Purchase tickets online for the State Opera House, Erkel Theatre, National Theatre and Budapest Festival Orchestra.

## THEATRE

Budapest has a strong relationship with the theatre, and while it would benefit further from greater financial support, there is a varied selection of plays, musicals and comedies to be found on over 40 stages around the city. The main cluster of these is just off Andrássy út, on Nagymező utca, which is known as the Pest Broadway. Alongside productions by domestic playwrights such as Mihály Babits and Ferenc Molnár, there is international drama including Shakespeare. However, the Anglo-Saxon visitor yearning to see *The Tempest* in Hungarian is a breed we've yet to meet, and only the Merlin is a safe bet for English-language drama. Curtains usually rise at 19.00.

**Buda Park Theatre** (*Budai Parkszínpad*) XI, Kosztolányi Dezső tér; tel: 1 466 9849 [3 D8]
T *19, 49;* B *7, 7A*

An open-air arena next to the 'Bottomless Lake' (see page 259), staging drama and concerts. The programme is listed outside the gates. *Ticket office open Wed–Sun 15.00–18.00.*

**Merlin Szinház** V, Gerlóczy utca 4; tel: 1 317 9338; www.szinhaz.hu/merlin [4 F5]
T *47, 49;* B *9*

There's contemporary dance at the Merlin, but it's also known for its classical, modern and alternative English-language productions. You can purchase tickets via the website (in English), and there's a 15% discount with a Budapest Card. Popular with ex-pats and foreigners. Tickets 1,000–2,000Ft. *Box office open 10.00–18.00 daily.*

**National Theatre** (*Nemzeti Színház*) XI, Bajor Gizi Park 1; tel: 1 476 6800; www.nemzetiszinhaz.hu
M3 *Kálvin tér;* T *47, 49*

The National Theatre was for some time a subject of drama. Thirty years after the communists demolished the splendid original in Blaha Lujza tér, an almighty slanging match erupted over its replacement. As the Fidesz government bickered with the Budapest mayor over costs (see page 13), the enormous foundation hole at Erzsébet tér was tagged the 'National Pit' by city wags. Eventually a new site was chosen near Petőfi híd and the theatre – a bold, self-consciously modern building, resembling a ship's prow – opened in 2002. It is a showcase for Hungarian drama – and very Magyar – but Sándor Román's ExperiDance (a famous local company) also performs dance here. *Ticket office open Mon–Fri 10.00–18.00, Sat–Sun 14.00–17.30.*

**Palace of Arts** (*Művészetek Palotája*) XI, Bajor Gizi Park
T *2, 24*
A concrete cube has just sprung up between Lágymányosi híd and the National Theatre (some say to make the latter shine by comparison). It is intended that this will become the new centre of arts for the city. When it officially opens in March 2005, the Palace of Arts will become a permanent home for the Ludwig Museum (there's no word on whether it will contain the whole collection) and the National Philharmonic Orchestra; it will first operate on a trial basis (Jan–Mar 2005), with concerts by the National Philharmonic and other orchestras.

**Puppet Theatre** (*Bábszínház*) VI, Andrássy út 69; tel: 1 342 2702; www.budapest-babszinhaz.hu [2 G3]
M1 *Vörösmarty utca;* B *4*
Puppets to some extent transcend the language barrier, and perform in a dirty black building next to the Liszt Museum (page 327). There are shows for children in the mornings and afternoons, and for adults on some evenings; starting times vary. Tickets around 350–600Ft. *Ticket office open 09.00–18.00.*

**Thália Színház** VI, Nagymező utca 22–24; tel: 1 312 1280; www.thalia.hu [2 F3]
M1 *Opera*
Well-respected theatre, recently refurbished. Links up with the Operetta Theatre for musicals and operettas (see page 179). *Ticket office open Mon–Fri 10.00–18.00, Sat–Sun 14.00–18.00.*

**Vígszínház** XIII, Szent István körút 14; tel: 1 329 2340; www.vigszinhaz.hu [1 E2]
T *4, 6;* B *26, 91, 191*
Budapest's oldest and biggest (seating 1,000) stands on the Great Boulevard, its pale lemon façade bursting from the surrounding browns and greys. For Hungarians, a visit to the

Comedy Theatre is a time to polish shoes and consider with more care than usual whether shirt matches trousers. The neo-Renaissance building was constructed in just one year, opening in 1896, and now shows a diverse range of Hungarian and foreign productions, all in Hungarian. *Ticket office at side of the building (on Ditrói Mór utca) open 11.00–19.00 daily, or at Pannonia utca 8 open Mon–Thu 10.00–18.00, Fri 10.00–17.00.*



## MUSIC

### Opera and classical

**Operas** in Budapest are full-blown affairs, with elaborate sets and luxuriant costume. They are also often performed in Hungarian, which is considerably less romantic than Italian but probably no worse than English. Opera buff or not, you should take advantage of some of the cheapest ticket prices in the world (from as low as 300Ft, but around 3,000–4,500Ft for a good view), and a sumptuous setting at the State Opera House. You don't need to wear top hat and tails, but jeans distress the usherettes. The 'father of Hungarian opera' was Ferenc Erkel, who conducted his own *Hunyadi László* and *Bánk Bán* at the opening of the State Opera House. Both operas remain popular today; there are also performances throughout the year by foreign masters like Mozart and Wagner.

Hungary has good reason to be proud of its **classical** heritage. Concert performances are two-a-penny, offering home-grown and international talent, although in the hot months these are more likely to be outdoor. The **Budapest Philharmonic Orchestra** was founded by Erkel in the mid-19th century; when it is not touring, its home is at the State Opera House. **Buda Castle Summer Nights** – opera, classical and jazz concerts in the Hotel Hilton's Dominican Courtyard (see pages 101–2) – run every other evening for much of July (book tickets through the hotel or on the website below), while there are concerts every five days or so in July in Szent István tér, the Basilica providing a stunning backdrop. In addition, regular organ recitals, choral performances and classical concerts are hosted in the city's churches – including the Lutheran Church (V, Deák tér), Mátyás Church (Castle District), and Szt Anna Church (I, Batthyány tér 7) – as well as at the Vajdahunyad Castle in City Park and the Dome Hall of the Parliament building. Information is available from Tourinforms, ticket offices or listings magazines (see pages 81–2); alternatively, details are given at www.viparts.hu, where you can also reserve tickets online, and in the *Koncert Kalendárium* (www.koncertkalendarium.hu, in Hungarian).

**Béla Bartók Memorial House** (*Bartók Béla Emlékház*) II, Csalán út 29; tel: 1 394 2100
See page 321.

**Budapest Operetta Theatre** (*Budapesti Operettszínház*) VI, Nagymező utca 17; tel: 1 269 3870; www.operettszinhaz.hu
M *Opera*
Along with Vienna, Budapest is a capital of operetta (light musicals); this is the best place to watch one, in glamorous art-nouveau surroundings and beneath a magnificent century-old chandelier. Classic Magyar operettas (usually subtitled in German) and modern musicals (usually subtitled in English). (See also Thália, page 177.) Tours available at weekends – call in advance. *Ticket office (next door) open Mon–Fri 10.00–19.00 (closed 14.30–15.00), Sat–Sun 13.00–19.00.*

**Duna Palace** (*Duna Palota*) V, Zrínyi utca 5; tel: 1 317 2754 [1 E4]
B *15*
Neo-baroque palace and base for the distinguished Duna Symphony Orchestra. Classical performances are held every Saturday at 20.00 May–Oct and once/twice monthly the rest of the year. There is also folk dancing by the Duna Folk Ensemble.

**Erkel Theatre** VIII Köztársaság tér 30; tel: 1 333 0540 [4 H5]
B *7, 7A;* T *37A, 37, 28*
Ugly home – along with the State Opera House – to the city's leading ballet company. There are also opera and musicals here. *Ticket office open Tue–Sat 11.00–17.00 (or show start), Sun11.00–13.00, 16.00 to show start.*

**Hungarian State Opera House** VI, Andrássy út 22; tel: 1 332 8197; info tel: 06 60 594594; www.opera.hu [2 F4]
M1 *Opera*
The Austrians apparently only agreed to the construction of Budapest's opera house on the condition that it was smaller than that in Vienna. When completed in 1884, it was certainly relatively small in size; however, Ferenc József lamented that he hadn't stipulated it be less pretty too. Designed by Miklós Ybl, it's a breathtaking neo-Renaissance building. The entrance hall has a winding staircase, swirling blue pillars and an opulent ceiling that undulates like a choppy ocean, while the horseshoe-shaped auditorium glows golden-red. The historicist artists Károly Lotz, Bertalan Székely and Mór Than painted the frescos, influenced by those of Paris and Vienna in illustrating music's power, while Alajos Stróbl created the sculptures of Erkel and Liszt in alcoves at the entrance. As well as looking great, it sounds pretty good too, the acoustics reputedly second only to La Scala. And it's cheap. Box office inside main entrance

(also selling tickets to Erkel and Thália theatres); guided tours at 15.00 and 16.00 daily. *Open Mon–Sat 11.00–19.00, Sun 16.00–19.00.*

**Liszt Music Academy** (*Liszt Zeneakadémia*) VI, Liszt Ferenc tér 8; tel: tel: 1 462 4600; www.musicacademy.hu [2 F4]

M1 *Oktogon;* B *4*

Situated on the lively Liszt Ferenc tér, this turn-of-the-20th-century art-nouveau music academy has two auditoriums – the huge Nagyterem (closed in Jul–Aug), seating 1,200 people, and the smaller Kisterem. The acoustics are fabulous, like the décor; pop your head into the entrance hall, with its greens and golds, mosaics and marble columns. A seated bronze of Ferenc Liszt is positioned above the entrance, and gargoyles leer at passers-by. The academy's central library contains the country's most extensive music-related collection.

**Pesti Vigadó** V, Vigadó tér 2; tel: 1 317 5067 [3 D5]

T *2, 2A*

The 'place of merriment' – one of Pest's foremost 19th-century historic buildings – was erected in 1865 on the site of Mihály Pollock's Redoute, which was destroyed during the Independence War. The architect made a self-conscious attempt at a 'Hungarian' style, and it is consequently ornamental and highblown. The acoustics are notoriously average, but that didn't deter composers like Liszt, Bartók, Kodály, Wagner, Strauss and Brahms from holding concerts inside. It's the city's second largest. The Hungarian State Folk Ensemble also dances here, and there's a gallery inside hosting temporary exhibitions by contemporary artists (tel: 1 318 7070; open Tue–Sun 10.00–18.00).

## Jazz and easy listening

There are several excellent jazz clubs in which to tap your toes, representing Hungarian and foreign talent. The Budapest Jazz Orchestra travels the country, and usually performs in the capital during the Autumn and Spring festivals (see page 34).

**Cotton Club** VI, Jókai utca 26; tel: 1 354 0886/1341; www.cottonclub.hu [2 F3]
An old-fashioned speak-easy club, bar and café with a determined whiff of 1920s America. There are varied live performances of music and dance at the weekends and on some week nights, featuring jazz, blues and revue-style shows. *Open daily 12.00–01.00.*

**Fat Mo's Music Club** V, Nyáry Pál utca 11; tel: 1 267 3199; www.fatmo.hu [4 F6]
Early 20th-century-themed club whose Saturday disco is popular with prowling meat marketeers. However, there are live jazz, blues and country performances on other evenings (Sun–Wed). *Open Sun–Fri 12.00–02.00, Sat 12.00–04.00.*

**Jazz Garden Music Club** V, Veres Pálné utca 44/A; tel: 1 266 7364; ww.jazzgarden.hu [4 F6]
The outside's in at this romantic little club, decorated to feel like a pavement café under a starry night sky. A firm favourite among jazz lovers, it attracts top Hungarian and international musicians who perform live in the evenings between 21.00 and 24.00. *Open 12.00–24.00 daily.*

**New Orleans Jazz Club** VI, Lovag utca 5; tel: 1 451 7525; www.neworleans.hu [2 F3]
A classy modern club that features big international jazz names, who perform at 21.00 every evening except Sun and Mon. The website (in Hungarian) lists the monthly programme. *Open 18.00–02.00 daily.*

## Contemporary

The electronic music scene is strong. As in western Europe, some musical events are managed by the same company at different locations, while other venues run consistently interesting programmes.

For electronica and dance-music fans, **Cinetrip**, a regular party whose venue varies, is just as remarkable for its large screens and VJs (improvisational video-based DJs) as its music. It has been staged at the Railway Museum and at Turkish baths, where fans take along a towel and a swimsuit to change into. You might also try **Trafó** (page 187) or **A38** (page 184). The municipal government-owned **Petőfi csarnok** is a large 'youth leisure centre' in City Park, which aims for more mainstream appeal. Large international acts appear at the Puskás Stadion or at the smaller arenas in the vicinity (such as the Kisstadion).

In warmer weather, the **Sziget Festival** is an August staple of the partying calendar (pages 35–7), while the day-long **Budapest Parade** is a huge rave similar to the Berlin Love Parade (page 37). In addition, outdoor clubs like **Zöld Pardon**, **Rio**, and the roof of the **A38** boat take advantage of the summer months.

The music scene is inevitably in a perpetual state of flux. For up-to-date information, see www.port.hu, www.index.hu or www.est.hu. Tickets for performances are available from the city-centre ticket offices (see page 174-5).

**Almássy téri Szabadidő Központ** VII, Almássy tér 6; tel: 1 342 0387; www.almassy.hu [2 G4] Located just north of Blaha Lujza tér, this cultural centre offers a varied selection of live music.

**A38 Club** XI, Állóhajó, near Petőfi híd; www.a38.hu [4 F8]
Opened in 2003, the A38 is a beautifully renovated Ukrainian stone-carrier ship moored near Petőfi Bridge, which serves as an innovative live-music venue, restaurant and nightclub. The website lists a monthly programme including jazz, rock, drum 'n' bass, hip hop and classical. Recent acts have included Anima Sound System, Erik Marchand and the Holmes Brothers.

**Millenáris Park** II, Fény utca 20–22; www.millenaris.hu [1 B2]
Two concert halls, one a vast brick hangar (the Teátrum) and the other a more informal space, that host world music and folk. Always a diverse programme of music, dance and entertainment.

**Morrisons Music Club** VI, Révay utca 25; tel: 1 269 4060 [2 F4]
A smoky old pub off Dalszínház utca that's inexpensive and popular with students. Check out the miniature train circling above the heads of the barmen. There's a dance floor and a chill-out room, and karaoke on Wednesday nights. Admission from 500Ft. *Open Wed–Sat 21.00–04.00.*

**Old Man's Music Pub** VII, Akácfa utca 13; tel: 1 322 7645; www.oldmans.hu [2 F4]
A lively basement bar in the Jewish quarter, with friendly staff and live jazz, blues, Latino, swing or rock acts between 21.00 and 23.00 most nights. *Open Mon–Thu 15.00–04.00, Fri–Sat 15.00–04.30.*

**Petőfi Csarnok** XIV, Zichy Mihály út 14; www.petoficsarnok.hu [2 J2]
Concert venue in City Park. Also has an open-air stage and arena, with folk-music performances in summer and bands like Massive Attack, Placebo, and Earth, Wind and Fire.

# DANCE

## Folk

The dance-house (*táncház*) movement began 30 years ago as a reaction against sanitised state ensembles, a sense of national pride and a concern for the Magyar minority in Transylvania (where the best music was concentrated). Young urbanites travelled to rural communities in an attempt to learn and preserve dying traditional music and dances. They then played and taught these to those in cities. Such dance houses continue. They are usually held in cultural centres, where traditional dance is accompanied by folk music played on traditional instruments by groups like Muzsikás.

Visitors take an active part in the dance, or sit around with glasses of *pálinka* and watch as musicians play and dancers dance. Dance houses take place less often in the summer. Entertainment listings magazines will show what's on, or log on to www.tanchaz.hu. If you want a polished performance rather than a workshop, it's worth checking the programmes at the National Dance Theatre, the Vigadó or the Duna Palota.

**Aranytíz Youth Centre** (*Ifjúsági Centrum*) V, Arany János utca 10; tel: 1 311 2248
Every Saturday evening, the Kalamajka táncház is found here, with Béla Halmos (the founder of the dance-house movement) and his band playing. Listen while enjoying *pálinka* from the makeshift bar.

**City Cultural House** (*Fövárosi Művelődési Ház*) XI, Fehérvári út 47 [3 E6]
A concrete block with regular dance houses, featuring Balkan and Moldavian troupes.

**Fonó Buda Music House** (*Zeneház*) XI, Sztregova utca 3; tel: 1 206 5300; www.fono.hu
T *41, 47, 18;* B *14, 103, 114 stop near by*
Slightly out of the centre, Fonó is a cultural centre and live-music venue. There are regular performances by Hungarian and eastern European folk bands and dance troupes – including Muszikás – as well as modern concerts. Dance-house events take place on Wednesdays, and there's an excellent CD shop. Closed in high summer (Jul 1–Aug 31).

**Marcibányi tér Cultural Centre** (*Muvelődési Központ*) II, Marcibányi tér 5/A; tel: 1 212 0803/4885 [1 A2]
Performances of Csángó music (the ethnic Hungarians from Moldavia), as well as informal sessions by Muzsikás on some Thursdays from 20.00 and a weekly dance house every Wednesday evening.

## Other

Ballet has been popular in Hungary for 200 years; the most prestigious of today's companies is the National Ballet Company, the country's first ensemble, which is based at the State Opera House. The National Dance Theatre also includes ballet among its repertoire. There are several venues offering contemporary dance.

**Central Europe Dance Theatre** (*Közép Európa*) VII, Bethlen Gábor tér 3; tel: 1 342 7163; www.cedt.hu [2 H4]
B *78, 7;* M2 *Keleti, then short walk along Bethlen Gábor utca*
Quality contemporary dance, with frequent workshops. Alongside the modern dance, there is a strong folkloric heritage with traditional dances deriving from the Carpathian Basin.

**National Dance Theatre** (*Nemzeti Táncszínház*) I, Színház utca 1–3; tel: 1 356 4085 *(theatre)*, 1 201 4407 *(ticket office)*, 1 375 8649 *(box office)*; www.nemzetitancszinhaz.hu [1 C4]
This is the country's only 18th-century theatre still functioning as such. Previously a Carmelite monastery, it became a place of drama when József II dissolved the religious order in 1784. Although the theatre primarily catered to the German population, the first professional Hungarian-language theatrical production (of *Igazházi* by Simai Kristóf) was staged here in 1790. Haydn attended a performance of his own 'Creation' oratory in 1800, and Beethoven played a concert in the same year. Since 2001, the theatre has specialised in dance and related performing arts – ranging from folklore to classical ballet and contemporary dance. There are two auditoriums, and during August performances (usually folkloric) are held outside in the Carmelite courtyard. Stands next to the Sándor Palace. *Ticket office (at front) open Mon–Fri 10.00–17.00, box office (behind theatre) Mon–Fri 13.00–18.00.*

**Trafó House of Contemporary Arts** (*Trafó Kortárs Művészetek Háza*) IX, Liliom utca 41: tel: 1 456 2040; www.trafo.hu [4 G7]
M3 *Ferenc körút;* T *4, 6 Üllői út*
Housed in a former electrical transformer station, Trafó is now a contemporary cultural centre and nightclub with a diverse programme. It hosts international-standard contemporary dance, theatre and music, as well as temporary exhibitions of graphic art. *Ticket office open daily 17.00–20.00 (gallery 16.00–19.00); tickets also available from Ticket Express (see page 175).*

## NIGHTCLUBS

While Budapest isn't a clubbing mecca in world terms, and you'll come across the odd trashy Euro-pop track, there are some excellent nightclubs to be sought out – both indoor and out – and some talented Hungarian DJs (see page 33). Clubbing is popular and nightclubs crowded, particularly after midnight. There is sometimes (although not always) an admission charge, which varies between about 500Ft and 5,000Ft depending on the event and venue. It is unjust, but not uncommon, for clubs to make just the men dip into their pockets at the entrance. Jeans are usually acceptable, although trainers may not be. When it comes to the clubbing uniform, Hungarian women seem to believe that 'less is more' when dressing and 'more is more' when applying make-up! Many clubs are connected to a bar, and so open for most of the day; the remainder open between 18.00 and 21.00, and usually continue until 03.00 or 04.00. If you like a club to have warmed up by the time you arrive, don't bother getting there until at least 22.30. Clubs can appear and disappear very quickly – criminal gangs have their fingers in the pie of nightclub ownership, and as a consequence the scene can be unstable.

## Buda

**Bed and Bed Beach** III, Szentendrei út 89–93 and Római part 7; tel: 06 70 2088389
Bed is something of a blend of warehouse and basketball court, with bleachers stacked around the main dance floor. The atmosphere is heady but friendly, the music a contemporary fusion of funky house and dance played by DJs who know how to work a crowd and attract more serious clubbers than those at the Dokk. During the summer, the club moves outside to a man-made beach on the Római part. *Bed open Sat 21.00–06.00 (end of Dec–May 2 only); Bed Beach open Sat 21.00–06.00 (May 3–Sep/Oct).*

**Dokk and Dokk Beach** III, Hajógyári-sziget 122; tel: 1 457 1023; www.dokkbistro.com
An uber-cool club that drags Budapest's young élite to its breast, Dokk is *the* party destination for the beautiful people. Follow the trail of parked sports cars lined outside, don your top togs and be prepared to be the view. Come July and August, the action is al fresco (Dokk Beach), with a bridge leading to a timber platform on the water, and a venue that rivals the Ibiza beach clubs. *Terrace bar and restaurant open Mon–Wed 12.00–24.00; dance club open Thu–Sat 12.00–05.00.*

**Rudas Romkert** XI, Budapest, Döbrentei tér 9 [3 D6]
This sunken paved garden set slightly behind the Rudas Baths is popular for coffee and snacks during the day; come evening, partygoers flood the al-fresco bar and dance floor as the DJ takes over (from 22.00 daily). There's a lively buzz and a notable lack of elbowroom on Friday and Saturday nights. (Note that this was closed during 2004 for renovations.) *Open May–Sep Sun–Mon 12.00–02.00, Tue–Sat 12.00–04.00.*

## Pest

**Bahnhof** VI, Váci út 1; tel: 1 302 4751; www.bahnhofmusic.hu [2 F2]
A thumping train-themed dance club, located behind McDonalds in Nyugati station (just off Teréz körút). *Open Thu–Sat 21.00–04.00.*

**Bank Dance Hall** V, Terez körút 55; www.bankdancehall.hu [2 F2]
Right up your street if you want to let go to banging bass lines in a huge and sweaty dance hall. There's a range of dance genres, including rap, R&B, funk, house and trance, played over three levels and across four separate rooms. Popular with teens and early 20s. Situated within the Nyugati train station building. *Open Fri–Sat, with smaller theme nights on some week nights.*

**Buddha Beach** IX Fővám tér 11–12, tel: 1 476 0433 [4 F6]
Sitting on the riverbank behind Big Market Hall, Buddha Beach features three cocktail bars, Thai 'sungalows' to chill out on and a giant golden statue of Buddha. *Open daily 11.00–05.00 (in summer).*

**Club Seven** VII, Budapest, Akácfa utca 7; tel: 1 478 9030 [2 F4]
Doesn't come to the boil until at least midnight; there are occasionally live jazz acts. Stands on the other side of Dohány utca from the Old Man's Music Pub. *Café part open Sun–Thu 10.00–04.00, Fri–Sat 10.00–05.00; disco open 20.00–04.00/05.00 daily.*

**E-Klub** X, Népligeti út 2; tel: 1 263 1614; www.e-klub.hu [4 K8]
Hedonists should follow the blue neon strip running along the outside of this large club in the wooded Népliget park. DJs spin the usual Euro-trashy dance, trance and house music, but there's also a floor that features more retrospective tunes from the '80s and '90s. *Open Fri–Sat 20.00–05.00.*

**Zöld Pardon** XI, Goldmann György tér; www.zp.hu. Outdoor club in the shadow of Petőfi Bridge, frequented by those at the younger end of the spectrum who come for music at the harder jungle and drum 'n' base end. *Open 09.00–06.00 daily (May–Sep).*

## GAY BUDAPEST

After a slow start the gay scene has perked up somewhat in the capital, and several bars and clubs have opened. Most clubs either charge an entrance fee or require a minimum drinks spend (running a tab that you settle on leaving). Some of the baths are established gay meeting points. For information on forthcoming events, log on to www.gay.hu or www.gayguide.net.

**Angyal Privát Club** VII, Szövetség utca 33; tel: 1 351 6490 [2 G4]
Budapest's best-known gay club has an inconspicuous exterior but a decidedly harder core. There are three bars, a downstairs dancefloor and a restaurant with cross-dressing staff. Saturday nights are male-only, but women are welcome at other times, and Sunday is popular with heterosexuals. Located halfway between Erzsébet körút and Rákóczi út. *Open Thu–Sun 22.00–05.00.*

**Capella** V, Belgrád rakpart 23; tel: 1 318 6231 [3 E6]
A dark and dingy spot that doesn't take itself seriously, revelling in drag acts and occasional foam parties. The crowd is mixed – in age, gender and sexual preference (many straight people enjoy the atmosphere). Live acts start at around midnight on Fridays and Saturdays; there is an entrance fee after 23.00. It is also a good place for picking up information about other gay events taking place in the city. *Open Tue–Fri 21.00–04.00, Sat–Sun 21.00–05.00.*

## CINEMA

If you want to watch a Hollywood blockbuster in a mainstream cinema, head for an American-style shopping mall, which often holds multiplexes. Many are in the original English with Hungarian subtitles, although comedies are frequently dubbed. If a film is advertised with its English title, you can assume it will be subtitled; alternatively look for *feliratos* (or *fel*) in the listings. Dubbed films are indicated by *magyarul beszélő* (or *mb*). Be wary of the peculiar Hungarian way of displaying times (see *How to use this book*). It is a source of great shame that some of Budapest's art-house cinemas have been forced to close. Nevertheless, investment by the

Budapest Film Company has meant that many others have been renovated to their former splendour, and they showcase art films from Hungary and other countries, often in intimate screening rooms. The *Budapest Sun* has a listings page containing all English-language movies; *Pesti Est* and *Pesti Műsor* have information in Hungarian. The art-cinema website is www.artmozi.hu. Tickets cost from 600Ft (for fading art-house cinemas) to 1,150Ft (for multiplexes).



**Corvin Film Palace** (*Corvin Film Palota*) VIII, Corvin köz 1; tel: 1 459 5050; www.corvin.hu
Revolutionaries of '56 scored a strategic victory here when the Russians were unable to pass down the narrow Corvin köz. A tram conductor held a tank up with a handgun; there's a statue of a boy martyred during the uprising outside.

**Mammut Budai Moziközpont** II, Mammut II, Third Floor, Lövőház utca 2–6; tel: 1 345 8140; www.mammutmozik.hu [1 B2]

**Művész Mozi** VI, Terez körút 30; tel: 1 332 6726 [2 F3]
There's an 'ethnic' ambience here; stalls in the lobby sell beaded jewellery, as well as books and CDs. Five screens show popular and less-mainstream productions.

**Palace MOM Park** XII, Alkotás út 53; tel: 1 487 5670 [3 B6]

**Palace WestEnd** VI, Váci út 1–3; tel: 1 238 7222 [2 F2]

**Puskin Mozi** V, Kossuth Lajos utca 18; tel: 1 429 6080 [4 F5]
This restored cinema is housed in a neoclassical building, with a carved vine motif around the entrance and gilded finishing to the interior. It shows Hollywood films alongside art-house releases in its cosy screening rooms. There's also a video club (open 10.00–22.00 daily).

**Uránia National Film Theatre** (*Nemzeti Filmszínház*) VIII, Rákóczi út 21; tel 1 486 3400; www.urania-nf.hu [4 F5]
Henrik Schmal's art-nouveau design and Venetian-Moorish interior are stunning. The seats lack padding, but – numb bum aside – this makes a film an experience.

## CASINOS

The demise of communism has seen a surge in casinos and gaming arcades. You'll usually need to present photo identification (like a passport) and pay a joining fee of 2,000–3,000Ft, for which you'll be given some complimentary playing chips.

**Las Vegas Casino** V, Roosevelt tér 2; tel: 1 317 6022; www.lasvegascasino.hu [1 D4]
Opened by Sylvester Stallone, this popular casino is inside the Sofitel Atrium Hotel. *Open 14.00–05.00 daily.*

**Royal Revue and Casino** VII, Erzsébet körút 43–49; tel: 1 413 1413 [2 G4]
Lavish casino in the Corinthia Grand Hotel Royal (page 103). Also stages cheesy variety shows. *Open daily 22.00–05.00.*

**Tropicana Casino** V, Vigadó utca 2. tel: 1 266 3062 www.tropicana.hu
Looking like a jungle, this casino is more lighthearted than most. If you lose your shirt, borrow one of the Hawaiian ones worn by the croupiers. *Open daily 11.00–05.00.*

**Várkert Casino** I, Ybl Miklós tér 9; tel: 1 202 4244; www.varket.com [3 D5]
The movers and shakers court luck's lady in the city's most elegant gambling den, originally designed by no less a hand than Miklós Ybl's (page 257). You don't need to arrive glammed to the gills, but avoid trainers, shorts or jeans. A complimentary taxi will return you to your hotel. On the Buda bank between the Chain and Elizabeth bridges. *Open 24 hours daily.*

# Shopping

Budapest is no Rome or Paris. The shops don't have the expensively labelled flocking from afar. Nevertheless, the variety of shops has grown significantly in the last decade, and elegant boutiques are now as much a part of the scene as the noisy market halls. The city is a fun-time place to browse and buy. Pest is where the retail action's at. The touristy Váci utca, Vörösmarty tér, Petőfi Sándor utca and the streets branching from them are lined with glamorous international designer outlets, and stores selling antiques, paintings, folksy items and cosmetics. Products here are pricier than elsewhere (and beyond the means of many Hungarians), but what stroll isn't enhanced by a spot of leisurely window shopping? Get your nose up to the windows, work yourself into the narrow aisles, and cast a curious eye over coloured glass, quirky antiques and hanging lace.

Budapesters target the **Great Boulevard** and streets stemming from or out towards it, such as **Rákóczi út** and **Kossuth Lajos utca**. Shops here are lower key, generally a touch shabbier, and more affordable. In addition, **American-style shopping malls** have sprung up like mushrooms; they are not particularly cheap, but they open late, have everything under one roof – including restaurants, bars and cinemas – and have inevitably placed pressure on small independent retailers.

**Popular gifts or souvenirs** include foods and spices (see box, pages 200–1), and folk art (embroidered tablecloths and napkins, decorated boxes, hand-made dolls and wooden toys, and painted vases, jugs and mugs). You won't have difficulty finding a piece of porcelain either, contemporary or antique. There are delicate

Hollóháza ceramics and chunky Sárospatak pots. However, Herend and Zsolnay are the premier manufacturers, each established for over 150 years, and producing hand-moulded dishes, bowls, figurines and, in the latter's case, vivid majolica roof tiles. Herend is classy and conservative, while Zsolnay Is distinctive for the dark iridescence of some of its pieces, like the feathers of a cormorant. These two are the dinner-service favourites of quality restaurants; discreetly check the maker's mark under your next *gulyás* bowl. Ajkas produces quality leaded crystal.

**Non-food shops** are usually open 10.00–18.00 on weekdays and 09.00–13.00 on Saturdays, while **those selling foodstuffs** are open 07.00–19.00 during the week and 07.00–14.00 on Saturdays. **Malls** will often keep longer hours (that include Sundays), and **markets** shorter ones that vary from site to site. International stores and malls accept credit cards, but you're best to carry cash to be guaranteed of closing deals elsewhere. See pages 68-69 for details of tax that non-European can reclaim on goods. The shops that follow tend to fall into the bracket that will interest those after a Hungarian speciality; for clothes etc you should head to the areas described above or the shopping malls listed later, while other everyday items are available all over the city.

## ANTIQUES, ART AND FURNITURE

Just off Szent István körút, Falk Miksa utca is the first stop for those in quest of antiques. The street is lined with commanding six-storey residences, and a rash of shops selling collectibles. You'll find galleries, auction houses, clock specialists, purveyors of antique porcelain, paintings, French art-deco furniture…

Elsewhere there are a number of shops selling antiques in both the Castle

District and on Váci utca, but these tend to be significantly overpriced. Instead look out for BÁV stores and auction houses, outlets of a well-respected Hungarian chain that are dotted all around the city. These usually have a range of period furniture, porcelain, fine art and glassware, and also stage auctions throughout the year. For more information, log on to their website www.bav.hu (with English language). Some BÁV stores and others are listed below. Remember when making purchases, however, that antiques require a permit for export (*kiviteli engedély*), so be sure to pick up the necessary paperwork at the shop. The form requires a special stamp of permission if antiques are over 70 years old. (See page 49 for further details.)

V, Kossuth Lajos utca 1–3; tel: 1 317 3718; email: info@bav.hu; www.bav.hu [4 F5]
*Open Mon–Fri 10.00–18.00, Sat 09.00–13.00.*
V, Falk Miksa utca 21; tel: 1 353 1975 [1 E2]
A small gallery. *Open Mon–Fri 10.00–18.00, Sat 09.00–13.00.*
VI, Andrássy út 43; tel: 1 342 9143 [2 F3]
Good for antique jewellery. *Open Mon–Fri 10.00–18.00, Sat 09.00–13.00.*
**Nagyházi Galéria** V, Balaton utca 8; tel: 1 475 6000; www.nagyhazi.hu [1 E2]
Collectible works of art. *Open Mon–Fri 10.00–18.00, Sat 10.00–13.00.*
**Polgár Galéria és Aukciósház** V, Kossuth Lajos utca 3; tel: 1 318 6954; www.polgar-galeria.hu [4 F5]
Gallery and auction house, specialising in fine art and furniture. *Open Mon–Fri 10.00–18.00, Sat 10.00–13.00.*

Superior modern furniture and furnishings can be found on VI, Király utca.

## FOLK-ART CENTRES

The centres of folk art lean very heavily towards the kitsch, and they are marketed firmly at the tourist; nevertheless, the craftsmanship is often good, and folk items make super souvenirs.

**Folkart Kézművesház** V, Régiposta utca 12; tel: 1 318 5143 [3 E5]
A busy craft house, with quality evident in the hand-painted plates, traditional clothes and textiles. *Open daily 10.00–19.00.*

**Handmade Studio** I, Tárnok utca 1; tel: 1 212 7050 [1 C4]
Traditional costumes and jewellery in the Castle District. *Open daily 10.00–18.00.*

## FOOD AND DRINK

(See also *Markets*, pages 199–206.)

**A Magyar Pálinka Háza** VIII, Rákóczi út 17; tel: 1 338 4219 [4 F5]
Throat-rasping drops of traditional brandy and other spirits. *Open Mon–Sat 09.00–19.00*

**Aureum Vinum Pincészet** V, Belgrád rakpart 19; tel: 1 483 1456; www.aureumtokaji.hu [3 E6]
A pince-style wine shop specialising in Tokaji from a family-owned winery. Also organises wine-tasting (phone a week in advance). *Open Mon–Fri 10.00–18.00, Sat 10.00–14.00*

**Bortársaság** I, Batthyány utca 59; tel: 1 212 2569; www.bortarsasag.hu [1 C3]
Knowledgeable staff and free tastings on Saturdays make this Wine Society shop an inevitable favourite. There are actually now five outlets: IX, Ráday utca 7; XII, MOM Park, Alkotás út 53; II, Budagyöngye shopping centre, Szilágyi Erzsébet fasor; II, Rózsakert

shopping centre, Gábor Áron utca 74–78. *Open Mon–Fri 10.00–20.00, Sat 10.00–18.00.*

**House of Hungarian Wines** (*Magyar Borok Háza*) I, Szentháromság tér 6; tel: 1 212 1030; www.magyarborokhaza.hu or www.winehouse.hu [1 C4]

Claims to be the sixth-largest wine-tasting establishment in the world – and after a two-hour session you'll find the boast seems rather credible. Its brick cellar (which is chilly, so take a sweater) showcases over 600 wines from the country's 22 wine regions, 60 bottles of which are open at any one time. The company also organises wine-tasting challenges and courses. Two-hour tasting 3,500Ft, with or without a guide (book ahead for the latter). Opposite the Hilton. *Open daily 12.00–20.00.*

**La Boutique des Vins** V, József Attila utca 12; tel: 1 317 5919; www.malatinzky.hu [1 E4]

A decent selection of wines from the southern region of Villány and some very fine French vintages. *Open Mon–Fri 10.00–18.00, Sat 10.00–15.00.*

**Librairie Gourmande** VI, Budapest, Szív utca 32; tel: 1 302 4039 [2 G3]

Read it and eat, fat boy! A proper gourmand's place, selling fresh deli stuffs alongside books on Hungarian and European cooking. Adjoins the Chez Daniel restaurant (see page 150). *Open 11.00–21.00 daily.*

**Portéka Hungaria** V, Magyarok Háza, Semmelweis utca 1–3; tel: 1 486 0336 [4 F5]

Shelves heave with traditional foodstuffs – Hungarian breads, pastries, salamis, jams and wines. Locals shop here. *Open Mon–Fri 10.00–18.00, Sat 10.00–14.00.*

**Szeged Pick Salami Shop** V, Kossuth Lajos tér; tel: 1 331 7783 [1 D3]

A salami show-house for the famous Pick company. *Open Mon–Thu 06.00–19.00, Fri 06.00–18.00.*

# MARKETS

The run-away winners in the shopping stakes, both in terms of value for money and all-round atmosphere, are the bustling market halls (*vásárcsarnok*) and flea markets (*piac* or *ócskapiac*). In most cases – and particularly if buying fresh food – it is best to get there early. It's strictly cash only; your flexible friend will be laughed all the way to the nearest bank ATM. You should not try to haggle in market halls, but you can do so in flea markets – although Hungarians are not very enthusiastic traders, and tend to seem a bit fed up with the process.

During December, festive markets pop up in many of the city's squares. The biggest is in Vörösmarty tér, where wooden booths are draped with fairy lights, and you can choose from handicrafts and wooden Christmas toys while clasping a plastic cup of piping mulled wine. Gerbeaud (page 162) revels in the Xmas atmos, transforming its frontage into an overblown advent calendar. Each of its windows represents a calendar date, and at 17.00 daily one of them is ceremoniously opened.

## Market halls

When the Nagycsarnok opened in 1897 (see page 202), four smaller roofed markets were also opened on the same day. Each was given a number (the Nagycsarnok was No I); look up for the numeral carved in stone or forged in metalwork above the *csarnok* sign and the entrance/exit. The other four markets can be found at: Rákóczi tér (No II), Klauzál tér (No III), Hunyadi tér (No IV) and Hold utca (No V). There is also one on Batthyány tér.

## FOOD GIFTS

If you seek a tasty gift or a flavoursome reminiscence of your trip, there are a variety of specialities available in the shops, market halls and supermarkets. How about:

**Sausage/salami** (*kolbász/szalámi*) You'll find a wide selection behind the supermarket's meat counter or hanging from market stalls, ranging from mild to spicy (*csípős*). The best-known brand is Pick salami, manufactured in Szeged (on the border with Serbia). Some *kolbász* needs to be cooked, rather like standard English sausages. Be aware that meats brought into the UK must be vacuum packed – you can be fined for having a bare *kolbász* in your suitcase.

**Red paprika** (*piros paprika*) The crimson spice of Hungarian life can be bought as a dried whole or in finely ground form. There are seven strengths: mild (*különleges*), also mild (*csípősségmentes*), mildish (*csemege* – the most commonly used in Hungarian dishes), medium (*édes-nemes*), slightly hot (*félédes*), hot (*rózsa*) and very hot (*erős* or *csípős*). You'll pay more for a fancy presentation bag.

**Goose liver** Available in the market in black-and-gold tins. The liver is produced by the Merian Orosháza Rt of Orosháza (southeast of Budapest, in the heart of goose-gagging country), who have a monopoly on the goose-liver market. A 200g tin costs 4,400Ft.

**Caviar** A popular offering among the tins of goose liver and the Tokaji in market halls. It's not Hungarian, but it is cheap by Western standards – ranging from 3,800Ft to 19,800Ft (and small tins of Russian Astrakhan caviar for 3,500Ft). Tins are usually marked '*malosol*' (meaning 'little salt').

**Wine** (*bor*) 'Wine is sunlight, held together by water', Galileo once observed. He very probably hadn't been to Kecskemét. However, there are some among the country's 22 regional wines that are very worth drinking; those particularly favoured by connoisseurs internationally are the sweet, white Tokaji Aszú (in its distinctive long-necked bottle) and Bull's Blood (Bikavér) from Eger or Szekszárd. (For further information on wine, see page 129.)

**Spirits** Brandy or grappa (*pálinka*) is a popular digestif. Kecskemét redeems itself with an apricot brandy (*barack pálinka*), and there are other fruity flavours that'll take the skin off your tongue (see page 128). Alternatively, take back some Unicum, a 'healthy' spirit concocted from a secret recipe of herbs. The branding is striking, with its dark orb of a bottle and a disconcerting poster of a man emerging from water that has become an advertising classic, but the taste is of the 'acquired' variety.

**Fény utcai piac** II, Lövőház utca 12, tel: 1 345 4100 [1 B2]
A buzzy daily market next to Mammut (page 209) sheltered by a glass-slatted roof. Fresh fruit, flowers, paprika, meat and vegetables. *Open Mon–Fri 06.00–18.00, Sat 06.00–14.00.*

**Lehel-csarnok** XIII, Váci út 15 [2 F1]
*T 14 terminus directly outside;* **M3** *Lehel tér*
A garish-toy-ship of a building selling super-cheap fresh produce, flowers, olive oils and wines. *Open Mon–Fri 06.00–18.00, Sat 06.00–14.00, Sun 06.00–13.00.*

**Nagycsarnok** IX, Vámház körút 1–3 [4 F6]
*T 2, 47 and 49 stop directly outside*
The Big Market's art-nouveau styling, with patterned bricks and coloured ceramic roof tiles, was the work of architect Samu Pecz in 1897. It was designed as a sheltered area for traders, who previously sold their wares from beneath umbrellas on the Danube bank. When first constructed, the hall had an indoor canal running through it along which goods were delivered to the stalls. It's a privilege to shop beneath its girders.

On the ground and lower-ground floors are fresh produce (vegetables, meats of all shapes and sizes, chickens' feet, river fish mouthing furiously in cramped tanks), pickles, wines and spices, while upstairs are stalls selling Hungarian handicrafts. Prices are good by Hungarian standards and cheap by those of western Europe, and there is usually a little room for negotiation (a 10% reduction the limit). There are also some cheap and hearty *büfés*. One of the ground-floor stalls proudly displays a photo of Margaret Thatcher haggling over some paprika in 1984; the Iron Lady was the first foreign dignitary to visit the hall. Southern end of Váci utca. *Open Mon–Fri 06.00–18.00, Sat 06.00–14.00.*

## Flea markets

**Hasznalt cikk piac (Ecseri Flea Market)** XIX, Nagykőrösi út 156

*B 54 from Boráros tér to the Autópiac stop; M3 Határ út, then B 154*

Treasure hunters usually try the Ecseri Market, in a southeastern suburb (40 minutes by bus from the centre). The place comes alive on Saturday, when serious collectors mingle with tourists. The chance of finding an antique bargain is increasingly slight – traders have wised up and prices will no longer have you panting with excitement – but haggle and you might find yourself winning. There's a mixed porridge. Jeans and leather jackets starting at 6,000Ft fight for space with heaps of machine parts. There's a huge selection of furniture and you'll still find oddities like communist badges. *Open Mon–Fri 08.00–16.00, Sat 07.00–15.00.*

**Józsefvárosi piac** VIII, Kőbányai út 16 [4 16]

*T 28 from Blaha tér; B 9 from Deák tér*

Situated close to Kerepesi Cemetery, behind the yard of Józsefvárosi railway station, Józsefvárosi piac is known these days as the 'Chinese market' because of its Far Eastern vendors. The city's largest marketplace, the lines of stalls are endless. Sportswear is the primary focus. Every sign shows two prices – '*egy*' (one) and '*sok*' (many), the latter for bulk buying. You'll find rock-bottom prices, but also some strange spellings – stereos by 'Panasoanic' and trainers by 'Adiads'. Prick a keen ear for cries of '*Vigyázz!*' ('Look out!') from traders pushing sharp-edged trolleys. *Open Mon–Fri 06.00–18.00, Sat–Sun 06.00–16.00.*

**Kőbánya bazár** X, Maglódi út 18

*T 37, 28 from Blaha Lujza (Népszínház út) to Sibrik Miklós út*

If you're after electrical goods, take tram 28 almost to the end stop, and alight at what used to be known as the 'Russian market'. Many traders still travel here daily by bus from

## THE DEATH OF CRAFT

Budapest's artisans – workers taking pride in using their hands to make beautiful things or fix what's broken – are representatives of a declining species. Shoe menders, boot makers, zip and watch repairers, goldsmiths, engravers, milliners and ladies who stitch up ladders in stockings once crowded the backstreets of Budapest. No longer.

Traditional shoemaking was a thriving industry, but there are just a few exponents of the craft now. Lajos Pető is in his 60s, and makes fashion shoes for women with extra-small feet. His signboard on Wesselényi utca was first used by his father in the early 20th century, and still reads '*czipész*' (the old word for 'shoemaker'). His clients come from far and wide – he claims that no other shoemaker in Europe specialises in such teeny sizes (of 30 to 35).

Magdolna Szabó followed her father into the engraving profession, gaining her master's qualification in 1971. She too now works on Wesselényi utca. 'I make everything with my hands; I do not use machines, although more and more people in our trade do. It is a profession that follows the whole life circle – I make plaques for births, marriages and cremation urns,' she explained. Sadly, unless there is an increase in the appreciation of, and demand for, such traditional skills, the economic epitaph of artisans like Szabó will be etched into the ledger of the capital's history. If you've lost a lens from your specs or your fly gets stuck, consider visiting the artisans opposite:

**Spectacle repairs** (*látszerész*) V, Veres Pálné utca 7 (Libál Lajosné)

**Master goldsmith** (*ötvös mester*) VII, Wesselényi utca 11 (György Falk)

**Engraver master** (*vésnök mester*) VII, Wesselényi utca 11 (Magdolna Szabó)

**Stocking repairs** (*szemfelszedő*) V, Kamermayer Károly tér (with huge plants in the window)

**Umbrella maker** (*ernyős*), V, Vitkovics Mihály utca 10

**Shoemaker** (*czipész*) VII, Károly körút 3 (István Priska)

**Watch and clock repairs** (*órás*) V, Ferenciek tere 5 (the sign on the door reads 'We do not repair quartz watches! We don't stock batteries either!') or VIII, Bródy Sándor utca 22 (Tibor Feig)

**Zipper, shoe, lock repairs** (*cipzár csere, cipő javító, lakatos* ) XIII, Pozsonyi út 35

**Locksmith** (*lakatos*) XIII, Csanády utca 16 (József Horváth and son) Also mend window blinds and mosquito nets!

**Piano repairers** (*zongora javító mester*) IX, Mester utca 5 (János Heigli and son)

**Baba Klinika** (doll and teddy-bear repairs) V, Múzseum körút 5. Also does leather working.

**Furrier** (*szűcs*) XIII, Pozsonyi út 13 (Ica Nagy) Cleaning, dying and repairing of leather and fur. (Fur is very popular among elderly women in Hungary in winter.)

Slovakia, Ukraine, Romania and Croatia. At one time, the market was a good source of unusual bric-a-brac from Russia and Ukraine, but these days training shoes and tools predominate. *Open Mon–Fri 07.00–17.00, Sat–Sun 07.00–16.00.*

**Novák piac** VIII/XIV (district border line), Dózsa György út [2 I4]

M2 *Keleti, then 5-minute walk up Verseny utca, behind the station*

Probably the best place in Budapest for bargain tat. Go at the weekend for the best atmosphere, when everyone enjoys numerous cups of *nagyfröccs* (white wine and soda) – and is generally three sheets to the wind by lunchtime! In the shade of the Puskás Stadion. *Open Mon–Fri 07.00–18.00, Sat–Sun 06.00–18.00.*

**Petőfi Csarnok** XIV, Zichy Mihály út 14, Városliget [2 J2]

M1 *to Széchenyi fürdő*

A little flea market in City Park, where hobbyists, collectors and traders gather at weekends. *Open Sat–Sun 07.00–14.00.*

## NEWSPAPERS, BOOKS AND MAPS

**Bestsellers** V, Október 6 utca 11; tel: 1 312 1295; www.bestsellers.hu [1 E4]

One of the city's best English-language bookshops, stocking a range of general-interest titles, academic books, international newspapers and lifestyle magazines. The staff can order books in for no additional charge. *Open Mon–Fri 09.00–18.30.*

**Bibliotéka Antikvárium** VI, Andrássy út 2; tel: 1 475 0240, 1 331 5132; www.bibliotekaantikvarium.hu [2 F4]

Housed in a lovely 19th-century building – with staggered corner balconies piled above the entrance and topped with dragon statuettes – this shop sells a fair selection of English-language publications among its antique and second-hand collection. *Open Mon–Fri 10.00–18.00, Sat 09.00–13.00.*

**Cartographia Map and Globe Shop (I and II)** VI, Bajcsy-Zsilinszky út 37; tel/fax: 1 312 6001 *and* XIV, Bosnyák tér 5; tel: 1 221 4407; www.cartographia.hu [2 F3]
Two stores stocking national and international maps and globes by Hungary's leading cartographic company. A detailed street map of Budapest costs around 630Ft. *Open Mon–Thu 09.00–18.00, Fri 09.00–17.00.*

**Freytag and Berndt** V, Kálvin tér 5; tel: 1 318 5844; email: bolt@freytagbrendt.hu [4 F6]
Travel bookshop. *Open Mon–Fri 10.00–18.30, Sat 10.00–13.00.*

**Hungaro Press** V, Városház utca 3–5 [4 F5]
Magazine and newspaper shop with an excellent choice of international daily, weekly and monthly publications. European weeklies and American newspapers sit alongside a full range of English broadsheet and tabloid dailies, available – oh, sweet contemporaneousness – on their day of publication. Of course, you'll pay handsomely to be up to speed (as much as 1,600Ft). *Open Mon–Fri 07.00–19.00, Sat 07.00–16.00, Sun 07.00–14.00.*

**Könyvesbolt** VI, Liszt Ferenc tér 9 [2 F3]
Fair selection of books in English. *Open Mon–Fri 10.00–18.00, Sat 10.00–13.00.*

**Központi Antikvárium** V, Múzeum körút 13; tel: 1 317 3514 [4 F5]
One of the largest and best-regarded antique bookshops in the city. English-language, as well as Hungarian, books. *Mon–Fri 10.00–18.00, Sat 10.00–13.00.*

**Oxford University Press Könyvesbolt** V, Gerlóczy utca 7; tel: 1 318 8633 [4 F5]
OUP publications, including academic and fiction. *Open Mon–Fri 09.00–17.00.*

## PORCELAIN, POTTERY AND GLASS

**Ajka Kristály** XIII, Szent István körút 18; tel: 1 340 5083 and V, József Attila út 7; tel: 1 317 8133 [1 E2]

Elegant, extraordinarily detailed, hand-crafted, lead-crystal drinking glasses, vases and table centrepieces. *Open Mon–Fri 10.00–18.00, Sat 10.00–13.00.*

**Art-Agora** I, Országház utca 15; mobile: 06 120 365 4413 [1 B3]

Small glass shop in the Castle District that sells patterned, coloured glass – goblets, vases, wine, champagne and shot glasses. *Open 09.00–19.00 daily.*

**Herend Porcelain** V, József nádor tér 11; tel: 1 317 2622 [1 E4]

Beautiful examples of Herend porcelain; you'll part with some cash and walk away with a delicate treasure. *Open Mon–Fri 10.00–18.00, Sat 10.00–13.00.*

**Herend Village Pottery**; II, Bem rakpart 37; tel: 1 356 7899 [1 C3]

Squashed beneath a block of flats between Bem rakpart and Fő utca, this store sells hand-painted Hungarian majolica from the Herend factory. It specialises in the more 'rustic' – rather than refined – pieces. *Open Tue–Fri 09.00–17.00, Sat 09.00–12.00, closed Sun and Mon.*

**Zsolnay** V, Kígyó utca 4; tel: 318 3712 [3 E5]

An array of hand-made Zsolnay pieces, including vases, plates, cups and saucers. The unique reflective design may be a little 'bling' for some, but there are less extravagant bits to be unearthed. *Open Mon–Fri 10.00–18.00, Sat 10.00–13.00.*

## SHOPPING MALLS

These enormous, self-contained centres are stuffed with the usual high-street outlets selling clothes, electrical goods, mobile phones and books, as well as cafés, restaurants, bars and multi-screen cinemas. Popular with young Budapesters, the shopping malls keep their own hours and often open at weekends and late into the evenings to accommodate the film-goers, eaters and drinkers.

**Mammut** II, Lövőház utca 2–6; info tel: 1 345 8020; www.mammut.hu [1 B2]
Just off Moskva tér, Mammut is a beast, comprising two buildings (I and II) that straddle Lövőház utca and are connected by a walkway. Alongside the shops, you'll find a cinema, bowling alley, tonnes of trendy bars and a nightclub. *Shops open 10.00–19.00 daily; bars often open until 04.00 at weekends.*

**MOM Park** XII, Alkotás út 53; tel: 1 487 5501; www.mompark.hu [3 B5]
The city's newest complex provides a calmer shopping experience than some of its rivals. There is a fitness centre here, as well as Budapest's first Virgin megastore. *Open Mon–Sat 07.00–24.00, Sun 08.00–24.00.*

**Rózsakert** II, Gábor Áron utca 74–78; tel: 1 391 5998
Smart, glass-fronted shopping mall in a residential area of Buda, containing all the usual shopping suspects, and numerous restaurants (including a sushi bar), a post office, a beauty salon and a medical centre (see page 62). *Open Mon–Fri 10.00–20.00, Sat 10.00–19.00, Sun 10.00–16.00 (restaurants until 22.00 daily).*

**Westend City Center** VI, Váci út 1–3; www.westend.hu [2 F2]
Style-conscious locals flit about central Europe's biggest shopping mall, which contains 400 shops, 40 cafés and restaurants, a cinema, a hotel and a 3ha roof garden. A sign at the entrance asks you not to eat ice-cream or bring bombs into the precinct. *Shops open Mon–Sat 10.00–20.00, Sun 10.00–18.00.*

## SMOKES

**Cigar Towers** V, Erzsébet tér 7–8; tel: 1 266 0945 [1 E4] A cigar-shaped smoker's paradise, where you can pick up a decent stinker. Expert staff can offer advice. *Open Mon–Fri 10.00–18.00, Sat 10.00–15.00.*

# Baths and Sport 9

## BATHS

A British novel was once much derided for its description of love's 'liquid nolses'. Well, there may be no shoreline, but the sounds of Hungarian passion are those of splashing and soaking and dripping and gulping, all liquid noises with bells on. The nation has Olympic swimming and water-polo champions, a reverence for wines and beers, and pensioners who spend their days sitting in mineral baths. Hungary is afloat on a hot reservoir of water that breaks the surface through natural springs and drilled wells. The thermal water absorbs minerals from the earth's crust, and the Ministry of Health has recognised the medicinal properties of 50 of the country's baths. Budapest itself stands on a fault line dividing the Buda hills from the Great Plain; three million litres emerge daily, feeding around 40 baths and seasonal pools, 15 with medicinal ranking. It is surely unique among the world's capitals in offering such a plethora of places for warming wallows.

### History

The **Romans** were the first to take advantage of Hungary's hot springs in any sophisticated sense. There were 14 baths in Budapest alone. Aquincum holds stretches of an aqueduct that channelled spring waters from the hills, and the central military complex at Florian tér is the largest of the country's 21 Roman baths. Many centuries later, Buda became Hungary's courtly centre and a bathing culture bloomed once more. Zsigmond built the Imre Bath (today called Rác fürdő) in the 15th century, and Matthias even added a corridor linking them to the palace. However, it was the Turks who constructed a baths network. They blended Roman bathing traditions with their own, and remains of these bathhouses – with main halls and pools – are the period's noticeable surviving monuments. Eight were recorded by a 17th-century English traveller, and of these the Császár, Király and Rudas still stand.

Advances in engineering and the development of '**balneology**' (the science of medicinal waters) provided fresh impetus in the 19th century. Baths were built or renovated by some of the country's greatest architects. In 1937 Budapest received the official title 'Bath Town/Spa City' from the first International Balneological Congress. In the aftermath of World War II, many were subsumed into the social-security system and rendered dull by socialist-style renovation. However, Hungary embarked on a huge programme in the '60s and '70s to develop hotels offering facilities focused around medicinal water. In the past ten years, therapies have come to include gymnastics, massage and electrotherapy, but healing waters remain the mainstay in this natural approach to treatment. In addition, there are numerous (usually seasonal) outdoor pools (*strand*), which are particularly popular on steamy summer days. While some of these have medicinal waters, and are occasionally linked to hotels or day-time hospitals, they are more properly areas for relaxation and recreation.

## Therapy

The medicinal spring waters are usually over 30°C (although there are a few outdoor medicinal baths that are cooler), and contain a range of minerals. **Spa**

**treatments** are recommended for those suffering from arthritic and rheumatic pain (muscle tension, aches), blood-circulation or breathing difficulties, for those requiring injury rehabilitation, and those with chronic gynaecological problems or certain skin conditions. And some baths have drinking halls where you can swallow as well as wallow (see box, pages 218–19).

Visitors can choose how they approach these soups of minerals. Some just enjoy spending a few hours sitting in the regenerative waters and enjoying their warmth. Others take advantage of the packages available at thermal hotels (see below). Treatments beyond general dips in the pools or tubs, or refreshing massages (such as mud or weight baths, healing massages, etc) require a medical referral. Hungarians receive prescriptions from specialised physicians, and they pay a small fee to the cashier (subsidised under the country's social-security system). However, professional bath physicians on site provide consultations for other visitors (for a charge).

Besides the public bathing complexes, there are also **hotels** offering treatment packages. These divide into two types – thermal hotels (*gyógyszálló*) and 'wellness' hotels, which cater for the modern interest in health tourism. Thermal hotels are based at the sites of thermal springs, and have spa therapy centres. They provide traditional Hungarian remedies, and have tended to cater to the older market; however, most offer fitness centres and other 'luxuries', and are increasingly attracting a younger crowd. In Budapest, you can choose from the Gellért, Margitsziget, Helia or Corinthia Aquincum hotels (see pages 108, 107 and 101). While wellness hotels are generally located in spa cities, they have neither on-site

## *BEAUTY IN A BUDAPEST BATH*

*Edith Pearlman*

My bath – I think of it as mine, though I always share it with at least 30 strangers – is for women only. That for men is on the other side of the clamorous hall of the Gellért Baths. A yellow-paned skylight allows beams to stream down into the seraglio-without-a-sultan. It doesn't really flatter, but this is not a beauty parlour or a convent for nudists. It is instead an allegory. At Tettuccio, a pump room at Montecatini Terme in Tuscany, painted tiles represent the stages of life. At the Gellért Baths there is no need for representations. Life's stages are here in the naked flesh.

There are the Old, breasts lying like envelope flaps against chests. Proud and unsmiling, these embodiments of La Vecchiaia rest their respected heads against the rim of the pool. The Mature, slightly younger than the Old, are not so bent of back. La Forza – strong, in the middle of the journey – are ample of hip and generous of bosom. They sometimes talk to one another in the water, but their exchanges are not secrets. Conversations do echo in the ceramic chamber, so gossip has to be restrained. And anyway, the baths are meditative places. The youngest women – they do chatter a bit – come late in the day, after work and before parties. They cast off their skimpy clothing and sweep their abundant hair into shower caps.

And the water is warm. One half-moon pool is 36°C, the other 38. We are all in this balm together: the Old, the Mature, the Strong, the Young. The Beautiful? That adjective belongs to everyone. The nubile bodies are arousing, as Nature meant them to be for Her impersonal purpose. The broader bodies are confident, the mature ones promise compassion, and the old are models for perseverance and resilience. They have been tried by life; life has declared them qualified to continue. They give a new meaning to the word 'fit'.

As I leave the warm pool to try the warmer one, I pause on the tiled area between the waters. I am naked and dripping. At home, I know myself to be shamefully saggy – an ambler through life who has never quickened her pace. But here – high on skin, warmth, moisture and the blessed absence of a Trainer – I glory in my flesh, in our flesh. We are not touching, but we are together nonetheless, one body, Body itself: its idea and its promise and its memory. We bathe shoulders, breast, bellies and feet. We think of motherhood, childhood, toil and love; we think of anything we damn well please. The old see what they once were. The young see what – if they are lucky – they will become.

*An abridged version of an article that appeared originally in* The New York Times medicinal waters nor medical centres. Instead they represent non-medical health retreats, where the focus is upon the promotion of well being through pampering and exercise.

## Baths and the bathing experience

A decade or so ago, **thermal baths** were primarily frequented by the mature lady or gent; however, these days you'll find wrinkled palms among younger Budapesters too. Indeed, the pools in some ways fulfil the same function as coffee houses, allowing people to gather, chat and relax.

Thermal baths are very different from recreational swimming pools. Some have the forbidding aspect of a sanatorium, with white tiles and staff in starched uniforms, while others have fabulous ornamentation, such as mosaics and fluted columns. Complexes usually comprise several pools or bathtubs, together with saunas or steam rooms. Bathing is often mixed, although some establishments offer same-sex bathing on different days of the week and the Gellért has different pools. You will be provided with a **changing cabin or a locker** (for extra security, the locker number differs from the tag you are issued with – the tag number is chalked on the inside of the locker door – so be sure to memorise the locker number itself), and sometimes a bathrobe on getting changed. **Swimming costumes** are usually worn (you can hire a costume or towel if you have come without) – although same-sex pools may allow nude bathing, and men are issued with aprons at baths like the Rudas and Rác. You will on occasions be required to don a **swimming cap**. The medicinal pools are peaceful places for sitting and soaking. There is usually a **swimming**

**pool** on the same site, however, for those of a more energetic disposition.

It is generally recommended that you spend 20–30 minutes in the **medicinal pools**, depending upon the concentration of the minerals. For the purposes of healing, regular visits are important. Doctors provide patients with prescriptions, and Hungarians receive state-subsidised discounts for up to two courses of 15 visits. Without a doctor's prescription, visitors cannot receive specialised treatments beyond healing massages and bathing; as a tourist, you'll need to join the queue of those with prescriptions to arrange a consultation with the **on-site physicians**. Those who receive treatment will often be expected to **tip** 'gate keepers'. If you are simply taking a dip in the baths, tip the locker *néni* about 50Ft; masseurs make little in wages, and should be tipped 200Ft or so. Beware, though, that queues to buy tickets can be long because patients with social-security referrals often use the same entrance as 'temporary' visitors. Cashiers rarely speak English.

Where the entrance price to the baths exceeds 1,000Ft, there may be a graded system of **refund** whereby a certain portion of money is returned if the visitor leaves within four hours. Note that children can only use recreational facilities, such as swimming pools, and are prohibited from the medicinal pools.

## *Buda*

**Csillaghegy** III, Pusztakúti út 3; tel: 1 250 1533
HEV *Csillaghegy*

'Star Hill' is the oldest *strand*, or open-air lido complex, in Budapest, fed by a karst-water spring and situated on the side of a hill in northern Buda. The swimming (24°C) and lido

(22°C) pools are found on the first terraced level near all the *büfé* stalls, while the children's paddling pool (28°C) and the grassy sun terrace are situated on the upper level. The main

## THE MINERAL WATER STORY

### A bit of bottle

Hungarians do not just sit in the life-enhancing mineral springs that bubble beneath them – they also sometimes drink them. Twenty-one are bottled nationwide, and four in Budapest itself (Apenta, Óbudai Gyémánt, Margitszigeti Kristályvíz and Gellérthegyi Kristályvíz). Of course, Magyars generally prefer beer and wine, but they still get through an average of 50 litres of mineral water a year. There are strict rules governing the sale of mineral water; it must be bottled at source, cannot be treated (beyond removing excess iron), and must have a minimum mineral content of 1000mg/litre. Check the label – if a bottle reads '*asványi anyaggal dúsított*' (enhanced with minerals), you'll be paying good money for purified tap water.

### At smelly source

Mineral-water aficionados or those with health problems should head for drinking halls (*ivócsarnok*), where they can taste the water at its warm and sulphurous source. It's an acquired taste, like drinking a stink bomb; pinch your nose and toss it quickly down your throat. Some find that chilling the pool remains open in winter, covered by a tented roof. Adult 1,000Ft, concessions 800Ft. *Swimming pool open daily 07.00–19.00 (May 1–Sep 15), Mon–Fri 06.00–19.00, Sat*

water makes it more bearable.

The **Rudas ivócsarnok** (beneath Erzsébet híd, on the Buda side) sells glasses for 25Ft; the marble-lined hall is filled with pensioners supping *korsós* (half-litre mugs) and chatting as if they were down at the pub. The Rudas offers three of the mildly radioactive waters: Hungária is good for stomach and kidney problems, water from the Attila spring helps those with bronchial, stomach, intestinal, gall-bladder and liver ailments, while Juventus is good for high blood pressure, rheumatism and even premature ageing!

The **Lukács Baths** have a drinking market set in a stylish stone structure near the entrance. The water is effective for treating stomach and kidney problems. At the southern side of the **Széchenyi Baths** you'll find an *ivócsarnok* in an elegant pavilion (built in 2003) called the 'Szent István forrás' (spring). A *korsó* costs just 18Ft, and reputedly assists with nervous stomach problems, chronic gall-bladder disorders and inflammation of the kidneys.

A new addition to the family of curative waters gushes outside the **Dagály Baths** from the mouth of a gargoyle named 'Well of Peace'. A group of elderly men surrounds the fountain, one by one filling plastic bottles from the steaming pipe. 'My wife drinks this water every day,' says one, 'and the best thing is it's free.'

*06.00–16.00, Sun 06.00–12.00 (Sep 16–Apr 30); lido pool open daily 07.00–19.00 (May 1–Sep 15).*

**Gellért Baths** (*Gellért fürdő*) XI Budapest, Kelenhegyi út 4–6; tel: 1 466 6166 [3 E7]

T *18, 19, 47, 49*

Here, one feels, a decadent of ancient Rome could draw contented breath, cast off toga and sandals, and plunge in with a hearty 'Carpe diem!' The domed entrance hall, frescoed ceilings, neo-Romanesque columns and spouting gargoyles ooze opulence; a visit here is as much about gawping as soaking. There is a pool for mixed bathing, as well as separate areas for men and women – where you can choose between your moon and your costume. Outside is a summer terrace and pool replete with vigorous wave machine. Guests of the adjacent Gellért Hotel may use the baths gratis. Entrance 2,200Ft/2,700Ft (with locker/cubicle), with reduced afternoon rates (1,600Ft/1,800Ft after 17.00); discount with Budapest Card. A sliding refund is paid on stays of under 4 hours – retain the coupon issued as you enter and collect your refund from the cash desk on leaving (ensure you ask for this – the notoriously unhelpful staff here tend to 'forget'). *High season (May 1–Sep 30) indoor and outdoor pools open 06.00–19.00 daily, and Fri–Sat 20.00–24.00 (Jun 13–Aug 16); low season (Oct 1–Apr 30) indoor pools open Mon–Fri 06.00–19.00, Sat–Sun 06.00–17.00.*

**Király Baths** (*Király gyógyfürdő*) II, Fő utca 82–86; tel: 1 201 4392 [1 C2]

B *60, 86*

Set back slightly from the road, its green cupolas like a pair of helmeted soldiers peeking over a wall, the Király (King) Baths date to the 16th century. Some swear that bathing here is a mystical experience. The baths are certainly the most atmospheric of any in the country, with lowly shafts of daylight from the original Turkish dome casting a murky, steamy haze. Open to men or women only on alternate days, visitors may go 'full monty' if they wish. Be aware that the baths are popular with gays and lesbians; there'll be some harmless strutting on male days, although the women tend to be middle-aged and matronly, and less inclined to pose. There are just two warm indoor pools, with a dry and wet steam room and saunas (under the smaller dome). The main pool is on the cosy side, so it is best visited on weekdays to avoid the crowds. Tickets are sold in 1½-hour slots. On purchasing your ticket, go upstairs and take a bath towel from one of the uniformed staff members. Choose a cabin along one of the long corridors; ensure that you return within 90 minutes or you will be charged extra. The shower facilities are next to the pool, under the second dome, and so it is probably worth taking your shampoo and soap with you on heading down to the baths. Adult 1,100Ft, no concessions; children prohibited. *Open Mon, Wed and Fri 07.00–18.00 (for women), Tue, Thu and Sat 09.00–20.00 (for men), closed Sun.*

**Lukács Baths** (*Lukács gyógyfürdő*) II, Frankel Leó út 25–29; tel: 1 326 1695 [1 C1]
T *4, 6, 17;* B *6, 60, 86*

The Lukács Baths is the elegant watering hole of the Buda literati. Facilities include eight pools – among them a fancy whirlpool and weight baths – a roof-top sunbathing terrace and mineral drinking cures. There is separate bathing for men and women. Thermal baths adult 1,400–1,600Ft, swimming pool adult 1,400–1,600Ft, with sliding discounts and cheaper entrance in the later afternoon. Close to the bridgehead of Margit híd. *Open daily 06.00–19.00 (some facilities shorter hours at weekends). Mud and weight baths open Tue, Thu and Sat for men, Mon, Wed and Fri for women.*

**Rác Baths** (*Rác fürdő*) I, Hadnagy utca 8–10; tel: 1 356 1322 [3 D6]

Named after the Serbian population that occupied the Tabán during the 18th century, the building was reconstructed in 1869 by Miklós Ybl, and only a stone pool remains of the original complex established here by the Turks. The baths will re-open after their makeover in 2005, and will (as before) receive men and women on alternate days. A popular meeting place for homosexuals. Entrance costs not yet published. *From 2005: open (women) Mon, Wed, Fri 06.30–19.00; (men) Tue, Thu, Sat 06.30–19.00.*

**Római Strandfürdő** III, Rozgonyi Piroska utca 2; tel: 1 388 9740
HEV *Római fürdő*
There used to be a Roman bath here. The water is 22°C – chilly compared with many of the other baths in town. The long-haired must wear swimming caps. There are saunas, slides and outdoor pools. Modern and well equipped. Adult 1,400–1,800Ft, concessions 1,200Ft; adult with changing cubicle 1,800Ft. *Open 09.00–20.00 daily (summer only).*

**Rudas Baths** (*Rudas gyógyfürdő*) XI, Döbrentei tér 9; tel: 1 375 8373 [3 D6]
Constructed by the Turks in the mid-16th century, the Rudas has an octagonal thermal pool and turquoise cupola, and is open only to men (who are issued with aprons to spare blushes). It is the favourite of many of the city's male bathers. This is a forthright gay cruising zone, and new arrivals may experience a friendly grapple under the water. The indoor swimming pool is open to members of both sexes. Immediately to the south of Erzsébet Bridge. Thermal baths 1,000Ft (no concessions); swimming pool adult 700Ft, concessions 600Ft (with cabin 1,000Ft); massages from 1,500Ft. *Open Mon–Fri 06.00–20.00 (swimming pool 06.00–18.00), Sat and Sun 06.00–13.00.* Note that the thermal pools are closed for renovation until 2005, although the swimming pool should be open sooner.

## Pest

**Dagály Baths and Strand** (*fürdő és strand*) XIII, Népfürdő utca 36; tel: 1 452 4500
T *1 to Árpád híd;* M3 *Árpád híd, then short walk up Váci út and left along Dagály utca*
A marvellous *strand*-lido complex in the working-class district of Angyalföld (Angel Land) in northern Pest. Open all year, the smaller swimming pool is covered in winter, but the outdoor Olympic-length pool is heated and you can do lengths in December with the snow falling gently on your bathing cap. The thermal pool also stays open in all seasons; sit in the eggy water at dusk on a cold autumn evening and watch the steam rise through the surrounding pine trees. There's also a curling fun slide and massive communal saunas. A real Magyar experience. Adult 1,400Ft, concessions 1,200Ft. *Open daily 6.00–19.00.*

**Széchenyi Baths** (*Széchenyi gyógyfürdő*) XIV, Állatkerti körút 11; tel: 1 363 3210; www.szechenyifurdo.hu [2 H1]
Opposite the circus in City Park is the mustard-yellow, neo-baroque edifice housing one of Europe's largest spa complexes. Built in 1913, the sitting-pools are based in enormous halls, suggestive of the Roman bathing culture, while steam rooms and cold-water tubs draw on Turkish and Nordic traditions. There are 9 pools in total, all of which (including those outside) are open all year. Prepare for hot, hot water, and bathers playing chess on floating boards. The daytime hospital at the back of the complex offers treatments, including drinking cures and Finnish saunas. Head for the entrance facing the circus – it doesn't accept those with medical referrals, and you are less likely to become caught up in queues. Cheaper and less intimidating than the Gellért Baths. Adult 1,900–2,200Ft, sliding refunds and reduced entry fees from 15.00 onwards (make sure you ask on leaving). *Open 06.00–19.00 daily (May–Sep), Mon–Fri 06.00–19.00, Sat–Sun 06.00–17.00 (Oct–Apr).*

## *Margaret Island*

**Palatínus Strand** XIII, Margit-sziget; tel: 1 966 6453
The biggest open-air lido complex in the capital, with numerous pools, waterslides and bathing areas, as well as fountains and snack shacks. Adult 1,400–1,800Ft, concessions 1,200–1,600Ft; discount after 17.00 or with Budapest Card. *Open daily 08.00-19.00 (May 1–Aug 20), daily 10.00–18.00 (Aug 21–end of season).*

## *Beyond*

**Visegrád-Lepence Baths** (*strandfürdő*) H-2025 Visegrád-Lepence; tel: 26 398208; www.castrum-visegrad.hu
*Yellow Volán bus from Árpád híd bus station, on the Esztergom route*
Pedants will doubtless point out that Lepence fürdő is actually outside Budapest – 42km outside, to be exact – and beyond the remit of this book. Well, a fat raspberry to them all. Set in woods at the point where the Danube breaks through the Börzsöny and Visegrád hills in a sharp bend, this is a fabulous complex at one of the country's most picturesque points. Adult day ticket 1,100Ft, concessions 750Ft; morning or afternoon ticket 500Ft. *Open daily 06.00–08.00 (morning swim), 09.00–18.30 (day swim) and 16.00–18.30 (afternoon swim) (May 1–Sep 30).*

# SPORT

Hungary has no preening, globally recognised sporting icon in the David Beckham mould, but the country actually punches above its weight on the sporting stage. At the 2004 Athens Olympics, the country finished in 13th place overall, with a highly respectable haul of 18 medals.

For offices selling **tickets** to sporting events, see page 174.

## Football

Football is the country's favourite game, and Hungary was once a round-ball heavyweight. Between 1950 and 1954, under the leadership of Ferenc Puskás, the national team went unbeaten; its most heralded victory came when pummelling England 6–3 during a friendly at Wembley in 1953. This is now but a distant 1950s memory, a sepia-tinted time of pig-skin balls and long shorts. Poor funding and financial problems have crippled the sport to such an extent that Hungary hasn't qualified for the World Cup for over 20 years. The most-successful club side is Budapest's Ferencváros, who play at the FTC Stadium (IX, Üllői út 129; see www.ftc.hu for information on fixtures).

## Hungarian Grand Prix

Undoubtedly the biggest event in the sporting calendar, the annual Hungarian Grand Prix is held at the Hungaroring racetrack 20km northeast of the capital in Mogyoród. The second week of August sees an invasion of F1-lovers and an astronomic hike in hotel and restaurant prices. If the latter doesn't put you off, log on to www.hungaroring.hu for ticket and visiting details.

## Budapest Marathon

The annual marathon (on October 3) starts and finishes in Heroes' Square; if you don't mind the blisters and dehydration, it actually provides an excellent sightseeing circuit of the city. Alternatively you can relax among the spectators lining the streets and enjoy the sight of dehydrated people with blisters. See www.budapestmarathon.com for information.

## Swimming and watersports

Hungary has made quite a splash in the international pool. The country's most-successful individual athlete of all time is swimmer Krisztina Egerszegi, who won gold and silver medals in Seoul, becoming the youngest-ever Olympic champion at just 14 years of age (and a delicate 41kg in weight). She added three further golds to her display case at the 1992 Barcelona Games. The water-polo team has dominated the world, winning gold in every one of the last eight Olympics. (Incidentally, did you know that water-polo players throw the ball at 80km/h?) If you're looking for a proper swim rather than a thermal soak, try one of the following. In addition, several sports centres (see opposite) have swimming pools.

**Császár Komjádi Swimming Pool** (*uszoda*) II, Árpád fejedelem útja 8; tel: 1 326 1478 [1 C1] T *17*; B *6, 60, 86*

Once a medicinal bathing institution, dating originally to the Turkish era, restored in classicist style and famous for its social jamborees, this is now a complex of three swimming pools favoured by professional competitors. It famously hosted the first European swimming, diving and water-polo championships in 1926. Adult 800Ft, concessions 500Ft. *Open Mon–Sat 06.00–21.00, Sun 06.00–19.00.*

**Hajós Alfréd National Sports Swimming Pool** (*Nemzeti Sportuszoda*) XIII, Margit-sziget; tel: 1 340 4946 [1 D1]
A belly flop from Margit híd, this specialist pool is named after Hungary's first swimming Olympic gold medallist and respected architect, and hosted the European Water-Polo Champs in 2001. One indoor and two outdoor pools (the latter May–Sep only). Admission from 600Ft. *Open daily 06.00–19.00.*

## Sport centres

**Lido Sports Centre** III, Nánási út 67; tel: 1 242 4479
Well-equipped, modern fitness centre located on the Római part on the Buda bank. Facilities include an indoor swimming pool, whirlpool, sauna, five air-conditioned squash courts, two tennis courts, a fitness suite and a gym. *Open 07.00–23.00 daily.*

**MOM Wellness Center** XII, Alkotás út 53; tel: 1487 5600; www.mom-wellness.hu [3 B5]
Massive fitness emporium with two aerobics studios, an indoor swimming pool and state-of-the-art gym. *Open Mon–Fri 06.00–22.00, Sat–Sun 09.00–20.00.*

## Squash and tennis

**City Squash and Fitness** II, Marcibányi tér 13; tel: 1 325 0082; www.squashtec.hu [1 B2]
Eight squash courts, a fitness centre and gym. Squash courts 2,000–4,000Ft/hour, fitness centre 1,200Ft/daily ticket. *Open Mon–Fri 07.00–22.00, Sat–Sun 09.00–21.00.*

**Margaret Island Tennis Club** (*Margitszigeti Teniszpályak*) Tel: 1 340 4484
Eight outdoor, well-cared-for clay courts on the southeastern side of Margaret Island. Courts 500–1,800Ft/hour. *Open 07.00–22.00 daily.*

**Match-point Tennis Club** II, Marcibányi tér 13; tel: 1 214 5433; www.matchpoint.hu [1 B2]
Numerous covered courts, next to City Squash (see previous page). Courts from 1,500Ft/hour. *Open daily 08.00–21.00.*

**Park Teniszklub** I, Bartók Béla út 63–65; tel: 1 209 1595; email: info@parktenisz.hu; www.parktenisz.hu [3 D8]
Near Feneketlen-tó; 13 clay tennis courts. Costs 900–1,500Ft/hour in summer, and double that in winter (heating expenses). *Open all year daily 06.00–22.00.*

## Horse riding and racing

There's a strong historic link between Hungarians and horses. Their ancestors were admired as accomplished horsemen; the *kocsi* (horse-drawn coach) was a Magyar invention. If your interests are equestrian, you're in the right country.

**Kincsem Park Galopp-pálya** X, Albertirsai út 2, tel: 1 263 7818 [2 J4]
M2 *Pillangó utca*
If you'd rather watch than participate – a horse, after all, is dangerous at both ends and uncomfortable in the middle – there is horse racing and trotting (where riders sit in a two-wheeled buggy) at Kincsem Park, near the big Hungexpo site east of Kerepesi Cemetery. Of course, your wallet may end up frayed at both ends and empty in the middle, but you'll be able to sit down without wincing.

**Petneházy Horse Centre and Hussar Inn** II, Feketefej utca 2–4; tel: 1 397 5048; email: petnehazy-lovascentrum@matavnet.hu; www.mediaguide.hu/petnehazy
A horse centre and guesthouse in the hilly second district. Lessons for beginners from

1,200Ft/25 minutes; cross-country programmes for advanced riders from 3,000Ft/hour; pony rides for kids from 700Ft/15 minutes. The summer horse shows are also worth catching – check the website for details.

## Cycling

Budapest has 140km of marked cycle paths. There are pleasant rides along the banks of the Danube, around Margaret Island or into the Buda hills; grab a copy of the excellent *Biking in Budapest* (1:60,000) map, available free from Tourinform offices. For an additional charge, bikes can be taken aboard the suburban, state, cogwheel and children's railways. Hotels sometimes offer bikes for rent; alternatively, try:

**Charles Rent a Bike** I, Hegyalja út 23; tel: 1 202 3414 [3 C6]

**Palatinus Strand** XIII, Margaret Island; tel: 1 966 6453
From 600Ft/hour

**Yellow Zebra** V, Sütő utca 2; tel: 1 266 8777; email: yellowzebrabikes@yahoo.com [3 E5]
Costs 3,000Ft/1 day and 5,000Ft/2 days, along with a 20,000Ft deposit.

The **X-Factor** in MOM Park (XIII, Alkotás utca 53; tel: 1 487 5606; email: x-factormom@hu.inter.net [3 B5]) is a bicycle-repair shop.

## Fishing

You'll see many anglers on the Danube banks. For information, contact the **Anglers' Union Budapest Association** (*Horgászegyesületek Budapest Szövetsége*) at V, Galamb utca 3; tel 1 318 5472 or 1 486 1602 [3 E5]. Alternatively, the portal http://horgasz.lap.hu is a starting page with links to many fishing sites.

## Other sports

**Bobpálya** XI, Balatoni út 7; tel: 1 310 4122

*Take the 7 road leading out of Budapest to Balaton, and the course is on the left*

A dry bobsleighing course for the kids. *Open daily 11.00–16.00 (Apr–Sep).*

**Buda-Ring GoKarting** XI, Floracoop, Budaörsi út; tel: 06 30 311 9856

Go-karting track next to the main highway to Vienna. Adult 2,000Ft/8mins, child 1,500Ft/8mins. *Open Mon–Fri 14.00–22.00, Sat–Sun 10.00–22.00.*

**Canoe and Kayak hire** III, Római-part 29; tel: 06 20 943 6521/06 30 257 7457

**Lido Bowling Club** III, Nánási út 67; tel: 1 242 1937

New 6-lane 10-pin bowling alley and bar just off the Római-Part. Open 12.00–24.00 daily.

**Wakeboarding** XIII, Hajógyári-sziget; tel: 06 20 9228 328

Similar to waterskiing, you ride the wake as you're tugged around a ropeway circuit. For more information, log on to www.wakeboarder.hu/center_eng.htm.

# Discovering Buda

10

## CASTLE HILL

Castle Hill (Várhegy) rises 60m above the Danube, bears aloft the former royal palace, and is the master of the western bank. It is overpriced, often overcrowded, and a haunt for overbearing tour guides touting their services. However, visit at the right time of day (earlyish morning or lateish afternoon) and in a patient frame of mind, and this World Heritage Site's cobbled streets and baroque dwellings provide the backdrop for some of the city's most pleasant strolls and river views. The museums and galleries of Buda Castle Palace, the wonderfully extravagant Mátyás Church, and the natural caves running beneath also make this a short-break must-see.

Inhabited by humans since the early stages of pre-history, it was not until after the **Mongol invasion** of 1241–42 (see page 3) that Castle Hill was considered as a potential stronghold. King **Béla IV** (1235–70) resolved to protect his homeland; he moved the country's capital from Esztergom to Buda, and constructed a fort to the south of Castle Hill and a royal residence to the north, near Bécsi kapu. Citizens from the Víziváros and other vulnerable areas were moved to residences in a new burghers' town (the Castle District or Várnegyed) that occupied the remaining two-thirds of the hilltop, and which was surrounded by fortified walls.

Over the following centuries, a diverse community grew up around the hill's castle and churches. Hungarians were actually in a minority here; **Germans and other European traders** contributed to a community that flourished until the arrival of

CASTLE HILL
Bécsi kapu
National Archives
Church
Museum of Military History
Lutheran Church
Church of Mary Magdalene
FRANKLIN UTCA
DONÁTI UTCA
VÁM UTCA
ISKOLA UTCA
FŐ UTCA
Calvinist Church
BUDAI ALSÓ RAKPART
Danube
SZABÓ ILONKA UTCA
TOLDY FERENC UTCA
TÁNCSICS MIHÁLY UTCA
FORTUNA UTCA
IBOLYA UTCA
LOVAS ÚT
Museum of Commerce & Catering
Telephone Museum
Hilton Budapest
VÍZIVÁROS
ORSZÁGHÁZ UTCA
ÚRI UTCA
Mátyás Church
TÓTH ÁRPÁD SÉTÁNY
VÁR
LOGODI UTCA
HUNYADI JÁNOS ÚT
SZALAG UTCA
PONTY UTCA
BEM RAKPART
SZENTHÁROMSÁG UTCA
Fishermen's Bastion
BUGÁT U
French Institute
Vérmező
LOVAS ÚT
Golden Eagle Pharmacy Museum
TÁRNOK UTCA
ÚRI UTCA
Post office
KRISZTINAVÁROS
PALOTA ÚT
DÍSZ TÉR
National Dance Theatre
SZÉCHENYI LÁNCHÍD
MIKÓ UTCA
Sándor Palace
CLARK ÁDÁM TÉR
KRISZTINA KRT
PAULER UTCA
Police station
Funicular Railway
0km marker
SZT GYÖRGY UTCA
KUNY D UTCA
ATTILA ÚT
Post office
Szt György tér
Ludwig Museum
LÁNCHÍD UTCA
KOSCIUSZKO TADÉ UTCA
Krisztina Church
National Gallery
ALAGÚT UTCA
VARALJA UTCA
N
Bradt
Buda Castle Palace
PÁLYA UTCA
National Széchényi Library
History Museum
GELLÉRTHEGY UTCA
LISZNYAI UTCA
0 200m
0 200yds
DÓZSA GYÖRGY TÉR
© Bradt Travel Guides Ltd
University
MÉSZÁROS UTCA
ORVOS UTCA
KRISZTINA KRT
Semmelweis Museum
GYŐRI UTCA
NAPHEGY TÉR
LISZNYAI UTCA
DEREK UTCA
Sports Hospital
AVAR UTCA
NAPHEGY
TABÁN

the **Turks**. Of course, Castle Hill's fortifications did not deter conflict. There were over 30 sieges during subsequent centuries, and the district had to be rebuilt on numerous occasions. Following the **1686 siege** that drove the Turks from Buda, most of the houses were reconstructed over two (rather than the original three) storeys in baroque and Louis XVI styles by successive Habsburg rulers. Similarly, few buildings escaped unscathed after the last gasp of the German army here in 1945.

The **funicular railway** or cable car (*Budavári sikló*; open 07.30–22.00 daily, closed first and third Monday of month for maintenance; adult 500/400Ft uphill/downhill, concession 300Ft either direction) offers the most direct and sedate journey up Castle Hill, while also providing stunning views of Budapest. (Join the lowest of the carriage's compartments for the best of these.) It is accessed at the western side of Clark Ádám tér. There is also a **lift** running from Dózsa tér up to the palace complex, next to the Lions' Courtyard (same hours as Széchényi Library; see pages 316–17).

The '**Várbusz**' – a dinky little chap that bears a castle symbol rather than a number – runs from Moszkva tér to Dísz tér every six or seven minutes. Alternatively, bus 16 travels between Déak Ferenc tér on the Pest side and Dísz tér throughout most of the day.

Much of the Castle District is pedestrianised, and most **cars** can only drive as far as Dísz tér – via Palota út or the one-way Hunyadi János út – where you must park and disembark. Only authorised vehicles and hotel residents may enter via Bécsi kapu (Vienna Gate). Another option is to drive up below the Fishermen's Bastion and park on the street there. Drivers collect a ticket on entering the district and pay on leaving at a rate of 400Ft/hour. If you are staying in one of the hotels, the receptionist will stamp your card to allow you to exit through the barrier. Parking is free for guests at the Hilton, while the Kulturinnov charges a daily fee for the use of its car park (see page 115).

There are approaches from most sides for those with the energy to puff and pant up Castle Hill **on foot**. Several roads lead up to Bécsi kapu. Steeper flights of stone steps (*lépcső*) snake up the hill's eastern side and provide more taxing but ultimately rewarding routes to the top. One set finishes next to the upper station of the funicular railway, another at the Fishermen's Bastion; these can be picked up at various points on and around Hunyadi János út, including from Clark Ádám tér. Alternatively you can take a route up from Szarvas tér to the southern end of the hill, and there are further flights leading up the western slope.

## Walking around Castle Hill

### *The castle complex*

(For details of the palace itself, see pages 338–40. For the museums and galleries here, see pages 313–18.)

There are two points of access to the **Buda Castle Palace** complex (open 06.00–22.00 daily) in Szent György tér, near the upper terminal of the funicular railway. That immediately to the left – a black ornamental gate with an intricate stone-carved arch – is most striking for its fierce neighbour, a huge bronze ***turul*** (see box opposite) (Gyula Donáth, 1905). As it glares grumpily over the city from its prime perch, you'd be forgiven for thinking that it finds the view a little irksome.

### *THE TURUL*

This mythical bird, resembling an eagle, is said to have sired Árpád's father, Álmos, and thus brought forth the Árpád dynasty. It became a symbol of national identity during the millenary celebrations of 1896. The weapon in its talons is the sword of Attila. While elsewhere in the world he was about as popular as a garlic mouthwash, Attila became a heroic figure in Hungarian cultural consciousness during the 18th century because of theories of an ancestral link between the Huns and the Magyars.

If so, it's feathered of brain; on passing through the gate and down to the cobbled terrace, you can look unhindered over the river as it cuts forcefully between Buda and Pest, and sweeps away around the bend.

Once you've enjoyed the views, turn to the statues. In the first portion of the yard is a fountain ('**Fishing Children**', Károly Senyei, 1912) – brimming with energy and detail – of three children wrestling with an over-sized fish. Beyond it, in the shadow of the emerald-green egg in its cup, is the vast neo-baroque equestrian statue of **Prince Eugene of Savoy** (1663–1736). Prince Eugene led the armies that liberated Hungary from Ottoman rule, forcing the Turks to sign the Treaty of Karlowitz in 1699 that ceded Hungary to the Habsburgs. The citizens of the town of Zenta (133 miles southeast of Buda, and now part of Serbia), scene of a seminal battle in 1697, commissioned this statue by József Róna 200 years later. However, they subsequently discovered their pockets weren't deep enough to pay for the work. Fortunately Ferenc József stepped in with funds. Leaning back in his saddle, the general pulls his champing horse to a halt and surveys the battlefield around him. One of the plinth's reliefs shows us what he sees – the fighting at its thickest and Turkish slain littering the ground. Prince Eugene had attacked Sultan Mustafa II's forces as they crossed the Tisza River, overcoming an army twice the size of his own.

An archway behind the statue leads to another courtyard at the palace's rear. On the left is the bronze **Mátyás Well** (*Mátyás-kút*) created by Alajos Stróbl in 1904. Mátyás was one of the country's most renowned and respected kings. He was fond of donning the clothes of commoners and mingling among his people; when he died, it was said that truth had died with him. As such, he made the ideal subject for a legendary tale of romantic love, recorded originally by his chronicler and then woven into a 19th-century ballad by Mihály Vörösmarty. Here Mátyás is shown in hunting attire, a stag lying dead at his feet, and bloodhounds – all ears and tongues – slaking their thirst in the waterfall below. To the left sits his falcon-bearing chronicler, while to the right is the beautiful peasant girl, Ilonka Szép (Helen the Fair). The poem describes her seeing this handsome huntsman and falling deeply in love; on learning his identity, and the impossibility of a match, she dies of a broken heart.

The '**Fresh**' (*Friss*) **Palace of Zsigmond** of Luxembourg probably stood in this courtyard. The area in front of the Ludwig Museum was also the scene of medieval tournaments, as well as the execution of László Hunyadi. '**The Horseherd**' (*Csikós*), a statue by György Vastagh of a Hortobágy herdsman struggling to control

### *LIFE IMITATES ART*

Adam Koch, the Viennese painter, much admired the great horsemanship of the Hungarians. Upon returning to Austria he pushed artistic licence to the full in painting an imaginary scene in which a single horseman rode five steeds at the same time. Intent on further proving their skills of horsemanship, Hungarians successfully imitated the painting; the stunt became known as the 'Koch (or *puszta*) five'. Riders have raised the bar ever since – the current world record is for one man on 12 horses!

his excitable steed, was originally erected in 1901 outside the Castle District's riding school (destroyed in World War II). The theme of a man working to subdue an untamed horse was popular among neo-baroque sculptors of the 19th century.

To the right of the Mátyás Well is the entrance to the **Lion Courtyard** (*Oroszlános udvar*), guarded by a pair of kingly beasts looking faintly aloof. On the other side of the arch, which is topped by two angels and the Hungarian coat of arms, they roar violently at the temerity of those who have passed between them. With these two and the *turul* bird, it is surprising that the palace receives any visitors at all! A corridor to the right as you pass beneath the arch leads to a small exhibition of artefacts from the castle, together with a written history in English. (Opening hours are the same as the library; see pages 316–17.) The courtyard (János Fadrusz, 1904) is considerably more enclosed than the others of the complex. At its southern end is the **Budapest History Museum** (Wing E; see page 313), accessed via the Telegraph Gate, either side of which are sculptures of war and peace (Károly Senyei, 1900). On the eastern side is Wing D of the **National Gallery** (see pages 306–8), and opposite that the **National Széchényi Library** (Wing F; see pages 316–17).

Beyond the History Museum are the restored **Medieval southern fortifications**, including the Mace Tower (*Buzogánytorony*) and the Great Bastion, as well as the palace gardens. You can descend to the Tabán (see pages 257–8) via Ferdinánd Gate, next to the Mace Tower. However, if you wish to explore the rest of the Castle District, retrace your steps and brave the lions, continue northward past the herdsman and his horse – stopping briefly to look down upon the continuing excavations taking place below the courtyard's western side – and exit the complex via the **Corvinus Gate**. On the top of the web-like gate is perched a raven with a ring in its beak – the raven (*corvus* in Latin) was the heraldic symbol of King Mátyás.

## *The old town*

If the palace is the noble head of the hill, and the prime target of any knockout punch during the epic fights that have taken place here, the **Castle District** (*Várnegyed*) or burghers' town has inevitably suffered the sapping body blows. It has undergone the same cycle of destruction and reconstruction. Little of its medieval Gothic apparel remained after the siege of 1686; the town had to be pulled to its feet, brushed down and given a fresh baroque set of clothes. It gained in strength, and during the late 19th century even boasted splendid mansions like Sándor Palace (see below), the bowers of preening aristocrats jostling for position beside the newly grandiose main palace. However, the Russian bombardment at the end of World War II brought it to its knees once more. A quarter of the buildings were flattened, and a measly group of just four escaped unscathed.

Nevertheless, the streets still follow their original medieval routes, and the recycling of building materials means that the eagle-eyed will recognise pieces of earlier architectural features – sections of wall, Gothic arches, stone niches, and window and door frames. Furthermore, during the clear-up operation after World War II, many medieval remnants were uncovered, shedding fresh light on the appearance of the district's original buildings; we have learnt, for example, that they were elaborately painted in a range of striking colours. Excavation of such early constructions and their foundations are ongoing, but it is this architectural stew that endows the district with its charm and interest. For all the pretty restoration, it is in such historical flotsam that the area's violent past is revealed, together with the resilience of the people who kept on piecing it back together.

### *Szent György tér*

Szent György tér represents a broad breathing space, a place to toss a coin and tilt your cap at the palace to the south or the body of the old town to the north. Whether you choose to dive into the holdings of the museums or enjoy a leg stretch and a beer, spare a thought for the square's prouder past as the site of noble mansions, tucked snug in the shadow of the palace. The stony rubble of some of these buildings can be seen towards the back of the square. The **Sándor Palace** (Szent

György tér 1–2) still stands – squat, neoclassical, a vivid white that dazzles in sunlight – immediately to the right of the funicular railway. Built in 1806 for Vince Sándor, it even had marble mangers in the stables. Later used as the prime minister's official residence, it was the scene of Pál Teleki's suicide in 1941. Just months after signing a friendship treaty with Yugoslavia, Admiral Horthy committed Hungary to the Nazi attack on its new 'ally'; his prime minister felt unable to live with the dishonour. The building was gutted by fire during World War II; renovations costing two billion forints were completed in 2002, and it is now the president's official residence.

The square once held the **Heinrich Hentzi monument**, erected by Ferenc József I in 1852 as a memorial to the Austrian general who died defending the castle from the Hungarians in 1849. The column struck deep at Hungarian pride and was finally removed in 1899. Oral tradition speaks of a second former landmark here – a tree that once grew at the square's southern end, and was used by the Turks as a gallows from which to hang a captain of the hussars, **Ramocsaházy**. The tree bent under his weight and his toes reached the floor, allowing him to support himself until rescuers arrived. In time he was made Castellan by Emperor Leopold I, and was always careful to look after the failed 'hanging' tree. The trunk was apparently later placed in Iskola utca, and journeymen would hammer nails into it on passing through

The yellow **National Dance Theatre** (page 187) – graced by performers including Haydn and Beethoven – is next to the Sándor Palace. The promenade at the back of Szent György tér is popular with buskers, who entertain strollers heading towards or away from the palace. At the northern end, near the start of

Tóth Árpád sétány and the Fehévár Bastion, are the sculptures of a **medieval knight and his herald** by Károly Antal and that of **Artúr Görgey** by László Márton. The latter depicts the young commander of the Hungarian forces that took Buda Castle during the 1848–49 War of Independence.

### *Dísz tér*

Walking up one of either Szent György utca or Színház utca you will reach Dísz tér and the southern extent of the burghers' town proper. Here it was that market sellers plied their trades during the Middle Ages, and where parades by the palace guards took place in the years after the expulsion of the Turks. Today much of the square is given over to **parking**, and it is the main point of traffic access to the Castle District (see page 233). A barrier prevents the movement of unauthorised vehicles northwards on Tárnok utca. At the centre of the square is the **Honvéd statue** by György Zala, cast from cannon metal and erected in 1893 as a memorial to those 'defenders of the homeland' who fought in the 1848–49 War of Independence. Cardinal Angelo Rotta, the Vatican's ambassador, was resident in the building at **numbers 4–5** during World War II, and was credited with saving the lives of many Jews at this sickening time. On the eastern side is a handicrafts market (open daily 10.00–18.00) whose inflated prices make it worth avoiding.

Two roads forge away from the top of the square – Úri utca (see page 252), which hugs the remaining length of the district's western side as far as Kapisztrán tér, and **Tárnok utca**. Take the latter for the moment, with its collection of little shops to keep you interested as you head towards Mátyás Church. Keep an eye out too for the **Tárnok Café** – difficult to miss, with its swirling red and orange sgraffitoed walls – and **Arany Hordó Vendéglő** at numbers 14 and 16 respectively. Their Renaissance exteriors were exposed following damage during World War II.

The **Golden Eagle Pharmacy Museum** (page 314) originally housed the district's first apothecary. In an upper-storey niche of the neoclassical façade stands a curious painted statuette – almost a sculptured cartoon – of the Madonna and child. Its elongated form is reminiscent of the fantastical illustrations of *Alice's Adventures in Wonderland*. Welcome to the glorious, unmistakable world of Margit Kovács. Kovács died in 1977, and is considered Hungary's greatest ceramicist. Moving just beyond the museum, you pass the tiny side street of **Balta köz**. Claustrophobic and darkly romantic, 'Axe Alley' is said to be where the brothers Hunyadi (László and Mátyás) were captured by László V, and where they defended themselves with axes during the violent struggle. Shortly before Tárnok utca emerges into Szentháromság tér you will find a **Tourinform**. Here too is a pick-up point for horse-drawn-carriage rides (*fiáker állomás*).

### *Szentháromság tér*

We have now reached the highest point of Castle Hill and one of the pouting cover girls of Budapest's picture postcards – the bustling and asymmetrical Szentháromság (Holy Trinity) tér. It even displays a tactile bronze monument to its own monuments, worn blonde in places by intrigued fingers.

The Council of Buda erected the baroque **Trinity Column** (1711–14) on behalf of plague survivors. It was funded in part through a system of fines imposed on naughty citizens found guilty of offences like adultery. Around the column are carved saints who stand as guardians of the city; these are actually replicas – the original sandstone protectors are themselves protected from the elements in the Kiscelli Museum (page 322).

At the northern side of the square stands a **neo-Gothic palace** (Szentháromság tér 6) originally constructed in the early 20th century. It served as accommodation for students at the Technical University between 1954 and 1981, many of whom were heavily involved in the 1956 uprising. Here too was the Várklub (Castle Club), an influential youth music centre of the period. The Hungarian Culture Foundation owns most of the building, and hosts free arts and technical exhibitions here throughout the year (open 10.00–16.00 daily).

The two-storey building with the diminutive green clock tower across from the Burg Hotel is the **former town hall** (Szentháromság tér 2), constructed by the Italian architect Venerio Ceresola in the late 1600s. A chapel was later added specifically to hold a holy relic – one of the feet of Szt János the Charitable. Originally a gift to King Mátyás from the Turks, the foot now 'stands' in the church of his name (see page 342). Artúr Görgey (see page 241) stayed in the town hall after capturing the area from the Austrians in 1849. The statue in a niche at the building's corner is Pallas Athene, the 'Protector of Buda'. Above it is a corner balcony, examples of which are most famously found in Györ, with a carved face at its bottom edge that is an eerie mix of lion and man.

A few metres to the west along Szentháromság utca is a horsy **statue by György Vastagh** (1936). The noble animal's green-and-black colouring is broken by its golden 'crown jewels' (ahem!), polished by generations of students who give them a rub for luck. Such superstition is, of course, a load of balls, but at exam time those with imagination may notice a faint smile playing around the stallion's lips. The figure atop is the popular András Hadik (1710–90), a man who rose through the ranks to become a hussar general – and later chairman of the Vienna Military Council, the only Hungarian to reach such dizzy heights under the Habsburgs – and was a favourite of Maria Theresa. The original of the sabre at his side can be seen in the Museum of Military History (page 315). A document bearing the name of every soldier to fall during the life of the Third Royal and Imperial Hussars (1702–1918) lies in a glass case entombed in the statue's pediment.

The square's show stealer, of course, is **Mátyás Church** (page 342). Next to this is the **Fishermen's Bastion** (*Halászbástya*); you might think that its stones are too brightly white and its medieval silhouette too sharp and unworn to have weathered the storms of several centuries – and you'd be correct. It was erected by Frigyes Schulek in 1902 as a purely decorative companion for his church, and stands at the section of the hill supposedly defended in the past by the guild of fishermen. The coned turrets symbolise the tents of the nomadic Magyar tribes (see page 3). The largest of the seven represents the leader Árpád.

In front of the bastion is an equestrian **statue of Szt István**, the country's first king, founder of the Hungarian state and convert to Christianity. It was commissioned of Alajos Stróbl at the time of the millenary celebrations, although the great historicist sculptor took ten years over his masterpiece – he even researched the history of the 11th-century stirrup. The statue is hung with intricately crafted riding regalia, in particular a loose-hanging saddle cloth whose fringes sway when the wind picks up. The altar-like pedestal was designed by Schulek, a man whose fingers were in so many of the square's pies; it is inset with carved reliefs depicting defining moments in the king's reign, including his coronation and his founding of Székesfehérvár Church.

Steps behind the bastion lead down to Hunyadi János út and the Víziváros. Shrouded by trees at the base of these steps is a **statue of Hunyadi** himself (István Tóth, 1903), the Turkish flag at his feet marking his famous victory of 1456 (see page 4).

## *Hess András tér*

The funnel-shaped square immediately to the north of Szentharomság tér is named after the first printer of Buda who lived here in the 15th century. The Hess press printed the earliest Hungarian book in 1473, the only remaining complete copy of which is in the Széchényi Library (page 317). At the square's centre is a **statue of Pope Innocent XI**, who is known as the 'saviour of Hungary' because of his endeavours in funding the European forces that freed Hungary from Turkish rule. The house behind the statue once held the **Red Hedgehog Inn** (*Vörös Sün-Ház*; Hess András tér 3) – splendidly christened after the nobleman's coat of arms above its gate. Somehow one imagines that its snug was a cosy little nest. The inn actually hosted the first theatrical performances of Buda in 1760, while the building itself is one of the oldest of the district, dating back to 1390.

The **Budapest Hilton** at number 1 is a heady mix of baroque, Gothic and 20th-century tinted chic. Opened in 1977, it was built on the site of a Dominican church and monastery of 1252 and incorporates the remains of its walls, together with a 15th-century tower and the reconstructed baroque façade of a 1688 Jesuit college. The tower is topped with a very modern interpretation of a turret; the relief of Mátyás – a copy of one on a gatehouse in Bautzen (Silesia) – is a true likeness of the king. The Dominican courtyard, together with a Renaissance well and monks' gravestones, can be visited by non-guests; concerts are held in the former (see page 102). Opposite is the **House of Hungarian Wines** (page 198).

### *Táncsics Mihály utca and Fortuna utca*

From Hess András tér, streets strike out northwards in a two-pronged attack on Bécsi kapu tér. In taking that on the right, **Táncsics Mihály utca**, you follow a curving road of two-storey houses painted from a pretty pallet of fading pastel shades. From the 15th century, this street was the hill's **Jewish quarter**. The Castle District had traditionally been a haven for religious groups. Béla IV granted legal privileges to Hungarian Jews in the 13th century, attracting those suffering from persecution in western European countries. They eventually settled along Táncsics Mihály utca, remaining here throughout the period of Ottoman occupation – indeed, at that time the road was called Zsidó (Jew) utca. There is a **16-century prayer house** at number 26 (page 316).

The arched corridor at **number 7** leads to a beautiful courtyard, with pigmented cobblestones and iron lanterns. The **baroque mansion** surrounding it was built for Count Erdődy between 1750 and 1769, among whose guests here was Beethoven. Such peaceful areas – to be found nestling behind the house fronts of many of the city's avenues and boulevards, though rarely as stately as this – are simple pleasures that are worth hunting out.

Number 9 next door is believed to have been the site of the original royal residence, before the monarch's quarters were relocated to the hill's southern end. Much later it was transformed into a barracks whose armoury was used as a **prison** from the early 19th century. Behind the huge gates, still visible today, several prominent anti-Habsburg 'subversives' were confined, including Lajos Kossuth (1837–40) and Mihály Táncsics (1847–48 and 1860). The prison was stormed during the uprising of March 15 1848, and Táncsics was freed and carried through the streets by the revolutionaries. Jókai, the writer, was also held here in 1863 for a libellous article. There are literary connections at **number 13** too, where the poet Árpád Tóth lived from 1918 and died ten years later. Look out for the carved Turkish head – replete with turban and plump moustache – on the gateway of **number 24**.

The parallel left-hand road from Hess András tér is **Fortuna utca**, which features a sprinkling of shops and galleries selling prints, antique collectibles and curiosities. There are also several decorative touches on the 18th-century houses along its length that should encourage you to keep the blinkers off. The street is named after the goddess of fortune, and breaking the duck-blue façade at **number 9** is a white relief of her made by Ferenc Medgyessy in 1921. The goddess certainly appears to have favoured a previous inhabitant of **number 6**, where a large number of 16th-century coins emerged during excavations in the 1930s. Cupid lies lazily above the door, so maybe the householder had love to match. Number 4 holds the **Museum of Commerce and Catering** (page 314). Originally, however, it was

## IGNÁC MARTINOVICS

In the 18th century, Ignác Martinovics juggled life as a monk with shadowy work as a secret agent for Emperor Leopold II, before becoming deeply affected by the revolutionary wave breaking in France. He gathered like-minded Hungarian intellectuals and radicals around him, discussed dark plots of republican uprising and swore a freemasons' oath against the king. Unfortunately for them, the conspiracy was uncovered, and the prime movers executed in 1795 on the Vérmező – 'Field of Blood' – an area of park at the western lower slope of Castle Hill.

the site of the Fortuna Inn, and possibly the late-18th-century meeting place for Martinovics's Jacobin schemers (see box above).

### *Bécsi kapu tér*

**Bécsi kapu** (Vienna Gate) is the northern entrance to the old town. It has stood in its present incarnation since 1936; its medieval ancestor was reduced to gravel during the 1686 siege. The **glazed relief** outside bears the distinctive style of Margit Kovács (see page 242), who here depicts a violent assault upon Buda's walls. It is a fitting companion for Ostrom utca – or 'Siege Street' – and for the square it introduces, once site of the medieval Saturday market but later marked as a place of remembrance for those who fell for freedom in 1686.

The bulging side walls and staggered tower of the square's little **Lutheran church** were built in 1895 by Mór Kallina. The southern façade has a plaque dedicated to Sztehlo Gábor, a clergyman who saved the lives of thousands of children during World War II. An olive tree grows in his honour in Jerusalem's Grove of the Faithful.

Next to the gate is a drab academic in harlequin's headgear – the **National Archives** (*Országos Levéltár*; Bécsi kapu tér 2–4) building, its sombre stone blocks topped with a majolica-tiled celebration of colour. Raised between 1913 and 1920, its roof betrays its designer – Samu Pecz – who was also responsible for the Big Market Hall (page 202). Outside it is a **bronze statue** by János Pásztor dedicated to Ferenc Kazinczy (1759–1831), leader of the 19th-century language reform movement and later participant in Martinovics's conspiracy (see box opposite). For the latter he was given seven years to mull things over. The olive-green house at **number 7** displays carved allegories of the arts and sciences, together with reliefs of classical heavyweights like Virgil, Cicero and Socrates. Lajos Hatvany bought this house and in it hosted his literary soirées of the 1930s; Thomas Mann is believed to have stayed here.

Don't leave without taking in the sights from the **outer walls**. The fortifications were primarily the work of the Turks, who incorporated medieval walls wherever possible. One way of joining these is from Bécsi kapu tér, with access next to the archives building on to a promenade leading around the northern tip of the district. After 100m you will pass the **memorial to Abdurrahman** on the Anjou bástya, a symbolic grave dedicated to the last Turkish governor (pasha) of Buda. He was 70 years old when he was killed in battle, and with this monument the Hungarians honour a heroic adversary. Further up are some cannon. From this point onwards, as you walk beside the chestnut trees that line the path, the Buda hills are presented in all their splendour, with clutches of houses thinning out in the distance. It is a peaceful and reflective place to watch a day begin or end. Immediately below is the Vérmező, where on May 20 1795 Martinovics and his comrades faced the day's end knowing they would never see another begin (see box, page 248).

The entrance to the **Museum of Military History** (see page 315) can be found on Tóth Arpád sétány. Also along this western stretch is the **monument of the Second Transylvanian Hussars**, an inter-war interpretation of Leonardo da Vinci's Renaissance horse and rider (as seen in the Museum of Fine Arts; page 310). The promenade leads eventually into Dísz tér.

### *Kapisztrán tér*

Petermann Biró utca – named after a medieval magistrate (not a ballpoint pen), but for a time following the 1686 siege bearing the pithy and graphic title of Vér (Blood) utca – carries you westwards from Vienna Gate into the cobbled Kapisztrán tér. The square is striking for the lonely Gothic tower of the **Church of Mary Magdalene** (page 341). Near the church's skeletal window is one of the enchanting details so typical of this district. A **ghostly blue-robed nun** passes through the walls of the building at Petermann Biró utca 4, her upper body on one side and her feet the other. The figure is a reminder of the 18th-century convent that once stood at Országház utca 28. Next to the **town hall** (Kapisztrán tér 1) at the northern side of the square stands a neoclassical palace, built as a barracks in 1847. At its entrance are two formidable cannon, one pointing poignantly towards the shell of the church, and signalling that the **Institute and Museum of Military History** (page 315) are now housed inside. Cannon balls are embedded in the façade, signs of the Hungarian army's liberation of the Castle District in 1849. Also here is a **statue of János Kapisztrán** (1386–1456), stepping over the body of a slain Turk. The Italian Franciscan monk fought with his private peasant army alongside János Hunyadi in the famous victory at Nándorfehérvár in 1456, succumbing to the plague shortly afterwards. A fresco in the Mátyás Church (opposite the Loréto Chapel) also commemorates this battle; Kapisztrán actually used the church for a troop-recruitment speech in 1455.

### *Országház utca*

Országház (Parliament) utca runs between Kapisztrán tér and Szentháromság tér, and is so named because several parliamentary sessions were held in **number 28** at the turn of the 19th century. Before that the building had been the convent of the Order of the Poor Clares, the female arm of the Franciscans (see page 252). It is now occupied by the Hungarian Academy of Sciences, and joins Úri utca 49 at its rear (home of the Telephone Museum; pages 317 and 252). There are several Gothic features to be seen on buildings along the street, most obviously extant alcoves or '*sedilia*' set within the openings of gates. Such intriguing architectural characteristics – unique to Hungary – came to light all over the district during post-war excavations and have perplexed boffins ever since. The educated assumption is that they were covered niches for nightwatchmen or for citizens and servants to duck into for rest or shelter. Whatever their purpose, they became canvases for carved decoration and display, as neighbourly peacocks strove to out-strut each other. Among other nuggets to root out is the piece of bread carved on the keystone of **number 17**, which was once the residence of a master baker. The great 19th-century sculptor István Ferenczy lived for a decade at **number 14**. Our favourite house, however, is that in pea green at **number 22**, with its jutting closed balcony and sturdy entrance arch. It once belonged to a master chimney sweep. The present façade dates to 1770.

### *Úri utca*

Úri utca is the final piece in the district's jigsaw, the only street to last the course through the whole length of the town, and connecting Kapisztrán tér and Dísz tér. Its location next to the promenade overlooking the hills to the west was enough to make medieval estate agents drool, and noble residences were hot property.

Religious devotees once shut themselves away from earthly pleasures in the Franciscan monastery at **number 53**, while the followers of Martinovics were more reluctant detainees here in the 1790s (see box, page 248). **Number 49** is linked to number 28 on the parallel Országház utca (see page 251), and was donated to the Order of the Poor Clares following Buda's liberation from Turkish rule. After József II suppressed the order, the Diet and royal court moved into the buildings. The present wings – bordering a beautiful courtyard – were designed by Franz Anton Hillebrand, who rebuilt the cloister at the end of the 18th century. A century later it served as the Ministry of Interior and the castle exchange (see page 317).

The 15th-century house at **number 31**, looking down upon its neighbours, is something of a historical 'storey teller' – providing us with the only standing evidence that there were once three-floor houses on the hill. There are medieval *sedilia* sunk into the gateway walls at **number 32**. The massive lucky charm that is the Hadik statue (see page 243) is at the junction with Szentháromság utca, while further on at **number 19** József Eötvös, the novelist and minister, drew his first breaths in 1813. If you're hoping the district will throw up one last ornamental quirk, you won't be disappointed with the two lions at the corner of **number 13**, resting their shared head on a heraldic shield like a pair of watchful Siamese twins. Finish off with a visit to the dank **cave system** (page 363), and then on to the creamy offerings at **Ruszwurm** (page 160) – the café that has been serving buns to burghers since 1827.

## GELLÉRT HILL, THE TABÁN AND SURROUNDS
### Walking around Gellért Hill

Gellért Hill (*Gellért-hegy*) raised its granite head over 200 million years ago, a craggy henchman to the south of Castle Hill. From deep in its bowels spews water that feeds the three thermal baths (see pages 220–1), while at the top the fortress and monument to freedom represent rather unlikely bedfellows. Inhabited since Neolithic times, transcripts of witch trials during the 17th and 18th centuries reveal that the rock was a favoured gathering place for exponents of the dark arts, and this is also supposedly where the Venetian monk Gellért (see page 3) – after whom the hill was named in the 18th century – was martyred.

You are less likely now to encounter witches' spells or falling bishops, but it still takes a certain commitment to brave the 140m on foot. The panoramic views, however, reward any effort; if you're here on August 20, you can also catch the fireworks that mark St Stephen's Day (page 37). A series of stone steps and sloping paths lead up the southeastern side of the hill (from opposite the Gellért Baths), while there are walkways from the north too. If you'd prefer to have some breath left for the views to take there is a **car park** on Citadella sétány, while **bus 27** (from Móricz Zsigmond körtér) stops 300m below the Citadella (outside the Búsuló Juhász restaurant).

At the Buda foot of **Freedom Bridge** (*Szabadság híd*), **Gellért tér** is a beacon for those hankering after some stylish soaking or a turn-of-the-20th-century flourish to their hotel stay (see pages 220 and 108). The gurgling blue fountain outside the Hotel Gellért, fashioned from Zsolnay porcelain, makes a popular meeting point. Freedom Bridge, topped with *turul* birds (see box, page 235), was built for the millennial celebrations and initially bore the name of Ferenc József. While it would be an exaggeration to say that the latter was a key construction worker, he did push a button that activated a hammer that drove the final rivet into the bridge. The rivet was silver and bore his initials; unsurprisingly it was later stolen. A little to the south of the square is the mammoth **Budapest University of Technology and Economics** (*Budapesti Műszaki és Gazdaságtudományi Egyetem*; Műegyetem rakpart 1–5), designed by Alajos Hauszmann. The atrium inside contains a pantheon of the university's famous alumni, which includes Imre Steindl (architect of the Parliament building).

Across the road from the Gellért Baths is the romantic **Cave Church** (page 340) after which you can begin the ascent to the summit. With its 14m poker-straight woman thrusting high above the hill's peak, the **Freedom Monument** is visible from miles around. Finally erected in 1947, it was commissioned originally by Admiral Horthy as a memorial to his son, who had died during a wartime test flight. In an ironic twist, the Russians arrived before the sculpture was complete, and Zsigmond Kisfaludy Stróbl adapted the design to suit his new patrons. A palm frond (instead of the intended propellor) was placed in the hands of the woman, transforming the piece from a personal – if very public – tribute into a political symbol of Russia's role in liberating the city. After the demise of communism, the bronze soldier was moved to Statue Park (page 311), leaving the muscle-bound beast slayer and striding torchbearer to convey an allegorical message shorn of specific historical associations. The plinth's inscription now reads 'In memory of all of those who sacrificed their lives for Hungary's independence, freedom and prosperity'. Next to the monument is the imposing **Citadella** (page 342).

A little further down the hill's northern end, Gellért (or 'Gerard') flourishes a cross above the traffic passing back and forth over Elizabeth Bridge. A waterfall flows beneath **Gyula Jankovics's statue** of 1904, and a walkway – guarded by a pair of *turul* birds – begins directly below it. It is said that at this point in 1046 the bishop took a more direct and less leisurely trip down the hill in a barrel full of spikes. The Italian missionary had been appointed Bishop of Csanád by King István, before becoming the country's first Christian martyr during the power struggle and

### *HALLO EVERYONE!*

The name Puskás Tivadar may not ring any bells, but this ex-student of the University of Technology invented the telephone exchange in 1877 and was a colleague of the rather better-remembered Thomas Edison. He also brought us the world's most familiar greeting. On testing his invention, and hearing a voice at the other end of the telephone line for the first time, he cried out '*Hallom*!' meaning 'I hear you!' in Hungarian. A slight mishearing and a dropped consonant later, and the word 'hallo' was born.

pagan backlash that followed the monarch's death (see page 3).

A short walk to the northwest of the Citadella, near the junction of Orom utca and Sánc utca, is a grassed area. In the **Garden of Philosophy**, bronze statues of history's great religious figures form a circle of spiritual unity around a marble-floored fountain. The artist's promotion of 'better mutual understanding' in the face of global differences of belief is uncomplicated, and yet many will recognise in it a particularly contemporary significance. It was placed here in 2001, the year the modern world changed. Fifty metres away is one of our favourite public sculptures, a chunky **landscape of Budapest**. Symbolic of the marriage of the city's two sides, the kingly Buda reaches across to his bride on the other side of the Danube.

## The Tabán

Plugging the gap between the two hills on the river's bank is the Tabán, an area of grass, a large traffic junction and two of the city's thermal spas. In summer it is the site of al-fresco concerts, while sledding and snowballs are popular during the snowy season. In Turkish times, foreign artisans set up shop here, and in the 18th century a village was built by Serbian settlers (after whom the Rác Baths are named). It became a lively place, with many restaurants and bars, but in 1933 the bulk of the single-storey houses were demolished for hygiene reasons (open sewers and diseased grape vines). Just outside it, on the lower southeastern slope of Castle Hill, is the zigzagging ceremonial pathway of the **Várkert-bazár**. It's in a sorry state now – the crumbling balustrades shut to the public – but in its heyday this was a splendid pleasure garden designed by Miklós Ybl in 1872. A **statue of Ybl** (1814–91), laden with dividers and architectural plans, stands near the **Várkert Casino** (page 193), which was originally constructed as an engine house to power the palace's water-supply system, and was also Ybl's work. Near by too is the **birthplace of Ignác Semmelweis** (see page 318).

The provincial-looking **Parish Church of the Tabán** (*Tabáni plébaniatemplom*) presents its lopsided self in Szarvas tér. Built in the 18th century, it was preceded by a Turkish mosque; the western tower was added by the architect Máté Nepauer. Immediately to the north of Elizabeth Bridge is the pedestrianised Döbrentei tér, its paths leading away underneath the busy flyover that circles overhead. Here sits a **youthful Erzsébet** (1837–98), fondly sculpted in a flowing gown with roses lying beside her. She was a popular queen, who made determined efforts to engage with the Hungarian people, and her assassination by an Italian anarchist was met with genuine sadness. A statue of the ultra-right-wing politician **Gyula Gömbös** (1886–1936), who allied Hungary to the Nazi cause, once occupied this spot; it was destroyed by communist resistance fighters during the war. (There's still a small plaque to him in the grass, usually defaced with black paint.) Underneath the bridge is a **drinking market** (pages 218–19), while on the southern side are the **Rudas Baths** (page 222). The **Rác Baths** (page 221) a short distance to the west of Döbrentei tér are closed for renovation until 2005.

**Nine statues** – grim-faced toughs with axes in hand and violence in mind – stand with Dózsa György tér at their backs and the rear of Buda Palace looming above. They represent participants in the peasant uprising of 1514 (see page 5), and were sculpted in 1961 by István Kiss. Opposite them, across Attila út and Krisztina körút, is **Naphegy** (Sun Hill). Neither its cheery name nor the children's playground at the top properly compensate for the leg-sapping climb up Pásztor lépcső and Fém utca.



## The surrounds

From Gellért tér, Bartók Béla út strikes out through Móricz Zsigmond körtér, the primary traffic junction of southern Buda. When Bartók died in New York in 1945, his will decreed that no place in Budapest should be named after him so long as there were still places like Hitler tér (now Kodály körönd) and Mussolini tér (now Oktogon). As a result, with the demise of Nazism at the end of World War II, the city decided to rename Horthy Miklós út (this one) after their famous Hungarian composer, together with eight other streets around Budapest. On its way towards the city's southwestern suburbs, Bartók Béla út passes **Feneketlen-tó** ('Bottomless Lake'), something of a leafy respite from the traffic arteries around it. The pretty lake is bordered with rushes and gravelled walkways, as well as an open-air theatre (see page 176). At dusk, the lake is one of the most atmospheric parts of Buda, with illuminations and shadows thrown across the reeds. The sandy, twin-towered **St Emeric of the Cistercians Church** (*Budai Ciszterci Szent Imre plébániatemplom*; Villányi út 23–25) stands just outside the park's northern boundary, built in 1938 for the growing population of Lágymányos district. Outside is a large **statue of Count Klebelsberg Kuno** (1875–1932), a prominent interwar minister of religion and education. As well as several buses, trams run from Deák Ferenc tér (49), Batthyány tér (19) and Moszkva tér (61) to the nearby Kosztolányi Dezső tér.

## MOSZKVA TÉR

Moscow Square, a short distance to the north of the Castle District, is Buda's main transport junction, and as such a portal for getting elsewhere rather than a place of interest in itself. It's gritty and fume-filled, and an early-morning congregation point for black-market workers after labour. The turreted building to the west is a **post office** (its entrance at Krisztina körut 6), while **Mammut** shopping mall is a few short steps away (page 209). Also near by is the **Millennium Park** (*Millenáris Park*; II, Lövőház utca 37; www.millenaris.hu), a sterile modern recreation area based around an artificial lake. Among the entertainments for children are a plastic 'ice-skating' rink and a wooden fort, while two industrial buildings have been converted into spaces for exhibitions, concerts and dance performances (*Tánc és Színház a Millenáris*; Fény utca 20–22; tel: 1 438 5335). For further information, see page 184.

## WALKING THE VÍZIVÁROS

The Víziváros (Water Town) squeezes between Castle Hill and the Danube, before breathing out and filling the space northward to Margit híd and westward to Moszkva tér. The main street (Fő utca) follows the route of a Roman road that linked the hill and Aquincum, and retains a healthy dash of old-world romance. In the years prior to the Turkish occupation, fishermen and artisans dwelt here; today it offers a straight-lined, uncomplicated walk between Széchenyi Lánc and Margit bridges. If you do it one way, choose Fő utca; if you have the stamina for a return journey, walk back along the parallel Bem rakpart next to the river.

Start at **Clark Ádám tér**, named after the 19th-century Scottish engineer who constructed both Széchenyi Lánchíd (the Chain Bridge) and the **tunnel** through the hill that connects the city centre with the western parts of Buda. The tunnel is 350m long, large enough, it is said, to accommodate the beautiful bridge in bad weather. The **Chain Bridge** itself was designed by Englishman William Tierney Clark (think Hammersmith Bridge), replacing a pontoon that had to be dismantled with the arrival of winter's ice. In December 1820, István Széchenyi was called to Buda on learning of the death of his father; however, the bridge was down, he could find no ferryman willing to navigate the drifting chunks of ice, and he very nearly missed the funeral. He campaigned thereafter for a permanent structure; it was

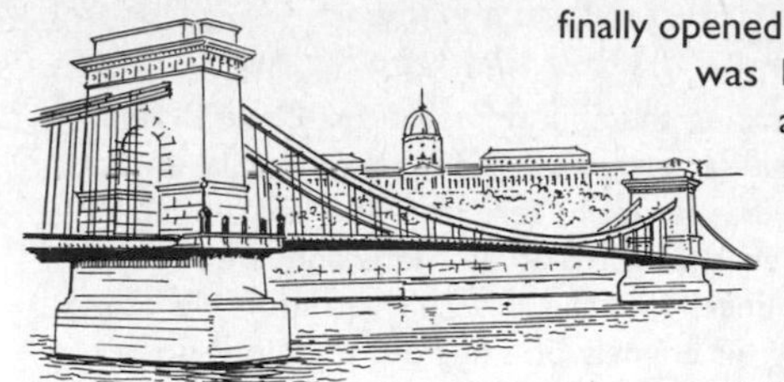

finally opened in 1849, although Széchenyi himself was by then incarcerated in a mental asylum, and unable to cross the bridge he had inspired.

Another member of the Széchenyi clan, István's son Ödön, suggested the construction of the **funicular railway** (*Budavári Sikló*; page 233) that trundles a 45° course up Castle Hill. It was built in 1870, and reconstructed after being smashed during World War II. Near the lower terminus is an oval-shaped monument – the **zero-kilometre stone** – from which distance markers along Hungary's main roads are measured. The sculptor intended to represent 'the birth of distance', which is why it resembles a woman's birth-giving parts.

**Fő utca** straddles districts I and II, carrying you north of Clark Ádám tér as far as Bem József tér. Some buildings appear sunk into the surface – this is because at the end of the 19th century the street level was raised by over a metre to reduce its vulnerability to flooding. Immediately on the right, at **number 1**, is a central court building designed by Miklós Ybl in 1867–69. The District I **cultural centre** (*művelődési ház*) stands at Fő utca 11–13, the building designed by István Lánzbauer in 1880 for Count Gyula Andrássy; a team of Polish doctors was killed here during fighting on March 19 1944. The **French Institute** is at Fő utca 17, while György Békesy (1899–1972), the Nobel Prize-winning scientist, lived and worked at **number 19** until

### *BEASTLY MOUTHS*

Take note of the four lions guarding the abutments of the Chain Bridge. Sculptor János Marschalkó was so proud of them that he challenged anybody to find fault; at the inauguration ceremony, an apprentice is reputed to have loudly criticised the fact that the lions appeared to be tongueless; Marschalkó threw himself into the river in frustration. He later wrote several articles defending his animals, pointing out that lions do not loll their tongues like dogs. He also responded to one critic by sniping 'Would that your wife had such a tongue as my lions!'



1946.

The **church** at the south side of **Corvin tér** (Fő utca 30–32) was originally constructed in the medieval period, used as a mosque during the Ottoman occupation (note the Turkish ogee-arched door in the southern wall) and then as a Capuchin monastery in the 18th century. A statue of Szent Erzsébet gazes down from high above the entrance. We love the butter-coloured house at **number 11**, packed with stone-carved window frames, while at the square's north is the faded but splendid **Buda Vigadó** (Corvin tér 8), built in 1900 and home of the Hungarian State Folk Ensemble and Civil Rádió.

You'll emerge for a few paces before disappearing into **Szilágyi Dezső tér**. The Hungarian-Indian artist Amrita Sher-Gil (1913–1941) was born at **number 4**, a house that Béla Bartók called home in the 1920s. Opposite stands the red-brick neo-Gothic **Calvinist church**, with a slender steeple – the tallest in Buda – and a roof adorned with ceramic Zsolnay tiles. A pint-sized statue of Samu Pecz, who clearly enjoyed playing with geometry in constructing the church in 1893–96, stands outside dressed in the garb of a medieval master builder. On the river bank is a memorial to the March 15 1848 revolution, bearing the message 'Steadfastly for your homeland'. It was at this place that the Arrow Cross murdered hundreds of Jews in 1945, dumping their bodies in the water.

**Batthyány tér** (named after the prime minister of the 1848 government) contains the baroque **Szent Anna Parish Church** (1740–62), twin clock-towered, dressed in gold and white and adorned with God's all-seeing eye. The church wasn't actually consecrated until 1805 because the finishing touches were hampered by an earthquake. Organ concerts are held inside (ticket information tel: 1 317 2754). On the northern side of the square is a **former hospital** run by Elizabethan nuns; a statue in front depicts Ferenc Kölcsey (1790–1838), the bald-headed Romantic poet who composed the Hungarian national anthem 'Hymn' ('Himnusz'). The adjacent pastel-blue **Church of the Elizabethan Nuns** (Fő utca 41–43) was built on the site of a Turkish mosque in 1731–57 by Jakab Hans, and has a rich baroque interior. Two centuries ago, the **Casanova bar** (page 167) – with its Rococco ornamentation – was the White Cross Inn, where the serial seducer Giovanni Jacopo Casanova is meant to have stayed while taking the Buda water cure. The high-pitched pop singer Jimmy Zámbó (who accidentally shot himself at a New Year's party in Csepel in 2001) began his musical career at the Casanova. Batthyány tér is served by both the metro (M2) and the HÉV, while tram 19 terminates here.

Cross Csalogány utca, spare a glance for the **socialist constructivist relief** at Fő utca 68 – depicting three masons struggling with a block of stone – and join **Nagy Imre tér**. Nagy was leader of the government during the 1956 revolution (see page 10); it was in the midst of the intimidating symmetry of the **military court and prison** building (Fő utca 70–78) to the square's north and northwest that he was sentenced to death two years later. Luckier was Attila Ambrus, the 'Whisky Robber', who in 1999 escaped from an upper storey with a rope he'd fashioned from bed sheets.

Just beyond the junction with Kacsa utca are the **Király Baths** (page 220), while on the other side of Ganz utca is the **Chapel of Szent Flórián** (*Görögkatolikus templom*; Fő utca 88). This tiny church – as yellow as egg yolk, and with just eight pews either side of a golden altar – was built in 1759–60 and later given to the Greek Catholics. After the raising of Fő utca, the church's portico slipped over a metre below street level; in the 1930s the church was itself lifted by 1.4m to minimise future flood damage.

Fő utca culminates at **Bem József tér**. The Polish General Bem József, known as 'Papa' (Apó), fought with the Hungarians in the 1848 revolution, scoring victories over Austrian and Russian armies in Transylvania. Bem fled to Turkey after the collapse of the uprising, and died in 1854 bearing the name Amarut Pasha after converting to Islam. The statue in the centre commemorates the 1849 Battle of Piski – 'I will take this bridge or I will die. Go Hungarians!' – and was a rallying point for students during the 1956 revolution. It was here that the Russian hammer and sickle was cut from the Hungarian flag, creating an instant gaping touchstone of the revolutionary cause.

From here you can visit the **Foundry Museum** (page 322) on Bem József utca, which leads away from the square's southwestern corner, while the Rózsadomb and **tomb of Gül Baba** (page 345) are a short but steep walk away. Alternatively make your way back along the river on **Bem rakpart**, running the gauntlet of speeding cyclists and enjoying the views of Parliament on the opposite bank.

## ÓBUDA, AQUINCUM AND THE RÓMAI-PART

The primary concentration of ancient history is to be found in Óbuda (Old Buda), which became 'old' in the 13th century when Béla IV shifted the centre of the region's power behind new walls on Castle Hill. Occupying a northern portion of the city, the early provenance is difficult to credit at a passing glance, for parts of District III sprouted high-rise flats during the '60s and a large carriageway was driven through the centre. However, two millennia ago the area was occupied by Celts and then Romans. The Danube represented the eastern boundary of the Roman empire; Flórián tér was the site of a camp supporting 6,000 legionaries, while to its north was a civilian settlement called Aquincum. The sites of interest are scattered between – and even sheltered beneath – highways and residential blocks, and as such it is best to move about by **public transport** if you want to avoid long treks through concrete jungle. You can travel here on bus 86 or tram 1 (over Árpád híd), but the HÉV suburban railway provides the simplest route; pick it up from Batthyány tér or Margit híd.

Alight at Timár út and walk eastwards to the corner of Nagyszombat utca and

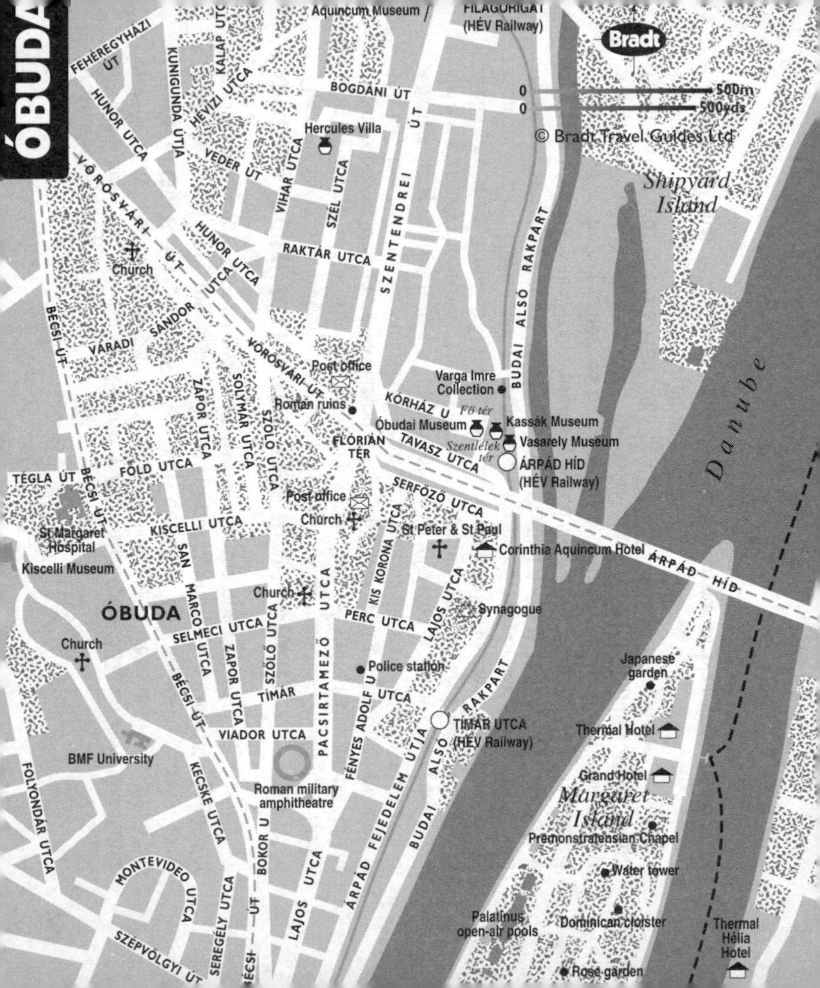
ÓBUDA
Aquincum Museum
FILAGORIGAT (HÉV Railway)
Bradt
500m
500yds
© Bradt Travel Guides Ltd
Shipyard Island
Hercules Villa
Varga Imre Collection
Post office
Roman ruins
Fő tér
Óbudai Museum
Kassák Museum
Vasarely Museum
Flórián tér
Szentlélek tér
ÁRPÁD HÍD (HÉV Railway)
Danube
Post office
Church
St Peter & St Paul
Corinthia Aquincum Hotel
St Margaret Hospital
Kiscelli Museum
Church
Synagogue
ÓBUDA
Church
Police station
TÍMÁR UTCA (HÉV Railway)
Japanese garden
Thermal Hotel
BMF University
Grand Hotel
Roman military amphitheatre
Margaret Island
Premonstratensian Chapel
Water tower
Palatinus open-air pools
Dominican cloister
Thermal Hélia Hotel
Rose garden
Church
FEHÉREGYHÁZI ÚT
HUNOR UTCA
KUNIGUNDA ÚTJA
HÉVIZI UTCA
KALAP UTCA
BOGDÁNI ÚT
VEDER ÚT
VIHAR UTCA
SZÉL UTCA
SZENTENDREI ÚT
VÖRÖSVÁRI ÚT
HUNOR UTCA
RAKTÁR UTCA
BUDAI ALSÓ RAKPART
SÁNDOR
VÁRADI
BÉCSI ÚT
ZÁPOR UTCA
SOLYMÁR UTCA
SZŐLŐ UTCA
KÓRHÁZ U
TAVASZ UTCA
TÉGLA ÚT
FÖLD UTCA
KISCELLI UTCA
SERFŐZŐ UTCA
KIS KORONA UTCA
ÁRPÁD HÍD
SAN MARCO UTCA
SELMECI UTCA
PERC UTCA
LAJOS UTCA
PACSIRTAMEZŐ UTCA
FÉNYES ADOLF U
TÍMÁR UTCA
VIADOR UTCA
KECSKE UTCA
BOKOR U
ÁRPÁD FEJEDELEM ÚTJA
FOLYONDÁR UTCA
MONTEVIDEO UTCA
SEREGÉLY UTCA
SZÉPVÖLGYI ÚT

Pacsirtamező utca where you'll find a 2nd-century **military amphitheatre**. Holding 15,000 spectators, this was the largest of its type north of the Mediterranean; here gladiators fought with beasts or took part in naval battles in the flooded arena.

Walk north up Pacsirtamező utca and you'll reach **Flórián tér**, straddling the western bridgehead of Árpád híd, and for the most part a monument to bleak 20th-century modernity with its roaring road and pre-fab buildings. There's a slight respite to the square's southeastern side, where stands the **Parish Church of St Peter and St Paul** (*Óbudai Főplébániatemplom*; III, Lajos utca 168), erected by the Zichy family (that owned much of Óbuda) in 1744–49. A stone's throw away is a **neoclassical synagogue** (*zsinagóga*; III, Lajos utca 163) designed by András Landherr in 1820–21, and boasting imposing pillars beneath its portico. There was a ghetto here during the war; it now houses a Hungarian television studio.

Duck under the Szentendrei út flyover and you'll enter a subway like no other, an unexpected trove of Roman ruins. These were the **legionary baths**, excavated in 1778, and the tiled heating courses are still evident. A few hundred metres east along Kórház utca is the former market place and present-day haven of **Fő tér** (behind Árpád híd station in Szentlélek tér). This pretty cobbled square contains a daffodil-yellow **town hall** (Fő tér 3) at its northern side, with a little balcony and acorn finials, while on the eastern edge is the 18th-century **Zichy Palace**. Inside its baroque wings, and those of an adjacent Trinitarian monastery, are the **Óbuda History Museum**, and collections of works by **Lajos Kassák** and **Victor Vasarely** (pages 320 and 321). Pass out of the square's northeastern corner

(Laktanya utca) and take a photo with the four ladies strolling towards you beneath their umbrellas. Imre Varga's intriguing sculpture is a taster for the fabulous exhibition of his layered and polished metal works near by (page 312).

There are mosaics a short walk north of Flórián tér at **Hercules Villa** (page 320), but head for **Aquincum** for the real orgy of Roman ruins. Take the HÉV to the Aquincum stop and you'll be at the heart of what became the principal town of the province of Pannonia Inferior until the soldiers (and consequently the civilians too) pulled out in 404AD. It was established as the base for those civilians associated with the military camp 3km to the south, but quickly became a major administrative and commercial centre in its own right, with an amphitheatre, law courts, baths and temples. Walk across the road to the neoclassical **museum** (page 319), which makes sense of the stone lines and piles, and displays other archaeological finds.

Go 1km north – or board the HÉV once more – to **Római-fürdő**, where you'll see the remains of the civilian amphitheatre and an aqueduct (which carried water through Aquincum and on as far as the military amphitheatre), and where there is an eponymous strand (page 222) on the site of original Roman baths. There is another swimming pool set in park land at **Csillaghegy** (Star Hill; page 217), one stop further on. Alternatively, walk east towards the river and the **Római-part** (Roman bank). This stretch of river is popular for cycling, canoeing and fishing, and has a resort feel to it in summer months. The small shacks and al-fresco tables are lively places in the evenings; take a pew and relish some of the tastiest fish you'll find in Hungary. The woody riverside is popular with mosquitoes too, so bring repellent. (A ferry runs between the Római-part, Boráros tér and Jászai tér from

March 1 to September 1; tel: 1 369 1359; www.ship-bp.hu.)

## BUDA HILLS AND BEYOND

With the exception of Pest's downtown, districts II and XII in the Buda hills hold the city's most desirable residences. There are some stunning detached houses, and these leafy suburbs are where the rich and famous choose to settle. Even the president and prime minister have homes here.

For tourists and workers sweating away in the streets of the Belváros, the hills – running in a semi-circle around the western edge of Buda – promise a little space and a cooling breeze. There are walking trails, cycling routes and viewing towers, conservation areas and a wildlife park, caves and quarries and birds and boars. This is where nature lives. The main mode of public transport is the bus, but there are also cogwheel and children's railways, and even a chairlift. For details of all these, see *Chapter 13 Natural Budapest*. In addition, there are a few interesting museums to visit, both among the hills themselves (the **Bártók Béla Memorial House** and the **Kiscelli Museum**; pages 321 and 322) and a little further out (**Statue Park** and the **Nagytétény Castle Museum**; pages 323 and 311). And don't miss **Wolf's Meadow Cemetery** (page 346).

# 11 Discovering Pest and the Islands

## WALKING THE DOWNTOWN

The downtown (District V) is Pest's beating heart, a gathering point for the city's shopping, commercial, banking and tourist centres. The bulk of the Belváros (inner city) portion is hemmed in by the Kiskörút (Small Boulevard), a near semi-circle of road running from Freedom Bridge along the original lines of the medieval walls (dismantled during 19th-century expansion) before becoming a little ragged on its way to the Chain Bridge. It is lanced by Kossuth Lajos utca, running from Erzsébet híd out to Keleti station. The Lipótváros (Leopold Town) north of József Attila utca holds two of the country's most significant buildings in the Parliament and Szt István Basilica. The tracks of tram 2 run alongside the Danube and circle the Parliament, offering views to rival those from public transport anywhere in Europe. Moving in from the tracks, though, the downtown is a compact area of one-way or pedestrianised roads that's best explored on foot.

### Belváros

There's no simple way of tackling the inner city – the chances are that you will start somewhere in the vicinity of Váci utca and dive off into those squares and side streets that take your fancy. No single linear walk properly covers the sights of interest; for the purposes of this guide, therefore, we've divided it into two chunks, south and north of Erzsébet híd. Pick and mix your way around.

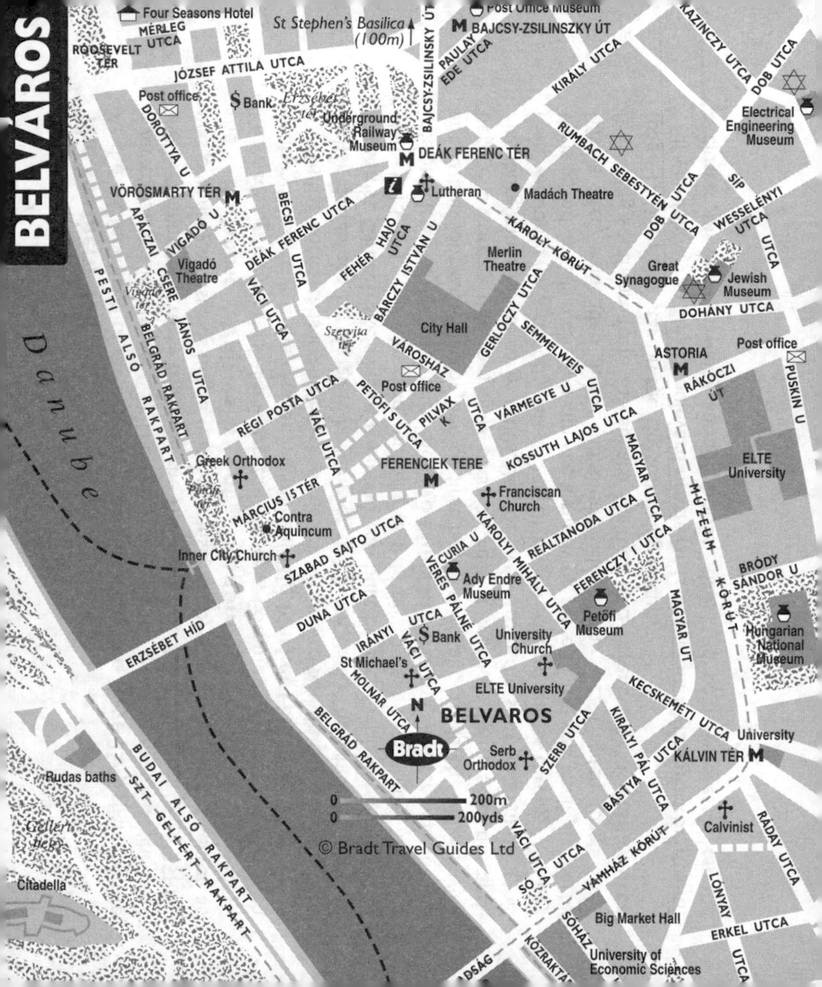
BELVÁROS
Four Seasons Hotel
MÉRLEG UTCA
ROOSEVELT TÉR
St Stephen's Basilica (100m)
Post Office Museum
BAJCSY-ZSILINSZKY ÚT
BAJCSY-ZSILINSKY ÚT
PAULAY EDE UTCA
KAZINCZY UTCA
DOB UTCA
JÓZSEF ATTILA UTCA
KIRÁLY UTCA
Post office
Bank
Erzsébet tér
DOROTTYA U
Underground Railway Museum
DEÁK FERENC TÉR
Electrical Engineering Museum
RUMBACH SEBESTYÉN UTCA
VÖRÖSMARTY TÉR
BÉCSI UTCA
Lutheran
Madách Theatre
SÍP UTCA
WESSELÉNYI UTCA
DOB UTCA
APÁCZAI
VIGADÓ U
DEÁK FERENC UTCA
FEHÉR HAJÓ UTCA
BÁRCZY ISTVÁN U
KÁROLY KÖRÚT
Merlin Theatre
Great Synagogue
Jewish Museum
Vigadó Theatre
Vigadó tér
CSERE
VÁCI UTCA
Szervita tér
City Hall
GERLÓCZY UTCA
SEMMELWEIS UTCA
DOHÁNY UTCA
PESTI ALSÓ RAKPART
BELGRÁD RAKPART
JÁNOS UTCA
VÁROSHÁZ
Post office
ASTORIA
RÁKÓCZI ÚT
PUSKIN U
Danube
RÉGI POSTA UTCA
PETŐFI S UTCA
PILVAX K
VÁRMEGYE U
KOSSUTH LAJOS UTCA
Greek Orthodox
Petőfi tér
FERENCIEK TERE
MAGYAR UTCA
ELTE University
MÚZEUM KÖRÚT
MÁRCIUS 15 TÉR
Contra Aquincum
Franciscan Church
REÁLTANODA UTCA
Inner City Church
SZABAD SAJTÓ UTCA
CURIA U
KÁROLYI MIHÁLY UTCA
FERENCZY I UTCA
BRÓDY SÁNDOR U
Ady Endre Museum
VERES PÁLNÉ UTCA
DUNA UTCA
Petőfi Museum
MAGYAR UT
ERZSÉBET HÍD
IRÁNYI UTCA
Bank
University Church
Hungarian National Museum
St Michael's
ELTE University
KECSKEMÉTI UTCA
University
MOLNÁR UTCA
N
BELVAROS
Bradt
BELGRÁD RAKPART
Serb Orthodox
SZERB UTCA
KIRÁLYI PÁL UTCA
KÁLVIN TÉR
Rudas baths
BUDAI ALSÓ RAKPART
SZT GELLÉRT RAKPART
0 200m
0 200yds
BÁSTYA UTCA
Calvinist
RÁDAY UTCA
Gellért hegy
© Bradt Travel Guides Ltd
VÁCI UTCA
SÓ UTCA
VÁMHÁZ KÖRÚT
LÓNYAY UTCA
Citadella
Big Market Hall
ERKEL UTCA
SÓHÁZ
KOZRAKTÁR
University of Economic Sciences

### *The southern half*

At the southern end of the inner city is **Szabadság híd** (page 254), spanning the river to Gellért Hill (page 253). The enormous, slightly grimy-bricked building near the bridgehead – actually falling on the Ferencváros side of the road (page 298) – was originally a customs house (*vámház*) designed by Miklós Ybl, but has served as the **Budapest University of Economic Sciences** (*Budapesti Közgazdaságtudományi és Államigazgatási Egyetem*; Fővám tér 8) since the mid-20th century. Next to it is the cleaner, magnificent **Big Market Hall** (page 202).

Vámház körút leads in an easterly direction around to **Kálvin tér**, a busy square rather dominated by the glass building of the Erste Bank. The white neoclassical **Calvinist Church** (*Református templom*) was built by József Hofrichter and József Hild (1813–51), while the sandy building (Kálvin tér 9) next to it – now holding a café and flower shop – was once the **Two Lions Inn** (see the weather-worn beasts above the doorway). Hector Berlioz first heard the 'Rákóczi March' while staying here – a stirring tune originally used to recruit freedom fighters to the anti-Habsburg cause in the early 1700s. Berlioz drew from the song in composing his own version over a century later. One of the **medieval gates** through the city walls stood at Kálvin tér; you can see a surviving piece of the wall itself on nearby Bástya utca, embedded in the northern side of the Jazz Garden (page 182). Branching southeast from the square (further into Ferencváros) is **Ráday utca** (page 172), a rising star on the city's drinking circuit.

If you follow the Small Boulevard northwards you'll join **Múzeum körút**, with a cluster of shops hawking antique books, maps and coins. Addresses on the opposite side of the road actually have a District VIII postcode (page 297), and these include the **Hungarian National Museum** (page 308). The museum is difficult to miss – it's the largest in the country – and you certainly shouldn't because it holds the Hungarian coronation mantle and some breathtaking ceiling frescos. It was from the museum steps that Petőfi's 'National Song' was recited at the outset of the 1848 revolution (see page 6), and from the **Radio station** on the adjacent Bródy Sándor utca that secret police fired the opening salvos at student demonstrators during the revolution of 1956 (page 10). A little further on, just before the Astoria junction where Kossuth Lajos utca meets the boulevard, is the faculty of arts of the prestigious **ELTE University** (*Eötvös Loránd Tudományos-egyetem*; Múzeum körút 4–8); designed by Imre Steindl, this was once the department of natural sciences and *alma mater* of Ede Teller, inventor of the hydrogen bomb (see page 86).

Cross the road and head back towards the depths of the inner city along Ferenczy István utca to **Károlyi kert**, an enclosed and peaceful park with well-kept flowerbeds and benches for rest and contemplation. This was a private garden belonging to the palace behind it, once home of Mihály Károlyi, the president of the 1918–19 Hungarian Republic. During the mid-19th century, the notorious Baron Haynau ('the Hyena of Brescia'; see page 25) took the place as his headquarters after crushing the 1848 revolution, and from here dictated those vengeful measures designed to dampen future thoughts of rebellion. It is now the headquarters of the **Petőfi Literary Museum** (page 325). (There's a further tribute to literature past at the **Ady Endre Memorial Museum** – page 323 – on the parallel Veres Pálné utca.)

To the right along Károlyi Mihály utca is **Ferenciek tere**, bordered by vast art-nouveau buildings funnelling traffic along the thoroughfare between Erszébet híd and Kossuth Lajos utca. Prime among these are the **Klotild Palaces** (Szabadsajtó út 5 and 6), identical six-storey twins guarding the western entrance. Built at the same time as the bridge, they once held an impressive café, but now stand empty. On the square's northern side is the **Párisi Udvar** (Ferenciek tere 5), commissioned of Henrik Schmahl in the early 20th century as a bank office and elegant Parisian shopping arcade. Its heyday is past, but the ornamented interior with stained-glass cupola is lovely still. (You can access Váci utca from the arcade, via Kigyó utca.) Across the road is the **Franciscan Church** (*Ferences templom*; Ferenciek tere 9) after which the square is named. The current church was completed in 1743, the Turks having trashed its 13th-century Gothic predecessor in 1526. Look out for the pew where Ferenc Liszt used to park himself while staying in the adjacent monastery. A relief on the wall outside shows the nobleman **Miklós Wesselényi** in action during the murderous flood of 1838 (se e page 6). His valiant efforts in a rowing boat saved many lives – and unlike others who milked desperate people by demanding payment for access to their boats, Wesselényi's bravery came free of charge. **Kossuth Lajos utca** runs away eastwards; the building at **number 3** was where the 'National Song' was printed, tog ether with demands for bourgeois reform (the 'Twelve Points').

Taking Károlyi Mihaly utca in the other direction from Károlyi Palace brings up **Egyetem tér** and the **ELTE**'s departments of law and political science (Egyetem tér 1–3). The **University Church** (*Egyetemi templom*; Papnövelde utca 9) needs a good bath, but beneath the grime of time and car fumes is a beautiful baroque surface of terracotta and white. It was constructed by the Paulines – the country's only indigenous monastic order – in 1748. They were booted out not long afterwards when József II dissolved the orders in 1782, and the church was taken over by the university. Parliament met for a short time here after the 1848–49 War of Independence. High above the altar, angels bear a copy of Poland's 'Madonna of Czestochowa'.

Moving southwest from the square along Szerb utca, the **Serb Orthodox Church** (*Szent György Nagyvértanú Szerb Orthodox templom*; Szerb utca 6) was constructed in 1698 by Serbs arriving after the Turkish occupation. The tower and façade were added in 1750, probably to the plans of the renowned architect András Mayerhoffer, and the nave divides male and female worshippers over two levels. The iconostasis is a replacement for an original that fell victim to the 1838 flood; a marker by the southern entrance shows the level the waters reached – fully two metres high.

The Serb Church is an incense whiff from Váci utca. (If you cross that road towards the river, you'll come to **Belgrád rakpart**, the embankment running from Fővám tér to Roosevelt tér and beyond. The views of the castle over the water make it a pleasant promenade, but those with less energy can climb aboard tram 2, which accompanies it all the way up to the Parliament building.) **Váci utca** is the vein pulsing through the whole of the Belváros, linking our northern and southern halves and marking the length of medieval Pest. It is the primary tourist street, pedestrianised most of the way, and characterised by cafés, restaurants, and shops selling goods from designer clothes to folk art and antiques (see *Chapter 8 Shopping*). Prices are as high as you'll find anywhere in the city, but it's busy and colourful and there are some sights worth seeing alongside the commercial outlets. The **City Council Chamber** (Váci utca 62–64), for instance, is a four-storey brick pile designed by Imre Steindl in 1870, with carved floral motifs and garlands, and dragons on its upper tier. **St Michael's Church** (*Belvárosi Szent Mihály templom*; Váci utca 47) has felt the lick of fire and flood since its foundations were laid in 1703, while Charles XII of Sweden rested his weary head for a night at **number 43** (now a school) on his frantic journey home from Constantinople in 1714. On meeting a sculptural tree of life – which actually looks more like a stick of celery – you'll have arrived at Szabad Sajtó út at the top of the inner city's southern segment.

### *The northern half*

Look to the left along Szabad Sajtó út and you'll see **Erzsébet híd**, crossing the river at its narrowest point. When originally opened in 1903, this was the longest single-span chain bridge in the world (at 380m). Destroyed by the retreating Germans in 1945, it was the last of Budapest's bridges to be replaced and – with its new cable design – the only one not restored to its former shape. A significant slice of medieval architecture was sacrificed to make way for the bridge, and the **Inner City Parish Church** (page 349) had to close its eyes and pray as the wrecking ball whistled past its left cheek. In front of the church in **Március 15 tér** are remains of **Contra-Aquincum**, a 3rd-century fort built by the Romans to protect their settlement on the other side of the river.

Duck under the subway (containing some 19th-century photographs of the city) to continue on Váci utca, which leads uninterrupted to Vörösmarty tér. If you take the direct route, keep your eyes peeled for the intricate blue façade of **Thonet House** at number 11, designed in 1888 by Ödön Lechner ('the father of Hungarian art nouveau'); the former **Inn of the Seven Electors** (Váci utca 9; now the Pesti Színház), where Liszt gave a performance in 1823 at the tender age of just 11; the well in Kristóf tér bearing a statue of the '**Fisher Girl**' ('Fischer Rézi'); and the jagged line of marble cobblestones just a little further on, which traces the position of the northern medieval **Vác Gate** before it was removed in 1789.

Alternatively, take a slight detour left into Régi posta utca, looking up to the painted relief of a stagecoach by ceramicist Margit Kovács (see page 242) on the building at **number 13**. When the McDonalds opposite opened in 1989, it was the first in the country and attracted a lengthy queue of locals; it's now just one of 13 in Budapest alone. At the end of the street you'll emerge into **Petőfi tér**, a square with strong symbolic significance and a favoured rallying point for both protest and celebration. The cloaked and goateed statue at the centre is Sándor Petőfi (see box, page 278), around which students gathered to denounce the Rákosi regime on October 23 1956. The **Greek Orthodox Church** was built by 18th-century Greek and Macedonian merchants; one of its two towers was destroyed in World War II and never replaced.

Move northwards along the Duna-korzó to **Vigadó tér**, a riverside eating and drinking spot with stalls selling woven, wooden, beaded and leather goods.

### *THE PEOPLE'S POET*

To this day, the nation's favourite versifier – the man who has made the deepest dent on the national and literary consciousness – is the 19th-century Sándor Petőfi (1823–49). He was a writer who brought the vernacular into Hungarian poetry, and a fervent patriot. Most of all, he was a newlywed who provided the voice and impulse for the revolution that broke out on March 15 1848. In his 'National Song' – recited from the steps of the National Museum – he pleaded 'Rise, Hungarians!' ('*Talpra, magyar!*'). And they did. A year later – at just 26 – he was dead, killed in Transylvania during one of the last battles of the War of Independence. His cult status was sealed as the young, passionate, revolutionary romantic – the eloquent James Dean of his age.

Some impish boys play by the fountain at the grassy centre, while on the railings next to the tram track sits the harlequinesque statue of the '**Little Princess**' ('Kiskirálylány', Marton László, 1989). The square takes its name, however, from the flamboyant **concert hall** (see page 181) at the eastern side. The promenade continues on to the Chain Bridge and Roosevelt tér, but we'll take a right down Vigadó utca to the side of the concert hall and on to **Vörösmarty tér**. It is broad and elegant, filled with portraitists and plane trees, with seasonal markets and performances of folk music. At its centre the poet **Mihály Vörösmarty** rests his pins; the opening line of 'Szózat' ('Admonition'), an appeal in 1836 for Hungarian unity, is inscribed on the statue's plinth – 'Be steadfastly faithful to your homeland, oh Magyars'. During winter the lucky chap surveys the world from inside a heated plastic bubble, designed to prevent his marble cracking. At the square's northern side is the celebrated **Gerbeaud** (page 162), while next to that is the western terminus of the city's **oldest metro** line (page 326). To the south is the Bank Palace of 1915, now holding the **Budapest Stock Exchange**.

Southeast of Vörösmarty tér is **Szervita tér**, which used to belong to the Order of Servites whose baroque church (*Szervita templom*) was consecrated in 1748. The relief above the portal's pediment depicts the order's founding saints – Julianna on the right and Peregrin (the patron saint of leg-pain sufferers) on the left. The square's three **art-nouveau façades** are wonderful, particularly Miksa Róth's allegorical mosaic of Hungary at number 3. **Petőfi Sándor utca**, a shopping street, leads south from the square, as does **Városház utca**. The latter is dominated by the salmon-pink and custard-yellow **City Hall** at 9–11, originally built in the 18th century to house disabled soldiers, Budapest's biggest baroque building and thought by Maria Theresa to better her own palace in Vienna.

North of Vörösmarty tér, **József nádor tér** is bordered by heavy neoclassical residences and the magnificent **Postabank Headquarters** (1860–61), which fills the entire western side. At the square's centre is a statue of Archduke József, the Habsburg palatine for 50 years from 1797. As palatines went, he was relatively popular in Pest; he loved the city, and made determined efforts to improve it – he was, for instance, the instigator for the planting of its greatest parks (at Margaret Island and City Park). The **British embassy** stands near by (Harmincad utca 6), regularly patrolled by armed police while the terrorist threat is high. East of that is **Erzsébet tér**, the site originally earmarked for the National Theatre before monumental squabbles put a halt to proceedings (see page 176). A modern park, with a glass-bottomed pool, has recently opened in its stead, with a car park and cultural and conference centre beneath. The square's bus terminal has now moved to Népliget, but some coach tours still depart from here. The **Danubius Fountain** is a replacement for a 19th-century original (Miklós Ybl and Leó Feszler, 1880–83) destroyed in World War II; its broad bowls are topped by an allegory of the Danube, with its half-naked tributaries seated around the base. Look out too for the statue of the shepherd piping to his sheep at the square's northern edge.

**Deák Ferenc tér** meets at the east, but feels more properly a part of bustling Pest. The simple **Lutheran Church** (*Deák téri evangélikus templom*) was designed at the turn of the 19th century by Mihály Pollock; the sons of Lajos Kossuth were baptised inside, and Sándor Petőfi was schooled here. The **Lutheran Museum** (page 324) is next door, while the **Underground Railway Museum** (page 326) in the station underpass tells the story of the continent's oldest metro line, one of several ambitious constructions built as part of the millennial celebrations. The beige and fading **Anker Palace** (Deák Ferenc tér 6), with its helmet turrets, was an insurance building that many felt a blight on the cityscape when it first appeared. It now contains a series of shops.

## Lipótváros and beyond

The area north of József Attila utca is known as Leopold Town, which developed following the construction of the Chain Bridge (page 260). It is still part of District V but a world away from the Belváros; colourful side streets make way for straight roads and broad squares, and shops and cafés for offices and 19th-century residential blocks. It feels a more serious place, one of industrious commerce and government, and holds pockets that resonate strongly with some of the city's tragic moments.

Start with the elliptical **Roosevelt tér** at the foot of the Chain Bridge. You'll risk life and limb in crossing the road running around it, but the grassed island in the centre was the site of **Coronation Hill**, a mound of soil gathered from points all over Hungary. Following the 1867 Compromise (see page 7), and the crowning of Ferenc József in Mátyás Church, Hungary's new king clambered the hillock, pointed to the four compass points with Szt István's sword, and pledged to be the country's defender – a symbolic act that harked back to pagan clan ceremonies. There was significant controversy when the **Four Seasons Hotel** (see page 104) constructed its car park underneath. The hotel itself has finally opened in the renovated Gresham Palace, an art-nouveau jewellery box originally built for an English insurance company. There are statues to Ferenc Deák, the architect of the Compromise, and István Széchenyi, who made possible the **Hungarian Academy of Sciences** (*Magyar Tudományos Akadémia*; Roosevelt tér 9) at the square's northern side. The count donated a year's income to the founding of the society in this neo-Renaissance palace, with its chunks of creamy-orange stone. A relief at one side of the building records the moment on November 3 1825; when asked how he'd live for a year with no money, Széchenyi replied 'My friends will help me'.

Zrínyi utca leads eastwards as far as **Szent István tér**, a pedestrianised space that seems rather undersized in the presence of the looming **Basilica** (page 352). Behind it is Bajcsy-Zsilinszky út – named after a politician who stood up to the Nazis and was executed for it in 1944 – which links Deák tér to Nyugati tér; the latter holds the iron-and-glass **Western Railway Station** (*Nyugati pályaudvar*), built by Gustave Eiffel's firm (1874–77). Adjacent is 'the world's most beautiful McDonald's', and to the rear the Westend City Center shopping mall (page 209).

If, instead of going east, you follow Széchenyi rakpart north from Roosevelt tér, you'll arrive at **Kossuth Lajos tér**. Imre Steindl was victorious in the competition to build **Parliament**, and his vision stands overlooking the river on the western side (page 350). Remarkably, however, the second- and third-placed entries were also constructed, becoming the Palace of Justice (number 12, now the **Museum of Ethnography**; page 324) and **Ministry of Agriculture** (number 11) respectively. At the northern end of the square is a **statue of Kossuth** (1802–94), leader of the ultimately failed 1848–49 War of Independence, while the Transylvanian Prince **Ferenc Rákóczi II** (1676–1735) – another anti-Habsburg freedom fighter of the previous century – is

*Parliament*

opposite. Also on the lawn are memorials – a **symbolic grave** and an **eternal flame** – to victims of October 25 1956 when ÁVO shooters fired on a peaceful crowd. Each metal 'bullet' set into the walls of the Ministry of Agriculture represents one of the dead. Two days before, revolutionaries had torn the Soviet emblem from the Hungarian flag during the uprising, and the gravestone bears a relief of this symbol of freedom.

Madonna sang 'Don't Cry for me, Argentina' from one of the balconies of **Alkotmány (Constitution) utca** – running east from the square – during filming of the Hollywood movie *Evita*. Leaving via the southeast corner, however, you'll pass through the tiny **Vértanúk (Martyrs') tere**; standing on a bronze bridge and looking westward for American support is a **statue of Imre Nagy** (1896–1958), the communist reformer and prime minister during the '56 revolution who the Soviets executed two years later (see page 11). Beyond it, at the end of Vécsey utca, is the lengthy **Szabadság (Liberty) tér**. Until the late 1800s, this was the site of a barracks, where significant participants in the 1848–49 War of Independence were incarcerated and then executed by Baron Haynau (see page 24). Among them was Lajos Batthyány, prime minister of the 1848 independent government, and close by on Aulich utca an **Eternal Light** in a greening casket glows perpetually in remembrance. The square's four corners once held allegorical representations of land stripped from Hungary by the Trianon Treaty, together with a central Monument to Grief. This was replaced in 1945 by the **Soviet monument**. After the fall of communism, the Russian government was allowed to nominate one public piece to remain in situ (rather than being carted off to Statue Park), and this was the choice. The hulking eclectic palace housing the Hungarian Television offices (Szabadság utca 17) is the **former Stock Exchange**, built by Ignác Alpár in 1905. Facing it across the square is another of Alpár's designs, the **Hungarian National Bank** (Szabadság tér 8), with reliefs showing personifications of art, industry and commerce. (Among these is Alpár himself, in the clothes of a medieval master builder.) The outstanding **Post Office Savings Bank** (1901) backs on to it (on Hold utca); Ödön Lechner fused art-nouveau and Magyar folk motifs into the façade, and ceramic bees – symbolic of saving – climb towards shiny honey pots. The lemon-yellow building (Szabadság tér 12), with coiling snake reliefs on its upper tier, is the **American embassy**; near it is a **statue of US General Harry Hill Bandholtz**, who prevented Romanian soldiers from looting the National Museum while serving with the peacekeeping force in 1919.

**Szent István körút** is the northernmost stretch of the Great Boulevard, joining Margit híd and marking the border with District XIII (Újlipótváros, or New Leopold Town). The beautiful **Vígszínház** (page 177) stands out among the otherwise grey eclectic buildings along its length. Prior to World War II, a high number of Jews lived in this district, and many of Wallenberg's safe houses were established here (one was at Pozsonyi út 14; see page 348). A tribute to the Swedish saviour by Pál Pátzay – comprising a half-naked man clubbing a hissing serpent – stands in **Szent István Park**, parallel with the southern tip of Margaret Island. The Jewish community is actually returning, and the area has been nicknamed 'Kis (Little) Tel Aviv'. Head up **Váci út** for the Westend City Center (see page 209) and the Palace of Wonders (page 325). Look out too for the concrete, neo-Romanesque **Parish Church of St Margaret** (*Szent Margit templom*; Lehel tér); its construction was funded by Lord Rothermere, whose family coat of arms are shown in one of the stained-glass windows.

## TERÉZVÁROS

Falling on the eastern side of Bajcsy-Zsilinszky út, and locked between Király utca, Dózsa György út and the tracks of Nyugati Railway Station, much of Theresa Town (District VI) is a touch shabby. **Király utca** (named after the king of England in 1860) was a major thoroughfare at the end of the 19th century, and has a thriving collection of shops selling second-hand clothes and electrical goods, some swanky interior-design showrooms at its western end, the Liszt Ferenc Academy of Music (page 181) at numbers 64–66, and the district's 19th-century parish church (where it meets Nagymező utca), with chapels by Mihály Pollock and spire by Miklós Ybl. Liszt Ferenc tér and Jókai Mór tér are popular drinking and meeting spots, and Nagymező utca contains the city's main clutch of theatres. However, the splendid big boy of the district is Andrássy út, the main avenue flying arrow straight from the Small Boulevard to Heroes' Square, and rated by many as the city's prettiest.

### A walk along Andrássy út

In the 1860s, politician and nobleman Count Gyula Andrássy returned to Hungary after a period in France with his head full of ideas. He was determined that Budapest should have its own Champs Elysées to complement the city's boom in building, transport and culture. The elegant avenue – declared a UNESCO World Heritage Site in 2002 – went some way towards fulfilling the dream; when the underground railway was constructed underneath in 1896 (three years before the Parisian metro), it could justifiably claim to have gone one better. The street is a showcase for turn-of-the-century star talent (including Alajos Strobl, Károly Lotz and Miklós Ybl). Writer and gourmand Gyula Krúdy noted the street 'lay in the body of Budapest like the Danube within Hungary. [I]t was the hope of the city.' The avenue stretches for over two kilometres; if you don't fancy strolling the whole length, break your walk by joining the metro for a stop or two, or hopping on bus number 4.

First called Sugár (Radial) út – and re-named variously Sztálin út, Magyar Ifjúság útja (Hungarian Avenue of Youth) and Népköztársaság útja (People's Republic Avenue) under communism – it was always popularly referred to as Andrássy út. Its buildings are neoclassical and strong-lined, with heavy doors and wide windows. The western portion features grand offices and apartments before it broadens after Oktogon into a tree-lined sweep of villas and gardens. Be sure to cast eyes into gloomy courtyards, and watch for portals supported by muscle-bound Atlases and graceful caryatids. To walk here is to peer into the life of the city and its history.

The **Postal Museum** (no 3; page 328) is your first stop, if only to see the frescoed stairwell. The breathtaking **State Opera House** (no 22; page 180) is a little further on. Strobl was just 26 when he carved the marble sphinxes outside; poet Endre Ady, who was fond of a drink, slipped off the back of one and cracked his head on the pavement. The literary world of the coffee house is well represented by the **Eckermann** (no 24, formerly a dirty dive frequented by Ady himself), the **Művész** (no 29; page 163), the **Lukacs** (no 70; page 162) and the **Media Club** on the terrace of the Hungarian Association of Journalists' headquarters (no 101, now occupied by the Premier Restaurant; page 152). The eclectic **Dreschler Palace** (no 25) was designed by Ödön Lechner (who famously explained that he decorated the roofs of his buildings to give the birds pleasure), and used to house the Ballet Institute. Just north of the opera house is **Nagymező utca**, the 'Hungarian Broadway', which also has a proliferation of hairdressing salons and sun-bed shops. The **Parisian Grand Department Store** (*Párizsi Nagyáruház*; no 39), with its bold art-nouveau façade, opened in 1911 as the city's most exclusive store; you could even ice-skate on the roof terrace in winter. Take a break at a café-bar on **Jókai Mór tér** or **Liszt Ferenc tér** (page 171), which straddle the avenue shortly afterwards. The **Liszt Music Academy** (page 181) is at the southeastern end of the latter; László Márton's statue near by shows the great composer in mid, manic flow.

In the eight-sided **Oktogon**, you may wonder why the **mayor's office** (Teréz körút 13) is adorned with six iron mooring rings. This is a hangover from the early 1800s, when a deep stream ran the length of the Great Boulevard – indeed, as the city developed, there was talk of transforming it into a canal with gondolas. Rather than Little Venice, however, Oktogon is today known as 'American Square' because of its fast-food restaurants (including the world's largest Burger King). Moving onward, the building at number 60 chilled hearts during much of the 20th century; it now holds a **museum to the terror regimes** (page 305). Ferenc Liszt lived in an apartment of the Music Academy at number 67 (the academy moved to its current location in 1907), and a **memorial museum** there allows you to have a snoop (page 327). The **Puppet Theatre** (page 177) and **Hungarian College of Applied Art** occupy the building at number 69, into which Adolf Láng crammed as many features of Italian Renaissance as he could muster in 1877.

**Kodály Körönd** is the most atmospheric circus in Pest, and the one in the worst state of repair. Its flaking buildings have dark turrets, rounded towers and Transylvanian-style boxed roofs. The statues gracing its four corners are fighters for freedom – the lyrical poet Bálint Balassi (who died in battle against the Turks), Miklós Zrínyi and György Szondi (16th-century heroes), and Vak Bottyán (a leader of the 18th-century anti-Habsburg independence war) – while the composer Zoltán Kodály lived at number 89, where there's now a **museum** (page 329). From here onward the spacious villas have fenced gardens, originally the homes of 19th-century industrial magnates but now belonging to embassies and law firms. Two collections of Asian art can be found at the **Hopp Ferenc** (no 103; page 326) and **Ráth György** (Városligeti fasor 12; page 328) museums, before the avenue reaches its dramatic climax in the vastness of Heroes' Square.

## HEROES' SQUARE, CITY PARK AND THE SPORTS DISTRICT

**Heroes' Square** (Hősök tere) was one of the millennial projects, constructed to celebrate the anniversary of the supposed date of the Magyar arrival in the Carpathian Basin. It is a monumental, triumphalist expression of Hungarian patriotism and confidence at a time when the Compromise had restored a nation's self-respect and the economy was buoyant; aside from the odd glaring omission (see below), its statues represent a chronological catalogue of the nation's first 1,000 years. In 1896, it also formed the gateway to the celebratory exhibition, whose 200 pavilions attracted visitors from all over the world.

At the square's centre is the 36m-high fluted column of the **Millennium Monument** (which wasn't completed until 1929), with the Archangel Gabriel atop bearing the Holy Crown that he is said to have offered to István in a dream. Around the base are the menacing Magyar tribal chieftains, their horses tossing and snorting, and the leader Árpád to the fore. A marble tablet in front covers an **empty coffin**, laid in 1989 to honour those killed during the 1956 revolution, and inscribed with 'In memory of our heroes'. All this is framed by a pair of colonnades bearing statues of the country's major leaders, starting with István and culminating in Lajos Kossuth, who headed the 1848 revolution before going into exile in America (and becoming a successful statesmen over there). One dynasty is noticeable by its absence; originally the last five statues in the sequence depicted the Habsburgs (Leopold II, Charles VI, Maria Theresa, Joseph II and Francis Joseph). The latter was an unpopular figure whose statue was quickly torn down when the monarchy fell at the end of World War I, and the others were later removed by the communists. The replacements are all heroes of the independence struggle against Turks, Habsburgs or both, with Ferenc Rákóczi II (see page 6) among the Transylvanian princes alongside Kossuth. The chariots charging above are allegories of work and welfare, war, peace, and art and science.

## *THE COMMIE TOUR*

The last Soviet soldier left in 1991, but there are communist reminders to be found in places other than Statue Park (page 311). Pest contains the odd shop with swirling neon sign, typical of the communist era. The former state-owned bookshops are still marked by a blue neon owl. A *közért* (literally 'for the public') is a local corner shop stocking traditional items. Try District VIII, which hasn't changed much, and you'll find unusual products in tins and jars – Traubisoda and Márka (fizzy drinks), Túró Rudi (a tube of cottage cheese with a hint of vanilla and covered in plain chocolate, found in the chiller cabinet), and Munkás (Worker) cigarettes.

In the garden at Puskás Ferenc Stadion are 16 socialist-realist statues, depictions of health and sport that lined the avenue leading to the stadium (built in 1953). On the corner of Dózsa György út and Városligeti fasor, near City Park, is a massive mural showing labourers on the wall of a former trade-union office. The Workers' Pantheon of Kerepesi Cemetery (page 349) is inscribed with 'They lived for communism and the people'; despite the law banning 'images of oppression', a nearby plot for fallen Soviet soldiers displays a hammer and sickle. This also features on the World War II monument in Szabadság tér (page 283). The island of Csepel in southern Budapest was always a stronghold of the workers' movement, and a statue called 'Olvasó

Munkás' ('Reading Worker') by András Beck adorns Béke tér. The Young Pioneers built what is now the Children's Railway (page 357) in 1950. A museum at Hűvösvölgy station has a charming collection of memorabilia, while Virágvölgy displays a plaque with three pioneers pointing towards a brighter socialist future.

Several restaurants preserve flavours of the socialist era. **Resti kocsma** (V, Deák Ferenc utca 2; tel: 1 266 6210; open Mon–Sat 12.00–05.00) takes its name from the railway-station buffets where you can buy lukewarm coffee and stale pastries. Communist signs urge the workers on, and everything in the cellar restaurant is red – down to the pioneer's tie draped over the beer pump. The food is too edible to represent a real *resti*, and the prices too high (mains around 1,500Ft). For details of **Marxim**, see page 140. **Menza** (VI, Liszt Ferenc tér 2; tel: 1 413 1482; open daily 10.00–24.00) – or 'Canteen' – opened in 2003, and evokes the socialist-realist dining-hall aesthetic of the 'Goulash Communism' period, with brown colours, polyester tablecloths and boarding to protect the walls from splashes of soup. The 'best-of' menu even includes socialist favourites like *lángos* (see page 132). **Paprika gyorsétterem** (V, Pilváx köz 1) was the Hungarian version of a fast-food restaurant, with goulash in plastic dishes and red wine sold in little paper cups. The restaurants gradually disappeared during the 1990s, but this last hanger-on is enjoying a renaissance.

Splendid examples of neoclassical architecture, the **Museum of Fine Arts** (page 310) and the **Palace of Arts** (page 332) stand to the north and south. A cross marks the point on **Dózsa György út** – which runs across the square – where a church once stood before it was dismantled by the communists in 1951 to make way for a parade ground. Here was placed a massive statue of Stalin that insurgents subsequently bashed to bits during the '56 revolution. The statue of Lenin that succeeded it is in Statue Park (page 311).

**City Park** (*Városliget*) is grassed and wooded, accessed from the back of Heroes' Square via a bridge (designed by Gustave Eiffel) over an artificial lake. The water is ideal for a summery splash around in a pedalo, or for a spot of ice-skating during winter when the southern portion is transformed into a rink (cost 300/600Ft per hour weekdays/weekends; open Mon–Fri 09.00–13.00, 16.00–20.00, Sat 09.00–13.00, 14.00–18.00, Sun 10.00–14.00, 16.00–20.00). Standing on an island, the **Vajdahunyad Castle** (*vára*) is as fantastical as any construction you are ever likely to see. Ignác Alpár used 21 buildings as the models for a design that incorporated all the styles of Hungary's architectural heritage. Its most striking sections were based upon the former castle of the Hunyadi clan in Transylvania, after which the creative mishmash is named. Originally fashioned from wood, the fairy-tale castle so enchanted those who saw it that it was rebuilt in stone as a permanent fixture. Just outside is a **statue of Alpár** surveying his masterpiece, and in the courtyard of the baroque wing (which holds the **Museum of Agriculture**; page 329) sits the hooded '**Anonymus**' (Miklós Ligeti, 1903). While his true identity is lost to us, the 12th- or 13th-century 'Anonymous' chronicled the country's early history in his *Gesta Hungarorum*, which is now held by the Széchényi Library (page 316). Touch his pen – it's considered good luck.

In summer, there are outdoor concerts at the castle, while at the park's eastern edge are the **Petőfi Csarnok** (page 184) and the **Transport Museum** (page 332). On the pathway leading from the rear of the castle is a **statue of US President George Washington**, donated in 1906 by Hungarian emigrants. America is home to a large number of Hungarian exiles, that in Cleveland representing the biggest population outside Europe. To the north of Kós Károly sétány are delights zoological, gastronomical and balneological; within a few hundred yards of each other are the country's biggest zoo (page 331), most famous restaurant (page 153) and largest spa (page 223), together with a circus (page 331) and an amusement park (page 333). It is difficult to find nothing to do.

To the southeast of City Park, on the other side of Thököly út, is the city's **sports district** (still part of District XIV). The main stadium among a sprinkling of sports halls and arenas is the **Puskás Ferenc Stadion** (or Népstadion), named after Hungary's iconic footballer (see page 225). It seats 80,000, and is where big football matches and concerts are held. Socialist-realist statues that once lined the avenue leading to its entrance are now in its garden (see box, pages 290–1), and there's a **Sport Museum** (page 330) near by, but in truth there is little else to draw you to what is otherwise a rather bleak area of the capital.

Hősök tere and Széchenyi fürdő stations are on the M1 underground line, while buses 4 and 30 and trolleybus 72 also serve City Park et al. Puskás Stadion is reached via Stadionok on the M2 metro line.

## ERZSÉBETVÁROS

District VII – Elizabeth Town – runs from the Small Boulevard's outer rim as far as Dózsa György út, and is bordered by Király utca to the north and **Rákóczi út** to the south. The latter is one of the city's main shopping streets, the route linking the Eastern (Keleti) Railway Station to the city centre a natural magnet for traders. It used to be a seedy area frequented by prostitutes, but it's cleaner now and the popular choice for well-priced clothes. While you're browsing the blouses and shirts, keep an eye out for the wonderful art-nouveau **Uránia film theatre** (no 21; page 193). At the corner with Gyulai Pál utca, the baroque **Szent Rókus Chapel** (no 31) was built in 1711 in the hope that it would secure saintly protection for the citizens of Pest during a period when the plague was hitting hard. The 1838 flood is commemorated in a relief on the façade; the street level was raised in 1846, which is why the church now sinks below the tarmac's tide. Next to the chapel, is the **capital's oldest hospital** (Gyulai Pál utca 2), constructed in 1796 – at that time well outside the city walls – to treat infectious diseases. It is named after the 19th-century head doctor **Ignác Semmelweis**, who was christened the 'saviour of mothers' after discovering that scrubbed staff reduced incidents of child-birth fever (see page 318). Further on, **Blaha Lujza tér** on the Great Boulevard is named after a 19th-century actress (who sang like a nightingale) and used to be the site of the National Theatre; a memorial stone marks where it stood before making way in the 1970s for the metro station. The nearby **New York Coffee House** (Erzsébet körút 9–11; page 163) is due to reopen in 2005.

The city's **Jewish quarter** falls in the area between the Small and Great boulevards. The first major influx of Jews to Budapest came during the tolerant reign of Béla IV in the 13th century, and they assisted with the process of rebuilding following the Mongol invasion (see page 3). There were periods of repression in centuries to come, but Hungary more usually represented a haven from harsher persecution elsewhere. The community's contribution has been valuable; during the 20th century, seven of Hungary's 12 Nobel Prize winners were of Jewish descent. By 1939 there were 200,000 Jews living in Budapest. Then came Adolf Eichmann and the **Holocaust** in 1944; 600,000 were murdered or deported nationwide, the population in the countryside obliterated. In Budapest, the Nazis established a ghetto between Dohány utca, Király utca and Erzsébet körút; 70,000 were crammed in here under brutal conditions, the majority around Klauzál tér. Bodies of the dead were kept in fridges at Klauzál tér market before burial in the square. Fortunately, however, annihilation was averted by the arrival of the Soviets. Today there are 80,000 Jews, less than half the pre-war number but still the largest community in central Europe.

## A walk along Dob utca

The district's prime sight is the **Great Synagogue** (Dohány utca 2; page 346), one of the city's foremost architectural works; the silver willow in its memorial park is both a striking sculpture and a touching tribute. The **Rumbach Sebestyén utca synagogue** (nos 11–13) – established in 1872 as a moderately conservative ('status quo' Jewry) alternative to the more reformist Great Synagogue – can be found on the road opposite the rear of the complex. However, if you fancy a walk through the district your best bet is **Dob (Drum) utca** (named after a former pub called the Three Drums), which traverses the very heart. Along its length a dying breed of craftsmen (see box, pages 204–5) ply their trades – goldsmiths, engravers, tailors and stocking repairers – and the cuisine available in its restaurants ranges from kosher to curry.

Keep an eye out early on for the **memorial to Swiss consul Carl Lutz** who, like Wallenberg after him (see box, page 348), saved many Jews from deportation. Placed at the one-time entrance to the ghetto, and looking like something out of the Cirque de Soleil, a gold angel stands perpendicular to a wall and offers a cloth lifeline to a figure lying prone below. An inscription from the Talmud reads 'He who saves one single person could also save the world.'

At number 16 is the gateway to the **Gozsdu udvar**, whose string of courtyards once represented a thriving centre for artisans' workshops, and which formed a wall of the ghetto. A modest sign at Dob utca 22 heralds one of the street's treasures; the **Fröhlich cukrászda** offers delicious cakes, and claims to be the only genuine kosher café in Hungary. At the corner of Kazinczy utca, look right to see Pest's **Orthodox Synagogue** (Kazinczy utca 29–31), designed by the Löffler brothers (Béla and Sándor) in 1913, and serving the city's small community of just over 3,000 Orthodox Jews. It looks dark and forlorn, but the Hebrew lettering at the top of the façade – 'This is the House of God and the Gate of Heaven' – remains in good condition. It isn't open to visitors, but you can get a closer look around the corner at Dob utca 35; through the courtyard by the kosher butchers (no 41) and the strictly kosher Hanna restaurant is the former **Orthodox school**. Further down Kazinczy utca is the **Museum of Electrical Engineering** (Kazinczy utca 21; page 333), while further up Dob utca is **Klauzál tér**, which was at the centre of the ghetto. Today, gypsies make up a high proportion of the residents in the single-room flats with outdoor toilets that are common in the area. There are some workshops immediately beyond the Great Boulevard, but thereafter the character of the street changes. Statues of István and others guard the giant post office on the corner of Hársfa utca, while next door is the **Stamp Museum** (Hársfa utca 47; page 334). Before leaving the district, be sure to run the gauntlet of a *néni*'s wrath by peering through the odd doorway to the leafy courtyards within; in these nooks you'll find children playing football, housewives beating carpets and grandmothers watching from balconies above. We're especially fond of that at Dob utca 82.

## JÓZSEFVÁROS, FERENCVÁROS AND BEYOND

The segment south of Rákóczi út to Üllői út is **Józsefváros** (Joseph Town, District VIII). East of the Great Boulevard has traditionally been the haunt of scoundrels and ne'er-do-wells, but as long as you keep your purse safe from wayward fingers, there are some real gems here. Appropriately enough, the **Crime Museum** (page 335) is in the vicinity. The **Eastern (Keleti) Railway Station** is surely one of the most beautiful and romantic in the world, a monumental eclectic structure in iron and glass. It was constructed in 1882 by Gyula Rochlitz, and outside are statues of the great English rail pioneers George Stephenson and James Watt. A short distance away is **Kerepesi Cemetery** (page 349), its paths the city's most peaceful, while there's nature to be had at the district's southern edge in the **Budapest Botanical Garden** (page 369) and **Natural History Museum** (page 337).

Several university buildings are located inside the sweep of the Great Boulevard, and this was a hot spot during the '56 uprising. **Bródy Sándor utca** was where it all erupted on October 23 after students were fired on outside the **Hungarian Radio headquarters** (no 7); there is a famous black-and-white photograph showing a Hungarian flag fluttering from an upper window of the building, the Soviet crest ripped from its centre. Opposite, a marble tablet commemorates 18-year-old János Vizi, who was the first to die that day. Sándor Bródy was a turn-of-the-20th-century writer, and while he didn't live here, many others of the literary world did. The street has an appropriately bookish culmination point at **Gutenberg tér**, named after the 15th-century printing-press pioneer; he is portrayed with wide-brimmed hat and open book on the house at number 4. Those who scurry between the square and Múzeum körút often miss the painted wooden **relief of the Last Supper** at Bródy Sándor utca 19, which can apparently be illuminated by an electric lamp above it on the wall. Múzeum körút, with its **National Museum** (page 308) and **antiquarian bookshops** (page 272), is dealt with under the Belváros.

**Ferencváros** (Francis Town, District IX), framed by Üllői út and the river, was flattened by the Great Flood in 1838; it is now an area dominated by blue collars and green-and-white flags, the latter the colours of the local football team Ferencvárosi Torna Club (FTC; see page 225). 'Fradi' has the best stadium in town and the most passionate (and at times thuggish) fans. The **Big Market Hall** (page 202) near Szabadság híd is an absolute must, and next to it is the **University of Economics** (page 272); we've dealt with these and **Kálvin tér** (page 272) during our walk around the downtown. **Ráday utca**, forging southeast from Kálvin tér, is a trendy night spot (pages 172–3). You'll generally witness the grubby Üllői út on your way to or from Ferihegy Airport (although if you're unlucky you'll discover that it also holds several clinics and hospitals). At the junction with Ferenc körút is the **Museum of Applied Arts** (page 336), a veritable art nouveau free-for-all. A new **Holocaust Memorial Centre** (Páva utca 39; page 335) is a short distance east in a former synagogue.

Around 3km further out is **Népliget**, founded in the 1860s and Budapest's biggest public park. It can be accessed via Népliget metro station (M3), but as a landscaped space it offers nothing that isn't available more centrally at City Park or Margaret Island. However, there is a Planetarium and laser show (page 337). The FTC stadium is opposite the bus and metro station. Another 20km away in District X is the **New Municipal Cemetery** (*Új köztemető*; X, Kozma utca), where Imre Nagy and other martyrs of the 1956 revolution were dumped by the communists in plots 300 and 301. Nagy was reburied in 1989, with great ceremony and political significance (see page 11). The grave is in the far northeast of the cemetery, a half-hour walk from the entrance; a microbus (marked *temető járat*) also runs visitors there at peak periods. A Jewish cemetery stands next to it. Take tram 28 or 37 from near Blaha Lujza tér or bus 95 from Keleti station.

# THE ISLANDS

## Walking Margaret Island

Margit-sziget is the city centre's prime piece of park. Ecclesiastical buildings, royal residences and aristocratic hunting grounds are now largely lost in history's mists, as are memories of the Turkish period, when the pashas' horses and 'women of ill repute' were kept here. Today shady chestnut trees, quiet walkways and open pieces of grass make it the playground of sunbathers, joggers and strollers without time to head for the hills. Formed from three islets that were artificially fused in the late 19th and early 20th centuries, the island now measures 2.5km long by 500m wide, and settles between Margit and Árpád bridges. Before World War II, 'undesirables' were deterred from the gardens and medicinal baths by an entrance fee, but you may now visit freely however undesirable you are.

Motorists can access the island via Árpád híd, and must pay to leave their vehicles in a car park at the northern tip. Bus 26 traverses the island on its journey between Nyugati station and Árpád híd; alternatively, alight from tram 4 or 6 on Margit híd. If you fancy sparing some shoe leather once there, you can hire a variety of bicycles, pedal cars or electronic buggies from near the southern end.

Approaching from **Margit híd**, you'll be using the city's second permanent river crossing, built 1872–76. It was designed in Parisian style by a colleague of Eiffel, and predictably became nicknamed the 'French Bridge'. Scores of pedestrians were killed when the retreating Germans blew up the structure during World War II. Follow the pedestrian bridge that runs from here down to the island, and ahead will be the **Centenary Monument**, erected on the 100th anniversary of the union of Buda,

Pest and Óbuda. A short distance beyond that is the country's largest **fountain**, a spectacular affair with shooting jets that rise to 25m; it is illuminated at night, and if you're lucky you'll catch its water spurts dancing to snatches of music.

Walk on past the **Hajós Alfréd Swimming Pool** (page 227) on the left, its indoor pool designed by an Olympic champion of the first modern games in 1896; water babies are also spoilt by the slides and pools of the enormous **Palatinus Strand** (page 224) a few hundred metres further up. Before reaching the Palatinus (which refers to the Habsburg palatines, who relaxed and sported on the island in the 18th and 19th centuries), to the right of the path lie the remains of a 13th- to 14th-century **Franciscan church** (*Ferences templom*), with a Gothic tracery window.

Leave the track and aim towards the centre ground, walk between the blooms of an **elliptical garden**, and then bear northeast a short while to the island's main archaeological site – the **cloister and church of the Dominican nuns** (*Domonkos kolostor*). When the Mongols sacked the country in 1241, Béla IV swore an oath that his future daughter would devote her life to God if his people were delivered from the hordes. Margit was born the following year, and the king had the complex built in honour of the Blessed Virgin. Margit lived a life of utmost piety here, and was famed for performing curing miracles; she was also known never to wash above the feet, so perhaps her greatest achievement was in persuading people to let her near enough to heal them. The cult of Margit began soon after her death at 28, although she wasn't finally canonised until 1943. The foundations – and the marble coffin of Margit's brother, István V, complete with golden funeral crown (now in the Budapest History Museum) – were discovered during the clear up after the Great Flood of 1838.

Look westward above the treeline to the 57m-tall **water tower** (*víztorony*), constructed in 1911 and a protected industrial monument. Beneath it is an open-air theatre. Directly northward is the reconstructed medieval **Premonstratensian chapel**, originally erected in the 12th century. In its tower hangs the oldest bell in Hungary, dating back to the 15th century; the bell lay hidden – probably from the Turks – until 1914, when a storm brought down a tree and revealed it among the roots. Near here too is the **Artists' Promenade**, a series of busts depicting greats of Hungarian literature, music and art.

The northern portion of the island contains the hotels **Grand** and **Thermal** (pages 106–7), which make use of the thermal medicinal waters that have been tapped here since the 1860s. The excellent spa is open to non-residents. From 1869, Miklós Ybl's magnificent neo-Renaissance **bathing hall** stood on the site, and it became a favourite retreat for aristocrats and poets; the writer János Arany (1817–82) spent his last summers on the island, and penned a host of poems from beneath the oak trees. It is a crying shame that, unlike the Grand Hotel, the hall was not reconstructed after the war. Beyond the hotels, on the western bank, is a **Japanese garden** whose plashing waterfall is a rare extant feature of the doomed bathing complex. Near by is a domed, music-playing **neoclassical well**, a replica of an 1820 original.

## Shipyard (or Óbuda) Island

The island to the north of Margit-sziget suffers something of an identity crisis, referred to variously as Hajógyári- (Shipyard) and Óbudai-sziget. Either way, this is where **palaces of the Roman proconsuls** stood when Aquincum was at its height, and much later where an industrial **shipyard** was sited. Today tourists will be less interested by the warehouses than by the wakeboarding lake (page 230), tennis courts, assault course, horse-riding opportunities and the achingly trendy Dokk nightclub (page 189). The island is invaded by music lovers during the Sziget Festival and by horsy types for the Budapest Equestrian Summer Festival in June (see page 35), while the Ladik Csárda puts on traditional banquets accompanied by performances of gypsy music and dancing. (The main banquets in its huge barn are primarily aimed at tour groups – telephone in advance to find out when the next one is taking place. Tickets can be purchased from hotels, and the entertainment usually kicks off at 20.00. A ferry will take guests from Vigadó tér to the island in summer.)

While cars can drive on to the island, buses 34, 42 and 106 only run as far as Szentendrei út, from where you'll need to walk on along Mozaik utca.

# Museums and More

Museums became popular in Budapest during the mid-19th century, when the middle class was emerging, the urban population was growing, and new-found political independence flamed a desire to reassert – and display – Hungarian nationhood and heritage. There was a particular boom between 1867 and 1914, prosperous years, and the period of the Millennial Exhibition. The legacies of these enlightened patrons among the upper-middle or noble classes remain, often framed by magnificent works of architecture. The Hungarian National Museum, the Hungarian National Gallery and the Museum of Fine Arts could float happily among the cream of European cultural houses, while individual attractions like the Varga Imre Collection are real treats.

Museums are generally closed on Mondays, and open between 10.00 and 18.00 on other days during high season (although ticket offices often close up to an hour before closing time). Hours are usually shorter in winter. You may be charged an admission fee (see note below), and permission to take photos or videos inside costs a significant amount extra. Guided tours may or may not be in English; museum attendants, often elderly ladies, may or may not speak English. For details of exhibitions during your stay, grab a copy of *Pesti Műsor PM Tárlat*, an A5-sized guide that is published quarterly, has English translations and is available free from tourist and ticket offices, coffee houses, museums and exhibition centres.

**Important note on prices** On May 1 2004, a government decree made admission to permanent exhibitions at museums free. The Culture Ministry subsidises the museums and the number of visitors has grown significantly. Many museums – like the Hungarian National Gallery – separate their permanent exhibitions (that are now free to enter) from their temporary exhibitions (for which there is a charge). However, this is not universally applied, and small museums especially may still charge entrance fees. Because museums are still reacting to this change, please be aware that there may be some differences regarding entrance costs.

## THE UNMISSABLES

**House of Terror** (*Terrorháza*) VI, Andrássy út 60; tel: 1 374 2600; www.houseofterror.hu [2 F3]
M1 *Vörösmarty utca;* B *4*
Among the stately apartments of Andrássy út is one painted in powder blue that bore witness to some of the blackest acts of the blackest years of the 20th century. During the short and bloody reign of the Arrowcross regime in 1944, the Hungarian Nazis set up their party headquarters here, torturing and murdering Jews in the former coal cellars. The address was subsequently used for interrogations and executions by the communist political police (the PRO, ÁVO and ÁVH) until 1956. Prisoners were beaten with rubber truncheons, given electric shocks and burnt with cigarettes; among the cells was one in which the occupant was forced to sit for days in water. Citizens as young as 15 were arrested for resistance to communist rule. Closer to a piece of installation art than a traditional museum, this represents a sensual assault more about atmosphere than artefacts; a

stylised use of light, space and music aims to educate through emotional engagement. The displays include video footage of communist propaganda, photographs of political leaders and prisoners, screen prints and props, and there are useful sheets in each room explaining the history of the terror regimes. Adult 3,000Ft, student 1,500Ft. *Open Tue–Fri 10.00–18.00 (last admission 16.30), Sat–Sun 10.00–19.30 (last admission 18.00); closed Mon.*

**Hungarian National Gallery** (*Magyar Nemzeti Galéria*) I, Budavári Palota, Épület B, C, D, Szent György tér 2; tel: 1 224 3700 or 1 375 7533; www.mng.hu [3 C5]
The National Gallery is daunting in size, sprawling across three wings of the Buda Castle/Palace. Of course, size isn't everything – it's what you do with it. Well, they've done well; this is one of the country's most significant museums.

The foundations of a public collection of Hungarian art can be traced to the middle-class reform drives of the early 1800s. There are now around 100,000 works in the gallery. On the ground floor of Wing D is a **lapidarium** containing medieval and Renaissance stone carvings, including fragments of 11th- to 15th-century architecture and marble carvings from King Mátyás's palace. The twin reliefs of the king and his wife by an Italian master are first-class examples of the craft. In vaulted rooms facing the Danube are **medieval panel paintings** and **wooden sculptures**, such as the *Madonna and Child from Toporc* of around 1420, with its milky-faced Mary and curly-haired Christ. In the first-floor throne room is an array of dazzling late-Gothic winged altars that adorned churches in northern Hungary.

Next door is the collection of **late-Renaissance** and **baroque art**. Among them are effigies of Esterházy family members, a 1712 portrait of the Transylvanian Prince Ferenc Rákóczi II by the court painter Ádám Mányoki, and 18th-century religious works by F A Maulbertsch. Towards the end of the period more secular genres emerged that embraced allegory and scenes of country life, thus anticipating the full flowering of Romanticism.

The same floor of Wings C and B holds the **19th-century collections**, which display the main parallel strains of Romanticism – the portraiture typical of the neoclassical form and the landscapes of Biedermeier (or middle-class Romanticism). Head for the works of János Donát and Károly Kisfaludy respectively for these genres at their early stages. Historical painting, another related branch of the Romantic tradition, is represented by Bálint Kiss and Mihály Kovács; the infusion of realism in the latter half of the century is embodied in works such as the *Condemned Cell I* (1870) by Mihály Munkácsy, itself strongly reminiscent of social commentary by other Europeans like Victor Hugo and Charles Dickens. Among the sculptors, Miklós Izsó was a true exponent of national romanticism in tackling both rural working life and portrait sculpture. National self-confidence after 1867 manifested itself in competitions to shape the city's buildings and public spaces. Many of the models on display by sculptors like Izsó, Alajos Stróbl, János Fadrusz and György Zala are the results of such competitions.

**Art of the first half of the 20th century** occupies the second floor of Wing C. Here you'll find works by Károly Ferenczy, the leading artist of the supremely influential Nagybánya artists' colony (an area now part of Romania); some vast canvases (such as *Ruins of the Greek Theatre at Taormina*, 1904–05) by Tivadar Csontváry Kosztka, visionary and drenched in colour; a range of post-impressionist paintings by József Rippl-Rónai, including the beautiful *Woman with Bird Cage* (1892), with her ivory-hued features (painted during the artist's 'black period'); and inter-war expressionist pieces by Gyula Derkovits and József Egry. Picasso was a fan of Csontváry, apparently requesting that he be left alone to admire the paintings during an exhibition of 1949. He was lucky to be able to see them at all; on Csontváry's death, his family had arranged to sell some of the pieces as tarpaulin before someone fortunately intervened to buy the canvases – to hang on walls rather than tent poles. On the third floor is a collection of **post-1945 art**. The **Habsburg Crypt** (*Nádor kripta*), the remaining part of the Chapel of St Sigismund, can also be accessed from the museum. It is here that Archduke József was buried, the son of Leopold II and the Habsburg representative in Hungary (the Palatine, or *nádor*) between 1796 and 1847.

The museum's main entrance is near the statue of Eugene of Savoy (see page 235) on the eastern side of the palace, although there is also access from the western side. Free entrance to permanent exhibitions; special shows adult 800Ft, concessions 400Ft. *Open Tue–Sun 10.00–18.00, closed Mon.*

**Hungarian National Museum** (*Magyar Nemzeti Múzeum*) VIII, Múzeum körút 14–16; tel: 1 338 2122; www.hnm.hu [4 F5/6]
T *47, 49 from Deák tér two stops to Kálvin tér;* M3 *Kálvin tér*

The largest museum in Hungary, and regal with it. Among its garden statues is that of Ferenc Széchényi (1754–1820), the enlightened rock on whose collection the museum was founded. The neoclassical palace, with its busty embodiment of Pannonia on the tympanum, was built in 1847 by Mihály Pollack and became a symbol of the Independence War a short time later. On March 15 1848, radical intellectuals gathered outside and demanded reform, and copies of Petőfi's 'National Song' were distributed.

Your entrance fee is justified immediately by the **rich frescos** that adorn the main stairwell. The work of Mór Than (1828–99) and Károly Lotz (1833–1904), those on the ceiling show allegories of virtues and learning, while the wall friezes depict a broad sweep of Hungarian history, from the Huns leaving Asia up to the birth of the museum. The collection at the top of the stairs charts the **period between 1000 and 1990**, from the Árpád dynasty (including goods buried with Béla III, the era's only royal grave to survive intact) to the collapse of communism. Descend from the foyer to a newish **lapidarium** and a 3rd-century mosaic excavated from a villa in Balácpuszta. To the right of the entrance hall is an exhibition with artefacts dating from the prehistoric **Palaeolithic Age to the Age of the Avars** (AD567–804), prior to the Hungarian conquest. To the left, though, is the museum's star attraction. You can take your Holy Crown and sceptre – the more lauded items of the coronation regalia that were moved from here in 2000 to the Parliament building; for us, the **cloak** is the true crowning piece. This semi-circular stretch of purple silk, shimmering with gold embroidery, is a textile masterpiece, and the sole item among the regalia that actually belonged to Szt István. He gave it to the church in Székesfehérvár in 1031, and he is included with his wife Giselle among the angels at the bottom of the cloth. Free entry. *Open Tue–Sun 10.00–18.00.*

**Museum of Fine Arts** (*Szépmuvészeti Múzeum*) XIV, Dózsa György út 41; tel: 1 363 2675; www.szepmuveszeti.hu/index.htm [2 H1]
M1 *Hősök tere;* B *4;* TB *79*
Indisputably Hungary's premier collection of international art, and very arguably one of central Europe's. The building has the look of a classical temple and the interior is a shrine to past masters. The place to head in a hurry is the renowned **Old Picture Gallery**; there are paintings by Raphael and Titian in the Italian collection, works by Breughel and Rubens in the Dutch one, and – featuring El Greco, Murillo and Goya – the richest group of Spanish pieces outside Spain itself. You'll find Monet, Manet, Renoir, Delacroix, Gauguin, Cézanne and Hungary's very own op-artist Vasarely (see page 321) popping their heads up in the modern department, while Pisano's marble 'Madonna and Child' is one of the darlings among the sculpture. If that isn't enough, the **Egyptian section** has mummies and painted sarcophagi, and there are statues and pottery in the display of **Greek and Roman finds**. The cream of the exhibition was gathered between the 17th and 19th centuries by the aristocratic Esterházy family; keep these princes fondly in your thoughts, for they left a wonderful, inspiring, sense-stirring hoard of art. Free entry to permanent exhibitions. Guided tours 4,000–5,000Ft, free (in English) on Tue and Fri at 11.00. *Open Tue–Sun 10.00–17.30, closed Mon.*

**Statue Park** (*Szoborpark*) XXII, corner of Balatoni út and Szabadkai utca; tel: 1 424 7500; www.szoborpark.hu
*B from Deák Ferenc tér (the stop has the Statue Park timetable), leaving at 10.00, 11.00, 15.00 and 16.00 in high season or red 7 (from Ferenciek tere to Etele tér), then yellow Volán bus (from stall 7–8 to Diósd-Érd)*
'Heroic' monuments to communism were not only symbols of ideology, but vast instruments of repression that bullied public spaces. The undersized Statue Park divests them of such registers, and makes them seem faintly pathetic. Of course, the setting is as much a product of its historical moment as the statues are products of theirs. When communism fell, this wasn't intended as a memorial; by contrast it was a dumping ground for beacons of the socialist period, an insignificant place 15km from the centre, a country's act of closure. And it feels like it. But don't be unimpressed; try to imagine the statues in their original political and historical context, as they stood on hills, on squares, on boulevards. Remember the backdrop to the 1956 publication of Gyula Illyé's poem 'One Sentence of Tyranny', which greets visitors at the gates. And remember that, because so many other nations destroyed such monuments as the Iron Curtain fell, these 42 bulky relics are rare extant markers of one of the significant periods of 20th-century European history.

To the right as you enter is the figure of the **Soviet soldier** by Zsigmond Kisfaludy Strobl that used to stand beneath the Freedom Monument (see page 255). You'll find statues of **communist martyrs**, memorials to Lenin, Marx, Engels, and **Hungarian communist leaders** like Béla Kun and Árpád Münnich. What you won't find is an image of Stalin; the city's only statue was cut off at the knees during the 1956 revolution, and many Budapesters still own fragments of the metal torso. The souvenir shop sells model Trabants (see box, pages 14–15), Soviet medals, CDs containing songs of the Movement, and T-shirts. Adult 850Ft, concessions 600Ft; free entry with Budapest Card. Return bus ticket (including entrance to park) 2,450Ft/person (discount with Budapest Card or student card). *Open daily 10.00–dusk.*

**Varga Imre Collection** (*Varga Imre Kiállítása*) III, Laktanya utca 7 [map page 266]
HEV *Arpád híd*
All that glisters is not gold; polished sheet metal glisters too, and in the hands of Varga is moulded, bent and folded into layered and textured works of art that delight those with eyes for shiny things. Varga came to major prominence in the 1960s and – despite being a favoured sculptor under János Kádár, crafting statues that were subsequently banished to Statue Park (see above) – sustained his popularity after the political changes. This concentrated collection shows why, a rich feast of statues, busts and sculptures that includes the gaunt figure of Szt István (the original of which is in St Peter's Basilica in Rome), the behatted Béla Bartók, and, leaning against a wooden gate, the tormented Jewish poet Miklós Radnóti, who was killed on a forced march from a labour camp in 1944. Varga often holds court here on Saturdays between 10.00 and 12.00, and speaks English. Greatly admiring his works, we try to forget that he is supposedly a rather unlikeable chap... Adult 400Ft, concessions 200Ft; free with Budapest Card. *Open Tue–Sun 10.00–18.00, closed Mon.*

# MUSEUMS, GALLERIES ETC

## Buda

### *Castle Hill*

**Budapest History Museum** (*Budapesti Történeti Múzeum*) I, Budavári Palota, Épület E, Szent György tér 2; tel: 1 224 3700 [3 D5]

The popularly known 'Castle Museum' can be found at the southern side of Lion Court. Reached from the basement below the museum itself are **remains of the medieval palace** at various stages and under various rulers. The greater share belongs to the Gothic **palace of Zsigmond of Luxembourg** (1387–1437), including the elaborately restored **Knights' Hall**, which now contains a series of Gothic statues (of contemporary courtiers and biblical apostles) that were unearthed from a ditch in 1974. Evidence of Mátyás's pad is largely restricted to stove tiles and fragments of red-marble balustrades, which can be viewed in the **Renaissance Hall**. The lower portion of the **Royal Chapel**, constructed by Nagy Lajos in the 1360s, also survives. Among the museum's other permanent displays are finds dating from prehistory to the end of the Avar period (second floor), and exhibits charting those moments that have caressed or buffeted the capital over the years since 1686, from transient domestic fashions to the devastating flood of 1838 and the tragic consequences of 20th-century war (first floor). Adult 1,400Ft, concessions 700Ft; free entry with Budapest card. *Open (May 16–Sep 15) daily 10.00–18.00; (Nov 1–Feb 28) Wed–Mon 10.00–16.00, closed Tue; (Mar 1–May 15 and Sept 16–Oct 31) Wed–Mon 10.00–18.00, closed Tue.*

**Golden Eagle Pharmacy Museum** (*Arany Sas Patika Múzeum*) I, Tárnok utca 18; tel: 1 375 9772 [1 C4]
Prior to the late 17th century, if you were struck by a jippy tummy in the Castle District you had little option than to adopt a steely grin, clench those glutes and run like the (proverbial) wind. In 1687, Ferenc Bösinger resolved to clear up this messy state of affairs by opening the district's first pharmacy at his home in Dísz tér. It was later moved to this 15th-century merchant's house. The museum includes original furnishings and instruments from the apothecary's shop, together with a reconstruction of an 'alchemist's workshop'. Pharmaceutical items date mainly from the 16th to 18th centuries, while some of the alchemist's ingredients suggest that he was a firm subscriber to the eye-of-newt school of medicine. Look out for the figurative wall and ceiling paintings, some of which survive from as early as 1500. Adult 150Ft, student 100Ft; guide in English 500Ft. *Open (Nov 1–Feb 28) Tue–Sun 10.30–15.30; (Mar 1–Oct 31) Tue–Sun 10.30–17.30, closed Mon.*

**Hungarian Museum of Commerce and Catering** (*Magyar Kereskedelmi és Vendéglátóipari Múzeum*) I, Fortuna utca 4; tel: 1 375 6249 [1 B3]
We can almost hear the excited squeals from catering students. The focus is the period from the Compromise of 1867 until World War II, when modern forms of trade emerged. It captures a snapshot of the period's atmosphere, lifestyle and fashions. Here are histories of two of Hungary's great foodies – Gerbeaud (see page 162) and Gundel. Károly Gundel was just 27 years old when he bought his renowned restaurant in 1911. Among exhibits in the second room is a mock-up of a

1938 general store (which served as a social hub in the way that the pub does today). The final item in the exhibition is a drawn blind marked 'Closed for Nationalisation' – an emphatic sign of the very different political and economic climate from 1948. Adult 500Ft, concessions 200Ft; taped guide in English 600Ft; free with Budapest Card. *Open Wed–Fri 10.00–17.00, Sat–Sun 10.00–18.00, closed Mon–Tue.*

**Institute and Museum of Military History** (*Hadtörténeti Intézet és Múzeum*) I, Tóth Árpád sétány 40; tel: 1 356 9522/9370 [1 B3]
There are enough boys' toys in here to satisfy the most macho of holidaying males. You'll find weapons dating from the Turkish period and before, as well as more modern machinery, medals and uniforms worn by the Hungarian Hussar regiment. The royal army of Regent Horthy is represented, together with an excellent exhibition devoted to the national army (*Honvéd*) of the 1848–49 War of Independence. The display related to the 1956 uprising will move even the stoniest of hearts. Admission to the museum is just behind the square's western side, on Tóth Árpád sétány, with its spanking views of the Buda hills (see page 249). Free entry to permanent exhibitions. *Open Oct 1–Mar 31 Tue–Sun 10.00–15.45, Apr 1–Sep 30 Tue–Sun 10.00–17.45, closed Mon.*

**Ludwig Museum Budapest – Museum of Contemporary Art** (*Kortárs Művészeti Múzeum*) I, Budavári Palota, Épület F, Szent György tér 2; tel: 1 224 3700 or 1 375 7533; www.ludwigmuseum.hu [3 C5]
Standing at the northern end of the castle complex, this museum was the first of international contemporary art in Hungary, and represents a bite-sized romp through

works by some of the 20th century's most flamboyant artists. It is based on donations and long-term loans by the German collectors Peter and Irene Ludwig. There are three late Picassos here (including *Matador and Nude*, 1970), examples of American pop art by Andy Warhol and Roy Lichtenstein, and European trans-avantgarde works. The Ludwigs were also among the first to collect from former socialist countries, and so there is material by artists from the Soviet Union, Bulgaria, East Germany and Hungary. In addition, an exhibition on the second floor charts Hungarian art in the 1990s, and there are regular temporary displays that are generally significant, interesting and worth a snoop. Adult 800Ft, student 400Ft; free entry with Budapest Card. *Open Tue–Wed and Fri–Sun 10.00–18.00, Thu 10.00–20.00, closed Mon.*

**Medieval House of Prayer** (*középkori zsidó imaház*) I, Tancsics Mihály utca 26
The exhibition in this 16th-century Jewish prayer house includes early gravemarkers and the late-Gothic keystone from a much larger synagogue of 1461, found in the garden of number 23 and yet to be properly excavated. Pictures and Hebrew inscriptions on the interior walls attempted to buoy up worshippers in the face of fears of persecution by Christians as power shifted during the 17th century. Adult 400Ft, student/pensioner 150Ft. *Open May 1–Oct 31 Tue–Sun 10.00–17.00, closed Mon.*

**National Széchényi Library** (*Országos Széchényi Könyvtár*) Budavári Palota, Épület F; tel: 1 224 3742; email: pr@oszk.hu [3 C5]
Some people collect stamps or beer mats; during the 18th century, Count Széchényi Ferenc, father of István (see pages 260 and 281), set himself the modest

task of collecting every available example of 'Hungarica' – literature by Hungarians or about Hungary. His obsession stemmed from a desire to reinforce Hungarian nationhood and establish the country's place as an 'intellectual' centre of Europe. Based on his hoardings, the national library opened in 1803 in Pest.

The library now occupies eight floors of the palace (the entrance in the Lion Courtyard is on the library's fifth floor). There are currently 10,000,000 items. Among the holdings are the only complete copy of the first book published in Hungary (the *Chronica Hungarorum* of 1473) and the *Gesta Hungarorum*, the early-13th-century work of an unknown chronicler (labelled Anonymus by the history books) charting the early centuries of Hungarian history. There are also 33 surviving 'corvina' codices from the acclaimed 15th-century library of King Mátyás (see page 338). A museum on the eighth floor includes a filing cabinet damaged by gunfire in 1956. Foreign-language tours of the library (by appointment only; tel: 1 224 3745) cost 200Ft. Day reader pass costs adult 400Ft, concessions 200Ft. *Reading rooms open Mon 13.00–21.00, Tue–Fri 09.00–21.00, Sat 09.00–17.00; closed Sun and August.*

**Telephone Museum** (*Telefónia Múzeum*) I, Úri utca 49; tel: 1 201 8188 [1 B4]
OK, OK, so you think you'd have to be an oxy*moron* to place 'interesting' and 'telecommunications' in a sentence free of the word 'not'. Well, a Hungarian, Tivadar Puskás, built the first telephone exchange in 1879, and this museum deserves a chance. In the 19th and early 20th centuries, the castle exchange (*várközpont*) was housed in this former convent (see page 252). Between 1928 and 1985, here operated – stay with us – the first mechanically switched automatic telephone

exchange. This immense piece of kit is preserved in its original splendour, and is the museum's *pièce de résistance*. The curator will kick-start it for you with a whirring and dinging of which Chitty-Chitty-Bang-Bang would be proud – and without a mention of tariff rates or network coverage. Other exhibits include phones belonging to Hungary's last two kings, and that of János Kádár, the communist ruler between 1956 and 1988. Adult 100Ft, concessions 50Ft. *Open Tue–Sun 10.00–16.00, closed Mon. Entry at weekends and holidays is via Országház utca 30.*

## *Gellért Hill, the Tabán and surrounds*

**Semmelweis Museum of Medical History** (*Orvostörténeti Múzeum*) I, Apród utca 1–3; tel: 1 201 1577; www.semmelweis.museum.hu [3 D5]

Ignác Semmelweis (1818–65) solved one of medicine's tragic mysteries by discovering that grime was the primary cause of puerperal (childbirth) fever. In pioneering hospital cleanliness and antiseptics, the surgical scrubber slashed mortality rates in his Viennese maternity hospital by 80%, and was labelled the 'saviour of mothers'. Fate and irony colluded to ensure that Semmelweis died of septicaemia in a mental asylum. The house in which he was both born and buried (the urn containing his ashes was placed in a wall of the building) stands to the south of Castle Hill, and charts the history of medicine from the Stone Age through to the 19th century. Along with medical instruments, a reconstructed 19th-century pharmacy and a medieval chastity belt, a memorial room preserves some of the man's furnishings. Adult 250Ft, concessions 100Ft, guided tour in English 1,500Ft; free entry with Budapest Card. *Open (Oct 15–Mar 15) Tue-Sun 10.30–16.00, rest of year 10.30–18.00.*

**TIT Urània Astronomical Observatory** (*TIT Urània Csillagvizsgáló*) I, Sánc utca 3B; tel: 1 186 9233/9171 [3 C6]

Observatory to the north of Gellért Hill where you can star gaze through a massive early-20th-century telescope, powered by mechanical (rather than electrical) movements. Cost 400Ft. *Opens after dark (hours vary; closed July and August).*

## Óbuda and Aquincum

**Aquincum Museum** III, Szentendrei út 139; tel: 1 250 1650

M2 *Batthyány tér, then* HEV *to Aquincum stop; turn right and the museum is 200m away, on the opposite side of the road*

The civilian Roman town of Aquincum was an important place, situated as it was at the eastern frontier of the empire (see page 265). The artisans, tradesmen and vintners left over a million artefacts for archaeologists to unearth, including early-Christian religious items, an altar dedicated to Mithras, and even a portable organ. The grounds surrounding the museum encompass one-third of the town, and there are remains of the courthouse, the great shrine, the public baths and the market, as well as evidence of a sophisticated sewage system – featuring flush toilets. The lapidarium has stone finds, while the civilian amphitheatre, which could hold 6,000 spectators, is near Aquincum station. Adult 700Ft, concessions 300Ft; free with Budapest Card. *Open (Apr 15–May 1 and Oct 1–31) ruins garden 09.00–17.00, exhibition 10.00–17.00; (Jun 1–Sep 30) ruins garden 09.00–18.00, exhibition 10.00–18.00; closed Mon and rest of year.*

**Hercules Villa** III, Meggyfa utca 19–21; tel: 1 250 1650
B *6, 86, 118, 106*
The imperial official who owned this urban villa clearly wasn't short of a gold coin or two. In the 3rd century AD he adorned his floors with a series of mosaics, imported from Italy and depicting events in the legends of Hercules and Dionysus. They are the cream of Pannonia's extant crop. On the corner of Meggyfa utca and Vihar utca, to the north of Flórián tér. Adult 700Ft, concessions 300Ft, family 1,200Ft; free with Budapest Card. *Open (Apr 15–31 and Oct 1–31) 10.00–17.00; (May 1–Sep 30) 10.00–18.00, closed every Mon and rest of year.*

**Kassák Museum** III, Fő tér 1; tel: 1 368 7021 [map page 266]
HEV *Árpád híd*
On the 1st floor of the pink baroque mansion – the 18th-century abode of the Zichy family, which owned Óbuda – is an exhibition of the works of Lajos Kassák (1887–1967), poet, author and leading artist of the Hungarian avant-garde. A working-class socialist, and of uncompromising artistic integrity, he was persecuted successively by Béla Kun in 1919, by the Horthy regime and by the Stalinists after 1945. Adult 400Ft, concessions 200Ft; free entry with Budapest Card. *Open (Mar 17–Oct 31) Tue–Sun 10.00–18.00, (Nov 1–Mar 15) 10.00–17.00, closed Mon.*

**Óbuda Museum** III, Fő tér 1; tel: 1 388 2534 [map page 266]
HEV *Árpád híd*
Adjacent to the Kassák Múzeum, this is an eclectic collection of items relating to the local history of Óbuda. *Open Tue–Sun 10.00–17.00, closed Mon.*

**Varga Imre Collection** See page 312.

**Vasarely Museum** III, Szentlélek tér; tel: 1 388 7551 [map page 266]
HEV *Arpád híd*
Yet another museum in a pocket of the Zichy Mansion, this one devoted to 20th-century Hungarian artist Victor Vasarely, famous for his optical, 3-D-illusion art. The extensive collection includes early Matisse-like sketches and distorted Picasso-like still-life paintings. Of most interest, however, are the stylised later pieces of the 1960s and '70s that make kaleidoscopic use of coloured geometrical shapes, playing with expectations of dimension and space. The effect can be giddying, almost psychedelic, as squares and dots swim before your eyes; take an anti-nausea pill before you visit. Adult 400Ft, concessions 200Ft, free entry with a Budapest Card. *Open Tue–Sun 10.00–17.00, closed Mon.*

## *Buda hills and beyond*

**Bartók Béla Memorial House** (*Bartók Béla Emlékház*) II, Csalán út 29; tel: 1 394 2100; www.bartokmuseum.hu
B *5 from Ferenciek tere to Pasaréti tér, then a short walk*
Set in a wooded garden, this villa was Bartók's home during the 1930s (prior to his emigration to America). Inside is the study where the composer composed, complete with writing desk and Börsendorfer piano, while rustic furniture and earthenware reflect his fascination with folk culture. His career as composer, performer and folksong scholar is laid bare in his life's flotsam. A circular theatre

in the garden hosts open-air concerts, and the indoor concert hall has an 18th-century cofferwork ceiling that originally graced a church in Tök. Concert tickets can be bought here or at Ticket Express offices (see page 175). *Open Tue–Sun 10.00–17.00, closed Mon.*

**Foundry Museum** (*Öntödei Múzeum*) II, Bem József utca 20; tel: 1 201 4370 [1 C2]
M2 *Batthyány tér;* B *11, 60, 86;* T *4, 6*
The Swiss industrialist and man of steel Ábrahám Ganz founded this chill-casting foundry in 1858. Adult 300Ft, concessions 150Ft; free with Budapest Card. *Open Tue–Sun 10.00–18.00.*

**Kiscelli Museum** III, Kiscelli utca 108; tel: 1 388 7817; www.btm.hu
T *17;* B *60, 165*
This crumbling baroque edifice once housed monks of the Trinitarian order; it's now filled with Hungarian art of the 19th and 20th centuries, featuring cubist works by János Kmetty, the puppet-themed paintings of Margit Anna, and avant-garde art of the 1960s, 1970s and 1980s. There is also an exhibition of antique printing presses, among them that on which Petőfi's 'National Song' was illegally published (see box, page 278), and there are Biedermeier furnishings from the Golden Lion Pharmacy, which stood in the Belváros between 1794 and 1945. Some of Hungary's foremost chamber orchestras perform concerts here in summer. Adult 600Ft, concessions 300Ft, family 1,000Ft; free for over-65s. *Open Tue–Sun 10.00–18.00 (Apr 1–Oct 31), 10.00–16.00 (Nov 1–Mar 31), closed Mon.*

**Nagytétény Castle Museum** (*Nagytétényi Kastélymúzeum*) XXII, Kastélypark utca 9–11; tel: 1 207 5462; www.museum.hu/budapest/nagytetenyi
B̄ *3 (from Móricz Zsigmond körtér to Petőfi utca), cross road and follow Pohár utca*
Fluted legs and well-turned feet aplenty in an exhibition of European furniture dating from the 15th to the 19th centuries. Admission free to permanent exhibitions. *Open Tue–Sun 10.00–18.00, closed Mon.*

**Statue Park** See page 311.

**Tropicarium-Óceanárium** XXII, Nagytétényi út 37–45; tel: 1 424 3053; www.tropicarium.hu
B̄ *3 from Móricz Zsigmond tér*
Flora and fauna of rivers, lakes and seas, together with a rainforest habitat containing alligators and iguanas. The sharks take luncheon on Wed and Sun. Adult 1,500Ft, concessions 900Ft; discount with Budapest Card. *Open 10.00–20.00 daily.*

## Pest

### *Downtown and beyond*

**Ady Endre Memorial Museum** (*Ady Endre Emlékmúzeum*) V, Veres Pálné utca 4–6; tel: 1 337 8563 [4 F5]
Documents and furnishings belonging to Ady (1877–1919), Hungary's premier *fin-de-siècle* poet whose collection of 1906 – *New Poems* – is said to have kick-started the country's 20th-century literary output. This apartment was his last residence.

Adult 150Ft, child 100Ft; free with Budapest Card. *Open (Mar 1–Oct 31) Wed–Sun 10.00–18.00; (Nov 1–Feb 28) 10.00–16.00 Wed–Sun, closed Mon–Tue.*

**Fine Arts Collection of the Hungarian Academy of Sciences** (*Magyar Tudományos Akadémia*) V, Roosevelt tér 9; tel: 1 411 6100 [1 D4]
They keep themselves tucked away, but the fine arts in the august Academy of Sciences are spoken of with reverence by those in the know. Spare a glance for the bas-relief of Empress Erzsébet grieving over the corpse of Ferenc Deák in the hallway before climbing the marble staircase. Alongside the portraits and sculptures on the uppermost floor, the 17th-century Flemish and Dutch landscapes are especially striking. No admission charge. *Open Mon–Fri 10.00–16.00.*

**Lutheran Museum** (*Evangélikus Országos*) V, Deák tér 4; tel: 1 483 2150 [3 E5]
Adjacent to the Lutheran church, the prize pupil of this collection is Martin Luther's last will and testament of 1542, a facsimile copy of which is on display (the original is in the archives). Adult 300Ft, concessions 150Ft; free with Budapest Card. *Open Tue–Sun 10.00–18.00 (10.00–16.00 in winter), closed Mon.*

**Museum of Ethnography** (*Néprajzi Múzeum*) V, Kossuth Lajos tér 12; tel: 1 473 2440; www.hem.hu [1 D3]
Like the Ministry of Agriculture next door, this building (by Alajos Hauszmann) was a losing entry in the fierce 19th-century contest to design Parliament. It was constructed nevertheless, destined to look greenly upon Steindl's victorious vision

across the square, and until 1949 served as the Supreme Court. Its interior includes a gorgeous fresco by Károly Lotz depicting 'The Triumph of Justice'. The present museum collection is founded on the late-19th- and early-20th-century interest in national folklore. The exhibition displays costumes, craftwork and photos of the peoples of historical Hungary, as well as artefacts gathered during expeditions further afield. There are frequent temporary displays too. Free entry to permanent exhibitions. *Open Tue–Sun 10.00–18.00 (winter 10.00–17.00), closed Mon.*

**Palace of Wonders** (*Csodák Palotája*) XIII, Váci út 19; tel: 1 350 6131; www.csodapalota.hu [2 F1]

M3 *Lehel tér, then walk north up Váci út*

An interactive science centre (in Újlipótváros) where children can bang, press buttons, take things apart, climb walls, ride a high-wire tricycle, and generally have a jolly good mess around while weary parents reassure themselves it's all in the name of learning. Young children revel in the energy and din; adults should take a cool flannel and a headache pill. Adult 650Ft, concessions 600Ft, family 2,000Ft; free with Budapest Card. *Open Mon–Fri 09.00–17.00, Sat–Sun 10.00–18.00.*

**Petőfi Literary Museum** (*Petőfi Irodalmi Múzeum*) V, Károlyi Mihály utca 16; tel: 1 317 3611; www.pim.hu [4 F5]

The national museum of modern literature is housed in the renovated Károlyi Palace, itself offering more than a sniff of historical interest. Queen Maria Theresa visited in 1791, Lajos Batthyány (the first Hungarian prime minister) was arrested here in 1849, and it was the birthplace of Mihály Károlyi (the first president of Hungary, in 1919). Bookworms will find some of Petőfi's personal items among the museum's exhibits. Note the wooden cobbles as you pass through the archway leading from Egyetem tér; these were common features of aristocratic mansions, dulling the din of horses' hooves. Adult 280Ft, concessions 140Ft; free with Budapest Card. *Open Tue–Sun 10.00–18.00, closed Mon.*

**Underground Railway Museum** (*Földalatti Vasúti Múzeum*) V, Deák tér underpass; tel: 1 461 6500 [1 E4]

Hungary can claim the first underground railway on mainland Europe and the second in the world (pipped by London's Metropolitan line), opened in 1896 to coincide with the millenary celebrations and running from Deák tér to City Park. In the subway (at the top of the escalators), this little museum displays original carriages and fixtures in telling the tale of the metro's history. On the walls are majolica tiles, manufactured in Pécs by the Zsolnay factory and a dainty feature of the stations on the oldest line. Adult 125Ft, concessions 90Ft; free with Budapest Card. *Open Tue–Sun 10.00–17.00.*

## *Terézváros*

**Hopp Ferenc Museum of Eastern Asiatic Arts** (*Kelet-Ázsiai Művészeti*) VI, Andrássy út 103; tel: 1 322 8476 [2 G2]

M1 *Bajza utca*

Much of the Oriental collection squirreled away by Hopp – whose villa this was – is in the Ráth György Museum (page 328). What remains here is Indian art inspired by the cult of Vishnu and Shiva, *wayang* puppets from Indonesia, and other works from Nepal, Tibet and Mongolia. Adult 300Ft, student 150Ft; free with Budapest Card. *Open same as Ráth György Múzeum.*

**House of Terror** See page 305.

**Liszt Ferenc Memorial Museum** (*Liszt Ferenc Emlékmúzeum*) VI, Vörösmarty utca 35; tel: 1 322 9804; www.lisztmuseum.hu [2 G3]
M1 *Vörösmarty utca metro station;* B *4*
One of music's masters, the silver-haired Liszt (1811–1886) was a symbol of Hungarian nationhood, his very concerts bold statements of opposition to the absolutism that followed the 1848–49 Independence War. He was elected president of the Academy of Music on its inauguration in 1875, and lived out his final years on the first floor of the academy's neo-Renaissance building. There's a bovine-legged Chickering grand piano, a gift to Liszt from the manufacturers, and a tailored writing desk with a pull-out keyboard. The man behind the music played whist (there's a card table and a card box); he smoked cigars (there's a case and a few coronas); he took snuff from a silver box. He needed a cognac snifter before a composing session. And his fingers! A bronze replica of his elderly hand – cast by Alajos Kisfaludy Stróbl – shows a thumb that reached to the knuckle of the forefinger! These lengthy digits cascaded over the keyboard; as one observer remarked, 'We had never been confronted by such passionate, demonic genius.' The building also holds a research library, and a small concert

hall. On the corner where Andrássy út meets Vörösmarty utca. Adult 360Ft, student 180Ft, foreign-language tour 7,000Ft. *Open Mon–Fri 10.00–18.00, Sat 09.00–17.00, closed Sun.*

**Postal Museum** (*Postamúzeum*) VI, Andrássy út 3; tel: 1 268 1997 [2 F4]
M1 *Bajcsy-Zshút*
Wooden doors flanked by winged figures open on to an eclectic mansion, built 1884–86 and owned formerly by the merchant Andreas Saxlehner (whose family fled to America in 1938). You'll have to buzz for entry; as you climb the stairwell to the first floor be sure to admire the ceiling frescos by Károly Lotz, which give an insight into the splendour of a wealthy 19th-century townhouse. The museum holds the trappings of postal history, and items relating to telecommunications and broadcasting. King Mátyás established the very first mail coach in 1458, which delivered missives between Buda and Vienna. Adult 100Ft, student 50Ft; free for under 7s, over 65s, and with Budapest Card. *Open Tue–Sun 10.00–18.00 (Nov 1–Mar 31 10.00–16.00), closed Mon.*

**Ráth György Museum** VI, Városligeti fasor 12; tel: 1 342 3916 [2 G3]
TB *70, 78*
The country's prime collection of Oriental art, based upon items accumulated by Ferenc Hopp during his travels (between 1882 and 1913). There are additional temporary exhibitions at the nearby Hopp Ferenc Museum (see page 326). Free entry to permanent exhibition. *Open Tue–Sun 10.00–18.00 (Jan 1–Mar 31 10.00–16.00), closed Mon.*

**Zoltán Kodály Memorial Museum** (*Kodály Zoltán Emlékmúzeum*) VI, Andrássy út 87–89; tel: 1 352 7106 [2 G2]
M1 *Kodály körönd*
Kodály (1882–1967) was one of the 20th century's most-influential composers, and a music teacher who devised the revolutionary 'Kodály Method'. This was his apartment for much of his life. Among his possessions are pieces of earthenware decorated with folk motifs; like Bartók (see page 321), Kodály embarked on a journeyman's crusade to collect folk music, and he picked up such ceramics on his travels. Press the buzzer in the courtyard for entry. Adult 300Ft, concessions 150Ft; free with Budapest Card. *Open Wed 10.00–16.00, Thu–Sat 10.00–18.00, Sun 10.00–14.00, closed Mon–Tue.*

## *Heroes' Square, City Park and around*

**Hungarian Agricultural Museum** (*Magyar Mezőgazdasági Múzeum*) XIV, Vajdahunyadvár, Városliget; tel: 1 363 1971; www.mezogazdasagimuzeum.hu [2 H2]
M1 *Hősök tere*
Europe's largest agricultural museum is held in the intriguing Vajdahunyad Castle, conceived in 1896 as a temporary flex of Hungary's architectural muscles. The building – into which Ignác Alpári wove a range of the country's structural styles – proved so popular that it was made a permanent fairy-tale fixture of City Park. The museum's collection is planted in the baroque and Gothic wings, and is devoted to animal husbandry (István Széchenyi imported English methods of horse-breeding during the 19th century), hunting and wine production. Adult 500Ft, concessions 200Ft, guide 5,000Ft; free with Budapest Card. *Open Tue–Fri 10.00–17.00*

*(10.00–16.00 in winter), Sat 10.00–18.00 (10.00–17.00 in winter), Sun 10.00–17.00, closed Mon.*

**Hungarian Railway History Park** (*Magyar Vasúttörténeti Park*) XIV, Tatai út 95; tel/fax: 1 450 1497/238 0558; www.vasuttortenetipark.hu and www.mavnosztalgia.hu

B *30 from Keleti Station to Rokolya utca;* T *14 from Lehel tér to Dolmány utca. Vintage diesel shuttle runs between Nyugati Station and museum (Apr 1–Oct 31, departing 09.45, 10.45, 13.45 and 15.45).*

Central Europe's largest outdoor railway museum is a real heavyweight. The bays of the former North Depot's 1911 roundhouse are crammed with carriages and engines dating back to the late 19th century. Among them are the Árpád rail car, which ran between Budapest and Vienna from 1937, and an *Orient Express* dining carriage. Many are used for tourist trips by MÁV Nosztalgia. You can drive a steam engine or a horse tram, and there's a model railway. Adult 900 Ft, concessions 300–400Ft, family 1,800Ft; interactive rides 100–1,000Ft. *Open (Mar 13–Apr 2 and Oct 25–Dec 19) 10.00–15.00, (Apr 3–Oct 24) 10.00–18.00, closed Mon and rest of year. The interactive rides are only open Apr 3–Oct 24 10.00–16.00.*

**Hungarian Sports Museum** (*Magyar Sportmúzeum*) XIV, Dozsa Gyorgy út 3; tel: 1 252 1696 [2 K4]

B *95, 130;* T *1, 1A;* TB *75, 77*

A utilitarian block profiling Hungarian sporting gods of the past. One room is dedicated to the winner of the country's first Olympic gold medal, Alfréd Hajós, who took up swimming after his father drowned in the Danube. Adult 300Ft, concessions 200Ft; free with Budapest Card. *Open 10.00–16.00, closed Fri.*

**Municipal Grand Circus** (*Fővárosi Nagycirkusz*) XIV, Állatkerti körút 12; tel: 1 343 8300 or 1 344 6008
M1 *Széchenyi fürdő;* TB *72;* B *4, 30*
Flanked by a pair of inflatable clowns in City Park, Pest's circus has a provenance dating to the 18th century. Tickets adult 900–1,400Ft, concessions 700–1,200Ft. *Summer performances (mid-Apr–Aug) on Wed, Fri, Sun 15.00 and 19.00, Thu 15.00, Sat 10.00, 15.00, 19.00.*

**Municipal Zoo and Botanical Garden** (*Fővárosi Állat-és Növénykerty*) XIV, Állatkerti körút 6–12; tel: 1 363 3797/3710
Few elephants around the world trumpet away beneath a turquoise domed roof. The Moorish enclosure – whose tower you can climb – was inspired by the remains of a Turkish mosque, but there is early-20th-century architectural adventure elsewhere, not least in the garish Secessionist entrance gate. At the western side of City Park (next to the circus), the zoo is also home to Hungary's only gorillas, and holds a good children's playground and a botanical garden. Adult 1,000Ft, concessions 750Ft, family 3,100Ft. *Open (Nov–Feb) 09.00–16.00 daily, (Mar–Apr and Sep–Oct) 09.00–17.00 daily, (May–Aug) Mon–Thu 09.00–18.00, Fri–Sun 09.00–19.00. Cash desk closes one hour earlier.*

**Museum of Fine Arts** See page 310.

**Palace of Arts** (*Műcsarnok*) XIV, Dózsa György út 37; tel: 1 460 7000/7014; 3-D film info: 1 460 7033 [2 H2]
M1 *Hősök tere*
One half of the exquisite neoclassical brace of buildings on Hősök tere, the Palace of Arts represents the country's largest gallery space and hosts temporary lashings of contemporary art. Regular screenings of a 3-dimensional film about Hungary's highlights take place in the exhibition hall. Adult 600Ft, concessions 300Ft; combined (gallery and film) ticket adult 990Ft, concessions 490Ft; free with Budapest Card. *Open Tue–Wed, Fri–Sun 10.00–18.00, Thu 12.00–20.00, closed Mon.*

**Transport Museum** (*Közlekedési Múzeum*) XIV, Városligeti körút 11; tel: 1 363 2658; www.km.iif.hu [2 J2]
T *1*; TB *70, 72, 74*
This is no 'tram, bam, thank-you ma'am' museum; the collection of trains, boats, motorcycles and vintage cars – both replicas and the real things – is vast. The model train engines, intricate and precise copies, are magnificent. In front of the museum are pieces of the Chain Bridge that was destroyed by the Germans during World War II. On the edge of City Park. Free entry. *Open Tue–Fri 10.00–17.00, Sat–Sun 10.00–18.00, closed Mon.*

**Vidámpark** XIV,Városligeti körút 14–16; tel: 1 363 3825; www.vidampark.hu/english/indexe.html [2 H1]
M1 *Hősök tere*
The 1906 merry-go-round (immortalised in the Rogers and Hammerstein musical *Carousel*) is a protected national monument encased in a glass building, and the roller-coaster terrifies not because of the dips and lurches, but because it is made of wood and a feels bit overly rickety... Generally quite deserted, this is a fun place on a dreary Sunday afternoon. Adult 300Ft, child under 120cm free! Rides cost 300–600Ft. *Open daily 11.00–sunset (winter), 10.00–20.00 (summer).*

## *Erzsébetváros*

**Hungarian Electrical Engineering Museum** (*Magyar Elektrotechnikai Múzeum*) VII, Kazinczy utca 21; tel: 1 322 0472 [2 F4]
M2 *Blaha Lujza tér;* TB *74*
Magyars have been to the fore in the highly charged field of electrical engineering. Ányos Jedlik – a monk at Pannonhalma – devised the commutator DC motor; Imre Bródy filled bulbs with krypton gas to create lights as we know them; and three Hungarians invented the transformer. As all this whizzed in one ear and out the other, we spent a happy hour in the former transformer station winding handles to light glass tubes and creating static thunder claps that made our hearts flop over. In fairness, there are some human stories to be dug out too. Jedlik, for instance, constructed the first dynamo (the original is here) but failed to patent it; seven years later someone else's version appeared, and Jedlik's achievement was forgotten

to history. Adult 300Ft, concessions 150Ft; free entry on Sat. *Open Tue–Sat 11.00–17.00, closed Sun–Mon.*

**Jewish Museum** (*Zsidó Múzeum*) VII, Dohány utca 2; tel: 1 342 8942 [2 G4]
T *47, 49;* B *7, 7A*
Little more than a decade after opening in 1932, the exhibits were destined for dark corners and dank cellars away from the keen eyes of German occupiers. The first of the two exhibitions focuses upon religious objects associated with Jewish holidays. As well as silver menorahs and chalices, borrow someone's reading glasses and take a careful look at the tapestry on the left as you enter. The words of the Torah are embroidered in tiny script; it was made in 1828, and used for covert worship during World War II. Contemporary photographs in the Holocaust exhibition bring up close the chilling plight of Hungarian Jews in 1944, many of whom perished in labour camps. There is also a more uplifting tribute to those who strove to help them, among them Raoul Wallenberg (see box, page 348). Next to the Great Synagogue (page 346). Adult 600Ft, concessions 200Ft; free with Budapest Card. *Open Mon–Thu 10.00–17.00 (Nov 1–Apr 14 10.00–15.00), Fri and Sun 10.00–14.00, closed Sat.*

**Stamp Museum** (*Bélyegmúzeum*) VII, Hársfa utca 47; tel: 1 341 5526 [2 G4]
T *4, 6;* TB *74*
Join the stampede of philatelists to view a collection of 12 million stamps. On the corner of Dob utca and Hársfa utca. Adult 150Ft, child 75Ft; free with

Budapest Card. *Open Tue–Sun 10.00–18.00 (Nov 1–Mar 31 10.00–16.00), closed Mon.*

## *Józsefváros, Ferencváros and beyond*

**Crime and Police History Museum** (*Bűnügyi és Rendőrség Történeti Múzeum*) VIII, Mosonyi utca 7; tel: 1 477 2183; www.policehistorymus.com [2 H4]
M2 *Keleti;* T *23, 24;* B *7, 7A*
The history of the Hungarian police force, with gruesome details of real 20th-century criminal cases. Free entry. *Open 10.00–17.00, closed Mon.*

**Dreher Beer Museum** *(Dreher Sörmúzeum)* X, Jászberényi út 7–11; tel: 1 432 9700; www.dreherrt.hu
A fun exhibition of the history of Hungarian brewing, in which you're transported on a little train. You'll need to book to tour the factory (tel: 1 432 9850). *Open Mon–Fri 09.00–18.00, Sat–Sun 10.00–16.00.*

**Holocaust Memorial Centre** IX, Páva utca 39; tel: 1 455 3333; www.hdke.hu [4 G7]
M3 *Ferenc körút*
Opened in April 2004, the exhibition halls and archive rooms are built around a restored synagogue that served as an internment camp – and form a deliberately angular and uncomfortable space. In the courtyard is a wall bearing the names of 60,000 victims. Over half a million Jews were killed after the Nazi invasion of March

1944. Those behind the centre strive for a fuller acceptance of the Holocaust as a part of Hungarian, as well as German, history. They invite discussion of the lack of resistance, the looting of property and the assistance provided by the authorities. In just 56 days, 437,000 Jews were deported, all but 15,000 to Auschwitz – the fastest and largest deportation of the Holocaust. They remind visitors of the nightly massacres by Arrow Cross troopers on the Danube's banks during the winter of 1944. And they pay tribute to the Roma people, who also suffered murderous persecution. By promoting a fuller understanding of, and accountability for, the past, the exhibition hopes to foster better relations in the present. Free entry. *Open Tue–Sun 10.00–18.00.*

**Hungarian National Museum** See page 308.

**Museum of Applied Arts** (*Iparművészeti Múzeum*) IX, Üllői út 33–37; tel: 1 456 5100; www.imm.hu [4 G6]
T̲ *4, 6*
Thoroughly, blissfully over the top, the art-nouveau building was designed for the millennial celebrations of 1896 by Ödön Lechner and Gyula Pártos. The pair clearly had some fun. Lechner – whose hunched statue sits outside – determined to create a uniquely Hungarian style, and there are folksy and oriental elements, as well as Indian influences deriving from the contemporary belief that the Magyar tribes arrived from the subcontinent. The portal looks like a piece of Moorcroft pottery, while the crown-like dome of the roof is coated with coloured ceramic scales. The

white interior contains arts and crafts, 17th-century costume, a selection of oriental rugs and examples of the art-nouveau movement. Free entry to permanent exhibitions. *Open 10.00–18.00 (10.00–16.00 Nov–Mar), closed Mon.*

**Natural History Museum** (*Magyar Természettudományi*) VIII, Ludovika tér 6; tel: 1 210 1085; www.nhmus.hu [4 J7]
M3 *Klinikák*
A permanent exhibition details man's often disharmonious relationship with nature. The museum, which has stood in the impressive Ludovika Military Academy since 1996, has certainly endured the wrath of the elements. Swathes of the collection were obliterated by the Great Flood of 1838 and by fire in 1956. It regrouped, however, and alongside the usual stuffed monkeys, there are reconstructions of ancient faces, a giant clam donated by the Hungarian storyteller Mór Jókai, a piece of moon rock from the Apollo expedition, and an extensive palaeontological display that includes dinosaur eggs and footprints. *Open 10.00–18.00, closed Tue.* Entrance to Nature Lover Hall/Exhibition building 400Ft/450Ft.

**Planetarium** X, Népliget Park; tel: 1 263 0871; www.lezerszinhaz.hu [4 K8]
M3 *Népliget;* B *103;* TB *75*
The paths of the planets are on show during the day, while in the evening there's a laser display in tune to music by galacticos of the pop world. 'The Wall' was the score to which the Berlin Wall fell, and Pink Floyd remains one of the laser theatre's best-loved shows. Tickets available from 18.30 or from city ticket offices;

alternatively book by telephone (tel: 1 263 0871). At the intersection of Könyves Kálmán körút and Üllői út. Planetarium 890Ft; laser show adult 1,890Ft, student 1,390Ft, child 600Ft; discount with Budapest Card. *Planetarium open Tue–Sun 09.00–16.00; laser shows start at 19.30 (closed Jun).*

## MAJOR SIGHTS

### Buda

**Buda Castle Palace** (*Budavári Palota*) I, Vár hegy [3 C5]

The vast pile that commands the southern end of Castle Hill is the last in a line of palaces built here since the early-medieval period. **Béla IV** first chose to construct a town here in the 13th century, surrounded by a defensive wall and with a fort to the south. After the demise of the Árpád dynasty, the **Angevin kings** also established strongholds, with Prince István 'the Angry' ('Haragos') building a keep whose foundations still exist, and Lajos Nagy (Louis the Great) erecting his palace on the same site.

However, the golden age of the royal complex came during the **15th century**. First Zsigmond of Luxembourg (1387–1437), King of Hungary and Holy Roman Emperor, established a considerably larger Gothic palace (featuring the renowned Knights' Hall; see page 313). After that the cultured and progressive Mátyás Hunyadi (also known as 'Corvinus'; 1443–90) expanded upon it with a Renaissance flourish. His second wife, Beatrice, was from Naples, and she brought with her a gaggle of Italian artists and a legendarily hospitable nature. Scholars and gentlemen from all over Europe flocked to the majestic palace, with its fine art and marble details. The king's library – the *Bibliotheca Corviniana* – was among the world's richest, holding 2,000 books and manuscripts. Scattered by the Turks, today only 200 remain worldwide (33 of them in the current National Széchényi Library; page 316).

The palace fell into decline under **Ottoman occupation**. It was finally put out of its misery in 1686, when Buda was liberated but its greatest building reduced to rubble. The country's **Habsburg rulers** began anew. Maria Theresa (1740–80) enlarged upon her father's baroque palace; it became the residence of the palatines, and from 1776 also held the Holy Right Hand of Szt István – the country's most prized and revered relic.

The palace's feathers were ruffled once more during the 1848–49 War of Independence, when it was occupied by Hungarian forces struggling against imperial rule. Restoration came on a grand scale following the Austro-Hungarian Compromise of 1867, first to the designs of Miklós Ybl and then, after his death, to those of Alajos Hauszmann. The expansion was an expression of a fresh sense of independence, and it was hoped that the splendacious palace would shift the dual monarchy's beating heart from Vienna to Budapest. Hauszmann doubled the length of the palace's façade (to over 300m) and added its outstanding feature, the central dome. Ferenc József, who had been crowned in Buda, laid one of the foundation stones during the millenary celebrations of 1896. Once completed, it formed the impressive backdrop to the coronation procession in 1916 of Károly IV, the last, short-lived Habsburg king.

In the **aftermath of World War I**, the newly elected governor, Admiral Miklós Horthy, moved into the palace and lived the right royal high life. Shortly after his removal in a German coup of 1944, the Buda Castle Palace was brought down for the 31st and final time. The German army's centre of operations was based here, and as the soldiers holed up in a doomed final stand, the palace was battered by Russian bombardment. The **post-war reconstruction** incorporated those walls that were still standing, and included Gothic and baroque elements, but paid little regard to many aspects of the original design. However, archaeological excavations went hand in hand with the reconstruction and revealed previously hidden medieval sections that can be viewed on the lower levels of the **Budapest History Museum** (page 313). A series of Gothic statues of saints, knights and bishops found in 1974 probably date to Zsigmond of Luxembourg's time. In 1959 the decision was made to devote the building to Hungarian culture, and, as well as the history museum, it now houses the **Museum of Contemporary Art**, the **Hungarian National Gallery** and the **National Széchényi Library**.

**Cave Church** (*Sziklatemplom*) I, Gellért tér [3 D6]
A jagged-walled cavern and rugged place of worship. Its hill was originally called Mount 'Pest', the Slavic word for 'cavity', while the cave itself was named Szt Iván after a medieval healing hermit who lived inside. In 1926 the grotto church was built, inspired by a pilgrimage to Lourdes. During World War II, Pauline monks disguised Jews in their robes and hid them in the adjacent turreted cloister. In 1950, however, the saviours turned victims when communists seized monasteries all over Hungary. In total, over 10,000 of the country's monks and nuns were forced out, and many executed or imprisoned. The cave entrance was blocked with concrete, the cloister

became a dormitory for students of the state ballet school and the Paulines had to wait almost 40 years for the political climate to permit their return. To the right of the cave entrance, a piece of the concrete wall remains as reminder of the enforced period of exile. A **statue of Szt István**, his toes curling over the plinth, is positioned outside. Masses are held daily at 11.00, 17.00 and 20.00, and on Sundays and holidays at 09.30 and 10.30. Non-observants may not visit at these times.

**Church of Mary Magdalene** (*Mária Magdolna templom*) I, Kapisztrán tér [1 B3] The first church was erected in Romanesque style in the 13th century, and traditionally served the Hungarian population of the burghers' town. During the Turkish occupation, for some time it was the only church in the Castle District where Christian services were permitted; making the best in difficult times, Protestants used the nave and Catholics the chancel. The Habsburg Ferenc I was crowned here in 1792, adorned in ceremonial Hungarian garb, and the neoclassical porch facing on to Úri utca was commissioned at the same time. Shortly afterwards Martinovics was stripped of his priesthood in the church, a further humiliation prior to his execution (see box, page 248). Massive World-War-II damage led to the demolition of most of the walls in 1952 and only the tower was preserved. The pathetic ruins of what was the church's main body lie behind it, culminating in an unsupported and fragile arched window, assembled from gathered fragments. It is said that if you look through the window your wishes will come true. This sounds laced with irony; in the face of this phantom of a church we're reminded of a dog with one ear and one eye called 'Lucky'.

**Citadella** I, Gellért hegy [3 D6]
Like the Freedom Monument (see page 255), the stronghold next to it had significant symbolic overtones when constructed by the Habsburgs following the 1848–49 War of Independence. Built with Hungarian forced labour, its forbidding presence against the skyline was designed to quash further rebellious impulses. However, tempers had cooled by the time the Austrian garrison took up residence, and the grey fortress began to look something of a white elephant. In 1894 it was handed over to the city, and parts of it demolished as a token of the country's unshackled self. It subsequently served, among other things, as a prison and a hostel for the homeless, but its walls now contain an **open-air exhibition** devoted to Gellért Hill, covering its history from ancient times up until the 20th century. There is a section on the martyrdom and cult of Gellért himself that challenges the traditional legend of the bishop's death (see page 255), arguing instead that the pagan insurgents of Vata tied him to a chariot, stoned him to death and pierced his heart with a lance. Infinitely preferable! Sellers of items irresistible to coach parties cluster outside the walls of the fort. Adult 300Ft; no concessions (except for groups). *Exhibition and panoramic views open 12.00–24.00 daily.*

**Mátyás Church** *(Mátyás templom)* I, Szentháromság tér 2 [1 C4]
Different brushstrokes for different folks. Some deplore the old town's centrepiece as a tattooed millionaire of a church, all chunky jewellery and no class; others see a triumphant marriage of 13th-century Gothic design and late-19th-century national pride. It is something of a miracle that there is anything left to argue about.

During World War II, tanks rammed through its main gates, the roof was burned out, and it was used alternately as a German field kitchen and a stable for Soviet horses. Mátyás was twice married here, and the walls – or parts of them – witnessed the coronations of Károly Róbert (the first Angevin king, in 1309), Ferenc József (for which Liszt's 'Coronation Mass' was composed, in 1867) and Károly IV (the country's last, in 1916).

The church was first raised on this site by Buda's **German population** in the reign of Béla IV. It was reconstructed by **King Lajos** in the 14th century (when the Maria portal was added) and **Mátyás** in the 15th (who oversaw the construction of the bell tower), and subsequently appropriated by the **Turks** as their main mosque during the 150 years of occupation. As part of the 1896 millenary celebrations, the architect **Frigyes Schulek** stripped away many of the later architectural layers in his quest to remain faithful to the spirit of the Gothic original. The result is a hall church characterised by its elegant Mátyás Tower, complete with lace-like stonework and bobbly spire, a fabulous Zsolnay-majolica-tiled roof, and interior decoration that thumps the eyeballs.

The **14th-century relief** above the southern Maria portal depicts the death and assumption of the Virgin Mary (after whom the church is properly named); the **raven** perched on the easternmost turret recognises the mighty impact of Mátyás Hunyadi's patronage. Inside, candy-sweet paints adorn every pillar of the nave and vaulted undulation of the ceiling. The geometric and floral designs were supposedly based upon Middle Age fragments, although the influence of Hungarian Secessionism (art nouveau) is also clear. Other frescos and stained-glass windows depict events of Hungarian history, and make the church as much a shrine to national consciousness as religious worship. These are the work of the renowned Romantic historicist artists Károly Lotz and Bertalan Székely, who were responsible for other paintings in the opera house and Parliament.

There are subtler details to be winkled out inside. Our favourites can be found near the Mátyás coat of arms, within the arch of the organ loft to the left after you pass through the Maria portal. Look carefully, and among the leafy motifs adorning two 15th-century capitals you will spot **four carved heads** – the wispy-bearded face of János Hunyadi, the curtain-haired Mátyás, the lopped-off noggin of László and, gazing towards the chancel, what is presumed to be a representation of the tower's builder. Next to the Hunyadi capital is the **Loréto Chapel**, the first of several side chapels. There's a legend attached to its statue. When the Turks converted the church into a mosque, they walled up a Madonna statue rather than taking the trouble to remove it. During the siege of Buda 145 years later, an explosion caused the wall to fall away, revealing the long-forgotten figure to startled Muslim worshippers. This was regarded as a sign, and a contributing factor in accelerating the Christian victory – although the current statue was sculpted later than 1686, and could not itself be the Madonna of the legend.

The **Szt Imre Chapel** is dedicated to the son of István (the first king of the Árpád dynasty), who died in a hunting accident in 1031. Without an heir, the monarch symbolically offered the crown to Mary. Next to it is the **Béla Chapel**, containing the remains of Béla III (1173–96) and his wife, moved here in the 19th century. The sarcophagus was paid for by Ferenc József, an act more political than benevolent: Béla's daughter had married a Habsburg, thus establishing a historic link between the dynasties, and justification for Habsburg claims to the throne.

The **Szt László Chapel**, to the altar's right, contains a replica of the reliquary – a stunning gold bust of László (reigned 1077–95) – held in Győr Cathedral. One fresco shows the famously tall king saving a Hungarian maiden from a pagan Cuman chief, while in another he summons water from a stone to quench the thirst of his soldiers. The **crypt** and **royal oratory** hold stonework remains, a collection of ecclesiastical art (none medieval, as József II auctioned most of this in 1785) and copies of the Hungarian crown and coronation regalia. In **Szt István Chapel** is the right foot of Szt János (see page 243). Adult 500Ft, concessions 250Ft, family 750Ft guide 2,000Ft. Holy Mass Mon–Fri 07.00, 08.30 and 18.00, Sun and public holidays 07.00, 08.30, 10.00, 12.00 and 18.00. Regular organ recitals and concerts; tickets can be purchased at the entrance. *Open Mon–Fri 09.00–17.00, Sat 09.00–12.00, Sun 13.00–17.00.*

**Tomb of Gül Baba** (*Gül Baba türbéje*) II, Mecset utca 14
B̲ *91, 191*

The cobbled stairway of Gül Baba utca leads you up the peaceful Rózsadomb (Rose Hill). In an octagonal mausoleum at the top lies the Turkish dervish Gül Baba, who took part in the capture of Buda but dropped dead during the thanksgiving service afterwards in Mátyás Church; Süleyman the Magnificent attended his funeral prayer. The dervish later became known as the 'Father of Roses', reputedly because he grew flowers on the hillside but more probably a reference to tributes left at his tomb.

The shrine was erected in 1548, the tablet pointing towards Mecca, and is a place of Muslim pilgrimage. Remove your shoes before entering. Adult 400Ft, concessions 200Ft. *Open Tue–Sun 10.00–18.00 (May 1–Sep 30), 10.00–16.00 (Oct 1–31).*

**Wolf's Meadow Cemetery** (*Farkasréti temető*) XI, Németvölgyi út 99 [3 A6]
*T̲ 59 (from Moszkva tér) to the terminus*
Draw a line west from Gellért hegy, pass the queue of mourners at the flower stalls outside, and you're among the chestnut and ash trees of a sprawling cemetery. This is the resting place of many former dissidents and refugees, among them Béla Bártók and the conductor Sir Georg Solti. Here too lies Mátyás Rákosi, the squat dictator – 'Stalin's best Hungarian disciple' – whose name is synonymous with mid-20th-century suffering; before being removed in 1956, he executed around 2,000 of his fellow citizens and incarcerated at least 100,000 more. The cemetery's focal point is the unprecedented mortuary chapel by Imre Makovecz, its winged doors opening on to a timber chamber fashioned like a torso. Caskets are placed where the heart would be. Makovecz was himself imprisoned at the time of the 1956 uprising, and went on to develop an organic, spiritual form of architecture that deliberately flouted the communist preference for regular, pre-fab blocks. *Mon–Fri 07.00–21.00, Sat–Sun 09.00–17.00.*

## Pest

**Great Synagogue** (*Nagy Zsinagóga*) VII, Dohány utca [2 G4]
The 'Tobacco Street' synagogue (named after a factory here) was raised in 1859, its Moorish minarets the work of Austrian architect Ludwig Förster. It is the world's

second largest (after that in New York), and seats 3,000. The magnificent interior – which caters for the Neolog community (a Hungarian denomination) – is unusual in several ways. As well as containing an organ, and 25 copies of the Torah (rather than the usual 12), it also has two pulpits from which the words of the rabbi are repeated so that all can hear (there are no microphones). Neglected under communism, renovation came in the 1990s, funded partly by the Emanuel foundation (established by actor Tony Curtis and named after his father, who emigrated in the 1920s). Today, festivals attract worshippers from all over Europe, and at other times there are concerts.

There was a ghetto here at the end of World War II, and a portion of the wall can be found in the **central courtyard**. The wall was demolished by the Soviets on January 18 1945, but a mass grave contains those who perished in the months before. Towards the back is **Heroes' Temple**, built in 1931 to commemorate Jews who died fighting at the front in World War I, often so poorly equipped that they didn't even have uniforms. The **Raoul Wallenberg Memorial Park**, behind the complex, is dedicated to the Swedish saviour (see box, page 348); its silver willow tree remembers the 600,000 Jews who died and the heroes of all faiths who risked their lives to save others. Relatives pay to have the names of victims inscribed upon the leaves. Next to the synagogue's main entrance is the **Jewish Museum** (see page 334); Tivadar (Theodor) Herzl (1860–1904) was born on this site, the journalist who founded the modern Zionist movement after witnessing anti-Semitism in Paris. Adult 500Ft, guided tour 1,900Ft. *Open Mon–Thu 10.00–17.00, Fri 10.00–15.00, Sun 10.00–14.00.*

## RAOUL WALLENBERG

Raoul Wallenberg is cherished as foremost among the 'righteous gentiles'. In 1944, SS officer Adolf Eichmann was arranging the annihilation of Hungary's Jewish population, and mass deportations were taking place daily. By summer, 400,000 had been carried away to concentration camps, the majority to Auschwitz. Wallenberg – a 32-year-old Swedish businessman – was sent to Budapest as secretary of the Swedish legation in the hope that he could stem the tide. He had no diplomatic experience, but was a tough man, ready to use bribery and extortion as necessary. He distributed protective passes to Jews that granted them protection as Swedish (neutral) citizens, and set up 30 safe houses in Pest under the Swedish flag. As deportations intensified, he even ran alongside the wagons, handing out passes and offering aid; German soldiers were so impressed with his bravery that they aimed high when ordered to shoot. It is estimated that Wallenberg saved the lives of 100,000. When the Russians arrived, however, he was taken to their military headquarters – and never seen again. It seems that he was arrested on suspicion of spying for the Americans, but his fate thereafter is unknown. The Russians claimed he had died of a heart attack, while many others claimed he was still alive in a Soviet prison. The likelihood, however, is that he was executed.

**Inner City Parish Church** (*Belvárosi plébániatemplom*) V, Március 15 tér 2 [3 E5]
Nestling tight against Erzsébet híd, the Inner City Parish Church is Pest's oldest building. It was first constructed in the 12th century over the southern wall of the Roman fort at Contra-Aquincum, and actually recycled some of the stones; the south tower contains remnants of this original. (There had been an even earlier church on the site, where the martyred Bishop Gellért was buried in 1046.) The current Gothic sanctuary was raised in the 15th century, although there was a baroque overhaul in 1739 and 19th-century renovation by Imre Steindl (at which time little shops operated from the spaces between the exterior buttresses). Work in the 1930s and 1940s uncovered *sedilia* in the sanctuary, together with a prayer niche (*mihrab*) that proves Turkish worship here during the occupation. The fragments of a medieval tabernacle were also found in the clear up after World War II; pieced together, it sits to the left of the high altar.

**Kerepesi Cemetery** VIII, Fiumei út [2 J5]
M2 *Keleti, walk down Festetics György utca and left into Fiumei út*
In our view, this is the city's prime haven – 54ha of parkland criss-crossed with paths and chestnut avenues, and history's movers all around. It's peaceful and fascinating. It's also one of the few places you'll see the red star and the hammer and sickle (officially outlawed as symbols of oppression). In one corner is the 1958 **Workers' Pantheon**, a white-stone piazza with socialist-realist statues and the words 'They lived for communism and the people'. The red-marble gravestone of **János Kádár** (see page 10) stands near by. Fallen revolutionary heroes of 1956 are

buried in a plot behind the pantheon; secret policemen (ÁVO) who died 'upholding the system' lie on the opposite side of the cemetery to prevent fights during memorial services. There are **magnificent mausoleums** for Ferenc Deák (see page 7), Lajos Kossuth (see page 6) and Lajos Batthyány (see page 7) – the latter raided by robbers in 1993, who stole a sword but overlooked the earrings of Batthyány's wife (now safe in the National Museum). József Antall – the first post-communist leader – is also here. Teenager Mária Csizmarovits is buried close to the Russian memorial; she died during the 1849 revolution, having disguised herself as a man to gain admission to the army. In the **artists' plot**, look out for sculptor János Pásztor, whose round-buttocked wife was the model for the statue on his grave; a widow was later so affronted to hear her husband was to be buried in the face of this peachy backside that she ordered the newly deceased be interred in another cemetery altogether! *Open (Jan–Feb, Nov–Dec 07.30–17.00, Mar and Oct 07.00–17.30, Apr and Aug 07.00–19.00, May–Jul 07.00–20.00, Sep 07.00–18.00.*

**Parliament** (*Országház*) V, Kossuth Lajos tér 1–3 [1 D3]

The symmetrical Parliament is a grandiose counterweight to the palace across the river, the symbol of democratic rather than aristocratic governance. (With this in mind, it is a typical irony of Hungarian history that for much of the 20th century, this 'democratic' institution simply rubber-stamped authoritarian decisions taken elsewhere.) It was the winning entry in a competition of 1882, its neo-Gothic aspect influenced by London's Parliament. However, Imre Steindl brought eclectic elements such as the central dome to the medieval-style buttresses, spires and archways. The statistics are staggering. The building took 17 years to construct, with 1,000 (often convict) labourers working at any one time; it is 268m long, its dome 96m high (a measured reference to the Magyar arrival in AD896), and contains 40 million bricks and 40kg of gold gilding. It is said that the cost of the project was equal to that of building a town for 60,000 people.

The true splendour of the place is evident as soon as you enter (via the south side, facing Kossuth tér). A **vaulted hall** is supported by eight columns carved from a single block of Swedish marble, a gift from the Swedish king (there are four of these in the English Parliament too); the imposing staircase carries you up to the **Dome Hall**, beneath frescos by Károly Lotz and an allegorical portrait of Hungary with István Széchenyi and Sándor Petőfi at her feet. The Dome Hall itself is surrounded by Zsolnay ceramic statues of the country's rulers (Árpád, the original Magyar, casting dagger eyes towards the Habsburgs to his right). The glass-cased centrepiece is the **coronation insignia**, with the Sacred Crown (Hungary's national symbol), sceptre, orb and sword, which were placed here in 2000 (the mantle remains in the National Museum; see page 309). While the legend goes that the crown was presented to István in 1000 as a sign of papal support for his rule, it was actually bashed together from two different pieces in the 12th century. Its skew-whiff cross is evidence of a turbulent history that saw it lost, dropped, buried in a bog and transported to various safehouses over the centuries, eventually ending up in America's Fort Knox before being returned in 1978. Since 1944, the legislature has been monocameral, and members sit in the **Chamber of Representatives** in the southern wing; the Upper House to the north is now used for international conferences. The **Hunter Hall** opposite the main staircase is the official dining area.

*Adult 2,000Ft, concessions 1,000Ft. Tourists may only visit on a guided tour; tickets are available from Gate X from 08.00 (ask the guard for permission to pass), and tours (in English) start at 10.00, 12.00, 14.00 and 18.00 daily.*

**Szent István Basilica** (*Bazilika*) V, Szent István tér [1 E4]

The Basilica got off to something of an inauspicious start. The first version of the capital's largest church, designed in 1845 by József Hild and constructed with inferior materials, had to be demolished after the dome collapsed. Miklós Ybl began anew, basing his Renaissance-inspired plan around a dome of 96m (like Parliament; see page 351) flanked by stocky towers. During World War II, the dome was hit by a bomb that mercifully failed to detonate, but a fire in 1946 brought it down once more. After restoration, Pope John Paul II took Mass here in 1991. As you move up the steps and through the entrance's triumphal arch, you'll pass beneath a tympanum of carved Hungarian saints worshipping Mary and Christ, a statue of Szt István (the founder of the Christian state) in Italian marble, and a gilded mosaic of Christ by Mór Than. The **interior** – laid out in the shape of a Greek cross – strikes you with contrasts, of light and dark, black and white, sturdy architecture and delicate art. Like the Mátyás Church (page 342), the artists present the Christian story very much in the context of Hungary's history, using Szent István as the focus. His statue (by Alajos Stróbl) graces the high altar, while major events in his significant life are played out in bronze reliefs on the walls behind. It is interesting to note that, for all the iconography portraying István's saintliness, he was actually a brutal and brooding king, merciless in suppressing perceived challenges to his authority. Look up to the dome, and mosaics by Károly Lotz, and to the Altar of the Virgin Mary at the southern end of the transept where Gyula Benczúr records the moment that István offered his crown to Mary on the death of his only son. There is a tiny **treasury** to the right of the entrance, and you can climb 300 steps (or take the lift most of the way) up to a **gallery** running around the outside of the Basilica's drum. However, the primary draw is the gnarled **right hand of István** himself, mounted in a casket in the Chapel of the Sacred Right. It is paraded through the streets during celebrations of the saint's day on August 20. Check listings magazines for details of concerts in the church or on the square outside. The church is free to enter (it has been known for conmen to try to charge tourists at the entrance); treasury 100Ft, Panorama Tower adult 500Ft, concessions 400Ft. *Open (Apr 1–May 31) 10.00–16.30, (Jun 1–Aug 31 09.30–18.00, (Sep 1–Oct 31) 10.00–17.30.*

# 13 Natural Budapest

There are few large cities where natural greenery is so readily accessible. The Buda hills are known as the 'lungs' of the capital, and – clichéd as it sounds – the woodlands and clearings really do promise kisses of life on stifling days. In winter, they are places to sledge, or even ski. The Buda Landscape Protection Area (*Budai Tájvédelmi Körzet*) covers 10,000ha in total, and is characterised by outcrops of white dolomite and limestone rock, by forested areas and grasslands, and by over 150 caves (themselves cool retreats). It contains the strictly protected meadows of Kis-Szénás hegy and Nagy-Szénás hegy, the only spots in the world that the yellow-flowered *Linum dolomiticum* calls home.

Some of the most fragile habitats are barred to the casual tourist boot, but Hármashatár, Kis- and Nagy-Hárs, Remete, János and Széchenyi hills are all within easy reach and feature trails for ramblers, families and cyclists. Over 100 species of bird breed up here, wild boar and deer (fallow and red) inhabit the forests, scarce reptiles like the Armenian whipsnake (*Coluber jugularis*) bask in the sun, and edible funghi are to be found such as the brown-capped common mushroom (*Agaricus sp*) – although check before guzzling a handful as there are also poisonous varieties. Botanical

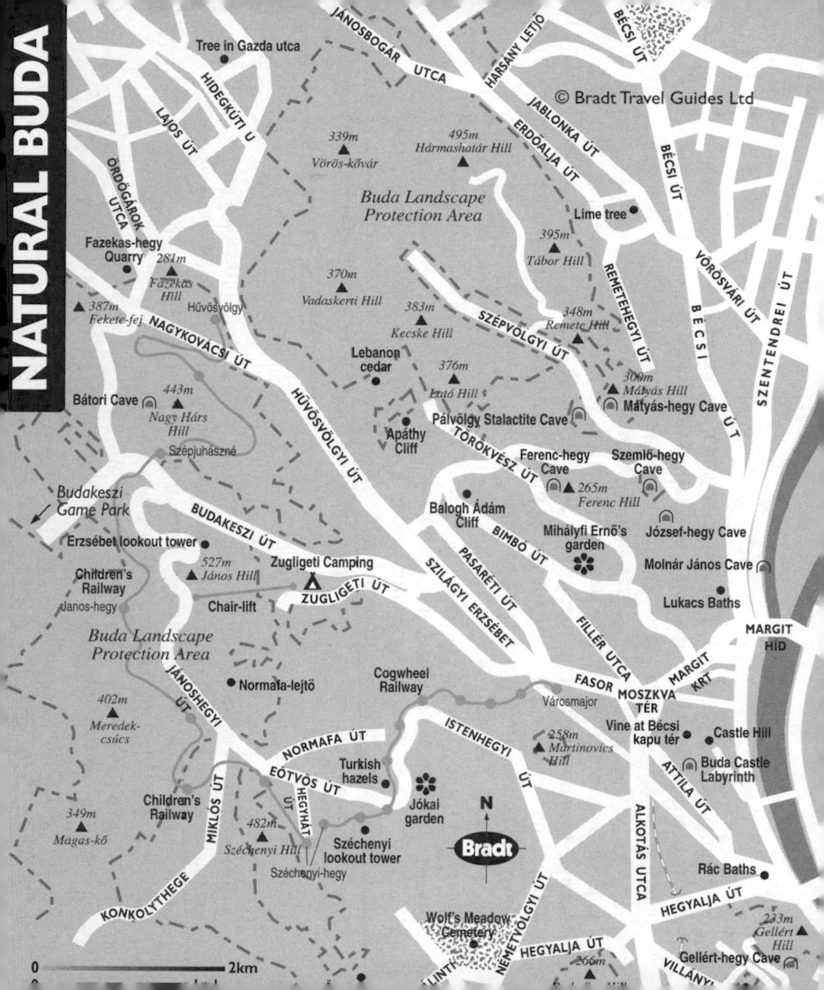

NATURAL BUDA
Tree in Gazda utca
JÁNOSBOGÁR UTCA
HARSÁNY LEJTŐ
BÉCSI ÚT
© Bradt Travel Guides Ltd
HIDEGKÚTI U
LAJOS ÚT
ÖRDÖGÁROK UTCA
339m
Vörös-kővár
495m
Hármashatár Hill
JABLONKA ÚT
ERDŐALJA ÚT
BÉCSI ÚT
Buda Landscape Protection Area
Lime tree
Fazekas-hegy Quarry
281m
Fazekas Hill
370m
Vadaskerti Hill
395m
Tábor Hill
REMETEHEGYI ÚT
VÖRÖSVÁRI ÚT
387m
Fekete-fej
Hűvösvölgy
NAGYKOVÁCSI ÚT
383m
Kecske Hill
348m
Remete Hill
SZÉPVÖLGYI ÚT
BÉCSI ÚT
SZENTENDREI ÚT
Lebanon cedar
376m
Látó Hill
300m
Mátyás Hill
Mátyás-hegy Cave
Bátori Cave
443m
Nagy Hárs Hill
HŰVÖSVÖLGYI ÚT
Apáthy Cliff
Pálvölgy Stalactite Cave
TÖRÖKVÉSZ ÚT
Szépjuhászné
Ferenc-hegy Cave
265m
Ferenc Hill
Szemlő-hegy Cave
Budakeszi Game Park
BUDAKESZI ÚT
Balogh Ádám Cliff
BIMBÓ ÚT
Mihályfi Ernő's garden
József-hegy Cave
Erzsébet lookout tower
527m
János Hill
Zugligeti Camping
ZUGLIGETI ÚT
SZILÁGYI ERZSÉBET
PASARÉTI ÚT
Molnár János Cave
Children's Railway
János-hegy
Chair-lift
Lukacs Baths
FILLÉR UTCA
MARGIT HÍD
Buda Landscape Protection Area
MARGIT KRT
JÁNOSHEGYI ÚT
Normafa-lejtő
Cogwheel Railway
FASOR
MOSZKVA TÉR
Városmajor
402m
Meredek-csúcs
ISTENHEGYI ÚT
258m
Martinovics Hill
Vine at Bécsi kapu tér
Castle Hill
NORMAFA ÚT
Turkish hazels
Buda Castle Labyrinth
EÖTVÖS ÚT
HEGYHÁT ÚT
ATTILA ÚT
Children's Railway
Jókai garden
N
349m
Magas-kő
MIKLÓS ÚT
482m
Széchenyi Hill
Széchenyi lookout tower
Bradt
Széchenyi-hegy
Rác Baths
ALKOTÁS UTCA
KONKOLYTHEGE
HEGYALJA ÚT
Wolf's Meadow Cemetery
NÉMETVÖLGYI ÚT
233m
Gellért Hill
HEGYALJA ÚT
266m
Gellért-hegy Cave
0
2km
VILLÁNYI

gardens and other sites of natural interest wait beyond the designated protection area too, and those who wish to go further can explore the footpaths of the Pilis, Visegrád and Börzöny hills in the Danube-Ipoly National Park (park directorate: II, Hűvösvölgy út 52; tel: 1 200 4033; www.dinpi.hu) to the north of Budapest. We've merely scratched a muddy surface with the following, and green fingers will find value in probing deeper. For operators running **nature-related tours**, see pages 47 and 84.

## THE RAIL TRAIL

Several buses run to points along the edge of the Buda Landscape Protection Area, but the train is an enjoyable way to ignore these limits and plunge straight on in. It also affords an easy introduction to a decent chunk of nature.

The **Cogwheel Railway** (*Fogaskerekű vasút*; XII, Szilágyi Erzsébet fasor 14–16) is the first stage of your two-track journey. Its lower end station (*vá*) is Városmajor, opposite the Budapest Hotel (page 113), and best reached by tram (18 or 56) from Moszkva tér. Trains run every 15–20 minutes to Széchenyi hegy (between 05.00 and 22.20 daily; last train back leaves around 23.30) and you can travel using an ordinary bus/train ticket. (You can also take your bike aboard, although it requires a ticket too.) Don't expect a quaint or relaxing ride; teethed cogs pull the carriages uphill, and it's something of a brain-sloshing 20 minutes.

On disembarking, signposts offer several options. You can walk a short distance along Rege út to the **Széchenyi kilátó** (a TV tower at the top of the hill), you can follow Golfpálya út on the considerably longer route on foot to János hegy (see page 359), or you can take a few steps to the second stage of the railway trail 200m away.

The **Children's Railway** (*Gyermekvasút*; Hegyhát út; tel: 1 397 5394/395 5420; www.gyermekvasut.com; adult 200/400Ft, child 65/130Ft; Oct 25–Mar 12 Tue–Sun 10.00–16.00 on the hour, Mar 13–Oct 24 Tue–Sun 10.00–18.00 on the hour, May 1–Aug 31 daily) is a narrow-gauge line that preserves the tradition – established by the communist youth movement and the Hungarian State Railway in 1948 – of giving work experience to children aspiring to a career on the railways. The kids collect and sell tickets conscientiously, but are not yet trusted with driving the engine. The carriages are wooden-benched and open-sided; they snake their way into the landscape protection area, and proceed northwards for 11km as far as Hűvösvölgy. The whole journey takes 45 minutes, but you may wish to alight at one of the eight stations along the way. The track passes Normafa lejtő, János hegy and Hárs hegy, while the Budakeszi Game Park (*Vadaspark*; see page 366) is accessible from Szépjuhászné. A nostalgia train also runs on the Children's Railway (an extra 100Ft for adults and 50Ft for child, one way).

## Normafa lejtő and János hegy

**Normafa** – Róza Klein once sang an aria from Bellini's *Norma* under a tree (*fa*) here – is a very popular walking, biking, jogging and picnicking spot, particularly at weekends. At 479m above sea level it is one of the highest points in town, and offers some snow sports in winter; in truth, though, the views are more thrilling than the skiing. Bus 21 runs here from Moszkva tér at regular intervals; alternatively, you can

***ONE MAN AND HIS MOP***

When we first saw a *puli* running down the street in Budapest, we looked around with some chagrin for the joker who was throwing mop heads around. It is one of the oddest dogs you'll see, a compact canine whose shaggy coat forms a series of natural cords – often mistaken for dreadlocks – that reach to the ground, covering its whole body. If the dog is standing still, it can be difficult to tell whether it is wagging a tail or shaking a head. When lying flat, you'd be forgiven for thinking it was a bath mat – although it would be a poor performer in this respect, for the *puli* can take three days to air dry, and will walk carefully around a small puddle.

Despite appearances, the *puli* is highly agile. It looks more sheep than shepherd, but was brought to Hungary by Magyar tribesmen over 1,000 years ago as a herder of livestock on the plains. The dogs gathered the stock from the

take the Children's Railway to Normafa station (and follow Eötvös út north). If you want to escape the crowds, and enjoy a gentle downward lope, follow the route marked with a green cross next to the final bus stop (on the other side from the Danube view). Cross the Children's Railway line, and head down the valley, through Budakeszi forest towards Makkosmária Church in its lovely clearing. After the church, continue down Makkosmária út towards the centre of Budakeszi. From here you can take bus 22 back to Moszkva tér, passing the wildlife park on the way (see page 366).

villages, and drove them between grazing areas or to market. *Pulik* differed from other working dogs, such as border collies, in having to move huge numbers of sheep – often upwards of 400, many with foot rot – in tall grass. As a result, theirs was a vigorous and less-refined method than other breeds – bouncing to see over the grass and yelping to spur the flock into motion. They are usually black in colour (originally to distinguish them from the sheep), highly intelligent, extremely active, and expressive watchdogs. Bred to be the sole companion of the shepherd during months of isolation, they are also affectionate and loyal. Indeed the bond was so strong between man and dog, that shepherds would only ever sell *pulik* between themselves, believing that others could never properly understand the dogs' unique temperament.

A more strenuous walk from Normafa is northwards to **János hegy**, the capital's highest peak (527m), along the blue-circle route. Up here you'll find the Erzsébet-kilátó, a viewing tower designed by Frigyes Schulek that takes you even higher for superb views, and further sign-posted walking routes (including a nature trail). Best of all, however, is the **chairlift** (*libegő*; open summer 09.00–19.00, autumn/winter 09.30–16.00, spring 09.00–17.00 daily; adult 750/400Ft, student/pensioner 550/300Ft, child 350/200Ft), which offers peaceful carriage down the hill to Zugligeti út (from where you can take bus 158 to Moszkva tér). It can get chilly up there, so take a sweater. There's a walking/cycling route running beneath the lift, but it's very steep.

## OTHER HILL WALKS

In addition to the walks suggested above, consider the few below, which are arranged in order of difficulty. Cartographia's *A Budai-hegység* (1:30,000; No 6) map shows the network of marked trails running through the Buda hills.

### Walk 1

*Route* Látó hegy–Mátyás király park–Vitorlázó mező–Remetekertváros–Hűvösvölgy
*Difficulty* Little shade; some uphill and some flat
From Batthyány tér, take bus 11 to the final stop, and follow the green-circle route for 1km as it weaves in and out of Görgényi út until it reaches a car park. A series of nature trails start from this point. The terrain is steep and covered with scrubby aspen and giant conifers. A long outcrop of smooth white rock forming the Hármashatárhegy and the lower Felső kecske hegy (Upper Goat Hill) dominates the skyline. All the coded trails are marked with the number of minutes ('p' for *perc*) they should take.

To reach the airfield (*Vitorlázómező és repülőtér*) where gliders and biplanes offer rides (usually for around 1,000Ft/5 minutes), take the red-circle route for about 1km, then turn left on to the yellow-cross track until you reach a large clearing with Homok hegy (Sand Hill) on your left. Climb the hillock to see the memorial to King Mátyás and watch the gliders take off opposite from Vörös kővár. After that, take an unmarked route across the airfield to the suburb of Remetekertváros. Go left at the border with the houses, and link up with Hidegekúti út; this leads to Hűvösvölgy, from where you can catch bus 56 back to Moszkva tér. (Hűvösvölgy was once the secret meeting place for the outlawed workers' movement, who avoided Horthy's police by pretending to be on picnics.)

## Walk 2

*Route* Fenyőgyöngye étterem–Árpád kilátó–Apáthy szikla–Napraforgó utca–Pasaréti tér
*Difficulty* Plenty of variety, with ups and downs
Take bus 65 from Kolosy tér (in Óbuda) as far as the Fenyőgyöngye étterem. Follow the blue-stripe trail up over Látó hegy towards Rózsadomb. This passes the Árpád kilátó (stone lookout lodge) and then meanders down to the end of Törökvész út. Crossing the road, head along the green-stripe route, which scratches along the side of a crumbly white cliff towards Apáthy szikla. If you follow the green-stripe trail down through the suburban roads, keeping the Franciscan church at Pasaréti tér as your marker, you can also take a stroll along the experimental showcase street, Napraforgó utca. Here 22 houses were built in the early 1930s, when some of Hungary's most inventive architects were commissioned to design homes for modern living. From Pasaréti tér, bus 5 runs to Március 15 tér in Pest.

## Walk 3

*Route* Fenyőgyöngye étterem–Hármashatárhegy–Udvarház étterem–Vihár hegy–Erdőalja út

*Difficulty* Strenuous, exposed, mainly uphill

Energetic climb up the television tower on Hármashatárhegy (Treble Border Hill); at 495m, it is a rival to János hegy across the Hűvösvölgy valley. It's wild and windswept, with little relief from the sun, but the Udvarház offers the chance for a drink on the terrace. From the Fenyőgyöngye étterem (see walk above), keep the valley road uphill to Újlaki hegy; turn to the right and follow the blue-circle trail up to Hármashatárhegy – and top-rate views. Continue along the blue-stripe route to Vihar hegy, and when you reach a chalet café at the hamlet of Gercsény, double back to the right along the blue-cross track. You will join Erdőalja út, from where bus 137 can drop you at Florián tér.

## CAVES

Budapest is unique as a world capital in being riddled with caves (*barlang*). There are over 60 thermal springs in Buda, welling up in groups at Gellért hegy, Hármashatár hegy and in the Csillaghegy-Rómaifürdő area; over thousands of years, the corrosive, toasty water broadened rock faults into chambers. The Bátori Cave on top of Hárs hegy was mined for iron ore during the Middle Ages, and the caves under the Castle District were used variously as cellars, burial vaults and air-raid shelters. Lime material deposited by the water as spring travertines at the surface was used in building the city, while the very name 'Pest' probably derives from the slavic word for cave.

Many other caves were only discovered during the urban expansion of the last hundred years (including most among the cluster of 80 in the Rózsadomb area). In their layers of limestone are preserved fossils that tell geologists about the ancient landscape, while mineral deposits provide both insights into the stages of cave development and weirdly wonderful sights. The five largest cave systems – Pál-völgy, Mátyás-hegy (a popular cavers' training site), Ferenc-hegy (a maze of narrow passages), Szemlő-hegy and József-hegy (only discovered in 1984) – are all located within an area of a couple of square kilometres, and are strictly protected. Despite this, there is limited access to a few of them for non-specialists. In addition to those below, some companies offer more active tours with qualified cavers, usually of the Mátyás-hegy system. For **further information** on caves, contact the Budapest Nature Conservation Directorate (*Budapesti Természetvédelmi Igazgatóság*; II, Szépvölgyi út 162; tel: 1 325 5722/7833).

**Buda Castle Labyrinth** (*Budavári Labirintus*) I, Úri utca 9; tel: 1 212 0207; email: labirint@mail.elender.hu; www.labyrinth.hu [1 C4]
The labyrinth has seen its share of wine, women and war. Once there were cellars, while during Turkish times, ladies past their prime from the pashas' harems were drowned in the pools. Corpses were brought down here following the 1686 siege; later it held first a World-War-II shelter and then a secret Cold-War military installation. Now organisers have tried to invest the complex with metaphysical meaning, adding stone-carved figures and taped heartbeats, and rather washy evocations of Hungarian history. Nevertheless, stumbling about with your oil lamp

is dank and thoroughly enjoyable. Cost (with or without guide) adult 1,200Ft, student 1,000Ft; free with Budapest Card. *Open daily 09.30–19.30. There is a second entrance outside the walls of the Castle District, at Lovas út.*

**Pálvölgy Stalactite Cave** II, Szépvölgyi út 162; tel: 1 325 9505 [map page 355]
B *65 (from Kolosy tér – alight at 5th stop)*
You'll need to scale a ladder and 417 steps in your tour of the stalactite cave (*cseppkőbarlang*), with formations that are crocodiles to the imaginative eye, and fossils of 40-million-year-old sea urchins in the limestone. At over 13km, this is the second-longest cave in Hungary; the public may see 500m of it. Guided tours (50 minutes) leave 15 minutes past every hour. (If you purchase a combined ticket for both Pálvölgy and Szemlő-hegy caves, the tour times suit a visit to the latter first.) Adult 700Ft, student/child 500Ft; combined ticket adult 900Ft, concessions 600Ft. Children under 5 may not enter. *Open Tue–Sun 10.00–16.00, closed Mon.*

**Szemlő-hegy Cave** II, Pusztaszeri út 35; tel: 1 325 6001 [map page 355]
B *29 (from Kolosy tér – alight at 5th stop, on Felsőzöldmáli út)*
The 2.2km-long cave is nicknamed 'the underground garden of Budapest' because of its popcorn-coralloid and other speleothems – in English, pretty mineral and crystal formations. The cave's glories were revealed in 1930, when a slim lady was passed through a narrow slit (later named the 'Needle's Eye'). Fat ladies (opera singers) now visit the 'Giant Corridor' to benefit from the curative effects of the cave's humid air. A 300m stretch is open to the public; tours (35 minutes) start on

the hour. Adult 600Ft, concessions 400Ft, free with Budapest Card, combined ticket (see opposite). *Mon and Wed–Fri 10.00–15.00, Sat–Sun 10.00–16.00, closed Tue.*

## OTHER SITES OF NATURAL INTEREST

The sites below vary in pomp and popularity, ranging from a wildlife park to a gnarled old tree. A couple are only accessible with a guide and a few have admission charges, but you can visit the majority freely and without your purse. See map, page 355.

### Buda

**Apáthy Cliff** II, Nagybányai út
B̲ *11 (from Batthyány tér to last stop)*
In the shadow of Látó hegy, the cliff offers pathway walks and capital views. There are fossiliferous rocks over the site's 6ha, and 26 protected plant species.

**Balogh Ádám Cliff** II, Balogh Ádám utca
B̲ *29 (from Kolosy tér),* B̲ *49 (from Moszkva tér)*
Something of a dolomite island wedged between the residences of Balogh Ádám utca and Endrődi Sándor utca, with rare botany and rarer views over the city.

**Buda Arboretum** XI, Villányi út 35–43 and Ménesi út 41
T̲ *61 (Móricz Zsigmond körtér to 2nd stop);* B̲ *27 (Móricz Zsigmond körtér to 1st stop)*
Two sites around the buildings of the University of Horticulture and Food, straddling

Ménesi út. There's an artificial pond and over 1,400 ligneous species, including several rare and exotic plants. Access may not be possible out of university term.

**Buda Sas hegy** XI Tájék utca 26; tel: 1 319 6789
B̄ *8 (Március 15 tér to Meredek utca stop), then walk left up Meredek utca and right into Tájék utca*
Much of Sas hegy is residential, but there are 30ha of protected landscape at the top of the 266m white block of rock. The reserve contains dolomite flora such as Hungarian meadow saxifrage (*Seseli leucospermum*), Buda knapweed (*Centaurea sadleriana*) and St Stephen wild pink (*Dianthus collinus*); this is also the habitat of the Pannonian lizard (*Ablepharus kitaibelii*) and many species of spider and insect. A lovely, elevated spot for a walk. You can only visit with a guide, by prior arrangement. Mr Siklósi Engelbert (tel: 06 70 3303 813) and Mr Halász Antal (tel: 06 70 3303 801) are the guides that facilitate entry; they live on site, but do not speak English. *Open Mar 15–June 15 and Sep 1–Oct 15 Sat–Sun 10.00–16.00.*

**Budakeszi Game Park** (*Budakeszi Vadaspark*) XII, Budakeszi; tel: 1 2345 1783
B̄ *22 (Moszkva tér to Szanatórium utca), turn right at hospital, a short distance from bus stop, and take forest path for 1km; Children's Railway (to Szépjuhászné), then* B̄ *22 (Budakeszi út to Szanatórium utca); by car along Budakeszi út, then Szanatórium utca to car park*
The wildlife park spreads over 327ha on the border of Budapest and Budakeszi, and contains game species (like wild boar and fallow deer), indigenous livestock and an

exhibition of small predators and birds. Several nature trails begin from the main entrance, taking walkers through woodland areas of beech, oak, spruce and pine. Pack some bread and sausage, and stop at one of the picnic spots. Adult 400Ft, child 200Ft, student/pensioner 250Ft. *Open (Mar 1–Oct 31) Mon–Fri 09.00–17.00, Sat–Sun 09.00–18.00; (Nov 1–Feb 29) Mon–Fri 09.00–15.00, Sat–Sun 09.00–16.00.*

**Ernő Mihályfi's garden** II, Bogár utca 25
B *11 (from Batthyány tér to Pusztaszeri út) or* B *91 (from Nyugati tér to terminus)*
Mihályfi was a journalist and botanist who died in 1972; he left a landscaped garden with rich rosebeds. Ask the current owner for a sniff around.

**Fazekas-hegy Quarry** II, Torda utca
B *63 (from Hűvösvölgy) to Széchenyi utca*
Heavy in fossils, the limestone was regrettably much plundered once work stopped in the quarry, and protection was very welcome in 1982.

**Jókai Garden** XII, Költő utca 21
B *21 (Moszkva tér to 11th stop); Cogwheel Railway to Költő utca*
There are vines and fruit trees in this garden, which was planted by – and contains a memorial room to – the romantic 19th-century author Mór Jókai.

**Lebanon cedar** II, Kondor utca
B *11 (from Batthyány tér to last stop);* T *56 (from Moszkva tér to Vadaskerti út)*

Standing here for 120 years, this Lebanon cedar (*Cedrus libani*) is one of the oldest cedars in central Europe. It is fenced off, but at 12m tall and 3m thick remains visible.

**Martinovics hegy** (Kis-Svábhegy) XII, Gaál József utca
*B 21 (from Moszkva tér), 39 (from Batthyány tér)*
Hemmed in by housing blocks, this is a popular place for residents to seek space. Valuable fossils have emerged from the limestone quarries in the reserve, while the habitat is home to grasses and karstic scrub forests, as well as protected plants like the pasque flower (*Pulsatilla grandis*) and the yellow adonis (*Adonis vernalis*).

**Ördög-orom Quarry** XII, Ördög-orom
*B 8 (Március 15 tér to Törökbálinti út), then walk north*
Excellent panoramic views from the dolomite hill and its abandoned 'Devil's Peak Quarry'. There are numerous protected plant species such as the yellow adonis (*Adonis vernalis*), which blooms on the southern slopes, the pygmy iris (*Iris pumila*), the black pulsatilla (*Pulsatilla nigricans*) and the lady orchid (*Orchis purpurea*). It is forbidden to leave the walking trails.

**Róka-hegy Quarry** III, Róka hegy
*HEV Csillaghegy (from Batthyány tér, on Szentendre line)*
'Fox Hill' is to the north of Óbuda, and the protected area extends over 9ha. The abandoned quarry is the largest in Budapest and its fissures provide breeding sites

for bats and birds. Butterflies and lizards can also be found. There is a panoramic trail around the top; keep to the paths (some of the flora is strictly protected).

**Rupp hegy** XI, Rupphegyi út
B *8 (from Március tér 15 to terminus)*
There are remnants of hornbeam and oak groves on the northern foothills, and patches of scrub forest on the top and on the southern slopes. Four species of mountain ash are also found here, together with rare plants like the small pasque flower (*Pulsatilla grandis*) and the pygmy iris (*Iris pumila*). The area covers 8ha.

**Tree in Gazda utca** II, Gazda utca 5
B *56 (from Moszkva tér to Hűvösvölgy), then* B *64 to Dózsa György utca*
You need permission from the private owner to enter the plot, but the linden (*Tilia cordata*) – the oldest tree in the city, at 500 years – can be seen from Nóra utca.

**Vine at Bécsi kapu tér** I, Bécsi kapu tér 8
Running around the yard of what is now a private house in the Castle District, this vine is 30m long and has been producing grapes since its planting in 1944.

## Pest

**Eötvös Loránd University Botanical Garden** (*Botanikus kert*) VIII, Illés utca 25
M3 *Klinikák or Nagyvárad tér*
The Budapest Botanical Garden will be familiar to Hungarians for its place in *The*

*Boys of Pál Street* (*Pál utcai fiúk*), a book by Ferenc Molnár about rival gangs of children fighting over this patch of land. There are 7,000 species of plant and tree in the 2.5ha, including tropical varieties in the greenhouse. Among the collection are orchids, the herbal remedy *Ginkgo biloba*, and the Chinese mammoth pine (*Metasequoia glyptostroboides*), found in 1950 after it was thought to have died out. Adult 300Ft, concessions 150Ft. (Purchase tickets from the porter's lodge, just inside the entrance.) *Garden open Mon–Thu and Sat–Sun 09.00–16.00, Fri 09.00–12.00; greenhouse open Mon–Thu and Sat–Sun 11.00–12.00, 14.00–15.00, closed Fri.*

**Merzse Marsh** XVII, Rákoskert
*Train to Rákoskert from Nyugati station, then walk 500m*
Considerable efforts have been made to preserve the wetland ecosystem of the marsh, which has dried up on several occasions. This is an important nesting site for waterfowl, immediately to the northeast of Ferihegy Airport.

**Naplás Lake** XVI, Cinkotai út
HEV *Cinkota (from Örsvezér on Gödöllő line), then* B *192 (to 3rd stop)*
At 150ha, this reservoir is the largest lake in Budapest, and the second-largest nature reserve. It sits on the eastern side of the city, to the north of the airport, and is rich in protected reeds, and species of amphibian, reptile and waterfowl. There are orchids in the bogs above and below the lake, while the reserve's forest supports over 150 species of nesting bird.

## Beyond Budapest

### Fót

*Take M3 motorway northeast and the Fót turnoff is signposted after 18km;* B *regularly from Árpád híd bus station or Újpest Városkapu terminus*

Famous for its church, naturalists also know that this village 25km northeast of Budapest is the place to see butterflies. The path starts at Fáy Présház (winery), which is signposted in the village.

### Nagy-Szénás

*Drive north towards Szentendre, fork left on route 10 towards Pilisvörösvár, and turn left after 10km to Pilisszentiván;* B *regularly from Árpád híd bus station*

Stands 25km northwest of the city, between Nagykovácsi and Pilisszentiván. It is a beautiful place, and one with a botanical rarity – the *pilis flax*. Contact Pál Kézdy (tel: 06 70 330 3812) for an English-speaking guide. Note that it is a strictly protected area, and if you come by bus or car you will have to alight and walk from the village. Follow the path marked with a yellow stripe heading south from the edge of the village for about 2km.

### Ócsa Landscape Protection Reserve

B *(every half-hour) from Népliget bus station to Ócsa, alight at Községháza, then go downhill and right, and look for the church*

Thirty kilometres to the southeast of Budapest, the Ócsa Reserve has a 13th-century Romanesque church. Moving outside, its protection area covers 3,576ha, the most valuable habitat being wet meadow. The depressions hold bogs and alder trees, while there are broad buckler ferns beneath ash trees and European mud minnows in the marshes. There is a visitor centre (Békési Panyik Andor utca 4–6; open May 1–Oct 30 Fri–Sun 09.00–17.00) next to the church, while twitchers make a beeline for the bird hide (tel: 28 454443). If you contact the hide in advance, you may also be able to participate in bird ringing. Ócsa's real treasures, however, are its spectacular orchids. Enjoy them on two walking trails, one of which (Selyemrét) is freely accessible. You'll need a guide for the second; contact Ágnes Pap (tel: 06 30 948 9150; email: tarnics@vipmail.hu), who can arrange one for 2,300Ft/hour (as well as offering bikes for hire). Earthwatch organises summer bird-ringing camps in Ócsa (including accommodation etc; see page 47), and Ecotours Hungary also runs excursions to the area (see page 84).

# Beyond the City

14

## THE DANUBE BEND

Just 45km to the north of Budapest, the Danube's course from its source in Germany is shepherded southwards by the Börzsöny and Pilis hill ranges. The sharp but graceful curve through a narrow valley is one of the prettiest stretches of Europe's second-longest river. The banks hold a collection of small historic towns, and these picturesque settlements represent ideal day-trip destinations from the capital. They are easily accessed, preferably on a weekday during the high season for they get busy at weekends. The hills are beacons for hikers.

### Szentendre

Located 20km outside Budapest, the charming old market town of Szentendre (St Andrew) opens the door and welcomes you to the Danube Bend. Now a thriving artists' colony, the town is spattered with galleries and art museums (such as one displaying the ceramics of Margit Kovács – see page 242); you can see why artists were drawn here, for the town is a picture itself, with cobbled pavements and colourful houses. The pleasant way to reach Szentendre is by ferry (see page 60), but the HÉV suburban railway from Batthyány tér station is quicker.

### Vác

A touch further north, and on the other bank, Vác is less favoured by tourists – a recommendation in itself. It has a mighty baroque cathedral, an embankment running alongside the river, and an ancient provenance. It was a significant centre during the medieval period. The MÁV nostalgia steam train runs here on most Saturdays between May and September (see www.mav.hu for the timetable); if you're after speed rather than romance, jump on a train from Nyugati station.

## Visegrád

Visegrád was once an important royal centre, its golden age during the rule of King Mátyás in the 15th century. You can visit the ruins of his magnificent Renaissance castle, as well as a hilltop citadel originally constructed by Béla IV that offers fabulous views over the bend's finest section. Take the ferry (see page 60), or one of the frequent buses from Árpád híd bus station.

## Esztergom

Esztergom is one of the country's most important towns. It stands 70km from Budapest, facing Slovakia across the water, and was the dearly loved King István's place of birth and coronation. The town served as Hungary's capital for over 250 years and has been the seat of the Hungarian Catholic Church for a millennium. The remains of the royal palace evoke the historical past of the town, while the colossal basilica – the largest church in Hungary – can be seen from miles around, and offers views back the other way from its cupola. You can get there by ferry (see page 60), train from Nyugati station or bus from Árpád híd station.

## GÖDÖLLŐ

Travel 30km east from Budapest and you'll reach the diminutive town of Gödöllő, the unlikely site for the country's biggest baroque mansion – the 18th-century Royal Grassalkovich Palace. In the 19th century, this sprawling building was a retreat for the popular Empress Erzsébet, who adored it and spent much summer time here. Take a tour of the mansion and eat a picnic in its splendid grounds. Regular buses to Gödöllő leave from Stadion bus station, while you can also take the HÉV from Örs vezér tere.

## LAKE BALATON

Pining for the beach? The 'Hungarian sea' is 95km southwest of Budapest, the largest freshwater lake in central Europe. Prices have escalated here in recent years, making it slightly less popular with Hungarians than it once was, but it still provides an escape from city heat and grime, and the opportunity to sunbathe and indulge in watersports. All around the lake are dotted towns and villages. The southern shore has a commercial Mediterranean-resort feel to it, popular with families and young party-lovers, and overrun with high-rise hotels, bars and nightclubs (the prime concentration at Siófok). The reedy northern shore has a peaceful charm, with sites of historical and natural interest, and wine cellars dug into rocky hills. If we were pressed, we'd name Badacsony and Tihany as our favourites – beautiful places and landscape protection reserves. Trains run to Lake Balaton from Déli and Kelenföld, and there are buses from Népliget.

# 15 Language

The Nobel-Prize-winning physicist Enrico Fermi was fascinated by the possible existence of extra terrestrials. 'Where are they?' he once blurted out. The Hungarian-born scientist Leó Szilárd paused from his lunch, looked up at his colleague, and replied, 'They are among us, but they call themselves Hungarians'. Alien speech betrayed these Martians in central Europe. Hungarian bears no relation to the Indo-European languages of neighbouring countries. Some argue a distant link with Finnish and Estonian (of the Finno-Ugric linguistic group), but we find the ET theory as credible as any other.

Staff in Budapest's restaurants and bars will usually speak some English, but you'll endear yourself by trying a word or two *magyarul* (Hungarian-ly). Small tourist dictionaries (*Magyar-Angol/Angol-Magyar útiszótár*) are available from bookshops, and should provide most of what you'll need. Don't worry about the grammar – life (and your stay) is too short. Good luck! – *Sok szerencsét!*

## PRONUNCIATION

Perfect pronunciation is a rare thing from beginners. No matter; be determined – and free with the odd descriptive hand signal – and you'll make yourself understood. The golden rules are that the stress should always fall on the word's first syllable, that there are no silent vowels, and that letters (or combinations of letters) are consistent in their sound values. Below is a list of letters with phonetic transcriptions; those not included are pronounced as in English, with the exception of *q*, *w*, *x* and *y*, which don't appear in Hungarian (except in foreign derivatives and some names). And did you know that every single word under *ty* in the Hungarian dictionary is related to, or begins with, the word for 'chicken' (*tyúk*)?

**a** as in d**o**t
**á** as in r**a**ther
**c** as the ts in ac**ts**
**cs** as the ch in bir**ch**
**é** as the a in d**ay**
**g** always hard as in **g**ood, never soft as in germ
**gy** as the dy sound in **du**ring
**i** as in sp**i**t, though slightly longer
**í** as the ie in n**ie**ce
**j** as the y in **y**esterday
**ly** as the y in **y**esterday (as above)
**ny** as the ny sound in **new**
**o** as the or sound in s**ore**
**ó** as above, but held for longer
**ö** as the u in **ur**n
**ő** as above, but held for longer
**r** rolled, as in the Scottish accent
**s** as the sh in **sh**opping

| | |
|---|---|
| **sz** | as the s in **s**ell |
| **t** | with the tongue |
| **ty** | as the tu in **Tu**esday |
| **u** | as in p**u**ll |
| **ú** | as the oo in m**oo**dy |
| **ü** | as in c**u**te |
| **ű** | as above, but held for longer |
| **w** | as the v in **v**an |
| **zs** | as the zs sound in trea**s**ure |

## WORDS AND PHRASES

### Numbers

| | | | | | |
|---|---|---|---|---|---|
| 0 | *nulla* | 5 | *öt* | 10 | *tíz* |
| 1 | *egy* | 6 | *hat* | 100 | *száz* |
| 2 | *kettő* | 7 | *hét* | 1,000 | *ezer* |
| 3 | *három* | 8 | *nyolc* | | |
| 4 | *négy* | 9 | *kilenc* | | |

### Days

| | | | |
|---|---|---|---|
| Monday | *hétfő* | Friday | *péntek* |
| Tuesday | *kedd* | Saturday | *szombat* |
| Wednesday | *szerda* | Sunday | *vasárnap* |
| Thursday | *csütörtök* | | |

## Months

| | | | |
|---|---|---|---|
| January | *január* | July | *július* |
| February | *február* | August | *augusztus* |
| March | *március* | September | *szeptember* |
| April | *április* | October | *október* |
| May | *május* | November | *november* |
| June | *június* | December | *december* |

## Basics

| | | | |
|---|---|---|---|
| hello (familiar) | *szervusz/szervusztok* (to one/more)<br>*szia/sziasztok* (to one/more) | | |
| hello/goodbye | *halló* (this tickles English speakers) | | |
| goodbye (polite) | *viszontlátásra* | Pardon?/At your service | *Tessék?* |
| good day (polite) | *jó napot* | | |
| good morning | *jó reggelt* | please | *kérem* |
| goodnight | *jó éjszakát* | sorry | *bocsánat* |
| no | *nem* | thank you | *köszönöm* |
| | | yes | *igen* |

## *Meeting people*

| | |
|---|---|
| Do you speak English? | *Beszél angolul?* |
| How are you? | *Hogy van?* |
| I am fine. | *Jól vagyok.* |

| | |
|---|---|
| My name is... | *Az én nevem...* |
| Pleased to meet you | *Örülök, hogy megismerkedhettem önnel* |
| What's your name? | *Mi az Ön neve?* |

## Transport

| | | | |
|---|---|---|---|
| bicycle | *kerékpár* | ticket | *jegy* |
| bus | *busz* | ticket office | *jegypénztár* |
| bus station | *autóbusz-állomás* | timetable | *menetrend* |
| bus stop | *autóbusz-megálló* | tram | *villamos* |
| car park | *parkoló* | underground/ metro | *metro* |
| railway station | *pályaudvar (pu)* | | |

## Eating and drinking

| | | | |
|---|---|---|---|
| A glass of... | *Egy pohár...* | goulash | *gulyás* |
| A table for two please. | *Egy asztal kettő személyre* | ice-cream | *fagylalt* |
| beer | *sör* | Is service included? | *A felszolgálás benne van?* |
| bread | *kenyér* | mineral water | *ásványvíz* |
| cake shop | *cukrászda* | One beer, please. | *Egy sört kérek.* |
| coffee bar | *eszpresszó* | pancake | *palacsinta* |
| coffee | *kávé* | pub | *söröző* |
| coffee house | *kávéház* | red wine | *vörös bor* |
| dumplings | *galuska* | restaurant | *étterem, vendéglő* |

## SOME PROVERBS

Like sayings around the world, Hungarian proverbs tend to be cautionary in nature. However, the tailored proverbs of a nation say much about its outlook. Those below are indicative of a character that is sceptical, but one that recognises everyday pitfalls for the minor inconsequences that they are. They also show a sharp, if dark, sense of humour.

| | | |
|---|---|---|
| *Aki korpa közé keveredik azt megeszik a disznók* | If you take risks, be prepared for the consequences | 'Those who get mixed up with bran will be eaten by pigs' |
| *A kutyából nem lesz szalonna* | You can't change a person | 'You can't get bacon from dog' |
| *A kerítés is kolbászból van* | They are doing really well | 'Even the fence is made of sausage' |
| *Több is veszett Mohácsnál* | It is not a serious problem | 'More was lost at Mohács' (defeat in 1526 that let the Turks into Hungary) |
| *Nem hajt a tatár* | We have time, no hurry | 'The Tatars are not chasing us' |
| *Sok beszédnek sok az alja* | Too much talk and no action | 'A lot of talk has a lot of dregs' |

| | | | |
|---|---|---|---|
| soup | *leves* | water | *víz* |
| tea | *tea* (pronounced *teya*) | White wine | *fehér bor* |
| The bill, please. | *Kérem a számlát* | winebar | *borozó* |
| The menu, please. | *Kérem az étlapot* | | |

## Accommodation

| | | | |
|---|---|---|---|
| bed and breakfast | *szoba reggelive* | for two people | *két személyre* |
| breakfast | *reggeli* | guesthouse | *panzió* |
| for one night | *egy éjszakára* | hotel | *szálloda* |

## Miscellaneous

| | | | |
|---|---|---|---|
| adult | *felnőtt* | entry | *bejárat* |
| and | *és* | exit | *kijárat* |
| big | *nagy* | gentlemen | *férfi* |
| boulevard | *körút* | hospital | *kórház* |
| bridge | *híd* | island | *sziget* |
| cash desk | *pénztár* | ladies | *nõk* |
| chemist | *gyógyszertár/patika* | no smoking | *tilos a dohányzás* |
| child | *gyerek* | open | *nyitva* |
| cinema | *mozi* | opening hours | *nyitvatartás* |
| city | *város* | police | *rendőrség* |
| closed | *zárva* | road | *út* |
| English (adverb) | *angolul* | street | *utca* |

| | | | |
|---|---|---|---|
| small | *kis/kicsi* | theatre | *színház* |
| square | *tér/tere* | toilet | *vécé* |
| swimming pool | *uszoda* | zoo | *állatkert* |

## And some slang ...

| | |
|---|---|
| *szellemi rövidnadrágos* | 'mentally short-trousered' (stupid) |
| *baromarcú* | 'cattle-faced' (annoying) |
| *kerítésszaggató* | 'fence ripper' (strong booze) |
| *lónyál* | 'horse's saliva' (soft drink) |
| *a béka* segge *alatt* | 'under a frog's arse' (in a poor financial state) |

# 16 Further Information

## BOOKS

### History and culture

Ardó, Zsuzsanna. *Culture Shock: A Guide to Customs and Etiquette in Hungary.* Times Media, 2003

Ash, Timothy Garton. *The Magic Lantern: The Revolution of '89 Witnessed in Warsaw, Budapest, Berlin, and Prague.* Vintage 1993

Balázs, Géza. *The Story of Hungarian: A Guide to the Language.* Corvina, 1997.

Fonseca, Isabel. *Bury Me Standing.* Vintage, 1996. The Roma (gypsies) in central Europe.

Kontler László. *Millennium in Central Europe: A History of Hungary.* Atlantisz, 1999

Lang, George. *The Cuisine of Hungary.* Penguin, 1985. Recipes and anecdotes.

Lang, George. *Nobody Knows the Truffles I've Seen.* Alfred A Knoff, 1998. Autobiography by Gundel co-owner detailing his escape from Hungary and love of cuisine.

Lázár István. *Hungary: A Brief History.* Corvina, 1989

Liddell, Alex. *The Wines of Hungary.* Mitchell Beazley, 2003.

Lukacs, John. *Budapest 1900: A Historical Portrait of the City and its Culture.* Grove, 1990.

Molnár, Miklós. *A Concise History of Hungary.* CUP, 2001

Móra, Imre. *Budapest Then and Now.* New World, 2001. Articles about Budapest.

### Literature

Bíró, Val. *Hungarian Folk-Tales.* OUP, 1992

Esterházy, Péter. *The Glance of Countess Hahn-Hahn.* Northwestern, 2000. A meditation on travel, the Danube and its history.

Esterházy, Péter. *Celestial Harmonies*. Flamingo, 2004. Dynastic saga of the Esterházys.

Fischer, Tibor. *Under the Frog*. Henry Holt, 1997. Ironic and humorous tale against the backdrop of the 1956 revolution.

Kertész, Imre. *Fateless*, 1992.

Konrad, George. *A Feast in the Garden*. Harvest, 1993. Boy escapes the Nazi horrors.

Kosztolányi, Dezső. *Anna Édes*. New Directions, 1993. Classic 1920s novel depicting bourgeois pretences in Budapest.

Márai, Sándor. *Embers*.

Petőfi, Sándor. *John the Valiant*. Hesperus, 2004. Epic Hungarian poem.

Various. *The Lost Rider: A Bilingual Anthology*. Corvina, 1997. Selection of works by famous Hungarian poets.

## Guidebooks and maps

*Budapest* map (1:22,000) Cartographia, 2004

Lőrinczi, Zsuzsa and Vargha, Mihály. *Architectural Guide, 20th Century*. Budapest, 1997

Németh, Gyula. *Hungary, A Complete Guide*. Corvina Books, 1992.

Phillips, Adrian and Scotchmer, Jo. *Hungary: The Bradt Travel Guide*. Bradt, 2005. If you've enjoyed the city guide, this is the full-country companion.

Pintér, Tamás K and Kaiser, Anna. *Churches of Budapest*. Corvina, 1993

Szatmári Gizella. *Walks in the Castle District*. Municipality of Budapest, 2001

Török, András *Budapest: A Critical Guide*. Pallas Athene, 2000. Eccentric look at Budapest.

## WEBSITES

**www.bbj.hu** Online edition of the *Budapest Business Journal* (see page 74)
**www.bkv.hu** Useful details on Budapest transport. English section.
**www.bortarsasag.hu** Website of the wine society and shops
**www.budapestinfo.hu** Budapest's official tourist website
**www.budapestpanorama.com** For events information
**www.budapestsun.com** Online version of the English-language newspaper
**www.elvira.hu** Useful timetable of the MÁV Hungarian Railway. In English.
**www.findagrave.com** Fascinating site holding 6 million grave records
**www.gay.hu** Latest information on the gay scene
**www.gotohungary.com** US website of the HNTO
**www.hotelshungary.com** Competitively priced accommodation
**www.hungarytourism.hu** Tourist office website
**www.insidehungary.com** From current affairs to entertainment
**www.inyourpocket.com** Online version of *In Your Pocket*
**www.longitudebooks.com** A good further-reading resource
**www.spasbudapest.com** Budapest's spas
**www.talkingcities.co.uk/budapest** Tourist sights and more
**www.tokaji.hu** Website of the association of top Tokaji estates
**www.tourist-offices.org.uk/hungary** UK-specific information
**www.volan.hu** Information on the Hungarian bus network. In Hungarian.
**www.wherebudapest.com** Online version of *Where Budapest* (see page 75)
**www.winesofhungary.com**

# Index

Fortuna utca, Castle District (AC)

Gellért Baths (LC)

Fishermen's Bastion (AC)

'Fishing Children', Buda Castle Palace (AC)

Chain Bridge (GAR)

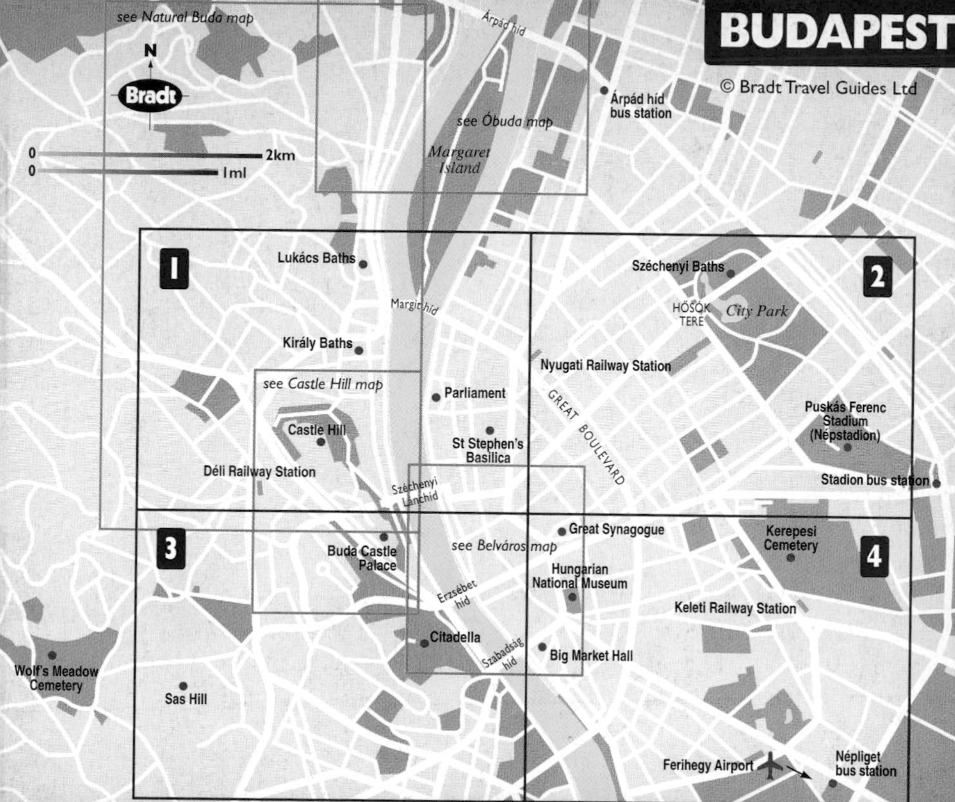
BUDAPEST
© Bradt Travel Guides Ltd
see Natural Buda map
N
Bradt
0
2km
0
1ml
Árpád híd
Árpád híd
bus station
see Óbuda map
Margaret
Island
1
Lukács Baths
Széchenyi Baths
2
Margit híd
HŐSÖK
TERE
City Park
Király Baths
Nyugati Railway Station
see Castle Hill map
Parliament
GREAT BOULEVARD
Puskás Ferenc
Stadium
(Népstadion)
Castle Hill
St Stephen's
Basilica
Déli Railway Station
Széchenyi
Lánchíd
Stadion bus station
3
Great Synagogue
Kerepesi
Cemetery
see Belváros map
Buda Castle
Palace
4
Hungarian
National Museum
Erzsébet
híd
Keleti Railway Station
Citadella
Szabadság
híd
Big Market Hall
Wolf's Meadow
Cemetery
Sas Hill
Ferihegy Airport
Népliget
bus station

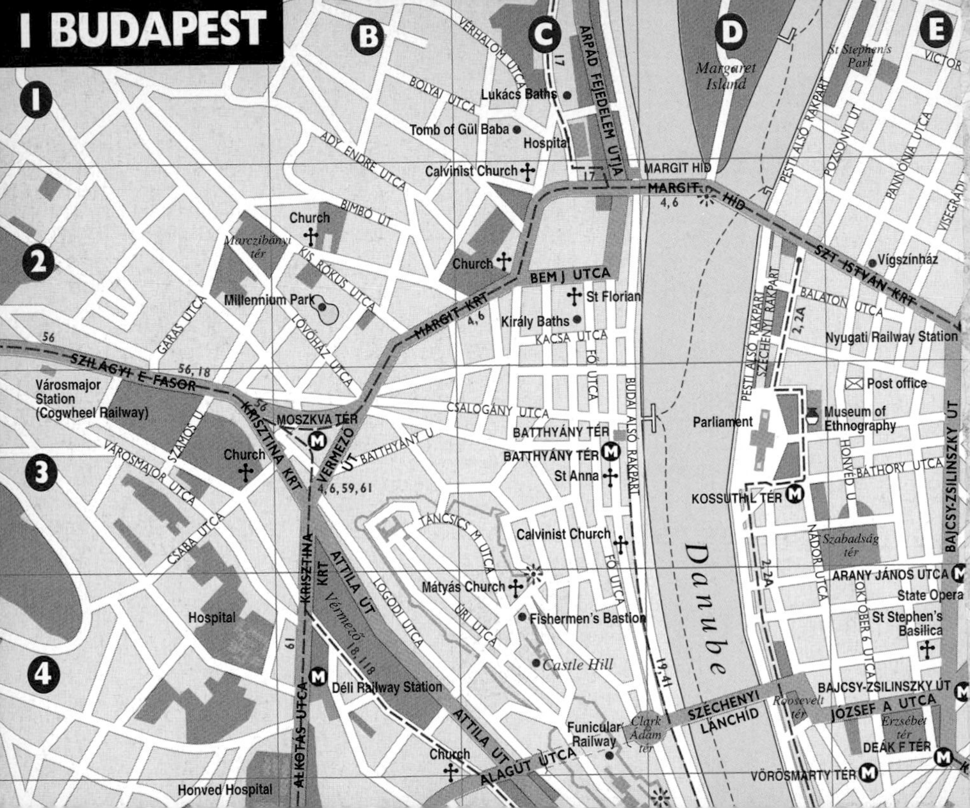
I BUDAPEST
B
C
D
E
1
2
3
4
Margaret Island
St Stephen's Park
VICTOR
VÉRHALOM UTCA
BOLYAI UTCA
Lukács Baths
Tomb of Gül Baba
Hospital
ÁRPÁD FEJEDELEM ÚTJA
Calvinist Church
ADY ENDRE UTCA
MARGIT HÍD
MARGIT HÍD
4, 6
PESTI ALSÓ RAKPART
POZSONYI ÚT
PANNONIA UTCA
VISEGRÁDI
BIMBÓ ÚT
Church
Marczibányi tér
KIS RÓKUS UTCA
Church
BEM J UTCA
SZT ISTVÁN KRT
Vígszínház
Millennium Park
St Florian
Király Baths
MARGIT KRT
4, 6
BALATON UTCA
2, 2A
Nyugati Railway Station
GARAS UTCA
LÖVŐHÁZ UTCA
KACSA UTCA
56
SZILÁGYI E FASOR
56, 18
Városmajor Station (Cogwheel Railway)
FŐ UTCA
BUDAI ALSÓ RAKPART
SZÉCHENYI RAKPART
Post office
56
MOSZKVA TÉR
CSALOGÁNY UTCA
Museum of Ethnography
Parliament
BATTHYÁNY TÉR
BATTHYÁNY TÉR
KRISZTINA KRT
SZAMOS U
VÁROSMAJOR UTCA
Church
VÉRMEZŐ ÚT
BATTHYÁNY U
St Anna
HONVÉD U
BÁTHORY UTCA
4, 6, 59, 61
KOSSUTH L TÉR
BAJCSY-ZSILINSZKY ÚT
TÁNCSICS M UTCA
Calvinist Church
CSABA UTCA
Danube
Szabadság tér
NÁDOR UTCA
ARANY JÁNOS UTCA
KRISZTINA KRT
ATTILA ÚT
Vérmező
LOGODI UTCA
Mátyás Church
ÚRI UTCA
FŐ UTCA
2, 2A
OKTÓBER 6 UTCA
State Opera
St Stephen's Basilica
Hospital
Fishermen's Bastion
18, 118
61
Castle Hill
19, 41
Déli Railway Station
BAJCSY-ZSILINSZKY ÚT
SZÉCHENYI LÁNCHÍD
Roosevelt tér
JÓZSEF A UTCA
Erzsébet tér
ATTILA ÚT
Funicular Railway
Clark Ádám tér
DEÁK F TÉR
ALKOTÁS UTCA
Church
ALAGÚT UTCA
VÖRÖSMARTY TÉR
Honved Hospital

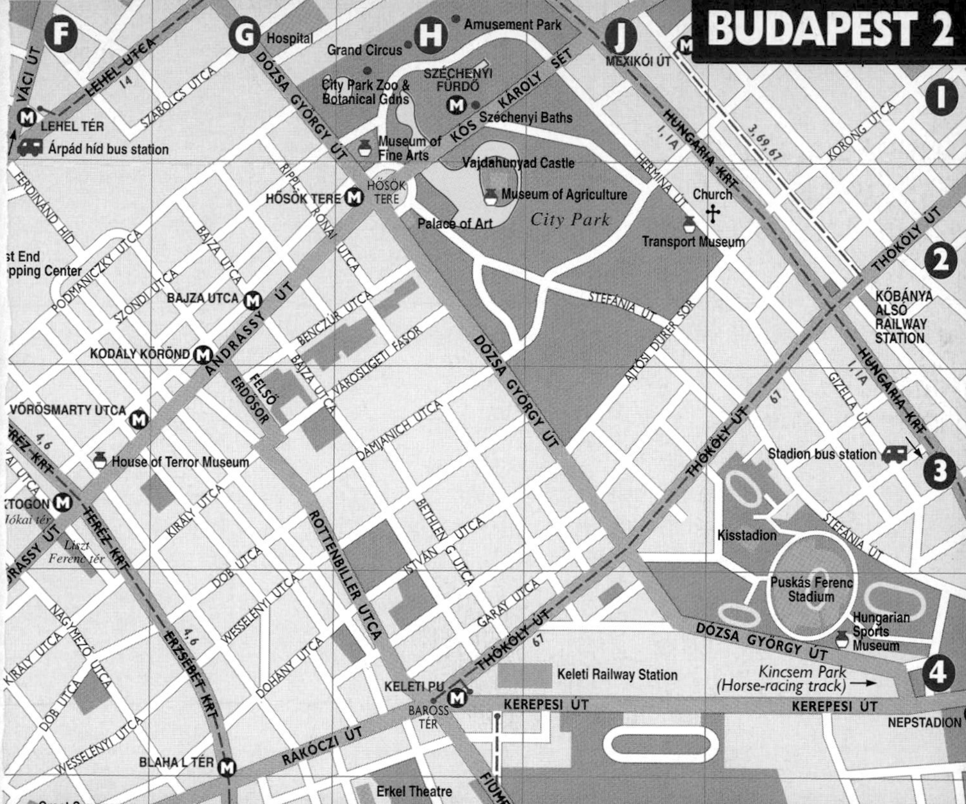

BUDAPEST 2
F
G
H
J
I
2
3
4
Hospital
Amusement Park
Grand Circus
SZÉCHENYI FÜRDŐ
City Park Zoo & Botanical Gdns
Széchenyi Baths
Museum of Fine Arts
Vajdahunyad Castle
Museum of Agriculture
City Park
Palace of Art
HŐSÖK TERE
Church
Transport Museum
MEXIKÓI ÚT
LEHEL TÉR
Árpád híd bus station
VÁCI ÚT
LEHEL UTCA
SZABOLCS UTCA
DÓZSA GYÖRGY ÚT
KÓS KÁROLY SÉT
HUNGÁRIA KRT
HERMINA ÚT
KORONG UTCA
3,69,67
1,1A
FERDINÁND HÍD
RIPPL-RÓNAI UTCA
BAJZA UTCA
PODMANICZKY UTCA
SZONDI UTCA
BENCZÚR UTCA
VÁROSLIGETI FASOR
ANDRÁSSY ÚT
KODÁLY KÖRÖND
FELSŐ ERDŐSOR
STEFÁNIA ÚT
AJTÓSI DÜRER SOR
THÖKÖLY ÚT
KŐBÁNYA ALSÓ RAILWAY STATION
GIZELLA ÚT
67
VÖRÖSMARTY UTCA
TERÉZ KRT
4,6
House of Terror Museum
DAMJANICH UTCA
Stadion bus station
Jókai tér
Liszt Ferenc tér
KIRÁLY UTCA
ROTTENBILLER UTCA
BETHLEN G UTCA
ISTVÁN UTCA
Kisstadion
Puskás Ferenc Stadium
DOB UTCA
WESSELÉNYI UTCA
NAGYMEZŐ UTCA
ERZSÉBET KRT
GARAY UTCA
Hungarian Sports Museum
DOHÁNY UTCA
Keleti Railway Station
Kincsem Park (Horse-racing track)
KELETI PU
BAROSS TÉR
KEREPESI ÚT
NEPSTADION
RÁKÓCZI ÚT
BLAHA L TÉR
Erkel Theatre
FIUME

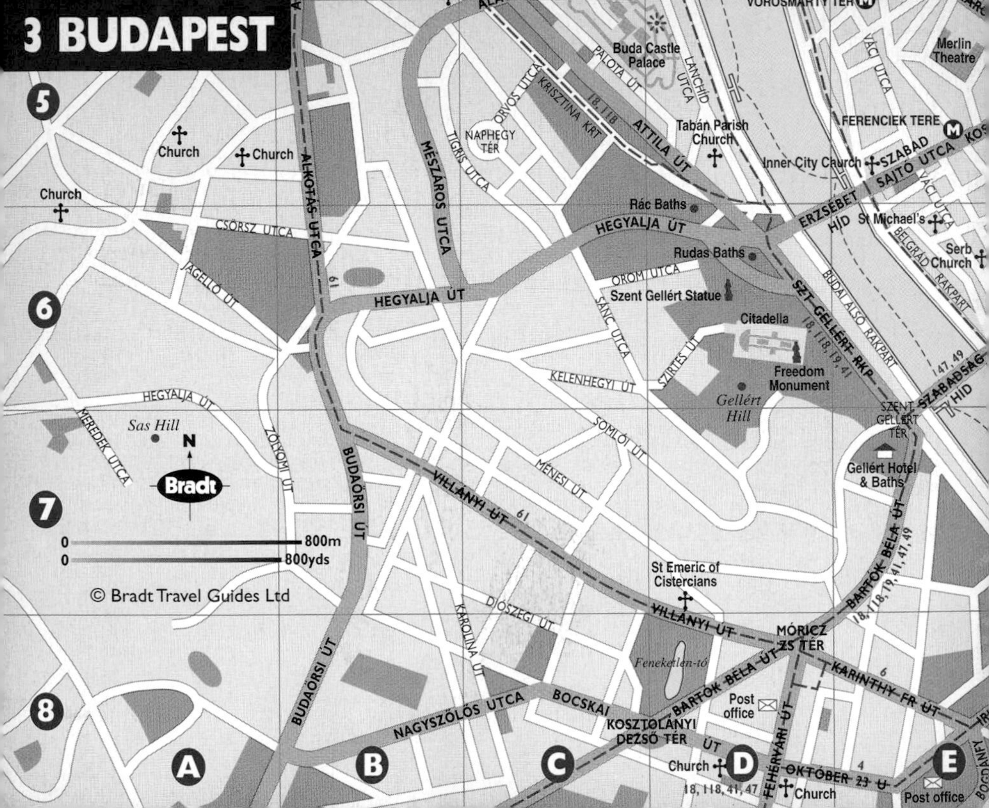

3 BUDAPEST
5
6
7
8
A
B
C
D
E
Church
Church
Church
Buda Castle Palace
Tabán Parish Church
Inner City Church
St Michael's
Serb Church
Merlin Theatre
VOROSMARTY TER
FERENCIEK TERE
NAPHEGY TÉR
Rác Baths
Rudas Baths
Szent Gellért Statue
Citadella
Freedom Monument
Gellért Hill
Gellért Hotel & Baths
SZENT GELLÉRT TÉR
St Emeric of Cistercians
MÓRICZ ZS TÉR
Feneketlen-tó
KOSZTOLÁNYI DEZSŐ TÉR
Post office
Post office
Church
Church
Sas Hill
N
Bradt
0 800m
0 800yds
© Bradt Travel Guides Ltd
ALKOTÁS UTCA
MÉSZÁROS UTCA
TIGRIS UTCA
ORVOS UTCA
KRISZTINA KRT
PALOTA ÚT
LÁNCHÍD UTCA
ATTILA ÚT
VÁCI UTCA
SZABAD SAJTÓ UTCA
ERZSÉBET HÍD
BELGRÁD RAKPART
HEGYALJA ÚT
CSÖRSZ UTCA
JAGELLÓ ÚT
ORÓM UTCA
SÁNC UTCA
SZT GELLÉRT RKP
BUDAI ALSÓ RAKPART
SZIRTES ÚT
KELENHEGYI ÚT
SOMLÓI ÚT
MÉNESI ÚT
SZABADSÁG HÍD
HEGYALJA ÚT
MEREDEK UTCA
ZÓLYOMI ÚT
BUDAÖRSI ÚT
VILLÁNYI ÚT
BARTÓK BÉLA ÚT
DIÓSZEGI ÚT
KAROLINA ÚT
KARINTHY FR ÚT
BUDAÖRSI ÚT
NAGYSZŐLŐS UTCA
BOCSKAI ÚT
FEHÉRVÁRI ÚT
OKTÓBER 23 U
18, 118
18, 118, 19, 41
47, 49
61
61
18, 118, 19, 41, 47, 49
6
4
18, 118, 41, 47

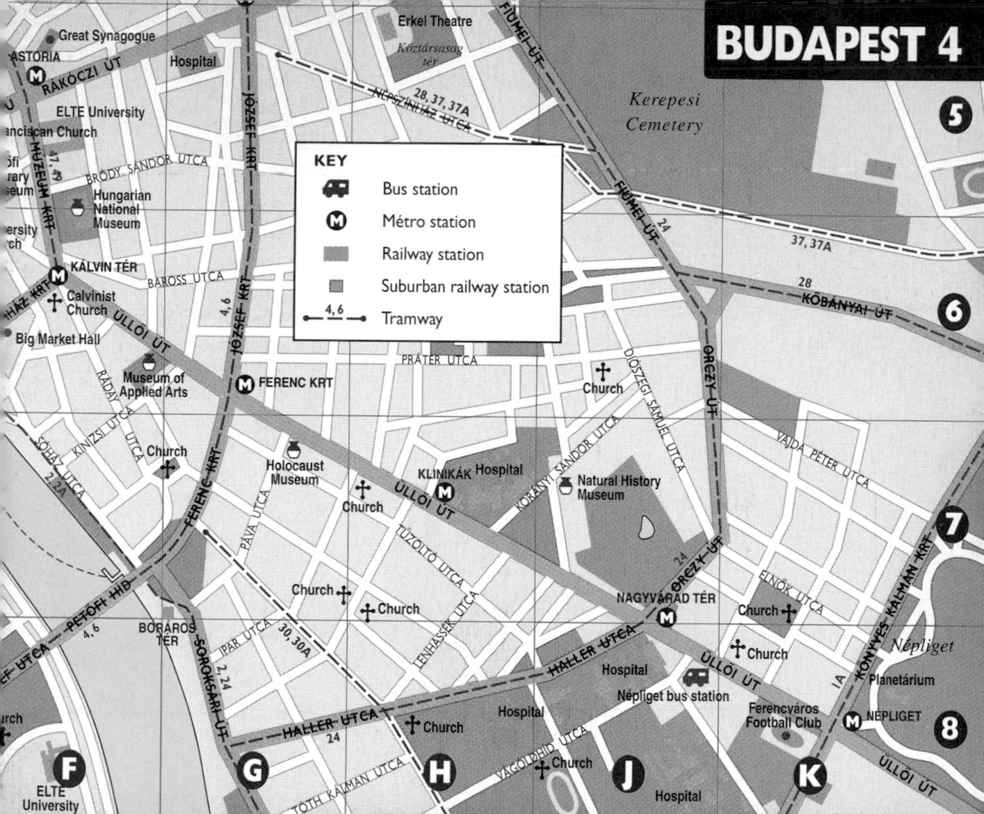
BUDAPEST 4
KEY
Bus station
Métro station
Railway station
Suburban railway station
Tramway
Great Synagogue
ASTORIA
RÁKÓCZI ÚT
Hospital
Erkel Theatre
Köztársaság tér
NÉPSZÍNHÁZ UTCA
28, 37, 37A
Kerepesi Cemetery
FIUMEI ÚT
ELTE University
Franciscan Church
MÚZEUM KRT
BRÓDY SÁNDOR UTCA
Hungarian National Museum
JÓZSEF KRT
KÁLVIN TÉR
BAROSS UTCA
Calvinist Church
ÜLLŐI ÚT
Big Market Hall
Museum of Applied Arts
RÁDAY UTCA
KINIZSI UTCA
SÓHÁZ UTCA
FERENC KRT
PRÁTER UTCA
KŐBÁNYAI ÚT
37, 37A
ORCZY ÚT
DIÓSZEGI SÁMUEL UTCA
Church
VAJDA PÉTER UTCA
KORÁNYI SÁNDOR UTCA
Natural History Museum
KLINIKÁK
Hospital
Holocaust Museum
PÁVA UTCA
TŰZOLTÓ UTCA
LENHOSSÉK UTCA
NAGYVÁRAD TÉR
ELNÖK UTCA
KÖNYVES KÁLMÁN KRT
Népliget
Planetárium
NÉPLIGET
PETŐFI HÍD
BORÁROS TÉR
IPAR UTCA
30, 30A
SOROKSÁRI ÚT
HALLER UTCA
Hospital
Népliget bus station
Ferencváros Football Club
VÁGÓHÍD UTCA
TÓTH KÁLMÁN UTCA
ELTE University
5
6
7
8
F
G
H
J
K

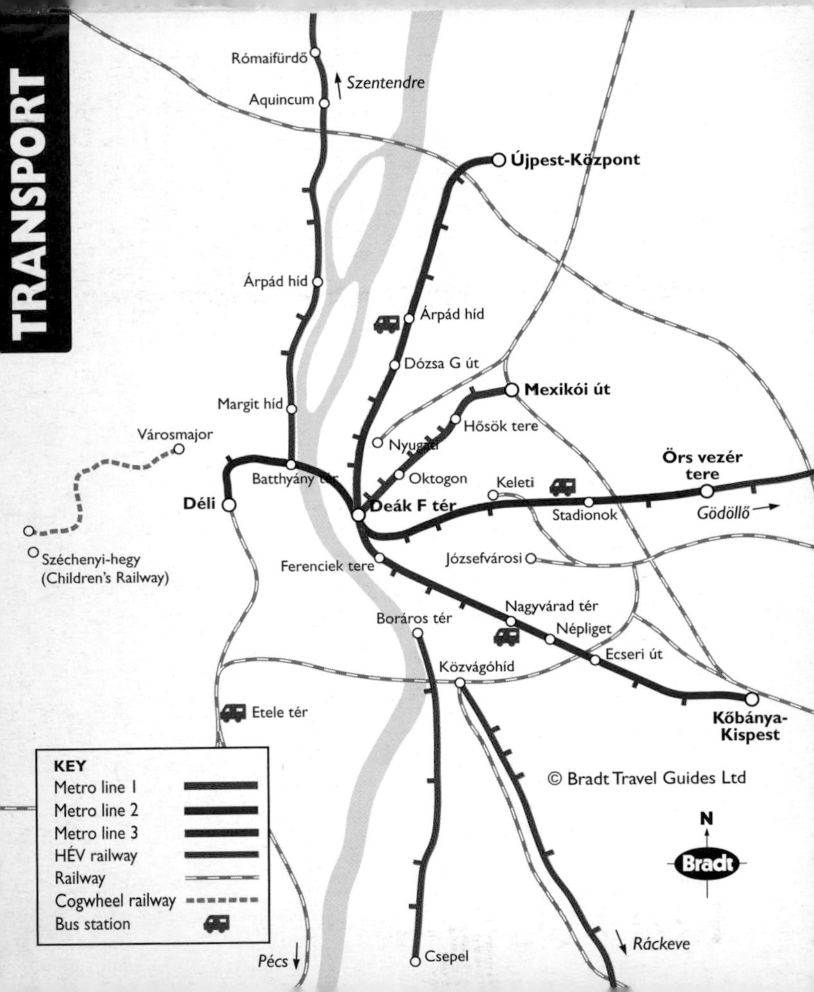

TRANSPORT
Rómaifürdő
Szentendre
Aquincum
Újpest-Központ
Árpád híd
Árpád híd
Dózsa G út
Mexikói út
Margit híd
Városmajor
Hősök tere
Nyugati
Örs vezér tere
Batthyány tér
Oktogon
Keleti
Déli
Deák F tér
Stadionok
Gödöllő
Széchenyi-hegy
(Children's Railway)
Ferenciek tere
Józsefvárosi
Nagyvárad tér
Boráros tér
Népliget
Ecseri út
Közvágóhíd
Etele tér
Kőbánya-Kispest
KEY
Metro line 1
Metro line 2
Metro line 3
HÉV railway
Railway
Cogwheel railway
Bus station
© Bradt Travel Guides Ltd
N
Bradt
Ráckeve
Pécs
Csepel